PRESERVING YOUR WEALTH

Expert Advice
You Can Use to
Protect Your Estate
from the
Risks of Litigation &
Ravages of
Taxes, Inflation &
Declining Asset Values

F. Bentley Mooney, Jr.

PROBUS PUBLISHING COMPANY
Chicago, Illinois
Cambridge, England

W9-CRS-916

© 1993, F. Bentley Mooney, Jr.

First printing 1991   ISBN 1-55738-208-5

ALL RIGHTS RESERVED. No part of this publication may be reproduced, stored in a retrieval system, or transmitted by any means, electronic, mechanical, photocopying, recording, or otherwise, without the prior written permission of the publisher and the copyright holder.

This publication is designed to provide accurate and authoritative information in regard to the subject matter covered. It is sold with the understanding that the publisher is not engaged in rendering legal, accounting or other professional service.

Authorization to photocopy items for internal or personal use, or the internal or personal use of specific clients, is granted by PROBUS PUBLISHING COMPANY, provided that the US$7.00 per page fee is paid directly to Copyright Clearance Center, 27 Congress Street, Salem MA 01970, USA. For those organizations that have been granted a photocopy license by CCC, a separate system of payment has been arranged. The fee code for users of the Transactional Reporting Service is: 1-55738-488-6/93/$0.00 + $7.00.

ISBN 1-55738-488-6

Printed in the United States of America

BB

   2   3   4   5   6   7   8   9   0

ACKNOWLEDGMENTS

Among the special contributions that distinguish this treatment of asset protection planning are those of four fellow attorneys: my tax associate, Matthew W. Goldsby, Barry Engel of Englewood, Colorado, W.J.H. Corlitt of Douglas, Isle of Man, and Charles Jennings of Grand Cayman, British West Indies. Thank you, gentlemen.

DISCLAIMER

Because law pertaining to the topics covered by this book changes from time to time, the author, publisher and all persons and entities involved in its preparation, publication, sale or distribution disclaim all responsibility for the legal effects or consequences of any legal document prepared or action taken in reliance upon any information contained in it. No representations, either express or implied, are made or given regarding those legal effects or consequences. Purchasers and persons intending to use this book for the preparation of any legal documents are advised to ascertain specifically the then-current applicable law for all jurisdictions in which they intend the documents to be effective.

CONTENTS

INTRODUCTION

Rick Johnson was at his desk, tie pulled loose, sleeves rolled up, and immersed in present value calculations for a client of his financial planning firm when the intercom sounded. "Mr. Johnson, a deputy sheriff to see you." With a puzzled expression, he rose and walked to the reception area. A uniformed deputy approached. "Richard D. Johnson?" he asked. "Yes, officer. What can I do for you?" "You are served," said the deputy, extending a thick, white envelope.

A wave of nausea swept over Rick as he took the envelope and stepped back. "What is this?" he thought. His mind raced over his business transactions of the last few years, searching for some recollection that could explain this bundle of papers in his suddenly shaking hand.

Back in his office, he hesitantly opened the envelope and unfolded the thick sheaf of photocopied pleadings. It was a complaint, naming him as the first of several defendants. The lawsuit was filed by a client who invested in a real estate partnership Rick sponsored a few years earlier. The partnership was ultimately dissolved and the property sale proceeds distributed to the investors after changes in the Internal Revenue Code stripped away the tax benefits for which his clients had bargained.

"Conversion, breach of fiduciary duty, breach of implied duty of good faith and fair dealing, conspiracy to defraud, everything but the kitchen sink," he thought as each word etched itself on his brain.

Rick is schooled in the ways of the world. He knows that predatory litigation haunts the dreams of every thinking professional engaged in private practice, every corporate director and of business owners in high-risk industries. In American society today, many will happily sacrifice a personal or professional relationship to recoup a loss if that friend or adviser is seen as a "deep pocket." This may be in part the direct result of a system that deems it the responsibility of society to provide a remedy for every misfortune. But however wrong-headed this cultural proclivity may be, the question for the Target Defendants of America is, "How do you protect yourself?"

Who is the Target Defendant? As I use this term, it means anyone whose vocation carries with it exposure to more than the usual risks of being sued.

Obvious examples are physicians, lawyers, accountants, architects, civil engineers, financial planners, stock brokers, investment wholesalers and syndicators. Others not so obvious include: plastic products manufacturers (the dropped bottle splits, spraying a caustic solution in a small child's face), real estate developers and builders (a trespasser on the development site falls in a trench), ladder or scaffolding manufacturers (ladder or scaffolding collapses, injuring or causing the death of the worker), electric gate manufacturers (a safety mechanism fails, causing someone to be crushed as the gate closes), and directors — both inside and outside — for companies forced into receivership or bankruptcy (negligent supervision, breach of fiduciary duty and other distressing allegations).

How do you protect yourself? Start with basics that are beyond the scope of this book. You must first identify the risks inherent in your business or practice, then develop a way to manage those risks. Here are some widely-applicable steps:

• Establish specific criteria for the selection of customers, clients or patients, as the case may be.

• Limit the volume of business to that which can be effectively managed, or alternatively increase your service capacity.

• Narrow the scope of the products or services provided, so as to enhance both expertise and economies of scale.

• Engineer the product with great care, or establish carefully-developed substantive systems for the provision of professional services.

- Examine all point-of-sale materials to be certain instructions are clear and complete, that implied warranties are disclaimed and that only justified claims of expertise are made.
- Seek information and assistance from consultants, liability insurance companies, trade associations and professional societies regarding software and other tools available to assist in reducing the risk of error.
- Purchase all the errors and omissions or professional liability insurance reasonably affordable.

This book, however, is not about preventing error: I assume that you have already taken the steps described above. Nor is it about lawsuit roulette. It is a book for the exposed. It addresses only ways to reduce the risk of losing the product of a working lifetime to a lawsuit that turns into a financial *blitzkrieg*!

The Steps. Here are the steps in the process: first, you establish or carefully recheck your estate plan; then you analyze proposed property transfers in light of fraudulent transfers law to establish the reserve ("Reserve"); then, if you cannot cost-effectively dispose of all your real estate investments other than your home, you convey them to either a land trust or to a family partnership; and finally, you transfer the remaining fungible assets to a tax haven trust, there to be invested in securities by the corporate trustee.

The Ethics. What about the ethics of asset protection planning? My greatest concern in going public with this information is that I may be seen as lawyer to the flakes of the world. So this book is not a treatise on how to avoid by any means the consequences of wild speculation, gross negligence or bankruptcy fraud, though certainly those so inclined may abuse this information to that end. Rather, it is about how to reduce the chances of being sued, and how to better position yourself for settlement when it happens.

The true professional prizes integrity above all; the accumulation of wealth is a happy but incidental consequence of practicing one's chosen profession with skill and diligence, not the principal objective. There is every cause to believe that most business persons chose their occupations with the same care and pursue them with the same principled zeal. Given this moral quality, you may reasonably question the propriety of so ordering your affairs as to present a less inviting target for the unhappy attentions of potential claimants. Among the many points of analysis, consider at least these:

- Thoughtful people may differ with societal notions of who should bear the risk of stumbling on a sidewalk crack, or neglecting to read safety instructions on a brazier, or undergoing surgery that carries known risks where the risks are fully described in advance, or failing to revisit the family attorney to periodically update an estate plan as facts and laws change, etc. Life is not without risk. Those who believe people should shoulder more responsibility for their lives may, with perfect logical and ethical harmony, arrange their affairs so as to discourage those claims deemed little more than the product of a lottery mentality.

- Attorneys advise daily on asset protection issues, and clients act on that advice; they just do not perceive it in quite the way it is presented in this book. For example, people routinely limit personal liability in the conduct of their business, practice and investment matters by conducting those affairs through corporations and limited partnerships.

- Every profession has lobbied successfully for favorable statutes of limitation. In some states, for example: a physician may not be sued unless the claimant first procures an opinion from an independent medical expert that the physician was professionally negligent; damages recoverable by the claimant (other than hospital-medical costs and loss of income) are severely limited; and attorney fees are so limited that only major claims produce fees large enough to justify the time and expense of suing. Asset protection planning is a fact of everyday life; it simply goes by another name.

- The type of planning we here contemplate has attracted some debate in the professions. The advocates fall generally into two groups: those who believe that it is immoral and degrades both the person and the profession to shelter assets in any way; and those who note the absence of any law or ethical rule on the point and take the position that there is no obligation to evidence financial responsibility for negligence in order to conduct business or prac-

iv

tice, so there can be nothing unlawful or unethical about sheltering assets against future claims.

Both schools acknowledge that transferring assets so as to hinder, delay or defraud known present and contingent creditors is both unlawful and unethical.

In this book, I address the needs and concerns of those holding the second point of view, those who have determined to place their obligations to family above those of unknown future creditors. The techniques are admittedly sophisticated, but they are also both practical and lawful. I hope you find them of value.

CHAPTER 1

Asset Protection Planning: The Process

Summary. *The steps in the process: establish or carefully recheck your estate plan; analyze proposed property transfers in light of fraudulent transfers law to establish your Reserve; if you cannot cost-effectively liquidate real estate investments, convey them into one or more land trusts or a family partnership; then transfer the rest to a tax haven trust. Violation of fraudulent transfers law puts all assets at risk. Familiarity with enforcement of judgment procedure enables you to plot your course with confidence. If the costs of liquidating real estate dictate keeping it, either the land trust or the family partnership is the best way to hold it. The tax haven trust surrounds your estate with both legal and practical protection. We are drowning in misinformation and sloppy advice in this asset protection area, so be careful who you believe.*

Section 1.1 An Overview, Q&A

A Perceived Remedy for Every Misfortune. The decades-long growth in claims against Target Defendants for product liability, noncompliance with securities law and professional negligence continues to boom. As a result, the Target Defendants of the world must either live with the risk that the product of a superior education and long years of diligent service may one day be carried out the door by a smiling claimant or leave their chosen field.

Insurance. For some, liability insurance is both available and affordable; for others, it is neither. If available at all, you should purchase it in at least low-six-figure amounts. The current trend is to apply defense costs to the policy limits, so having $200,000 to pay defense attorneys through settlement or trial is of real value, even if an asset protection plan is in place. It would be foolhardy to place so much faith in the plan that no need is seen for competent defense counsel.

Insured or not, asset protection planning is of critical importance to the task of preserving financial independence against that day when advancing age or declining health forces full or partial retirement.

Fully one-third of all physicians, lawyers and accountants practice without professional liability insurance. For architects, it is 58.6% at last count.[1]

Those claims that go to trial often result in six and seven-figure judgments, with the result that even insured Target Defendants face the risk of judgments exceeding policy limits. The policy limits issue becomes even more disturbing, considering claims based on conduct taking place many years earlier; *e.g.*, the $35 will prepared in 1968 that turns into a million-dollar claim in 1992. When that happens, sometimes years after the Target Defendant retired to the golf courses of Palm Springs, the $100,000 occurrence policy in force in the year the will was prepared looks puny indeed.

You. You are a Target Defendant, or you would not be this far into the book. Admit it. You know the risks associated with your chosen field, but it won't happen to you. Right? You are the lucky one. But what if you are the statistic? Can you afford to be wrong? Like most, you know the problem exists, but by hoping for the best, your anxiety is reduced to the point that you take no action. That anxiety level will rise to the skies, though, the first time you are served with a killer lawsuit. But planning **then** is fraught with greater legal and practical risks. So do it now!

Perhaps because of the supposed costs, perhaps because of discomfort arising from a sense of impropriety, you may have tried self-help. If so, you may now find yourself trapped by the results. Self-help is almost invariably wrong in some material respect. Do it correctly the first time by securing competent legal guidance and avoid the parade of horribles. The costs are often offset by liability insurance premium savings and are always offset by the peace of mind it provides.

Working Assumptions. In approaching the task of asset protection planning, I work on certain assumptions; planning strategies based on any others are beyond the scope of this book. Those assumptions are that you wish to operate entirely **within the law**, and that you wish to retain **direct control** over your property at all stages in the process. This eliminates:

• transferring property to a relative or friend as a purported gift, intending to retake it when the crisis passes; and

• transferring property to the asset protection trusts widely promoted in the tax havens (a phony irrevocable discretionary trust).

Given that our planning must be lawful and that you must stay in control, we rely on the art involved, on illusion, as the first line of defense. Solid barriers are raised only if and to the extent the claimant proves particularly tenacious.

The Steps. As noted in the Introduction, the asset protection planning process presupposes a sound business or practice methodology for reducing risk. It goes beyond that: to establish an effective estate plan by which to address estate tax reduction and management needs of the survivors; then to carefully evaluate claims, both those asserted and those known but unasserted, so as to ascertain the value of property to be maintained in your name and thereby avoid fraudulent transfer liability; then to remove your name from record title to the remaining assets. We will return to the process in a few pages, but first consider the reasons for these steps.

On terminology, I use the term "claimant" to denote the time period prior to trial, "plaintiff" during trial and "judgment creditor" or "creditor" after judgment.

Usually, a claim of the type experienced by Target Defendants is directed at multiple defendants. At some stage, the defendant group will collectively evaluate the merits of the claim and reach a conclusion about both the probable outcome and the costs of continuing the litigation through trial. Unless angered beyond belief by the unfairness of it all, the defendants will then pool their funds based on agreed levels of proportionate liability and make a settlement offer. At that time, the plaintiff's attorney must decide whether to recommend acceptance, a counteroffer, or that the plaintiff reject and try to better it at trial.

Plaintiffs are usually interested in settling so as to avoid delay, expense and the risk of losing. If the case is strong on both liability and damages, the case will usually settle for about two-thirds of the expected recovery; less of course if the case is weak. But if you disclose that you have no insurance covering the claim, or that your policy limit is too low to satisfy the settlement demand, the attorney faces a more difficult task in advising the plaintiff.

An inquiry into your personal finances is generally prohibited, because your ability to pay is not relevant to either liability or the determination of damages. Anything not relevant is inadmissible. Plaintiff's counsel is unable to subpoena your tax returns for insight into ability to pay; they are inadmissible for the same reason and also protected from disclosure by the privilege against self-incrimination under the Fifth Amendment to the US Constitution and local evidence law. The only way left for plaintiff's counsel to secure enough information for a settlement recommendation is to engage a private investigator to conduct an asset search.

The ingenuity of investigators knows few bounds. They will ordinarily discover each bank account, stock brokerage account and parcel of real property you own. But if you have an asset protection plan in place, the investigator's report will reveal only your home, furnishings, personal effects, an automobile or two, modest bank accounts and an incorporated business or practice.

Given homestead laws and other statutory exemptions from the claims of judgment creditors, results-oriented plaintiff's counsel will usually recommend acceptance of the offer. It is rarely worth the effort to prosecute a case to judgment against a defendant who may not be able to pay. Accordingly, most such claims are settled for little or no payment from the defendant who appears to have modest resources.

Where can this strategy break down? Let me count the ways:
• Most lawsuits do not result in punitive damages. That is because the required factual showing is unusual. To obtain punitive damages, the plaintiff must show that you breached an obligation (other than contract) where you were guilty of oppression, fraud or malice. As an employer, you may not be held liable for punitive damages based on the act of an employee unless you had advance knowledge of the unfitness of the employee and hired that person with conscious disregard for the rights and safety of others, or authorized or ratified the wrongful conduct for which the damages are awarded, or are personally guilty of oppression, fraud or malice.

Until the plaintiff can establish a basis for punitive damages, no inquiry may be made of your finances. Your financial condition is irrelevant, thus inadmissible.

If, however, the court on motion concludes that a case for punitive damages is established, an order to that effect is made and your net worth becomes relevant to — thus admissible on — the punitive damage issue. That is because such an award must be reasonably calculated to deter you from repeating the unlawful act. Given such an order, plaintiff's counsel may ask about your assets, and you must respond truthfully or face perjury or contempt of court charges.

- If the claim is ultimately reduced to judgment, the (now judgment creditor's) attorney may then freely inquire about your assets by written interrogatory or in an oral examination of judgment debtor proceeding. Again, you must respond truthfully or face perjury or contempt of court charges.
- Even though personal income tax returns are protected from discovery by the privilege against self-incrimination (because you have sworn under penalty of perjury that the information is true), that privilege may be inadvertently waived by providing copies to persons who have no "need to know" or by failing to move promptly to prevent their production. The latter is the most common, since people generally do not disclose tax returns to anyone but tax preparers, spouses and lenders, all of whom have a need to know.

Most states provide some protection by requiring the party seeking discovery of your tax returns to provide you notice; *e.g.*, when serving a subpoena on a bank for your loan file. That notice provides you the opportunity to file a motion to quash the subpoena and for a protective order, asserting the privilege. If your state does not have such a notice requirement, talk to your lender; have a note placed prominently in your credit file instructing all lender personnel to call you first if the lender is ever served with a subpoena for production of your records.

Historically, corporate documents (including tax returns) are unprotected because the corporation is a franchise — a creature of the state — and as such is deemed to have waived any such privilege. This is now supplanted by a new doctrine, one established by the US Supreme Court in 1984 and providing that the "act of production" of potentially incriminating personal records is itself an incriminating act protected by the Fifth Amendment. Innovative counsel now attempt to stretch this rule to corporate records, as well.

- If plaintiff's counsel identifies your assets by any of the above means or otherwise (ex-spouse, talkative neighbor, etc.), the attempt to recover under the judgment begins.

That attempt need not await trial of the main action: a present or potential judgment creditor may ordinarily file suit to set aside a purported fraudulent transfer whether or not the claim in the main action is yet reduced to judgment.[2] Real property held in land trusts and partnerships may be partially insulated from levy (see Section 1.4) and that held in the tax haven trust are insulated by various legal preconditions to recovery in those jurisdictions (see Section 1.6).

• Bankruptcy can defeat the asset protection plan where you use a trust domiciled in a common law jurisdiction (Bermuda, Cayman, Bahamas, Turks and Caicos, Isle of Man, Channel Islands, Hong Kong, etc.). This is because, under English common law, title to personal property of a debtor vests by operation of law in the bankruptcy trustee, wherever the bankruptcy proceeding is located. If you consider an involuntary bankruptcy petition filed against you by a judgment creditor to be a risk crying for a remedy, you should either use the irrevocable discretionary trust popular in the havens, with a provision removing you from the schedule of beneficiaries upon your bankruptcy, or establish the trust in Switzerland. Switzerland does not recognize or enforce the bankruptcy laws of other countries. This will keep you in control of your assets while you disclose your action to the bankruptcy court and negotiate a resolution.

Your best defense is confidentiality. Protect the attorney-client privilege and disclose the asset protection plan to others strictly on a need-to-know basis. Asset protection planning is like plastic surgery; you don't talk about your own.

Back to the Steps. Returning to our discussion of the process, the Reserve comprises non-exempt assets held in your own name and available to satisfy known asserted and unasserted debts and claims. Even if there are no such debts or claims, consider keeping your home, personal property and a few bank accounts in your name (and that of your spouse, if married) or in that of the family trust you establish for the usual estate planning reasons. To go overboard in transferring assets is to lose credibility, since no one will believe a successful Target Defendant owns nothing. Multiple trusts or limited partnerships formed to segment various assets usually have no legitimate reason to exist other than to frustrate creditors, so such an approach may be an open invitation to a fraudulent transfer claim. You can defend prejudgment transfers to land trusts and partnerships that you would utilize even in the absence of asset protection planning, but you will surely be called on to do so if it reduces nonexempt unsheltered assets to less than the amount necessary to satisfy known claims.

Finally, one of the tests for fraudulent intent in making a property transfer is whether it was made either at a time when you were insolvent, or where it made you insolvent;[3] the insolvency calculation is based on assets remaining in your name, after deducting the value of exemptions from the claims of judgment debtors, tenancy by the entirety property, liens (such as the home mortgage), and property that was transferred to the land and foreign trusts.[4] The Reserve serves to avoid liability under this rule. Your worksheet might look something like this:

SOLVENCY CHECK ON DATE OF TRANSFER

Asset Description	Fair Market Value	Exempt Portion, Sec.Debt	Beyond the Court's Jurisdiction	Balance
Residence	$850,000	$35,000 (a)		
		600,000 (b)	-0-	$215,000
Commercial Prop.	900,000	500,000 (b)	-0-	$400,000
Securities	200,000	-0-	-0-	200,000
Pension	500,000	500,000 (c)	-0-	-0-
Spousal IRA	10,000	-0-	-0-	10,000
Medical Prac.	500,000	-0-	-0-	500,000
Automobiles	70,000	1,000 (c)	-0-	69,000
Furniture, fixtures, appliances, personal effects	100,000	100,000 (c)	-0-	-0-
Total: must exceed all known debts and claims, whether or not asserted				$1,394,000
Reserve: settlement value of known asserted and unasserted claims				<150,000>
BALANCE AVAILABLE FOR TRANSFER TO TRUSTS				$1,244,000

Notes:
(a) Homestead exemption.
(b) Security interests in the property (mortgage, deed of trust, prior judgment lien, tax lien, etc.).
(c) Statutory exemption from the claims of judgment creditors.

Once putting the standard estate plan in place and completing the fraudulent transfers analysis to establish the Reserve, we turn our attention to property transfers.

The Land Trust. If you are a real estate investor, a poor market or capital gains taxes may make it impractical to sell properties in order to fully fund a tax haven trust. If so, you may transfer them to a family partnership or a land trust. Here, we consider the latter.

Few states grant reciprocity to the corporate trustees of their sister states. Absent reciprocity, a corporate trustee cannot hold title to real property outside its state of domicile. Technically, individual trustees may hold title to property anywhere, but both prudence and convention dictate that we use corporate trustees in land trust matters. Consequently, a separate land trust is required for each state in which your property is located.

The land trust provides privacy of ownership, nonresident ownership, avoidance of probate, less exposure to judgment liens, avoidance of marital interests in title, insulation from the hazards of individual ownership, transferability of beneficial interests, availability of the beneficial interest for use as collateral, an effective defense to partition proceedings by other beneficiaries, a way to easily integrate your estate and asset protection plans and serves a variety of business and property development needs. Detailed discussion is provided at Section 1.4.

If you enjoy a substantial net income from real property, or if your estate plan discloses a need for more tax liquidity, you may wish to borrow on or refinance the properties and transfer the proceeds to the tax haven trust. If you borrow, do it before conveying the property to the land trust. Outside those states where loan officers are familiar with them, lender discomfort with real and imagined loan underwriting concerns may otherwise complicate the transaction. If you borrow first then convey, you are still the beneficial owner and personally liable for repayment of the loan, so the conveyance in trust should not give effect to a "due on sale" or similar clause in the loan security instrument.

The major concern with the land trust (as with partnerships, business trusts and corporations, for that matter) is the possibility that a judgment creditor frustrated with results of a charging order on your beneficial interest may obtain a court order for the foreclosure and sale of that interest. If that happens, you could lose more than the amount of the judgment; you could lose your entire interest in the trust if the sale price is less than the value of the trust property. Nearly all states prohibit the execution sale of beneficial interests in land trusts, but not all of them. As an example, here is how it could come about in California:

"Code of Civil Procedure, Section 699.720. Types of Property Not Subject to Execution.
(a) The following types of property are not subject to execution:

• • •

(2) The interest of a partner in a partnership where the partnership is not a judgment debtor.

• • •

(8) The interest of a trust beneficiary."

The operative word is "execution." It is a term of art, meaning a levy based on a writ of execution that includes an order for sale of the levied property without special consideration by the court. This prohibition does not preclude sale upon further court order. Now consider this:

"Code of Civil Procedure, Section 708.310. Satisfaction of Judgment Against Partner Only by Order Charging Interest in Partnership.
If a money judgment is rendered against a partner but not against the partnership, the judgment debtor's interest in the partnership may be applied toward the satisfaction of the judgment by an order charging the judgment debtor's interest

pursuant to Section 15028 of the Corporations Code."

"Code of Civil Procedure, Section 709.010. Beneficiary's Interest in Trust Subject to Enforcement of Money Judgment

• • •

(b) The judgment debtor's interest as a beneficiary of a trust is subject to enforcement of a money judgment only upon petition under this section by a judgment creditor to a court having jurisdiction over administration of the trust as prescribed in Part 5 (commencing with Section 17000) of Division 9 of the Probate Code. The judgment debtor's interest in the trust may be applied to the satisfaction of the money judgment by such means as the court, in its discretion, determines are proper, including but not limited to imposition of a lien on or sale of the judgment debtor's interest, collection of trust income, and liquidation and transfer of trust property by the trustee."

"Section 709.020. Application for Order Applying Unvested Interest of Judgment Debtor's Property to Satisfaction of Money Judgment.
The judgment creditor may apply to the court on noticed motion for an order applying to the satisfaction of a money judgment a contingent remainder, executory interest, or other interest of the judgment debtor in property that is not vested in the judgment debtor. The interest of the judgment debtor may be applied to the satisfaction of the money judgment by such means as the court, in its discretion, determines are proper to protect the interests of both the judgment debtor and judgment creditor, including but not limited to the imposition of a lien on or the sale of the judgment debtor's interest."

At first blush, it appears that partnerships enjoy a major advantage in terms of enforcement of judgments protection; there is no clear statutory provision for a court order authorizing the execution sale of a partnership interest, either general or limited. Case law, however, construes certain statutes in a way that brings this remedy into existence. There, if the judgment creditor applies for the sale order, showing that the charging order did not lead to satisfaction of the judgment and that the debtor does not render unique services critical to the success of the partnership enterprise, the motion may be granted.

This treatment of land trusts is unusual. The land trust beneficial interest is usually subject to no more than a charging order, just like partnership interests. I point it out only to highlight the importance of checking local law as you structure your plan.

The Family Partnership. A detailed discussion of family partnerships is at Section 1.5. The land trust discussion overlaps in many respects, and to that extent is incorporated by reference. Separate considerations include the potential disparity in treatment under enforcement of judgments procedure as noted above and the special drafting considerations required by intrafamily gifts of partnership interests. I cite you to Section 1.5 except to mention that multiple land trusts where you use one for each state in which you own property should never present a problem from the standpoint of a creditor claiming that doing so constitutes evidence of an intent to hinder, delay or defraud creditors; after all, you have sound privacy and estate planning reasons for multiple trusts. That cannot be said, though, for multiple partnerships where the partners and their interests are the same in each; especially where one or more of them own unconventional assets like automobiles. That calls your credibility into account when you try to explain that such multiple partnerships were not created solely to make more difficult the collection task of the judgment creditor.

Remember the proviso at the beginning of the land trust comments above. You use these vehicles only if it is not cost-effective to liquidate the real estate. Your best protection is the tax haven trust, so weigh the cost question with that point in mind. *Et sic pendet.*

The Tax Haven Trust. The property sale or loan proceeds, all securities and most of your cash should then be transferred to a tax haven trust located in a carefully-selected jurisdiction, using a major non-US bank as trustee. Why a tax haven trust? You reach that conclusion by a process of elimination:

• If you use a domestic trust and serve as your own trustee, a routine asset search will disclose all the real estate, bank accounts and brokerage accounts because your name is on them.

• If you appoint a close friend as trustee, that friend may get sick, die, lose interest in the job or become a greedy former friend.

• If you form a corporation to hold the assets, you may face unhappy tax consequences: personal holding company tax penalties; unwarranted accumulation of surplus tax penalties; double taxation of appreciation on dissolution of the corporation (once to the corporation and once to you as distributee); and minimum state franchise tax. Moreover, your identity as shareholder may be ascertained by examining the file of the state department of corporations.

• You may use a corporate trustee (bank or trust company) to establish a domestic trust. Title is held in the corporate trustee's name, identifying the trust by number instead of by reference to the settlors. That will keep your name off the record for purposes of holding title to the various assets. Such a trust being revocable, however, any judgment creditor who discovers it may immediately levy. It is that weakness that leads to use of a tax haven trust as the preferred vehicle for holding the remaining assets in your estate. The creditor is usually discouraged by the complexity and the effort required to locate and levy on assets held offshore. A detailed discussion is found at Section 1.6.

Planning for the Business or Practice. Turning now to asset protection planning for your business or professional practice, here are a few fundamentals:

• Sole proprietors and practitioners are personally liable for all obligations arising from the business or practice.

• Partners are not only liable for all business or practice obligations, they are liable for the acts of the other partners to the extent committed in the course and scope of partnership operations.

• Those who conduct a business enterprise in corporate form are protected from business obligations except: where expressly assumed; where the obligation is personal because it arises from conduct not part of the employment relationship; or where the corporation serves as a sham and device by which the shareholder defrauds creditors (the Alter Ego Doctrine).

• Professionals operating in corporate form have the same protection, except for personal professional negligence. Practitioners are personally liable for their own professional negligence, but not for that of other professionals practicing as shareholder-employees of the corporation. A professional corporation must, upon formation and each year thereafter, satisfy its regulatory agency that it maintains some minimum level of professional liability insurance, or must otherwise provide its patients or clients some form of security for negligence.

Most of us leave more cash, receivables and equipment in the business or practice than necessary. By going through a corporate reorganization to remove excess assets, you reduce the amount available to satisfy future judgments, blunting the interest of many prospective claimants. Here are some examples:

• The contractor or manufacturer may form a new operating corporation, funding it with the necessary working capital and such work-in-process as then exists, and converting the predecessor corporation or partnership to a capital equipment leasing company. The leasing company sublets the facilities and rents the equipment to the operating company. The revenues of the operating company are drawn down as lease, salary and bonus payments so as to keep its assets at the irreducible minimum. If a judgment that puts the operating company out of business is taken, sale of the leasing company assets, or their use in a new — **different** — business provides a way of starting over.

In this context, a 1988 case is instructive. The 9th Circuit Court of Appeals, in an opinion dated January 13, 1988, addressed "a novel question involving principles of bankruptcy, labor and corporate law."[5] The court found that a US Bankruptcy Court cannot order the discharge of a corporate debt in a Chapter 7 (straight bankruptcy) proceeding. Under USC Sec. 727 (a) (1), the bankruptcy court is required to grant a debtor a discharge "unless ... the debtor is not an individual." Thus, corporations (and partnerships) cannot discharge their debts in a bankruptcy proceeding. The defendant corporation in this case incurred a liability to the National Labor Relations Board ("NLRB") for back pay damages arising from unfair labor practices. The shareholders ceased doing business through the original corporation, started a new one, were pursued by the NLRB, again ceased doing business through the second corporation and started a third, a process repeated several times and concluding with a Chapter 7 corporate bankruptcy proceeding. The court examined the history of the US Bankruptcy Code and concluded that a primary legislative concern was the evasion of liability by liquidating corporations that later resume operation in different form, free of debt. The legislature intended that corporations actually continuing in business may not avoid previously-incurred debt, so it forced the shareholders in that case to satisfy the NLRB claims from personal resources.

This ruling tells us that if you separate your company or practice into equipment leasing and operating entities, then lose a large lawsuit, your choices may be limited to two: commence a Chapter 11 reorganization proceeding for the operating entity under which some or a large part of the judgment may be effectively discharged under a court-approved partial-payment plan; or if the substantial court, administrative and legal costs put the reorganization option beyond your grasp, place the operating company into straight bankruptcy, liquidate the capital equipment company and leave that particular business.

•   Another approach is the "Reverse LBO." It involves: obtaining maximum loans against the assets and general credit of the corporation, limited only by the amount of debt it can service and by fraudulent transfer considerations; creating the most liberal possible pension or profit-sharing plan for the shareholder-employees; and paying the remainder out as bonuses. This approach leaves a highly leveraged business, a lower book value, a large amount tucked away in an exempt qualified pension or profit-sharing plan and any balance in the hands of shareholders who presumably have undertaken personal asset protection planning.

To reduce the risk of personal liability under the Alter Ego Doctrine and fraudulent transfers law, you should obtain an independent expert opinion on the amount of working capital required by the operating company in either of the two examples described above. That way, you blunt any argument that you deliberately rendered it unable to satisfy its obligations.[6] Beyond that, it is important that the corporate formalities be observed and that the operating company in fact function as a separate company.

Anyone who tries to impose personal liability on you for corporate obligations under the Alter Ego Doctrine must plead and prove some or all of the following elements: that the corporation was originally undercapitalized for the volume of business and liabilities assumed under normal business operations (a highly subjective judgment, drawn largely from industry practice and norms); that the shareholders commingled corporate and personal funds, or used corporate funds without characterization as salary, bonus, lease payments, expense reimbursements, etc.; that the claimant believed the business was unincorporated — and it appeared to be unincorporated — at the time the decision was made to enter into the transaction with it, that assumption being material to the decision; and that the shareholders failed to maintain certain minimum corporate records such as accounting journals, tax returns, authorization for corporate actions, minutes, stock, etc. To make the case for Alter Ego, the creditor must find multiple failures of this nature leading to the conclusion that the corporation serves only as a sham and a device by which the creditors are defrauded. That is a substantial burden of proof, and most such claims are unsuccessful.

In a related development, the California Supreme Court, in March 1990, clarified the rule that shareholders of a dissolved corporation may not be sued on a cause of action that arose after dissolution. The case involved a construction company, Penasquitos, Inc., sued for construction defects in work performed prior to dissolution, but which did not become known and lead to damage until later. The statutory exceptions to the rule did not apply. (Those exceptions are: actions pending at time of dissolution may still be prosecuted against the former shareholders; recovery is permitted from shareholders who received assets in dissolution without satisfying all corporate debts; and the shareholders of a dissolved corporation may be sued on a cause of action that arose prior to the date of dissolution.) The cause of action "arises" when damage is incurred and becomes known. This suggests a substrategy for those Target Defendants engaged in project-oriented occupations (contractors, developers, syndicators): form a separate corporation for each project, and dissolve it upon completion, taking account of the "collapsible corporation" rules.

In undertaking any corporate asset protection planning, it is important for legal counsel to review the business records and major contracts for preventive steps that may reduce ongoing business risks. The review may include point-of-sale materials, product or service warranties, invoice language, sales training materials, operating manuals, etc.

• There are certain similarities to the foregoing in the structure of a corporate professional practice. All the equipment and the office building should be owned outside the corporation and leased to it. It leaves the professional corporation owning nothing but cash, receivables, prepaid expenses and work-in-process. Partly as a matter of convenience in dealing with periodic negative cash flow, the corporation should establish and maintain its own line of credit with an institutional lender; avoiding shareholder loans to the corporation reduces the number of leads to personal assets.

Summary of the Strategy. Asset protection planning is the process of presenting for public consumption an estate that is both modest (a relative term) and protected to a substantial extent by exemptions from the claims of judgment creditors. The likely result is that you will not be seen as a "deep pocket" defendant. That may help you avoid being sued at all. If sued anyway, at least you will hold the strongest possible settlement posture. Asset protection planning is best done prior to the first claim, but can be successfully carried off even after a claim is threatened. As Robert Louis Stevenson said so well, "Life is not a matter of holding good cards but of playing a poor hand well."

You may be struggling with some questions at this point, so let us address those that arise most often:

Q. *Is asset protection planning a guarantee that I will never have to pay a judgment?*

No. Any plan offered as "bulletproof" under all circumstances must be based on the assumption that you will hide assets then lie about it. Such an assumption is morally, ethically and legally unacceptable. Asset protection planning will **reduce** the likelihood of being sued and will establish a useful settlement posture where the claim cannot be avoided; it will not **eliminate** every risk.

Once you have adopted this posture, anyone who conducts an asset investigation to evaluate whether to sue is likely to give up on the notion after concluding that recovery prospects are poor.

Q. *Is not your money at risk when you put it offshore?*

No more than keeping it here; probably less. The largest banks in the world maintain branches and subsidiaries in the major tax havens. They are as large and sophisticated as any American bank, and their records as portfolio managers are among the best in the world.

This brings up an important point. The second-stage defense to a fraudulent transfers attack is diffusing the appearance of *mens rea* (wrongful intent). We do that by using the asset protection planning process to address legitimate investment goals. For example: a typical and legitimate use of the land trust is insulation of the investor-owner from the complaints of tenants; and geographical investment diversification is effectively obtained by purchasing foreign securities through an offshore trust. Asset protection then becomes an **incidental** benefit. That position may become critical in persuading a judge or jury in any subsequent fraudulent transfer action that the planning and transfers were not undertaken to hinder, delay or defraud creditors. **Any time the circumstances surrounding an allegedly fraudulent transfer comport equally with a theory of honest and fair dealing, a finding of a fraudulent transfer may not be made.**[7]

Q. *Why do you worry so much about fraudulent transfer risk?*

In America, we have a constitutional prohibition against debtors' prisons. You will not be incarcerated merely because you fail to pay your debts. But you **may** go to prison if you willfully violate a lawful, known court order. It is called "contempt of court." A contempt of court citation is what issues if you are found guilty of a fraudulent transfer and you refuse the court's order to retrieve the assets and pay the judgment creditor.

Q. *Isn't it simpler to just transfer everything to my spouse or children?*

Not after you think about it for a minute. If you keep a string on it, it is probably a fraudulent transfer. Otherwise, it is a gift.

Assume for the sake of argument that you are willing to risk liability for fraudulent transfer. What if you become estranged from the transferee? It happens. When the spouse or children have the money and the power to keep it, strange things can happen to the relationship. What if the transferee predeceases you? It happens. What if the transferee is financially destroyed by a lawsuit or bankruptcy, losing your money to those creditors? It happens.

Whether fraudulent or not, the transfer takes the form of a gift; except where covered by the marital deduction, gifts are taxable at rates ranging from 18% to 55%.

At bottom, I have yet to meet a Target Defendant who seriously desires to give away the estate. To **pretend** to do so involves both loss of control and risk of prosecution for making a fraudulent transfer.

Q. *Is it easy to find qualified advice in this area of the law?*

No. To my eternal chagrin, most of the advice comes from non-lawyers promoting thinly-veiled tax evasion schemes, where asset protection planning plays a minor role. Much of the published asset planning material is even directed toward people who just choose not to pay their bills.

There are a few attorneys practicing in this area of the law who seem to have given these issues serious thought, but each relies heavily on the use of multiple limited partnerships, some of which are funded with things like automobiles, certificates of deposit and household bank accounts. Since the usual function of a limited partnership is to hold and manage only investment properties and active business interests, the only rational purpose for placing noninvestment holdings in them is to create as many judgment enforcement obstacles as possible. Put yourself in the position of the judge who must apply the badges of fraud (*infra*) to the facts and circumstances of such a transfer. You cannot afford that risk.

Q. *Should I use only corporate trustees?*

Yes. They do not get old, lose interest in the job or die. Just as important, if they make a mistake you can sue with some reasonable prospect of collecting on your judgment.

Q. *Are there any tax savings from using a tax haven trust?*

No. It is taxed under the grantor trust rules, just like your domestic family trust; the income and deductions are reported on your personal tax returns.

Q. *How about the land trust?*

Same thing.

Q. *Is this planning costly?*

It is invariably a small percentage of the asset values protected, and a one-time cost that routinely leads to superior investment returns on the assets transferred to the tax haven trust. This planning also rationalizes a reduction in the amount of professional liability or errors and omissions insurance. For physicians practicing in high-risk areas of medicine, for example, reducing coverage from $3 million to $1 million may reduce the premium by $60,000 every year.

Q. *It sounds as though this is a balanced approach for the professional or business person who wishes to keep control and operate strictly within the law.*

Yes, it is. You may hold in your own name a nice home, automobiles, furnishings and modest bank balances, maintaining a lifestyle commensurate with your station in life. Your wealth is held primarily in a land trust or partnership where you have effective control and all the benefits of outright ownership, and in a professionally managed portfolio of foreign securities where you have even more control; perhaps also in securities held and managed by the corporate trustee of your domestic family trust. No asset protection plan is foolproof, but this approach provides reasonable assurance of retaining the proceeds of a lifetime's work.

Section 1.2 Fraudulent Transfers

Its Origins. The first statute dealing with fraudulent transfers was *13 Eliz. c.5.*, the Statute of Elizabeth entitled *The Fraudulent Conveyances Act 1571* ("the 1571 Act"). It was enacted by England during the reign of Elizabeth I and is thought by legal historians to reflect then-existing English common law. Following the practice of the day, the 1571 Act was drafted in wide terms so as to enable judges to bring within its scope almost every kind of transaction used by debtors to the prejudice of their creditors. In *Twynes Case (1602)*, for example, the court stated:

> "Because fraud and deceit abound in these days more than in former times, all statutes made against fraud should be liberally and beneficially expounded to express the fraud."

The 1571 Act was partially repealed and superseded in 1925 by Section 172 of England's *Law of Property Act (1925)* ("the Property Act"), narrowing the view of transfers deemed fraudulent.

From an asset protection standpoint, the key element of the 1571 Act was the absence of protection against the claims of unknown future creditors; the precise meaning of "creditors and others" in that act was held in numerous early cases to include those who held unasserted or contingent claims at the time of the transfer, but whose claims were not known to the transferor. None of the cases dealt precisely with those whose claims matured and who became known only after the transfer. Unfortunately, the Property Act did little to clarify the question. The Property Act was later consolidated with the 1571 Act in *The Insolvency Act 1986*.

As a general proposition, your tax haven trust should be established in a tax haven that follows English common law; that gives you 800 years of trust precedent on which to rely for predictability. The principal havens in that category are members of the British Commonwealth. English law becomes the law of a Commonwealth member in any of several ways. The most common way is under Section 40 of the *Interpretation Law, c.70:*

"70. All such laws and statutes of England as were, prior to the commencement of I George II, c.1, esteemed, introduced, used, accepted or received as laws in the Islands shall continue to be the law in the Islands save insofar as any such laws or statutes have been, or may be, repealed or amended by any law of the Islands."

Thus, if the haven jurisdiction has enacted law on a particular topic, that enactment supersedes English law. If not, English law applies by default.

In America. Through the early part of this century, every state adopted various versions of the 1571 Act. In 1918, the National Conference of Commissioners on Uniform State Law ("the Conference") formulated the *Uniform Fraudulent Conveyance Act* ("UFCA") in order to encourage uniformity of law among the states. Sometimes with minor modifications, about one-half the states adopted UFCA. Because of changes made in the *Bankruptcy Reform Act of 1978*,[8] the Conference appointed a committee in

1979 to revise UFCA. The result is the *Uniform Fraudulent Transfer Act* ("UFTA"), adopted by eight states to date. The name was changed to emphasize the fact that UFTA deals with **all** property transfers, not just conveyances of real estate alone.

Throughout the following discussion, remember that transferring an asset so as to utilize an exemption from judgment creditor claims is not a fraudulent transfer; nor is the gift of an exempt asset; nor is the sale of a nonexempt asset, if made for adequate consideration; nor is your transfer of property to a trust where you are still the beneficial owner, as long as the transfer was made for reasons other than to hinder or delay the claims of creditors, even if the latter is the necessary result.

There are two tests by which your transfer of property or incurrence of an obligation may be deemed fraudulent. They are **actual** fraud and **constructive** fraud:

• **Actual Fraud.** Under the actual fraud test, the creditor must prove that you intended to "hinder, delay or defraud" one or more creditors. It is impossible to prove your state of mind in the absence of a confession, so the courts have identified certain factors indicating the necessary intent, characterized as "badges of fraud." UFTA contains certain specific badges for consideration in determining intent. The California version (which serves as our example) does not itemize those factors in the statute; rather, they are found in the Official Comments. The list includes: whether the transfer was to an insider, whether the debtor retained possession or control of the transferred property, whether the transfer was disclosed or concealed, whether the debtor was threatened with litigation before the transfer was consummated or obligation incurred, whether the transfer was of substantially all the debtor's assets, whether the debtor absconded, and whether the debtor removed or concealed assets.

The mere presence of one or more of these badges does not lead to a presumption of fraud, just an inference of possible fraudulent intent.[9] The courts are to consider all the facts and circumstances.[10] If the transfer is explained away as made in pursuit of some proper business, planning or investment purpose unrelated to hindering, delaying or defrauding creditors, the court should find the explanation persuasive. Under some state versions of UFTA, preferential payments to creditors may be made without being deemed fraudulent as to those whose claims are left unsatisfied.

As to property sales, so long as the person to whom the property was transferred bought it without debtor collusion, and received the property in good faith for reasonably equivalent value, the transferee is provided a complete defense to a fraudulent transfer claim.[11] The term "reasonably equivalent value" is not precisely defined, and proof of its payment rests on the transferee.

• **Constructive Fraud.** To find a fraudulent transfer under the constructive fraud test does not require proof of actual intent to defraud creditors. Instead, a court need only find that **both** the consideration given for the transfer (or obligation incurred) is inadequate, and that any one of three measures of financial condition is unsatisfied. If **either** adequate consideration is found or all three financial condition requirements are satisfied, the transfer is not fraudulent under the constructive fraud test.

• **Adequate Consideration.** The term "reasonably equivalent value" as used in UFTA no longer requires the court to examine the good faith of the transferee in determining the adequacy of consideration. Value is given for a transfer or an obligation if property is exchanged for it or prior debt is satisfied.[12] So where the debtor repays a loan, value is given, and an unpaid creditor cannot characterize the repayment as a fraudulent transfer.

Under UFTA, the grant of a security interest in property with a value substantially in excess of the amount of the obligation meets the fair consideration test, although it does not meet it under UFCA. Absent other factors, a finding of reasonably equivalent value is not foreclosed simply because the value of the collateral exceeds the value of the underlying debt.[13] The reason is that the difference between the value of the collateral and that of the underlying debt is available to unsecured creditors by operation of law after satisfaction of the transferee's debt.

• **The Three Tests.** The three measures of financial condition included in the constructive fraud test are: unreasonably small assets in relation to liabilities assumed, inability to repay debts and insolvency.

"Asset" is defined as property of the debtor, except to the extent of valid encumbrances, exemptions and tenancy by the entirety interests.[14]

The second financial condition measure is whether the debtor intended to incur, or believed or reasonably should have believed, that any debts incurred were beyond his or her ability to pay.[15] The new language holds the debtor to an objective standard as to the likelihood of satisfying the debts. A debtor is deemed insolvent if aggregate liabilities exceed the fair market value of assets.[16] For this purpose, contingent debts may be discounted based on the likelihood that payment will be required. The result could be a rebuttable presumption of insolvency based on the debtor's general nonpayment of debts.[17] In seeking to set aside a purportedly fraudulent transfer, creditors should find it easier to establish insolvency by gathering evidence of nonpayment than by trying to establish balance sheet insolvency from the debtor's records.

Although the term "fair value" is not defined in UFTA, it is construed by the courts as somewhere between liquidation value and the best price obtainable in a perfect market with no time constraints. Usually it will be something in excess of book value. In attacking the solvency of the debtor, plaintiff's counsel will move early to obtain a valuation of the assets at the time of the purportedly fraudulent transfer. The "unreasonably small assets" and "ability to pay debts" issues may be determined on the basis of cash flow projections; i.e., if cash flow projections based on the facts known when the asset was transferred or the debt incurred show the probability that the ability to pay debts existed, the court will usually find for the debtor. In making such a finding, the court in *Credit Managers' Association vs. Federal Co.*[18] introduced a reasonableness standard when it said:

"[T]he law does not require that companies be sufficiently well capitalized to withstand any and all setbacks . . . The requirement is only that they not be left with 'unreasonably small capital' at the time of a conveyance alleged as fraudulent."

Consequently, the financial status at the time of transfer or incurrence of an obligation showing the ability to operate or service the debt incurred may be sufficient to satisfy the financial status branch of the constructive fraud test, despite the debtor's ultimate financial difficulty arising from unforeseen events.[19]

Foreclosures. UFTA shields most foreclosures from attack as fraudulent transfers. It provides that the enforcement of liens, so long as there is no collusion with the creditor and so long as the foreclosure complies with applicable law, cannot be voided as a fraudulent transfer.[20]

Statute of Limitations. The statute of limitations on **actions** for fraudulent transfer is four years after the transfer is made or the obligation incurred, or one year after it was, or reasonably could have been, discovered, whichever last occurs.[21] The limitation on seeking a fraudulent transfer determination under enforcement of judgment law, so as to permit a **levy**, is four years after the transfer or obligation.[22] In no event may the claim be prosecuted, whether as an action or levy, more than seven years after the transfer is made or the obligation incurred.[23]

Under local law,[24] a prejudgment writ of attachment may be available as a provisional remedy for claims that are the subject of pending litigation.[25] This secures the status quo so as to assure full or partial satisfaction of the judgment, once obtained.

Even if the transfer is fraudulent, a transferee receiving the property in good faith and who has paid value for the asset or obligation is entitled to a lien on the asset or enforcement of the obligation to the extent value is given. The transferee who is also an insider will not qualify for that protection if the transferee had reason to believe the debtor was insolvent at the time of the transfer.[26]

Criminal Sanctions. In addition to the summary of UFTA here presented, bear in mind that criminal penalties apply to fraudulent transfers as well. As a general rule, every person who is a party to a transfer made with the intent to deceive and defraud others or to hinder, delay or defraud creditors is guilty of a misdemeanor.[27] Moreover, participation by an attorney in a scheme to defraud present or potential judgment creditors of the client is a crime and a proper subject for disciplinary action by the state bar.[28]

In Selected Tax Havens. To comment on fraudulent transfers law in each of the major havens would enlarge this book unnecessarily. Therefore I mention only three and discuss primarily one in order to provide a sense of the environment in which asset protection planning operates there:

   •   **The Isle of Man.** The Isle of Man as presently constituted under Tynwald, the Manx government, was established early in the 11th century, 500 years before the 1571 Act was enacted. Manx common law exists for fraudulent transfers, but it has no statutory law. Under these circumstances, the 1571 Act is not Manx law by default, so the Isle of Man finds the 1571 Act merely persuasive, not controlling. It goes its own way in several material respects.

   Keep in mind that our discussion of fraudulent transfers law in the Isle of Man, the Cayman Islands and the Cook Islands is tightly focused on your needs in asset protection planning. That leaves out a number of topics related but having only academic significance.

   The form of trust in common use here for asset protection (not the form I employ), is an irrevocable discretionary trust. This is one in which you make an irrevocable gift in trust, granting the trustee sole power to accumulate income and to distribute both income and principal to whomever it chooses from a list of beneficiaries you provide upon establishing the trust. You may be among the named beneficiaries, but a trust provision deletes you if you are ever the subject of a bankruptcy petition. You also provide the trustee a "side letter" by which you express your preferences on trust distributions. "Just in case," you may also appoint a "Protector" whose function is to see to it that the trustee honors your wishes. The discretionary trust (but not the side letter) is sanctioned by statute at Section 33 of *The Trustee Act 1961*.

   As a fundamental proposition, the courts of the Isle of Man

will recognize an order of a US Bankruptcy Court under the principle of "universality" discussed below. They will not, however, give effect to the judgment of a foreign court otherwise unless covered by *Judgments (Reciprocal Enforcement) Isle of Man Act 1968*. That act does not apply to the US. As a result, the US judgment creditor is required to file suit on the original cause of action (negligence, etc.) in the Isle of Man and prove the case all over again, this time under Isle of Man law. As a defendant nonresident in that country, the creditor must obtain leave of the Isle of Man court to serve process on you where you live. It will not do so. This presents an insurmountable barrier to filing a new lawsuit there, unless the creditor can serve you while you are visiting that country. The creditor's only meaningful alternative is to file a petition for involuntary bankruptcy, either there or in the US.

In considering the possibility that a trustee in bankruptcy could claim that selection of Isle of Man trust law was an artificial device serving as a "badge of fraud," note that *The Hague Convention on the Recognition of Trusts* was adopted in the Isle of Man through the *Recognition of Trusts Act 1988*. Under that act, the trust is governed by the law elected in the trust instrument. The law so chosen will govern its validity, its construction, its effects and its administration. The choice of Manx law will be recognized by the Isle of Man courts, and will not be viewed as circumstantial evidence of an intent to hinder, delay or defraud your creditors.

The *Recognition of Trusts Act 1988* is subject to conflict of laws provisions found elsewhere. This raises the possibility that a creditor could move to set aside your transfer in trust by claiming that the trust is invalid in accord with relevant state or federal law, or in accord with Isle of Man law. To avoid that risk, you must be certain that the trust satisfies the US criteria for recognition as a trust and that its funding does not violate fraudulent transfer law in either your state of domicile or in the Isle of Man. While your foreign grantor trust may not exist for tax purposes (see Section 1.6), it does exist as a legal relationship.

In addressing another aspect of the validity of a tax haven trust under Isle of Man law, you must recognize that it is a self-governing territory and never part of the United Kingdom. The United Kingdom (England, Scotland, Ireland and Wales) is responsible for its defense and foreign affairs, while Tynwald governs its internal affairs. Manx law is separate from English law, so English law is persuasive only in the absence of Manx law to the contrary. Therefore, it behooves us to consider both together.

In England, as in the Isle of Man, any creditor attack on a transfer in trust must be based either on bankruptcy or fraudulent transfer law.[29] The approach of the English courts is illustrated in the opinion on *In Re Butterworth (1882) 19 Ch.D. 588.*

There, the debtor was a successful baker until August 1878. He then decided to start a grocery store. Before doing so, he instructed his solicitor to prepare a trust for the benefit of his wife and children. The solicitor cautioned him that conveyance of his extensive property holdings to the trust would be void if he was unable to satisfy all his debts from property remaining in his name alone. The debtor prepared and presented to the solicitor a financial statement demonstrating that ability. The solicitor then prepared the trust and deeds. Apparently the debtor either misled the solicitor or was wildly optimistic about the value of his assets in relation to his liabilities, because the court found in the following bankruptcy proceeding as follows:

"Any settlement of property [*i.e.*, transfer in trust] made by a trader not being a settlement made before and in consideration of marriage, or made in favour of a purchaser or encumbrancer in good faith and for valuable consideration, or a settlement made on or for the wife or children of the settlor or property which has accrued to the settlor after marriage in right of his wife, shall, if the settlor becomes bankrupt within two years after the date of such settlement, be void as against the trustee of the bankrupt appointed under this Act, and shall, if the settlor becomes bankrupt at any subsequent time within ten years after the date of such settlement, unless the parties claiming under such settlement can prove that the settlor was at the time of making the settlement able to pay all his debts without the aid of the property comprised in such settlement, be void against such trustee."

Having held that the debtor's transfer in trust was void under bankruptcy law, the court went on to say that it was also void under the 1571 Act as a fraudulent transfer. This second finding was *dictum* (not necessary for the decision), but clearly enunciates the principle as follows:

"A man is not entitled to go into a hazardous business, and immediately before doing so settle all his property voluntarily, the object being this: 'If I succeed in business, I make a fortune for myself. If I fail, I leave my creditors unpaid. They will bear the loss.' That is the very thing which the Statute of Elizabeth was meant to prevent. The object of the settlor was to put his property out of the reach of his future creditors. He contemplated engaging in this new trade and he wanted to preserve his property from his creditors. That cannot be done by a voluntary settlement. That is to my mind, a clear and satisfactory principle."

Similarities in Isle of Man law to that of England are demonstrated by *In Re Corrin's Bankruptcy - Kermode, Trustee of Corrin's Bankruptcy vs. Craige (1912)*.

John Kermode bequeathed a share of his estate to Mr. and Mrs. Corrin, reserving a life estate to his widow, who died in January 1911. Mr. Corrin was then insolvent and being pressed for payment by his creditors. Prior to the death of Mrs. Kermode, Mr. Corrin assigned his share of the inheritance to a trustee for the benefit of his wife and children. In July 1911, he was adjudicated bankrupt. The question in the case was the validity of the assignment in trust. The parties conceded that the assignment was not void under then-existing bankruptcy law (Section 30, *Bankruptcy Code 1892*). The trustee in bankruptcy contended, however, that the assignment was void under the Common Law of the Isle of Man, which was on this point the same as the law of England under the 1571 Act. To this contention, the court ruled:

"The Common Law of the Isle of Man is substantially the same as the law of England under the Statute of Elizabeth, and a settlement by a man who was hopelessly insolvent at the time is fraudulent and void. There is nothing in the Bankruptcy Code to detract from the operation of the Common Law. Section 30 of the [Bankruptcy] Code simply says that such a settlement shall not be avoided by the Code. This settlement was void apart from the Code."

The court found the assignment void and ordered Corrin's trustee to pay over his share of the inheritance to the trustee presiding over his bankruptcy.

The 1571 Act was substantially altered by the *Law of Property (Amendment) Act 1924* which, in turn, was consolidated in *The Property Act*, the relevant portion being Section 72. *The Insolvency Act 1986* now contains the pertinent statutory law of England. The Isle of Man has not followed this with any specific legislation on fraudulent transfers. Note, though, Section 4(4) of *The Evidence Act 1736*:

"All fraudulent assignments or transfers of the debtor's goods or effects shall be void and of no effect against his just creditors, any custom or practice to the contrary notwithstanding."

This review of English and Isle of Man law leads us to the one unanswered question that matters: "Is the Common Law of the Isle of Man substantially the same as that of England's *Insolvency Act 1986*?" We have a court in 1912 saying it was the same as the 1571 Act at that time, but we have no modern case on point with respect to current English law. Here is a summary of England's law today:
   •   Where you transfer property in trust, either without consideration or for less than fair market value, and where the court is convinced that the transfer was made for the purpose of avoiding the claims of present or future creditors, it may fashion any order it deems fit in order to protect the interests of the creditors so prejudiced.

- The court may not, however, invalidate a sale made to a *bona fide* purchaser for value, whether the price paid was equal to fair market value or not, so long as that purchaser bought the property without knowledge of the transferor's intent to thereby defraud creditors.

Similar facts may produce different results. Asset protection may be the necessary effect of a transaction having another principal purpose, such as to facilitate international investing and diversification. Logic suggests that the determination of fraudulent intent would turn on the predominant purpose. There is no Isle of Man law on the point, however, so we are left to speculate.

While we are unable to determine whether the Isle of Man would find that England's *Insolvency Act 1986* reflects Isle of Man common law, it is safe to assume that a creditor or trustee in bankruptcy would leave no stone unturned in fashioning an argument that the act applies in the Isle of Man and that "predominant purpose" is irrelevant. So under present law, there is considerable risk of an adverse result. That leaves the procedural difficulties of prosecuting a fraudulent transfer claim in the Isle of Man as your best defense.

Turning our attention now to fraudulent transfer claims that may be asserted by way of bankruptcy proceedings, here is Section 30 of the *Bankruptcy Code 1892:*

> "Any settlement of property, not being a settlement made before and in consideration of marriage, or made in favour of a purchaser or encumbrancer in good faith and for valuable consideration, or a settlement made on or for the wife and children of the settlor of property which has accrued to the settlor after marriage in right of his wife, shall, if the settlor becomes bankrupt within two years after the date of the settlement, be void against the trustee, and shall, if the settlor becomes bankrupt at any subsequent time within ten years after the date of the settlement, be void against the trustee unless the parties claiming under the settlement can prove that the settlor was, at the time of making the settlement, able to pay all his

debts without the aid of the property comprised in the settlement, and that the interest of the settlor in such property had passed to the trustee of such settlement on the execution thereof."

Section 7 of *The Bankruptcy Procedure Act 1892* provides the following jurisdictional requirements for a bankruptcy proceeding filed in the Isle of Man:

• The debt involved must be at least £25 or such higher amount as the Treasury may require.

• The claim must be for a liquidated sum; *i.e.*, a specific amount of money, not a claim the amount of which is determined according to proof at trial.

• The "act of bankruptcy" on which the petition for bankruptcy adjudication is based must have occurred within three months prior to the filing date.

• The debtor must be domiciled in the Isle of Man or must have maintained either his principal residence or place of business there within one year prior to the filing date.

As is apparent, this presents little risk to you unless you decide to retire to the Isle of Man. If you do so, a bankruptcy proceeding commenced there within two years following your transfer in trust will invalidate the transfer unless the proceeding itself is successfully challenged.

Careful practice suggests that you deliver to your Isle of Man trustee, with your signed trust and conveyancing instruments, an affidavit to the effect that you are at that time able to satisfy all your obligations without the property being placed in the trust. The affidavit will be filed in the General Registry, which is a public Registry of Deeds. Doing so constitutes notice to the world and should be persuasive in satisfying the tests of *Bankruptcy Code* Section 30.

Because of the close geographic proximity of England and the Isle of Man, bankruptcy fraud information is exchanged between those two countries. It is authorized under Sections 1 and 5(i) of the *Bankruptcy Code 1892*. While reciprocal arrangements with other countries are possible, none yet exist.

The law provides for the conduct of discovery in the Isle of Man for litigation pending elsewhere. The *Evidence (Proceedings in Other Jurisdictions) (Isle of Man) Order 1979* is a statute extending to the Isle of Man the *Evidence (Proceedings in Other Jurisdictions) Act 1975* of the United Kingdom. Generally, it enables the Isle of Man courts to order or permit: the examination of witnesses, either orally or in writing; the production of documents; the inspection, photographing, preservation, custody or detention of any property; and taking samples of any property and carrying out any experiments on or with such property.

Finally, there is an English common law rule that operates alongside the Isle of Man statutes on bankruptcy. Under it, the orders of a foreign bankruptcy court are recognized. It requires only that the debtor be domiciled in the country where the order was made at the time the petition for bankruptcy was filed, and that the debtor subjected himself or herself to the jurisdiction of that court by either filing the petition or by appearing in the proceeding. The likelihood is that a US Bankruptcy Court order would be recognized.[30]

• **The Cayman and Cook Islands.** Late in 1989, the Cayman Islands enacted the *Fraudulent Dispositions Law 1989*. The Cook Islands passed its own statute around the same time, the *International Trust Amendment Act 1989*.

Both the Cayman and the Cook Islands statutes serve to protect the person transferring assets in trust and the trust company. The Cayman statute features the following:

• The law is given retroactive effect except for actions pending on the effective date and except for those filed within six months thereafter if based on transfers made prior to the law's effective date.

• The fraudulent transfer is voidable, as under prior law.

• The burden of proving fraudulent transfer is on the creditor seeking to void it, as under prior law.

• The statute of limitations is six years.

• Prior law voided the transfer *ab initio* (from the beginning) if the trustee had prior knowledge that the transfer was intended to hinder, delay or defraud creditors. The result was trustee liability for the return of all fees and for all disbursements made to beneficiaries. There was great uncertainty as to the nature of the proof required in order to avoid a finding of trustee complicity. This new statute grants the trustee the right to retain earned and collected fees (as well as a priority lien for those earned but not yet collected) and holds the trustee harmless from liability to the frustrated creditor for disbursements to beneficiaries, both so long as the trustee did not conspire with the transferor in the fraud. There are still no statutory elements of proof; presumably it is the customary steps of proof by the creditor that the transfer was fraudulent as to that creditor, then (separately and subsequently) that the trustee received the property with advance knowledge of the transferor's fraudulent intent.

• The fraudulent transfer is set aside only to the extent necessary to satisfy the creditor successfully asserting the claim.

The Cook Islands statute is the same in many respects. Here are the principal differences:

• The trust to which the property is transferred must be an "International Trust," domiciled and registered in the Cook Islands, in order to be governed by the law. Taken literally, that precludes locating your trust elsewhere and electing to have it governed by Cook Islands law.

• Proof of intent to defraud is limited to insolvency, either at the time of the transfer or brought about by the transfer, looking only at assets available to the creditor. Fraud may not be inferred from the timing of the transfer or from the retention of any powers over the trust.

• The statute of limitations period is one year after the transfer or two years after the underlying cause of action accrues, whichever first expires. Think, now. Assume the worst — that you funded your Cook Islands trust the day the cause of action accrued and that you failed to establish an adequate Reserve. If the usual course of events takes place, the underlying action (negligence, etc.) is filed by the plaintiff one year after the cause of action accrues, in order to avoid the bar of the statute of limitations where you live. Depending on the caseload of your local court, it will take from one to six years for the plaintiff to get the case to trial. It will then take at least a few months to get through the post trial proceedings and for plaintiff's counsel to discover that you transferred assets to a foreign trust. Upon landing in the Cook Islands to file a fraudulent transfer claim, counsel will discover that the local statute of limitations began to run two to seven years earlier, and plaintiff is out of court.

  • The Cook Islands will not recognize the judgments of any other country. As a result, all fraudulent transfer actions must be tried there *de novo* (from the beginning).

  The utility of Cook Islands law turns on the extent to which you feel the need to eliminate risk. It is clearly the best fraudulent transfers law in the world, guided to that end by Colorado lawyer, Barry Engel.

  Unless you select a strong trustee (in terms of portfolio management capabilities) and use the trust as a base for Far East investments so as to make a case for nonasset protection motivation, you may have trouble with the contention that you selected this jurisdiction for its one-sided fraudulent transfers law. Remember, most such actions and proceedings are brought in the US, relying on the court's contempt powers to secure compliance.

  The Cook Islands are remote and air service is weak, a negative for traveling there to meet with your trustee, but a positive to the extent the cost of litigating there discourages claimants. That aside, its economy is weak, the country is politically and economically dependent on New Zealand, its government is still at the Town Hall stage, and quality support services (lawyers, accountants, banks and management companies) do not compare well to the established tax havens.

  • **Cayman, Examined Separately.** Having now compared Cayman and Cook Islands statutory law, we return to related matters in the Cayman Islands; specifically, enforcement of foreign judgments, recognition of foreign bankruptcy proceedings, Cayman bankruptcy law and more on Cayman fraudulent transfers law.

  The *New York Convention on the Recognition and Enforcement of Foreign Awards* is a convention to which both the US and the

Cayman Islands are parties. It covers judgments made in the US to be enforced in Cayman.

Except for convention awards, recognition of foreign judgments is accomplished only as a matter of comity (principle under which the courts of one jurisdiction give effect to the laws and judgments of another, not as a matter of obligation but out of deference and respect). Cayman courts may also recognize US judgments as a defense to a claim there, or in connection with the assignment of property.

At common law, only those US judgments which meet the following tests are enforceable in Cayman:

• The foreign court must have obtained personal jurisdiction over you under the conflict of law rules applicable in Cayman; it cannot merely secure jurisdiction over your property.

• The judgment must be final; either all avenues for appeal or other review must be exhausted, or the time to appeal must have expired. Unless enforcement is stayed by the timely filing of an appeal bond, however, a trial court judgment will be considered "final" for enforcement purposes.

• The judgment must be for a liquidated sum — a specific sum of money; not for injunctive relief, not for taxes or any tax euphemism (e.g., "user fees") and not for punitive damages or any other form of penal recovery.

Only the issues listed above will be considered by the Cayman court in determining whether to enforce the foreign judgment in Cayman. The parties may not relitigate the merits of the claim.

In ruling on these issues, the Cayman court will recognize personal jurisdiction of the foreign court over you only under one or more of the following circumstances:

• Where you voluntarily submitted to the jurisdiction of the foreign court. That excludes a case in which you appeared in the other action solely for the purpose of challenging jurisdiction, or appeared solely to obtain the release of assets.

• Where you were a plaintiff in the proceeding leading to the foreign judgment (and lost on a cross complaint or counterclaim).

• Where the judgment was based in whole or in part on a

written agreement in which you agreed to submit to the jurisdiction of the foreign court.

• Where you resided in the foreign jurisdiction at the time the underlying action or proceeding began; or if your corporation is the target, where it had its principal place of business there and was properly served under the laws of that jurisdiction.

• Possibly, depending upon the equities as perceived by the Cayman court, where you maintained a place of business in the foreign jurisdiction and the judgment was based solely on a business transaction affected through that place of business.

Important defenses, given the right facts, are that the foreign judgment was obtained by fraud, or that its enforcement is contrary to Cayman public policy. In addition to asserting lack of personal jurisdiction as a defense, judgments dealing solely with specific property may be subject to the defense that the issuing foreign court lacked subject matter jurisdiction; *i.e.*, the property was not located within the court's geographic jurisdiction.

All the foregoing aside, the general principle underlying enforceability of foreign judgments in Cayman is whether the Cayman courts would render such a judgment against Cayman citizens. In that context, the considered opinion of local counsel is that punitive damages is both a prohibited recovery of "taxes, fines or other penalties" and violates settled public policy in Cayman.

Cayman Recognition of Foreign Bankruptcy Proceedings. At common law, such proceedings deal both with your **estate** and your **status** as debtor. All your property being vested in the bankruptcy trustee, wherever that property may be located, bankruptcy court orders are considered binding throughout the world as to: determination of insolvency; powers of management; disposition of assets and distribution of a dividend; and your discharge as debtor.

Cayman law is consistent with this worldwide enforceability theory of bankruptcy law. The Cayman courts regard assignment of a foreign debtor's property to the bankruptcy trustee as an assignment of **all** the debtor's property, including that located in Cayman. Accordingly, where the foreign bankruptcy trustee operates under a legal system consistent with this theory (a proceeding *in rem*, that is, with jurisdiction over the property and having extraterritorial effect), it will be recognized by Cayman without the need to have the foreign court orders first settled as Cayman orders.

US bankruptcy law is given recognition under this analysis. The bankruptcy orders of those countries adopting the "Territoriality" theory of bankruptcy (Brazil, for example) are not recognized. Switzerland expressly prohibits recognition of foreign court-appointed receivers and bankruptcy trustees.

There are some limitations to the Cayman court's willingness to recognize US bankruptcy trustee claims. One is that some of the rules applicable to the enforcement of foreign judgments will be applied. For example, claims for unpaid taxes will not be recognized.

Generally, though, the US bankruptcy trustee may take possession of your Cayman property (other than land) without the need to first settle its order as one of the Cayman court. As to your Cayman land holdings, the US bankruptcy trustee must first register title under Section 118 of the *Registered Land Law*, using an *ex parte* (no noticed hearing) domestication proceeding.

The Cayman court will not ordinarily inquire into the identity of the creditors in the US bankruptcy proceeding. Consequently, it is likely that assets recovered in Cayman will be applied to the satisfaction of any taxing agencies among them. That is not necessarily inconsistent with your desires, since the purpose of the bankruptcy proceeding is to dispose of all claims. Having said that, however, Cayman public policy may impose some limitations: the difficulty is in determining where the Cayman court will draw the line. Clearly, if Internal Revenue Service ("IRS") is the only creditor, the Cayman court will refuse recognition on the ground that the bankruptcy trustee is merely the agent of the US Treasury Department. Apart from the likelihood that the Cayman court will not inquire into the composition of the creditors, there is case law for the proposition that the court will enforce a tax claim where it is only one among many ordinary creditors. The cases are in conflict where there is only one creditor other than the taxing agency.

Cayman is an offshore financial center offering commercial secrecy. That term is broader than banking secrecy. Commercial secrecy does not, however, prevent a US bankruptcy trustee from locating your assets. Cayman law applies the assignment principle and treats the bankruptcy trustee as the owner. As a result, the duties formerly owed by the holder of the property (the Cayman trustee, in our working model) to you as the debtor are then owed to the bankruptcy trustee. That includes transferring funds upon order of the bankruptcy trustee and providing all requested account information, without the need for a Cayman court order. This principle applies with equal force whether you are the direct owner of the Cayman property or its beneficial owner through a trust or corporation.

The task of the US bankruptcy trustee is more complicated if you established a Cayman trust for the benefit of others. Under that circumstance, the bankruptcy trustee must present a case for setting aside the trust. Successfully doing so is difficult in the absence of investigation, and investigation is difficult under commercial secrecy. Unless large amounts are at stake, the cost of such an effort will discourage most claimants.

Once the bankruptcy trustee decides to press the claim, the commercial secrecy law presents only an obstacle, not an insurmountable barrier. The bankruptcy trustee will apply to the court, without notice to you or the trustee of your Cayman trust, and will request orders both enjoining the transfer of property and preventing the Cayman trustee from reporting the restraining orders to you or the other trust beneficiaries. Then, on noticed motion, the Cayman trust assets may be attached and an order for authority to conduct discovery made, leaving you unaware of what is taking place until it is too late to do more than respond.

So much for the effect of US bankruptcy orders in Cayman. We now turn to bankruptcy petitions filed directly in Cayman. Cayman jurisdiction to determine the estate and status of insolvent persons is found in the *Cayman Islands Bankruptcy Law (Revised)* statute. That pertaining to business enterprises is found in the *Companies Law*, cap. 22, referred to as a "winding up proceeding" or "liquidation." Since Cayman can adjudicate the bankruptcy of foreign individuals, but may not wind up or liquidate foreign companies, this comment addresses only the law pertaining to individuals.

Cayman bankruptcy law derives from the *Jamaican Bankruptcy Law 1879.* (Cayman was once a dependent of Jamaica.)

Section 14 provides that a creditor from within or outside Cayman may present an **involuntary** bankruptcy petition against a "debtor" who commits an "act of bankruptcy." The term "debtor" is cryptically defined under Section 2 as including anyone who, at the time the act of bankruptcy is committed is: personally present in Cayman; or ordinarily resides or has a place of business in Cayman; or is conducting a business in Cayman, personally or through an agent or manager; or is a member of a business entity which conducts business in Cayman.

Any debtor may present a **voluntary** petition in bankruptcy. There is no requirement of personal presence, residence or the direct or indirect conduct of a business in Cayman or elsewhere. Consequently, as a non-Caymanian debtor with assets in Cayman, you may file a voluntary petition in order to protect those assets from the claims of local creditors and to insure a ratable distribution among creditors internationally.

Returning to involuntary petitions, an "act of bankruptcy" includes certain acts committed outside Cayman. Here are some examples: conveyance of property, anywhere in the world, to a trustee for the benefit of your creditors; arguably, your filing of a reorganization petition under Chapter 11 of the *US Bankruptcy Code*; and fraudulent transfers made anywhere (that could include a transfer to a Cayman trust if made with the intent to hinder, delay or defraud known present and contingent creditors).

All this notwithstanding, bankruptcy jurisdiction is discretionary with the Cayman court. It may decline to exercise jurisdiction on your behalf if you do not come within the ambit of Section 2 and have no material connection with Cayman. While this presents a measure of uncertainty, jurisdiction will ordinarily be exercised if you transferred property to a Cayman trust, with or without any other Cayman connection.

Let us now turn our attention from foreign judgments and

bankruptcy law to some final observations on Cayman fraudulent transfers law. Its new statute is described earlier; we here discuss the effect of an order setting aside a transfer.

A transfer voided under Section 107 of the *Bankruptcy Law (Revised)* leads to radically different results than one rendered *void ab initio* (invalid from the beginning as though the transfer never took place) under fraudulent transfers law where complicity by your Cayman trustee-transferee is found. As to those voided in a bankruptcy proceeding, all acts prior to the date of the act of bankruptcy precipitating the bankruptcy proceeding (as much as six months prior to the filing date) remain valid. Thus, the fees paid to the Cayman trustee-transferee may be retained; only those received after that date are at risk. We noted earlier that lack of complicity by the trustee-transferee secures its fees to the date of the court determination, and holds it harmless from a duty to restore disbursements made from the trust. It is where complicity is found that risk remains.

The new fraudulent transfers statute does not expressly address the result of transferee complicity, except for a new limitation under which the fraudulent transfer made with transferee complicity is voided only to the extent necessary to satisfy the claim of the prevailing creditor. The result where the creditor's claim exceeds the value of the fraudulent transfer is that prior law continues to apply. Under prior law, generally believed to be the 1571 Act, the trustee-transferee is liable for the return of all trustee fees and for the restoration of all income and principal disbursements made to trust beneficiaries. As you may imagine, that is a frightening prospect for the trustee.

In addition to the financial risks, a claim of fraudulent transfer presents the trustee with an **ethical** dilemma: it owes a fiduciary duty to the trust beneficiaries to oppose the claim until its validity becomes clear; but the cost of resisting may well be paid by the trustee from its own resources if the transfer is found fraudulent with trustee complicity and the claim exceeds the remaining value of the property transferred.

On balance, it is clear that the trustee must act immediately to investigate the claim on receipt of notice. That usually requires entering an appearance in the claim proceeding so as to avoid a default judgment. If the course of action remains unclear, the trustee may (and should) seek instructions from the Cayman court by petition under Section 45 of the *Trusts (Foreign Element) Law 1987*. If the Cayman court directs it to defend, the trustee is likely to be able to recover defense costs from the trust estate, but only in the absence of a finding of complicity. If the transfer is found fraudulent with trustee complicity, any trust instrument provisions for indemnity are of no legal effect, leaving the trustee to bear all the costs of defense, fees disgorgement and disbursement restoration.

As is clear from the foregoing, a trust company offering asset protection trusts is engaged in a high-risk business enterprise. It understandably analyzes each prospective trust with the skeptical eye of a cargo insurance underwriter. In addition to the use of sound judgment as to customer selection, most have or will develop objective selection criteria for this type of business, Those initially imposed by NatWest, for example, include a two-year hold on all trust distributions.

Section 1.3 Enforcement of Judgments

The material in Section 1.2 above includes enforcement of judgments law in the tax havens because it is there more closely related to considerations of bankruptcy and fraudulent transfers. In this section we deal with enforcement of judgments in the US, an important subject if I am to fully acquaint you with the collection methods employed by plaintiffs seeking prejudgment attachment and creditors seeking satisfaction of their judgments. Forewarned is forearmed.

As you might imagine, this topic could be a book in itself if we attempted to examine the laws of every state. Instead, I will describe enforcement procedure in common use and leave it to you to check local law. This will thus serve the purpose of helping you better understand your options if called upon to engage local counsel for this purpose.

I will not deal with the *Uniform Commercial Code*, secured real property loans (mortgages and deeds of trust), statutory liens (those of repairpersons, innkeepers, bankers, mechanics and hospitals) or consumer statutes (retail installment sales, automobile sales financing and leasing).

Finally, you should consider this material in the context of assets held personally as well as those held in corporations, limited partnerships, land trusts and business trusts. Among the most widely-promoted asset protection vehicles are the latter three.

The business trust is an anachronism from the years following World War I when Massachusetts refused to recognize incorporated real estate development companies. Its function in that state, Texas and some other southern states was to secure the advantages of incorporating to operate an active business enterprise, without actually forming a corporation. I prefer incorporating such an enterprise, however. It is everywhere recognized and treated the same way for tax and liability purposes, whereas the subjective analysis of trust versus corporate features to determine tax and liability issues, plus the dearth of modern case law, make the legal effects of a business trust inherently less predictable.

As to limited partnerships, their conventional use is for multi-principal investments requiring management by a general partner. Its selection as an asset protection vehicle may be driven by the desire to make gifts to children or by the greater protection afforded it under the enforcement of judgments law of a given state.

Then there is the land trust, the conventional use of which includes not only those of limited partnerships, but passive property holdings of single investors as well.

Preliminary Considerations. At the outset, before the lawsuit is filed, the careful claimant will take the time to position the claim for mistake-free collection; correctly following the required procedure is critical to avoiding wasted time and attorney fees. Since a judgment is enforceable only against the named judgment debtor, your proper legal name and capacity as the Target Defendant must be determined by the claimant. It must appear correctly in the summons, the complaint, any writ of attachment, the judgment and any writ of execution. "Capacity" means trustee, partner, vice president, etc. One of your first defensive moves will be to see if this part of the claimant's task was correctly performed.

The careful claimant will also examine public records so as to build a list of your assets. Once obtaining that information, collectibility may be determined by analyzing applicable exemptions and security interests. Under the *US Bankruptcy Code*, only "natural persons" (not corporations or partnerships) are entitled to exemptions; many states follow the same rule. A search of your local secretary of state's records using a standard UCC-3 form under the *Uniform Commercial Code* will disclose those creditors who hold security interests in your personal property. A preliminary title report from a local title insurance company office will reveal your real property legal description, along with all liens and encumbrances.

The claimant's judgment lien (if, as or when obtained) has value only to the extent there is an equity after giving effect to all properly perfected senior liens. So the careful judgment creditor will closely examine the records to determine whether your other creditors properly perfected their security interests. If not, the claimant may acquire a lien superior to any unperfected security interests in the property.[31]

Prior to filing suit, the sophisticated claimant may contact you directly to request a voluntary security interest in property, installment payments under a promissory note, or both. Voluntary security interests confer a priority over exemptions from the claims of judgment creditors, thus serving the interests of the creditor more effectively. If you do not feel threatened at this stage, you may be inclined to talk freely about your assets and liabilities. If so, even if you choose not to agree to a voluntary lien, the information you provide may serve to facilitate collection. It is ethically permissible for either the claimant or claimant's counsel to contact you directly, so long as you do not have legal representation at the time.

The careful claimant will be certain the claim is made in the proper court. All states have separate courts for small, medium and large claims (*e.g.*, justice, municipal and superior trial courts). The amount of interest, costs and attorney fees claimed are usually (but

not always) excluded in determined the proper court where jurisdiction is determined by the amount in controversy. Your residence
as the prospective judgment debtor and the place where the alleged
act on which the action is based bear also on selection of the proper
venue (court location) for the lawsuit.

Between Filing and Judgment. Whether statutory or common
law, prejudgment remedies provided by state law are generally
enforceable in the federal courts, as well. That is because the
federal courts treat them as "substantive" law, rather than "procedural." (Federal courts follow their own procedure.) This includes
enforcement of judgments from sister states that are settled for
enforcement purposes as those of the state in which you as the
debtor reside or where your property is located.

As a general proposition, orders *pendente lite* (made between
the filing date and trial) and judgments may be enforced only
against property located in the state where they are given effect
(the one where made and those where settled as a sister state order
or judgment). California, however, has pushed the limits of this
rule into uncharted waters with its Code of Civil Procedure, Sec.
708.510. This statute allows the court (subject to applicable exemptions) to order you as judgment debtor to assign to the creditor
your right to income from elsewhere (wages from the federal
government, rents, commissions, royalties and the right to borrow
on life insurance), on pain of jail for contempt of court if not
obeyed. Check your local law for anything similar to this one.

The means by which your assets may be seized prior to
judgment is called a prejudgment writ of attachment. The purpose
is to secure collection of the judgment by putting the levied
property in the hands of the court pending a trial on the merits of
the claim. It is generally available only where the action is based
on: an express or implied contract; for a readily ascertainable
amount; an unsecured claim; where the plaintiff shows a substantial likelihood of prevailing at trial; and the action is against a
corporation or partnership, or otherwise arises from a commercial
transaction (sometimes where it arises from a continuing guarantee).[32] It is a creature of statute that must carefully observe the

findings of *Sniadach vs. Family Finance Corporation* 395 US 337 (1969). That court found the prejudgment attachment of wages in Wisconsin (without prior notice or opportunity for hearing) to violate the debtor's constitutional right to due process of law.

Prejudgment remedies are not generally available in the negligence claims that plague Target Defendants (not being business-to-business transactions for specified amounts of money), but check local law. The procedure is to file an application for attachment at or about the time the lawsuit is filed. It is set for hearing a few weeks later and proceeds on the supporting affidavits and memoranda of law. The successful plaintiff must post bond to protect the defendant against wrongful attachment. Any attached assets are held by the county until the claim is reduced to judgment. At that time, the assets (usually bank account proceeds) are released to the judgment creditor to satisfy the judgment. If you prevail instead, any assets so attached are released back to you.

As a tactic, prejudgment attachment can be a powerful tool in securing your willingness as defendant to settle. It may deprive you of necessary working capital and, depending on local law, may carry with it certain automatic injunctive orders that seriously impair the orderly conduct of your business or practice (*e.g.*, one that no shareholder-employee may receive more than $300 per week in compensation pending trial). The risk run by the claimant in using this tactic is that you as the defendant may be forced to defend the action rather than default, or that you may file for bankruptcy. In this context, an attachment lien on inventory, farm products and equipment filed with the secretary of state, or a recorded attachment lien on real estate, will not disrupt the business. They will, however, become "seasoned" in the ordinary course of business, thus avoiding invalidation as a "preference" in any subsequent bankruptcy proceeding.

Being inchoate, prejudgment attachment liens are subordinate to any federal tax lien attaching to the same property.[33] They may also be subordinate to preferred wage claims. This suggests that (if you are in this much trouble) you may effectively influence settlement negotiations by arranging for a tax levy on that property or by having unpaid employees file preferred wage claims.

After Judgment. A notice, order or other paper that must be served on you as the judgment debtor may be served instead on your attorney of record. Careful attorneys will therefore revoke any consent to service previously filed or will substitute you *in propria persona* (as your own attorney of record) once the representation ceases.

If personal service is necessary, the method used is the same as that required for service of a summons and complaint. Depending on local law, that may be personal service on you as the debtor, personal service on your attorney of record, or service on either of you by mail.

As a general rule, interest on *tort* claims (negligence, fraud, assault, etc.) begins on date of entry of judgment, and for contract claims from the date provided by the contract. Unless provided by agreement, the rate of interest is set by local law.

Costs of suit are awarded to the prevailing party where it is a clear victory; *i.e.*, one where there was no setoff against the plaintiff's judgment for claims of the debtor. Whether or not the plaintiff secures such a clear victory as to support a cost award, those reasonable and necessary expenses of enforcing the judgment are recoverable. Orders for their recovery are obtained by periodically filing a memorandum of costs (or similarly-titled filing under local law) itemizing them. Recoverable costs include statutory fees paid to the court clerk for issuing writs of attachment, fees paid process servers for service of process, and fees paid for issuing and recording an abstract of judgment as a lien on your real property. You are afforded an opportunity to contest the amounts or types of costs with a Motion to Tax Costs. Otherwise, the costs requested are automatically allowed and added to the judgment, where they accrue interest at the legal rate.

Judgments are usually enforceable for limited periods of time, as much for efficient judicial administration as anything else. The enforcement period may be renewed on timely application by the judgment creditor. A typical period of enforcement is 10 years, with renewal periods of 10 years each as long as the judgment creditor wishes to prosecute collection. Check local law carefully for any requirement that a certified copy of the notice of renewal of judgment must be recorded in order to preserve the judgment lien on your real property; if such a requirement exists, inattention by the judgment creditor may cause expiration of the lien, freeing you to sell the property free of it. All liens brought about by the judgment must be carefully monitored by both parties in order to avoid (or exploit) lapses arising from procedural mistakes.

As a general rule, all your property is available to satisfy the claims of a judgment creditor unless an exemption applies. In community property states, that will ordinarily include community property even if your spouse was not named in the lawsuit.

Certain types of property are often thought beyond the claims of creditors but on closer examination may not be so well insulated. For example, spendthrift trusts may be subject to certain kinds of claims (taxes, child support), Individual Retirement Accounts may be made available to the extent deemed by the court to be unnecessary for your "reasonable" retirement needs, leasehold interests are available (unless the lease flatly prohibits assignment),[34] your right to sue others "for money or property" unless assignment is prohibited under local law, and sometimes licenses issued by public entities (liquor, FCC, etc.).

Unlike inchoate prejudgment attachment liens (noted earlier to be subordinate to subsequent tax liens), judgment liens are finally determined, giving them a priority over other liens on a first-in-time, first-in-right basis. If a judgment **execution** lien is created based on the same action that led to a prior **attachment** lien, the judgment lien "relates back" for purposes of giving the creditor a priority based on the date of the attachment lien.

The county clerk where the judgment was rendered issues the abstract of judgment on application by the judgment creditor. Upon recordation of the abstract, the judgment lien attaches to all real property interests you then own and all that you acquire in that county for so long as the judgment remains in effect, **except** for an interest in rents, a leasehold estate with an unexpired term of less that two years or your interest as a trust beneficiary. Recordation and this lien effect takes place county-by-county. The lien may reach certain equitable interests, as well; *e.g.*, that of a purchaser under a land sale contract and redemption rights. It will also reach any surplus left over after satisfaction of senior liens, encumbrances and exemptions limited in amount.

The judgment lien is the least expensive and least disruptive to your affairs as judgment debtor. The abstract usually contains the date and amount of the judgment, the name and address of the parties and their attorneys of record and, for identification purposes, your social security and driver's license numbers. Enforcement against assets other than bank accounts is usually (but not always) by levy and sale under a writ of execution.

If you convey or encumber property that is subject to a judgment lien, the property remains subject to the lien. At least one court has held, however, that where the lien attached to the interest of only one joint tenant and that joint tenant died, the judgment lien is extinguished, leaving the surviving joint tenant holding title free of the lien. If this fact situation applies, the careful judgment creditor will check local law on this point; if the joint tenancy is not severed by the imposition of the lien, and if the lien is extinguished by death of the debtor, the creditor must levy and sell the property under a writ of execution before date of death.

As is the case with voluntary liens (mortgages and deeds of trust, primarily), the judgment creditor may release the lien in exchange for valuable consideration (payment or other security) and may subordinate the lien priority to another (a construction loan, for instance), and will usually do so if it will aid in satisfying the judgment. This is accomplished by means of an agreement to that effect and in recordable form. Most commonly, a release or subordination agreement is deposited in a sale escrow or given to a lender with delivery and recordation conditioned on payment of a specific sum to the judgment creditor.

After the judgment creditor is paid in full, or a compromise is reached and payment made under it, the creditor signs a form of Satisfaction of Judgment. That form is filed with the court, usually by the debtor, who wants to be certain the task is properly and promptly completed. A clerk's certificate is then issued by the court and recorded so as to remove the lien from all properties encumbered by it. In some states, the form is prepared in recordable form and recorded directly, rather than being first filed with the court.

A levy on real property under a writ of execution creates an execution lien on that property for a period of time set by local law (typically one or two years) not exceeding the remaining period of judgment enforceability. Except for foreclosure sale by a senior lienholder, the execution lien follows the property any time it is transferred. Personal property in the custody of a levying officer also remains encumbered by the execution lien on transfer. As to personal property **not** in the custody of a levying officer, the lien remains in place on transfer or sale subject to certain exceptions arising from the *Uniform Commercial Code* and, perhaps, local law. Those exceptions include a *bona fide* purchaser for value who takes without knowledge of the lien and various purchasers, banks and factors described in the code.

If the judgment creditor dies, the judgment is enforced by the creditor's executor, administrator or successor in interest. If the creditor is a partnership or corporation that dissolves, the judgment is enforced by the assignee of the partnership or corporate assets as successor in interest. If enforcement is sought against your estate after your death, the need for a creditor claim is determined by local probate law.

The execution process begins with issuance of a writ of execution by the court clerk. The writ sets forth information similar to that in the abstract of judgment. Local law will often require that it be returned within a certain period of time.

In general, nonexempt property that is assignable may be reached by some procedure to satisfy a money judgment. In most community property states, the community is liable for the debts of either spouse, and those incurred for "the necessities of life" may also be satisfied from the separate property of either spouse.

Certain types of intangible property may not be subject to direct levy under local law; *e.g.*, your partnership interest, a cause of action not yet reduced to final judgment, a debt (other than earnings) owed to you by a public entity, the loan value of your life insurance policy, a license issued to you by a public entity (*e.g.*, liquor, FCC), your interest as a trust beneficiary, your nonvested interest in property and property in a guardianship or conservatorship estate. In order to levy on such property, the creditor must use a different procedure; *e.g.*, a charging order, lien, assignment order, etc.

To aid in following this material, three definitions bear repeating. "Levy" means to take the property physically, including money, with the money applied to satisfaction of the judgment and possession of the property by the levying officer. "Execution" is a levy that includes an order of sale, so as to reduce the property taken by levy to cash and apply the proceeds to satisfaction of the judgment. A levy under a prejudgment writ of attachment, for example, may not include execution, whereas one made after judgment might; the phrase is "levy on a writ of execution." A "charging order" is one imposing a judgment lien on a debtor's asset; when that asset is protected from automatic levy or execution, a separate court order is required. Under it, all distributions made on account of that asset are to be delivered to the judgment creditor, but the asset remains in the possession of the debtor. Unless exempted, it may be subject to a further order for execution sale.

Acting on the creditor's instructions, the officer levies on your personal property in one of the following ways: by serving the writ of execution and notice of levy, taking physical possession of the property; by service of the writ and notice alone; by filing or recording the writ and notice; or by delivery of the writ and levy instructions to the officer in possession under a prior writ of attachment.

The notice of levy is used to inform you of the capacity in which you are served, of the personal property subject to the levy, of the right of a person in possession to assert a third-party claim, of your right as debtor to make a claim of exemption, and of your duties under the levy.

The levying officer holds the property or money for a period determined under local law (typically 10 days) in order to provide both you and any third-party holder time to file your claims. If none are filed, or if filed and denied by the court, the property is sold and the proceeds delivered to the creditor to the extent necessary to satisfy the judgment. Any money subject to the levy is paid over in the same way. Excess funds are, of course, returned to you. Upon receipt of instructions from the creditor or an order from the court for release of the levied property, the levying officer will release the property to you.

Usually, the levying officer will take possession of personal property under a writ without a breach of the peace. If the person in possession refuses to deliver up the property, the officer may procure a seizure order from the court and break into the premises to take possession of the property. If faced with the risk of physical harm, the officer will return to the court for such other orders as are necessary to bring about a relatively safe levy. Another approach is to apply to the court for an order directing you as judgment debtor to transfer to the levying officer the property sought for levy, documentary evidence of title to the property, or both.

If the need for the order is shown and the order issued, a copy is then served personally on you, along with a notice that refusal to comply with the turnover order will subject you to incarceration for contempt of court. This approach to dealing with the uncooperative debtor is superior to the order for levy in a private place, since it permits turnover of evidence of title that will facilitate the eventual sale of the property.

Where the judgment creditor seeks to levy on personal property in which a third party holds a secured interest, the secured party must also be served copies of the writ and notice. The levy reaches not only your equity (in the surplus after satisfaction of the secured interest of the third party), but may reach your right to redeem the property from the security interest, as well.[35] Subsequent judgment creditors may levy on property already subject to a levy, thus participating in any surplus after satisfaction of the first creditor's judgment.[36]

The levying officer may take possession of the personal property of a going business, unless the judgment creditor instructs that levy be made by placing a keeper in possession. The costs of doing so may be substantial, but if enough cash can be collected from gross receipts of the enterprise in a relatively short period of time, it can be a cost-effective collection technique.

Various forms of notes and other negotiable instruments may be the subject of a levy. If in your possession as debtor, the levying officer takes possession as above. If in the possession of a third party, service is made there and the obligor is instructed to make payment to the officer instead of you. If payment is made to you anyway, the obligor is not relieved of the obligation to make them again, this time to the officer.

Deposit accounts and safe deposit boxes are subject to levy. The levying officer serves the institution and takes possession of the account funds and the box contents to the extent necessary to satisfy the judgment. If the account or box is held in joint tenancy or in the name of another person, the judgment creditor may have to file a bond in an amount set under local law. That bond protects the interest of the nondebtor holder of the account or box if and to the extent it is proven that you have no interest in the funds or contents. Any such levy is subject to the institution's right to set off against the balance or contents any debt you may owe the institution. Local law may provide for some specific amount that is not subject to the banker's setoff right. If account funds are traceable to your wages or the sale of an exempt asset, you may have a proper claim of exemption.

If the property to be taken for satisfaction of the judgment is personal property used as a dwelling (*e.g.*, mobile home or camper), the levying officer serves a copy of the writ and notice on one occupant personally, or by substituted service, or by posting and mailing. While a keeper may be placed in charge at the expense of the creditor, occupants may be removed only after a court hearing where those occupants are given an opportunity to appear and explain why they should not be evicted.

Vehicles and boats are simply taken by the levying officer, following which notice is given to the legal owner and you as judgment debtor.

As with obligors under notes payable to you, those who owe you money as accounts payable, money judgments, from decedent's estates, etc. are personally served with the writ and notice and are instructed to pay the creditor instead.

Levy on securities usually requires seizure in the manner

provided by *Uniform Commercial Code*, Sec. 8317.

What about the liability of third persons in possession of your property ("Garnishees") who are properly served with the writ and notice? Proper service establishes a lien on the property and imposes a duty to pay or deliver possession, along with all documents necessary to transfer title, unless the Garnishee claims the right to possession. If such a claim is asserted, the creditor may file an action for possession. If the Garnishee is found to have refused without good cause, he or she will be liable to the creditor for the value of your interest in the property or payments owed, or the balance owed under the judgment, whichever is less, plus reasonable attorney's fees and costs of suit. Before filing suit for delivery of the property and title documents, the levying officer may demand a memorandum from the Garnishee supporting the claim to possession. If not delivered within 10 days, the creditor may recover attorney's fees and costs incurred to obtain that information as well.

Property subject to a security interest is handled in various ways. Whoever is in possession may be required to either sell it or deliver it to the levying officer for sale and must apply the net sale proceeds to satisfaction of the various claimants in the order of their lien priority.

Cash (*e.g.*, silver dollars) may not be sold unless its market value exceeds its face value. Checks, drafts and money orders payable to you as the debtor are endorsed by the levying officer and presented for payment. Receivables are generally collected as they become due, rather than sold for present value.

The sale of personal property to satisfy a judgment requires notice sufficient to satisfy the requirements of constitutional due process. Local law will generally require that the notice: be in writing and contain the date, time, place of sale and a description of the property to be sold; be given to you at least 10 days prior to sale; be given to those requesting it, including the clerk of the court that issued the judgment; and be posted or otherwise adequately exposed to the market so as to procure the best price reasonably obtainable under the circumstances. The levying officer may be liable for failing to give proper notice of the sale where the price obtained is inadequate, and an extreme case may give rise to equitable redemption allowing you to regain property sold for a fraction of its value, relying on defects in the sale notice or procedure.[37]

The sale of real property to satisfy a judgment may or may not be subject to a right of redemption. It will turn on the length of the notice period for the sale. If sold on 10 days' notice, for example, the buyer may take subject to the debtor's right to buy it back ("redeem" it) within a year following the sale. If, however, the minimum sale notice period is 120 days, the right of redemption may exist only until the date of sale. Check local law. Filing a bankruptcy proceeding will further delay the sale, but you should think long and hard about the ripple effect on taking that step; apart from the effect on reputation and the risk that you will be sued for abuse of process, it may trigger defaults under other obligations (notes, contracts, leases, etc.). The notice contents and service requirements for lien foreclosure on real property are similar to those for the sale of personal property but also require publication and notice to occupants and others holding liens on it. The sale is made at auction to the highest bidder, with any personal property in plain view and in such groups or lots as are likely to bring the best price. Payment is all cash, except that the judgment creditor may make a credit bid in a sum equal to all or part of the balance under the judgment and the senior liens of others.

If paying more than $2500 for personal property or $5000 for real property, the buyer may pay 10% on the date of sale and the balance with interest within 10 days thereafter. On such deferred terms, no possession is given the high bidder until the price is paid in full. If not so paid, the property is resold, with the defaulting bidder liable for costs of resale plus or minus any price differential. The levying officer may not have any direct or indirect interest in any purchase at an execution sale. The minimum bid must exceed aggregate preferred labor claims, state tax liens and applicable exemptions. If a minimum bid is not received, the levying officer must release the property back to you. As is the case in any foreclosure sale, junior liens not satisfied from the sale price are extinguished.

If the judgment under which the writ is issued is later vacated or reversed on appeal, you may recover the proceeds of the execution sale plus interest at the legal rate.

If the sale is irregular for any reason and the property was purchased by the judgment creditor, you may bring an action to set it aside at any time within six months. If successful, two things happen: the judgment is revived to the extent of the money so recovered, plus interest accruing to the creditor for the period between the sale and the recovery; and you may also recover damages arising from the improper sale. One is set off against the other.

The proceeds of the sale must be distributed within 30 days, and are applied in the following order:
- Preferred labor claims.
- State tax liens senior (*i.e.*, recorded prior in time) to that of the judgment creditor.
- Any deposit made with the levying officer by the judgment creditor to bond around third-party claims.
- To you as judgment debtor, a sum equal to any applicable exemption.
- To the levying officer, any costs of sale advanced on behalf of the judgment creditor.
- To the judgment creditor, first to costs of sale and second to costs, interest and principal (in that order) under the judgment.
- To any other judgment creditors who delivered writs to the levying officer with instructions to levy on the same property and whose lien priorities are junior to that of your judgment creditor, in order of their priorities.
- Any balance remaining is paid to you as judgment debtor.

Exemptions. Exemptions from the claims of judgment creditors do not apply to the foreclosure of voluntary liens; *e.g.*, a mortgage, deed of trust or UCC lien. They may be asserted only by natural persons, not by artificial persons like partnerships and corporations. Only you as judgment debtor and your spouse may assert them, and the spouse need not be a judgment debtor to do so.

Certain property may be regarded under local law as exempt

without the need for claim. That aside, the general rule is that your property is set aside as exempt only if the exemption is timely claimed. The court may have either statutory or "inherent" power to provide relief from failure to timely make the claim. In most states, exemption waivers cannot be enforced as a matter of public policy.

Exemption amounts are not increased by being married, but each spouse may claim their own separately, effectively doubling them where applicable. In ruling on claims of exemption based on need and support standards, the court will take both marital and separate property of the spouses into account, whether or not such property is exempt on other grounds.

The claim of exemption is made by filing it in the court that issued the judgment for which satisfaction is sought. Notice is given and the claim set for hearing, usually within 10 days following levy on the property.

A separate set of exemptions is provided under the *US Bankruptcy Code* for use in bankruptcy proceedings.[38] The code reserves to the states whether to permit an election between the federal and state exemptions; but remember, this is only where you file for bankruptcy.

Under California law, for example, judgment debtors filing for bankruptcy may elect either all those exemptions provided under the *US Bankruptcy Code* or those provided under California law, but may not pick and choose between them.[39] Illinois law takes the other tack, prohibiting its citizens from choosing the federal exemptions.[40] The predecessor to California's statute was found unconstitutional by Bankruptcy Judge Calvin K. Ashland in 1982, who felt its citizens should be able to use the most liberal exemptions of both without being forced to an either-or election. The present statute is substantially the same, so if it is found unconstitutional as well, the right to elect may be replaced by denial of the state exemptions to bankruptcy debtors.

In taking steps to deal with difficult financial circumstances, you may sell one or more exempt assets. If the exemption is thereby lost, the opportunity to recover financially by redeploying the proceeds into productive resources (tools, inventory) will be lost if the creditor takes the money. The general rule, then, is that such funds remain exempt as long as they can be traced back to the exempt source. The tracing methodology will vary from state to state, but the result is substantially the same. The burden of proof, if challenged, is on you as debtor and is presented in a claim of exemption.

The majority rule on available exemptions is that you may claim only those in existence at the time the obligation was incurred. The minority rule is that exempt property and amounts depend on the statutes in effect at the time the judgment lien (or the earliest in a series of overlapping liens) attaches.[41] This is an important consideration. As an example, a 1990 unsatisfied California judgment based on a 1968 promissory note would be subject to a $15,000 homestead exemption under the majority rule and either a $45,000 or a $75,000 homestead exemption under the minority rule.

Exemptions from the claims of judgment creditors vary widely from state to state. They generally, however, cover all or part of the following: an automobile; household furnishings and personal effects; building materials for use in repairing or improving your principal residence; jewelry, heirlooms, works of art; health aids; tools of your trade (with no overlap between this and other exemptions, like the automobile); deposit accounts containing social security benefits; prisoner's funds; life insurance cash surrender value, and sometimes (but not always) the loan value; qualified corporate and self-employment pension and profit-sharing plan accounts (but subject to spousal and child support claims);[42] individual retirement accounts (but some states may not fully extend this exemption if a court finds that not all of it is "necessary" to your reasonable retirement needs);[43] employee vacation credits; unemployment and unemployment disability benefits; disability income and hospital-medical insurance benefits; personal injury cause of action and award; wrongful death cause of action and award; workers' compensation benefits; charitable financial aid; homestead; relocation benefits; student aid; and a cemetery plot.

The homestead exemption is much discussed and little understood. Where available (repealed in Ohio, for example) it covers your "dwelling," whether that dwelling is a house, a mobile home, a boat, a condominium or cooperative apartment or a community apartment project. In Texas, it can also be a place of business.[44] If local law provides multitiered levels of exemption depending on marital and dependent status, it will also define the family on which the exemption turns.[45] Some states may provide the exemption only if and for so long as you reside on the property,[46] while others allow it even after you move out.[47] Most states require a homestead in a real property dwelling to be established by recording a declaration of homestead, but others make it available without that requirement.[48] The homestead exemption for dwellings other than real property is asserted as a claim of exemption, just like any other. The exemption may be limited in various ways; a specific amount or amounts; the amount of land involved; or both. Generally, it is a specific amount of equity which may be retained from foreclosure proceeds after satisfaction of voluntary liens. Some state laws on this topic seem to serve as an open invitation to abuse; *e.g.*, Texas, where no declaration need be recorded prior to execution by the judgment creditor, where a single adult may homestead 100 acres of rural property and all improvements, where married persons may do the same with 200 acres, and where the city dweller may own a high-rise apartment building on no more than one acre and live in the penthouse with the homestead exemption extending to the entire building.

The foreclosure of a judgment lien on real or personal property subject to a homestead declaration is substantially the same. The writ is levied with or without a court order, depending on local law. Levy creates a lien preserving priority if not previously established by recording an abstract of judgment.

A personal property dwelling (mobile home, motor home, etc.) may be sold on notice and with adequate exposure to the market in the same manner as other personal property. The only difference as to other personal property is that you receive the homestead exemption amount after satisfaction of the voluntary liens and senior involuntary liens in addition to receiving anything left of the sale proceeds after satisfaction of the judgment.

After levy, a court order is usually required for sale of a real property dwelling subject to a homestead declaration. You are entitled to notice of any application for the court order. Time limits for securing it may apply, and the lien may be released as a matter of law if those time limits are not satisfied. The application may be presented as an order to show cause why the property should not be sold to satisfy the judgment. You have the burden of proof on entitlement to the homestead exemption, although if one is timely recorded (or otherwise procured under local procedural requirements), the burden is on the creditor to prove that it should not be given effect. The sale will go forward, whether or not the homestead is effective. After appointing an appraiser to report on fair market value, the court must order the sale and specify the amounts to be paid to the various holders of liens and encumbrances. The price must exceed all liens, encumbrances and the amount of the homestead exemption, and must be at least 90% of appraised value. If no adequate bid is received, the judgment creditor may not recover any of the costs incurred for the levy and attempted sale.

• **Wage Garnishment.** This topic is of minor relevance to you as a Target Defendant, but is included so as to present a complete discussion of the methods by which judgments are enforced.

Wage garnishments are applicable only to compensation for services by an employer to an employee. That eliminates the self-employed and encompasses only those employed by and drawing salaries from their corporations.

There are two ways to reach wages and salaries: wage assignments and earnings withholding orders. The former is used for payment of court-ordered child and spousal support; the latter for all other money judgments. We will address only withholding orders.

Based on a writ of execution, the withholding order is served on the employer. It requires withholding for a period specified by statute and is payable by the employer to the levying officer at specified intervals. In terms of priority over other such orders, wage assignments often have a super priority, with withholding orders for support next and all other withholding orders last.

Wages and salaries may not be reached by prejudgment attachment. Federal government employees enjoy a 75% exemption for "disposable earnings" and a little less for support obligations.[49] Otherwise, an exemption is generally provided for that part of the debtor's income proven necessary for support of the debtor and dependents. Without such an exemption, debtors would be thrown onto welfare; the public policy is that the creditor should bear that cost rather than society.

Procedure for obtaining the withholding order will vary from state to state, but the order is generally issued on request if a writ of execution is first issued and has not expired. In some jurisdictions, the order is issued by the levying officer. Service may be made personally or by registered or certified mail. The papers served will include the withholding order, a form of employer's return and a notice to the employee-debtor.

Special Procedures. The two principal procedures are written interrogatories and oral examination of the judgment debtor.

Interrogatories are written questions to be answered (typically within 30 days) in writing and under oath. This discovery procedure is generally available as long as the judgment remains unsatisfied. Interrogatories may not, however, be used during such time as enforcement is stayed pending an appeal nor within some reasonable period prescribed by local law following your last previous examination.

If you fail to timely respond, the court may impose sanctions. Those sanctions are usually financial, though contempt is available, and include the cost of attorney fees incurred by the creditor in seeking the sanctions order. Where the examination constitutes harassment or is unduly burdensome, you may seek a protective order in such form as the circumstances dictate.

Oral examinations may include both you and any third person. It comes about on application to the court by the judgment creditor. The resulting order is for you, the third person, or both, to appear before either the court or a court-appointed referee to be examined under oath in aid of enforcement of the judgment.

The court or referee may issue, modify or vacate any order

relating to enforcement of the judgment; it may also make a protective order, issue a warrant, grant adjournments and subpoena witnesses. The court, but not the referee, may punish for contempt, award attorney's fees, determine a contested claim of exemption or determine a third-party claim.

At least in California, spousal privileges do not apply, so your spouse may be called as a witness and required to testify. Check local law to see if you have an aberration like this.

If the order to appear is directed to an organization, it must send someone familiar with the property and the debts. You may, of course, be represented by counsel at that hearing.

As with interrogatories, failure to comply may lead to sanctions, including incarceration for contempt of court. The proper court is the one that entered the judgment for which enforcement is sought. A geographic limitation is usual; e.g., you may not be required to travel outside the county of residence unless it is less than 150 miles from home in order to appear at an oral examination of the judgment debtor.[50]

If someone claims an interest in the property the creditor seeks to take, that claimant may intervene in the examination hearing to assert it.

The order for your oral examination is issued *ex parte* and personally served on you at least 10 days before the hearing. It creates a lien on all your nonexempt personal property lasting as long as does the judgment.

The procedure for examining a third party in possession of property thought to belong to you is substantially the same. The differences are that the affidavit supporting the *ex parte* application may be based on information and belief, and the third person must be offered witness fees in the statutory amount.

Service on the third person creates a lien on your interest (if any) in the property held by that party. To prevent "fishing expeditions," the creditor must accurately describe the property thought to be held by the third person. If the court finds that you indeed have an interest in the property held by the third person, the lien priority in that property dates back to the date on which the third person was served with the order to appear for examination. If the third person makes a good-faith claim to the property adverse to yours and establishes that the court lacks jurisdiction to hear the claim, or that another action is pending in which the adverse claim will be adjudicated, the court may not determine it.

The court may also decide on its own that the claim should be determined in a creditor's suit. Otherwise, any adverse claim of the third person is decided in the examination hearing. On a proper finding, after determination that the third person has no interest in the property, the court may then order the property delivered to the creditor.

If the court cannot or chooses not to determine an adverse claim of a third person in possession of property thought to belong (at least in part) to you, the creditor may file suit. This may also be the preferred method where the creditor anticipates non-cooperation or where the third person is an employer who fails to garnish wages as ordered.

As a general rule, the creditor may file suit any time a third person is the obligor under a debt owed to you or holds possession of property in which you have an interest.

The suit is to compel delivery of the property to the creditor to sell, or to make payment to the creditor instead of to you. Some states require the creditor to first levy under a writ of execution; others permit direct action at the discretion of the creditor. The latter seems the more enlightened, in view of the sophistication of some debtors.

In some states, the creditor's suit must be filed within certain time limits (*e.g.*, while the judgment is still enforceable, before the expiration of any statute of limitations on a suit by you to recover the property, and in any case within one year after creation of the judgment creditor's lien). If timely filed, it may be prosecuted to judgment even if doing so takes longer than the time remaining in which to enforce the underlying judgment.

Because the remedy (turnover of the property upon a court determination that you have an interest in it) is equitable in nature, there is no right to a jury trial.

Finally, costs incurred by the creditor in recovering property from a third person may not be charged to you as a cost of enforcing the judgment.

Charging Orders. Charging orders are those used to reach your interest in assets exempted from automatic sale under a writ of execution. They are available to the creditor only if specifically authorized. For example, a statute may exempt a list of property interests that include partnership and trust interests, but give the court discretion to issue a charging order against a partnership interest and to order the sale of a trust interest or distribution of the trust assets if appropriate. When you find a list of property interests exempted from automatic sale under writs of execution, look for statutory exceptions. California law on this point gives family partnerships no edge over land trusts.

The order is obtained on noticed motion and creates a lien in favor of the creditor from the date of filing.[51] The lien is either continued or extinguished at the hearing on the motion, depending on whether the motion is granted. As is discussed more specifically in Section 1.4 on land trusts, the charging order obtains for the creditor only the right to receive distributions otherwise payable to you by virtue of your partnership, stock or trust interest. To get more, the creditor must obtain an order for foreclosure. In the absence of an authorizing statute or case law, the exemption prevents it.

If foreclosure would result in statutory dissolution of the partnership, the judgment creditor is paid from the liquidation distribution. A thoughtful amendment of the partnership agreement (providing for continuation of the partnership with the creditor as assignee of the debtor-partner) may deal effectively with this risk; at a minimum, it may make the partnership interest unsaleable as non-income producing.

Though the required elements may preclude it, the creditor who forecloses on stock in a corporation may acquire thereby a position from which to force dissolution of the corporation. See local law for the requirements.

If the creditor becomes a partner, shareholder or trust beneficiary by foreclosing and purchasing your interest with a credit bid, then expiration, nonrenewal or satisfaction of the judgement is no longer an issue, since the creditor gets whatever the interest is worth. That partnership, stock or trust interest may be worth a great more than the balance of the judgment. **This is the risk you assume when you decide to keep the real estate instead of selling it to fund the tax haven trust. The risk applies equally to property held in a partnership, whether general or limited, and to that held in a business trust.**

Where you are the plaintiff in another action, the judgment creditor may preserve lien priority on any recovery under it by filing a notice of lien in that action, together with an abstract or certified copy of the creditor's judgment. In some states it is accomplished by a noticed motion. All parties in the other action must be served in order to bind them, but failure to do so does not affect the validity of the lien.

Assignment Order. The nonexempt portion of certain kinds of assets may be reached most effectively by means of an assignment order. Such assets include: wages due from the federal government; rents; commissions; royalties; and an insurance policy loan value. The order is obtained by the creditor on noticed motion in which the court considers your needs as debtor and those of your dependents, your other obligations, the balance unsatisfied under the judgment and the amount sought by assignment.

Receiver. Appointment of a receiver can be a draconian collection method if not used selectively. Accordingly, it is imposed only after the court is satisfied that it is the most reasonable under the circumstances. For example, it may be the only way a liquor license can be sold to satisfy a judgment and is the most cost-effective way to collect rents (so as keep them from the defaulting borrower) during foreclosure proceedings. Some states require a showing that the writ of execution was returned unsatisfied before appointment of a receiver will be ordered.

Trust Interests. As to enforcement against trust interests, we deal here only with written voluntary express trusts, not "Totten Trusts," investment trusts, deeds of trust, constructive trusts or resulting trusts. Specific discussion of land trusts and foreign situs trusts are found at Sections 1.4 and 1.6, respectively.

In the absence of a valid spendthrift provision, judgments are generally enforceable against any trust interest, including contingent interests. It is usually exempted from automatic execution, so it will require a court order fashioned to suit the circumstances. Such special orders may include charging and execution sale orders, and in some states the court may order liquidation of the trust in order to force distributions from which the judgment may be satisfied.[52] Protection is afforded beneficiaries protected by a trust spendthrift clause (generally, those who lack the power to compel distributions).[53]

Probate Estate Claims. As to claims made against your probate estate, there is a "creditor claim period" during which claims must be filed with the court or presented to the executor. Those not timely filed or presented are usually barred. Some states impose on the executor a duty to make a reasonable effort to identify the creditors and give them notice of their right to file or present their claims. Other states leave it up to the creditors to discover the death and perfect their claims without assistance.

Modern law will also address the problem of the creditor who is diligent about prosecuting but is hindered by the absence of a probate administration proceeding, or is faced with one in which the assets are insufficient to satisfy the claim. There the creditor may go first against the probate estate, then against the family trust if the probate estate is insufficient to satisfy the claim; if no probate administration proceeding is commenced, the claimant may often go directly against the family trust.[54] Where no such protection is provided the claimant, you should deliberately plan for a small probate administration proceeding in order to bar creditors from reaching past the probate estate into your family trust.

Payment and Release. After settling with the claimant or judgment creditor, you must be certain to properly document the matter. Before judgment, it takes the form of a release agreement and dismissal of the lawsuit with prejudice. After judgment, make certain the levying officer returns any outstanding writ of execution fully satisfied and that the judgment creditor acknowledges satisfaction with the court. If an abstract of judgment was recorded as a lien on your real property, be certain to record a certified copy of the filed satisfaction of judgment so as to extinguish the judgment lien. If the judgment creditor fails to provide you with a satisfaction of judgment, you may serve on the creditor a demand for it. If there is no timely response (usually 15 days), you file a motion for a court order compelling it. If the creditor's failure was without just cause, the court may impose sanctions that include reimbursement of the attorney's fees and costs incurred to procure the order.

The rules for enforcement of judgments may never become a matter of concern for you. If a claim ever gets this far, however, having the information at your fingertips will provide two major benefits: knowing the procedures available will avoid nightmarish speculation, so as to reduce your anxiety level; and you may be able to enlighten your attorney as to defensive measures that may not be obvious.

Section 1.4 Land Trusts

Like an oxcart driver in monsoon season or the skipper of a grounded ship, we sometimes must go forward by going back.

Except for two or three transactions over the years involving the conveyance of Illinois property, I had not heard or thought of Illinois land trusts since law school; until, that is, a client asked about its use in his estate and business planning. Upon researching the matter, I concluded to my delight that, indeed, land trusts may be used in California and that they may fill some important asset protection planning needs.

Except for those states where the land trust is a popular title-holding device (Illinois, of course, Indiana, Virginia and Florida), research on its availability in your state may be complicated by the absence of both statutory and case law. Backing up to those old cases to polish off and update an old idea, however, may prove to be a worthwhile endeavor indeed.

In this subsection, we examine the nature of this form of trust and its benefits, then we review certain points of analysis your attorney must research if you are not in a state where this vehicle is in popular use.

Nature and Use of the Land Trust. Following are the principal characteristics of the land trust:

• **Beneficiaries Not Identified.** It is used to hold title to real property, identifying the representative capacity of the trustee, but without identifying the other parties to the trust. This conveyance in trust is accomplished through a custom-drafted form of grant deed called a "deed in trust."

• **Beneficiaries Hold Full Management Powers.** The trust agreement is not recorded. Under it, the settlor-beneficiaries retain full powers of management and control over the trust property, and the trustee acts only at the direction of those beneficiaries to convey, encumber or take any other action affecting title to the property. The trustee has no duties relating to the trust estate other than those affecting title to the land.

• **Real Property Interest Converted to Personal Property Interest.** By express provision, the interest of each beneficiary is characterized as personal property, in much the same way as is stock in a corporation. Evidence of ownership is a certificate of beneficial interest, similar in form and content to a stock certificate.

• **Nonprobate Designation of Beneficiaries.** The trust agreement usually establishes a specific term with an option to extend. At the end of the term, the trust either expires or is extended. It may also specify who will receive the interest of a beneficiary who dies during the term of the trust.

• **Independent Trustee.** For practical reasons, the trustee is invariably a bank or independent trust company. You need an independent trustee, and the fees are so low as to be inconsequential.

• **Beneficiaries Assume All Liabilities.** Under the trust agreement, the settlors (creators of the trust) absolve the trustee of any liabilities arising from the operation of trust property by the settlor-beneficiaries.

Use and Benefit of the Land Trust. Following is a review of the benefits attributable to the land trust:

• **Privacy of Ownership.** Often, the beneficial owners of real property have a legitimate need to avoid disclosure of their interest: *e.g.*, in the acquisition of contiguous parcels of land by developers so that sellers do not realize what is taking place and collude to raise their prices; judges need anonymity for protection from unhappy litigants; celebrities protection from enthusiastic fans; and persons of means prefer not to attract the attention of those prospecting for wealthy individuals.

Privacy of this nature is sometimes criticized. Slumlords hide their ownership so as to make it difficult for public agencies to enforce municipal codes. On balance, however, the legitimate interests of those seeking privacy by this means outweigh any such criticism.

• **Nonresident Ownership.** Probate administration of an estate takes place in the county in which the decedent resided at the time of death. The estate there subject to probate administration includes real property in the state of domicile and personal property everywhere. By converting the interest of a land trust beneficiary from real property to personal property, an ancillary probate proceeding in the state where the real property is located may be avoided, along with estate or inheritance taxes in that state.

• **Avoidance of Probate Administration.** The property of the decedent passes to whoever is going to receive it in one of three ways: by **title** (typically joint tenancy), by **contract** (life insurance, trusts, preretirement death benefits of a pension, etc.) and by **probate administration** (whatever is left). Inclusion of a land trust interest in a probate estate may be avoided by at least two means: one is to issue the certificate of beneficial interest to the decedent-beneficiary's family trust, and the other is to provide in the land trust agreement itself who is to receive that interest on death of the beneficiary (other than the probate estate, of course).

• **Limited Exposure to Judgments and Liens.** Where several people are beneficiaries of a land trust, there is continuing risk that one or more may encounter difficulties resulting in a personal judgment. No such judgment will impair the interests of the other beneficiaries because they will not constitute liens on the real property itself, only on the beneficial interest of that beneficiary-judgment debtor. As a consequence, the other beneficiaries (perhaps with the foreclosure sale purchaser of the beneficial interest now included) may continue to deal freely with the rent, refinancing and sale of trust property without title concerns.

• **Avoidance of Marital Interests in Title.** The real property comprising the land trust is not, in and of itself, subject to the dower, community property or other marital rights of the beneficiaries. Consequently, instruments dealing with title to the property need not be executed by a spouse, only by the trustee. That permits continued property operations, notwithstanding marital strife among the beneficiaries. Such strife will involve only entitlement to the certificates of beneficial interest in the trust estate, not to the trust property itself.

• **Insulation from Hazards of Individual Ownership.** Under other methods of holding, managing and developing real property, the death or incompetence of an owner will invariably produce delays as an executor or conservator is appointed by the court and authorization is sought to continue with the project. Not so with a land trust drafted to anticipate the problem. Similarly, the bankruptcy of a beneficiary will not hinder trust operations, since the bankruptcy trustee and ultimate creditors simply step into the shoes, and assume the benefits and burdens of the former debtor-beneficiary.

• **Transferability of Beneficial Interest.** By converting the beneficial interest in the trust estate from one in real property to one in personal property, that interest (in the form of certificates) may be transferred using a simple written assignment. This permits sale or transfer without any public record of the transaction and without the expense and delay of procuring title policies. Securities law issues are present here but are capable of satisfaction.

• **Use of Beneficial Interests as Collateral.** While it may strain the imagination, given typical banking practice, it is at least theoretically possible to make a collateral assignment of a certificate of beneficial interest for the purpose of securing a personal loan. Any such transaction will not impair the continued operation of the trust property.

• **Partition Unavailable.** Partition is a legal proceeding by which one of several owners of real property may force division or sale of the property in order to liquidate the interest of the petitioning party. The property in the land trust, being owned by the trustee and not the beneficiaries, is not subject to a partition proceeding, thus sparing the other beneficiaries this risk of disruption to trust operations.

• **Estate Planning Uses.** By providing in the trust agreement for distribution on death of a beneficiary, the land trust may be fully integrated with personal estate planning needs.

• **Apartments.** The land trust lends itself nicely to protecting the beneficiaries in the operation of apartments. Tenants do not know the owners' identity, thus cannot bother them with complaints.

• **Partnership Uses.** An especially attractive feature of the land trust is its utility in holding property for partnerships, both general and limited. By this means, property operations may be protected from interference by liabilities of the partnership or by disputes between the partners. The governing provisions of the partnership agreement also permit it to serve as an effective substitute for the beneficiaries' agreement otherwise used in instructing the trustee as to matters affecting title.

• **Corporate Uses.** Using a corporation as beneficiary creates liability protection for the shareholders and, by means of the officers appointed by its board, also serves as an effective substitute for the beneficiaries' agreement noted above. There may be some other unhappy consequences, though. See the tax discussion later in this section.

• **Agricultural Uses.** In many states, the land trust is in wide use for holding title to agricultural property. It is of special interest to farming families who wish to pass the property through succeeding generations without risk of partition by dissident heirs.

Legal Characteristics of the Land Trust. It is necessary to

understand the basic legal characteristics of the land trust in order
to determine its utility in your state. Those characteristics are listed
and discussed below:

• **Validity.** In the absence of a statute authorizing the land
trust, its validity must be determined by an analysis of existing case
law in your state. The principal impediment is ordinarily the
Statute of Uses. This statute was enacted in 1536 by King Henry
VIII of England to invalidate gifts of land in trust. That act was
modified by the English courts nine years later, holding the Statute
of Uses was not applicable to an active use or trust; *i.e.*, where the
trustee is given active duties to perform, the trust is valid and not
impaired by the Statute of Uses.

While the Statute of Uses is the law in many states, it is not in
some.[55] Even where not recognized, however, the courts consistently hold that a "dry" or "passive" trust (one in which the trustee
has no duties to perform and the purpose of the trust is accomplished) may be terminated.[56]

Even if no cases can be found in your state where the trustee's
duties are limited in the manner contemplated for the land trust,
that trustee clearly has duties precluding termination as a dry trust;
e.g., it must, at the instruction of the beneficiaries, convey title and
perform any other acts that affect title, and only upon expiration
of the trust term will the trustee be relieved of its duties. Under
Restatement (Second) Trusts Section 69 (1959), the majority view
in the US is that a duty on the part of the trustee to convey the trust
estate, and nothing more, is sufficient to avoid classification as a
dry trust.

• **Relationship Between Trustee and Beneficiary.** In order
to understand the utility of the land trust, we must clearly distinguish the roles of trustee and beneficiary. The trustee owns the
property, subject to the right of the beneficiaries to instruct on all
matters affecting title. The beneficiaries hold only the right to give
those instructions and to enjoy the rents and profits from the
property.

The trustee is not the agent of the beneficiaries. A superficial
analysis of the relationship between trustee and beneficiary suggests an agency relationship. Under trust law, however, the courts

uniformly hold that reserving or granting a power of direction does not create an agency. Consequently, the trustee acts, even though at the direction of the beneficiaries, only as a principal and not as their agent. This legal characterization leads to personal liability on the part of the trustee. It is for that reason that the prudent corporate fiduciary serving in this capacity carefully protects itself with hold-harmless and indemnification provisions in the trust agreement. A second legal consequence is that the trustee cannot create a liability enforceable against the beneficiaries without their consent.

The beneficiary is also not the agent of the trustee. In managing the property and giving instructions to the trustee, the beneficiaries act on their own behalf, not as its agent. So any obligations incurred are enforceable against them alone and not against the trustee or the trust property. The beneficiaries may not sign anything — including leases of the property — on behalf of the trustee. The result is that the beneficiaries negotiate leases, loans, etc. for the signature of the trustee, but provide it an opportunity to review the proposed transaction in advance, so it may reflect on whether the trust agreement adequately protects it from liability.

• **Relationship Between Beneficiaries.** In the absence of a provision in the trust agreement characterizing their legal relationship, the trust beneficiaries are likely to be viewed as partners or joint venturers in the conduct of business related to the trust properties.[57] A partnership or joint venturer relationship is both good and bad. As such, each owes the other a fiduciary duty (*i.e.*, to act in the best interests of the other with full disclosure and no unconsented-to adverse or conflicting interests), but each is fully liable for the acts of the other where the other acts within the course and scope of the reserved powers and duties in managing and operating the trust property. If appropriate, risk may be reduced by a provision authorizing one beneficiary to act as agent for the others in managing and operating the trust property. This is efficient, but raises the possibility that the beneficiaries may be taxed as an "association taxable as a corporation." See the tax discussion later in this section.

• **Relationships with Third Parties.** Beneficiaries may not bind the trustee in dealings with others when managing and operating the trust property. Consequently, only they are bound by any unconsented-to commitments.[58] Beneficiaries make the decisions and present the documentation to the trustee for approval and execution. The trustee then assures itself that it is held harmless or provided indemnity from liability before signing.

Third parties dealing with the trustee may have no reason to appreciate this interplay, however, so they may rely on the powers and restrictions found in the deed under which the trustee holds title. Those powers and restrictions provide that the trustee has full powers affecting title, and third parties need not examine the trust agreement to ascertain whether the trustee is acting consistently with its duties and obligations. Deed provisions of this type are neither contrary to law nor to public policy, and are given effect as a means of enabling third parties to deal with real estate in reliance upon the record title of the land trustee.[59]

Any beneficiary may, of course, act alone in dealing with beneficial interests in the trust (sell, gift, collaterally assign, etc.). It is personal property, just like stock in a closely-held corporation.

Points of Analysis on Adaptation of the Land Trust to Use in Your State. If you live in a state where land trusts are routinely used, you may be skimming this section. If not, the following points must be presented to your attorney for research in order to be certain you can make use of this planning tool. The list is not exhaustive, but covers the key elements. Here are the points:

• **Is the Trust Terminable by the Courts as a Dry Trust?** As already mentioned, a dry trust is one in which the trustee has no more duties to perform and the trust purposes are accomplished. The land trust should survive this test handily in any state, but check the case law in yours to be sure.[60]

• **Are the Certificates of Beneficial Interest Personal Property Under Local Law?** You will need a clear statement under the cases in your state. This is too important a point for guesswork.[61]

• **Is the Land Protected from the Judgment Creditors of Beneficiaries?** Here, there may be some interplay between trust law and enforcement of judgments law. Starting with the assumption that the interest is converted from real property to personal property, enforcement of judgments law may provide direct or inferential guidance on whether judgment creditors are limited to charging orders. Look at trust law, though; it might contain a surprise.

In California, for instance, we find that if the judgment debtor-beneficiary has the power to revoke or otherwise appoint the trust property acting alone, the creditor may reach the underlying property to satisfy the judgment. So in this state, the trust should either be irrevocable or should have two or more beneficiaries who are not married to each other and all or a majority of whom must consent to any amendment, revocation or appointment of property.[62]

• **May the Beneficiary Transfer the Beneficial Interest in the Trust?** If local law recognizes recharacterization of the trust interest as personal property, it is assignable. The right to assign, however, should be subject to modest restrictions for the tax reasons discussed later in this section.[63]

• **May a Purchaser for Value Rely on a Deed from the Trustee?** Check both property law and trust law, looking for the main point and for peculiarities in presumptions, burden of proof, actual knowledge (or lack thereof) by the purchaser and the legal consequences of each.[64]

• **Where the Beneficial Interest is Community Property, Must Both Spouses Sign Everything?** The rules vary widely among the nine community property states.

As a general guide, separate property is that acquired prior to the marriage, accumulations from earnings after the date of separation and property received by gift or inheritance. Community property is earnings and accumulations therefrom during the marriage and prior to separation, and separate property transmuted to community by agreement or conduct. The transmuting agreement must usually be written and in recordable form, but it may be oral in some states if supported by conduct evidencing the alleged agreement. Conduct may also include depositing separate property funds in a joint account or otherwise commingling separate and community property. With certain exceptions, either spouse may be the manager of all or some part of the community property, including the beneficial interest under a land trust. The manager-spouse must notify the nonmanager-spouse of any intended sale, lease, exchange, encumbrance or other disposition of all or substantially all of the personal property separately managed. Failure to do so will not invalidate the disposition but may subject the manager-spouse to liability to the other spouse for breach of the duty of good faith and fair dealing.[65] It is prudent for both spouses to hold title to the certificates of beneficial interest and for both to sign forms assigning or encumbering that interest. Otherwise, the nonmanager-spouse should consent in writing to each transfer or encumbrance of that interest.

So, for most purposes, the manager-spouse may sign alone, the only exceptions being for those acts which could be detrimental to the community interest of the nonmanager-spouse. Remember, this may vary widely between Arizona, California, Idaho, Louisiana, Nevada, New Mexico, Texas, Washington or Wisconsin.

• **What Are the Options on How the Certificate of Beneficial Interest May Be Held?** The certificate may be issued to a partnership, corporation, trust or individuals. If there is more than one beneficiary and trust management issues are not sufficiently addressed in the trust agreement, a separate beneficiary agreement is used.

Consolidating management authority in a corporation, managing general partner or trustee could raise corporate taxation risks (see tax discussion, *infra*), though that risk seems manageable.

If the tax haven trust is the land trust beneficiary, distributions offshore are subject to 30% withholding, but distributions directly to you are not.

• **What Are the Securities Law Issues, if Any?** Federal securities law is found in *The Securities Act of 1933* and *The Securities Exchange Act of 1934.* (The "'33 Act" and the "'34 Act") There, Congress defines the term "security" in a way that includes not only stock, bonds and notes, but "investment contracts, certificates of interest or participation in any profit sharing agreement" as well as any related warrants or subscription rights.

The regulatory purpose is protection of the public from fraud, so the Securities Exchange Commission ("SEC") will look to substance, rather than form, in determining whether a given investment constitutes a "security." The principal tests are: the investment of funds in a common enterprise, where the investment return is to be earned from the "efforts of others." The states generally apply the same two tests.

The foregoing suggests for purposes of our present concern that securities issues arise only where:

 • two or more people (or entities) "invest" by contributing real property (or cash to purchase it) to a land trust; and

 • one or more of them will rely on others to manage the property.

Given that circumstance, the beneficial interest in a land trust may well be a "security." If so, an exemption must be found from the duty to either register the "offering" with the SEC, or to qualify such interests as an intrastate public offering with your state regulatory agency.

Without an applicable exemption, the purchasers of unregistered or unqualified securities have an absolute right to rescind the transaction and recover their investment with interest. There is no need to prove fraud, material misstatement or material omission. The statute of limitations on enforcement of that right is three years following issuance.[66]

The federal exemption most useful is Rule 506, Sec. 4(2) of the '33 Act for private placement of securities. Look for a similar provision under your state securities law, because you must deal with both.[67] Rule 506 provides a "safe harbor" as to what constitutes a private placement of securities. There, the trust may issue certificates of beneficial interest for an unlimited amount of consideration to any number of "accredited" investors and (if specific information is provided them) to as many as 35 other "sophisticated" purchasers. Under the federal rule, an accredited investor is an institutional investor, a private business development company, a charity with assets of $5 million or more, insiders (here, a

director, officer, trustee or general partner of the sponsoring beneficiaries), wealthy investors or a wholly-owned subsidiary of any
accredited investor.[68, 69]

The 35 sophisticated investors under the federal exemption are
those whom the issuer (sponsoring beneficiaries) reasonably believes to have (directly or through a "purchaser representative")
enough knowledge and experience in financial and business matters to be capable of evaluating the merits and risks of the investment.[70] That determination requires the use of certain investor
suitability standards, written appointment of the personal representative (if one is used) and specific qualifications of that representative.[71] Additional requirements include full disclosure,
limitations on advertising, resale restrictions and reports to the
SEC on securities sales.

If both federal and state requirements are satisfied, you need
only to prudently document the transaction (investment letter,
disclosure document and written acknowledgment by the investor
that the applicable investor criteria are satisfied).

The statutory requirements are not exclusive, however. A non-
complying issuer (the trust) may still claim the private placement
exemption by relying on the conclusion that the investors need no
protection.[72] That may leave the final determination to the courts,
an inherently unpredictable endeavor if dissension arises in the
investor ranks.

At bottom, certificates of beneficial interest in a land trust
where the beneficiaries all participate in trust property management are not securities. (There is no reliance on "the efforts of
others.") Certificates issued by land trusts in which a beneficiary
delegates the management functions to others probably are securities.

As a precaution, the certificate of beneficial interest should
contain language similar to that found in investment letters for
private placements of securities. Just in case.

• **How Is the Land Trust Taxed?** Only five types of entities
are recognized for tax purposes: individuals, estates, partnerships,
trusts and corporations. Associations of various kinds (including
trust arrangements) which have the characteristics of corporations

may be so classified and taxed by the IRS. That result is undesirable, since it imposes a separate tax at the trust/corporate level and deductions may be denied the trust/corporation for amounts deemed by IRS to be dividends or unreasonable compensation for services.

In the absence of corporate tax treatment, the right to income retained under a land trust causes it to be taxed as a "grantor trust."[73] As such, the beneficiaries report both earnings and deductions of the trust on their personal tax returns.

In its corporate tax treatment analysis, IRS applies several major characteristics ordinarily found in a pure corporation which, taken together, distinguish it from other organizations.[74] The characteristics are: associates; an objective to carry on business and divide the gains therefrom; continuity of life; centralization of management; liability for corporate debts limited to corporate property; and free transferability of interests.

An organization will be treated as an association taxable as a corporation if the corporate characteristics are such that the organization more nearly resembles a corporation than a partnership or trust.[75]

Since associates and an objective to carry on business for joint profit are essential characteristics of all organizations engaged in business, the absence of either characteristic precludes classification as a corporation for tax purposes.[76]

Certain characteristics of corporations are also found in trusts; others are common to both corporations and partnerships. Characteristics common to both trusts and corporations are not material in determining whether a trust should be classified and taxed as a corporation. For example, since centralization of management, continuity of life, free transferability of interests and limited liability are generally common to both trusts and corporations, the determination depends on whether there are associates and an objective to carry on business and divide the gains from that enterprise.[77]

In the case of a limited partnership, for example, if it has centralized management and free transferability of interests but lacks continuity of life and limited liability with no other characteristics significant in determining its classification, it will be taxed as a limited partnership. Although the limited partnership also has associates and an objective to carry on business and divide the gains from it, those characteristics are not considered because they are common to both corporations and partnerships.[78]

If the trust agreement expressly provides that the trust may be terminated at will by any beneficiary, it is clear that it lacks continuity of life in the sense that corporations have that characteristic. However, if it provides that the trust is to continue for a stated period of time or until the completion of a specific transaction, the trust has continuity of life if the effect of that provision is that no one settlor-beneficiary has the power to dissolve the organization in contravention of the trust agreement.[79]

As to centralization of management, the organization has it if any person (or any group of persons other than all the beneficiaries), has continuing exclusive authority to make the management decisions necessary to the conduct of the business for which the trust was formed. Centralized management means a concentration of continuing exclusive authority to make independent business decisions on behalf of the beneficiaries without their ratification. There is no centralization of management, however, where the authority is merely to perform managerial acts as the agent of the others. The centralization contemplated by the regulations requires sole authority to make major decisions.[80]

Considering the limited liability question, a trust has that characteristic if under local law there is no beneficiary who has personal liability for the debts of or claims against the trust. Personal liability means that a creditor of the trust may seek personal satisfaction from a beneficiary to the extent that the assets of the trust are insufficient to satisfy the creditor's claim. A beneficiary who is personally liable for the obligations of the trust may make an agreement under which some other person, whether or not a beneficiary, assumes all such risks or agrees to indemnify the beneficiary. However, if under local law the beneficiary remains liable to the creditors notwithstanding the hold-harmless agreement (*i.e.*, where the guarantor fails to perform), personal liability is established for the purpose of keeping this characteristic from attaching to the trust.[81]

The free-transferability-of-interests characteristic is established if any beneficiary has the unrestricted right to assign the
beneficial interest without the consent of the trustee or other
beneficiaries and to substitute the assignee in the trust with all the
powers held by the assignor-beneficiary. Thus, this characteristic
does not exist in a case where each beneficiary may, without the
consent of the others, assign only the right to share in profits but
cannot so assign the right to participate in the management of trust
operations. Another, less radical, approach to excluding this characteristic is to provide in the trust agreement that each beneficiary
may transfer the interest to a nonbeneficiary but only after offering
to sell it back to the other beneficiaries at its fair market value.
Under such a provision, the IRS will recognize a modified form of
free transferability and, in making its determination whether to
classify the trust as a corporation, the presence of this modified
corporate characteristic will be accorded less significance than if
transferability is unrestricted.

   • **Must the Trust be Irrevocable?** The practice generally is
to leave the trust agreement silent on this point, probably more as
a result of old habits than considered legal analysis. Even if
expressly made irrevocable, it may be effectively revoked by
simply instructing the trustee to convey the property to a new land
trust containing the desired new provisions. For that reason, trustees routinely accept amendments that do not add to their administrative burdens.

   As a general proposition, leaving such a point unaddressed may
lead to a presumption at law that the trust may be altered, amended
or revoked,[82] so the decision to make it irrevocable will be driven
by local law.

   California serves as an example. Its Probate Code Sections
18200 and 18201 deal with creditor protection as follows:

**"18200. Creditor's Rights Against Revocable Trust During
Settlor's Lifetime.**

"If the settlor retains the power to revoke the trust in whole or in part, the trust property is subject to the claims of creditors of the settlor to the extent of the power of revocation during the lifetime of the settlor."

"18201. Creditor's Rights Against Revocable Trust After Settlor's Death.

"Upon the death of the settlor who had retained the power to revoke the trust in whole or in part, the property that was subject to the power of revocation at the time of the settlor's death is subject to the claims of creditors of the decedent settlor's [probate] estate and to the expenses of administration of the estate to the extent that the decedent settlor's estate is inadequate to satisfy those claims and expenses."

With California's statutory presumption of a power to alter, amend or revoke, and the absence of any comparable statute excepting land trusts from the ambit of the creditor protection provisions cited above, the first level of analysis suggests that land trusts in this state should be made irrevocable. Given that the power to order the sale of trust property and distribution of the proceeds, even where the trust agreement is irrevocable, may constitute an effective power to revoke under which the creditors may reach the trust property, something more is needed. For the single settlor-beneficiary land trust, you may permit distribution of net income in the discretion of the beneficiary, but nothing else until the trust term expires. Multiple settlor-beneficiary land trusts would permit, by unanimous or majority consent, distributions of income and principal. By this means, the creditor who obtains a charging order on the certificate of beneficial interest may receive income to apply to satisfaction of the judgment (if the debtor-beneficiary who retains the management powers deigns to order distribution) but nothing else. The hoped-for result is that the judgment will either be satisfied from trust income distributions, or will expire and become unenforceable because the discouraged creditor declines to renew it.

If the creditor is able to procure a court order and foreclose on the beneficial interest, and to buy it at the sale and wait for the trust term to expire, the game is up; some negotiation is needed.

• **Gift Taxes.** The beneficiary's transfer of property to an irrevocable trust while reserving only the right to income for the trust term raises a gift tax issue.

A gift is incomplete, thus nontaxable, where the donor in trust reserves a power to give it away by will,[83] or where the donor in trust reserves the right to take back the property,[84] or where the donor in trust reserves the right to change beneficiaries or to change their interests in the trust.[85]

To retain the right to take back the property may suit your purposes, but not if you live in California. (See the discussion of its creditor protection law above.) It renders meaningless any provision purporting to make the trust irrevocable. It also places a judgment creditor who becomes a beneficiary by acquiring the interest in foreclosure in a perfect position from which to satisfy the judgment (presuming the credit bid was less than the judgment balance).

The other two gift code provisions noted above, however, offer simple ways to avoid gift tax exposure without material loss of asset protection: as an individual beneficiary you may avoid gift tax liability by reserving the right to take back the property when the trust term expires, or if you die first, for the property to be distributed to your estate or revocable trust or under the provisions of your will; an artificial entity (partnership, corporation, etc.) or its successor as beneficiary, may take back the property upon expiration of the trust term, or otherwise provide for it to go to those designated with the unanimous consent of its principals.

• **Real Property Reassessment for Property Tax Purposes on Conveyance from the Beneficiaries to the Trust. On Assignment of the Certificate of Beneficial Interest.** This is clearly a local law issue, but where applicable can have a material effect on certain decisions. In November 1978, Californians circumvented their state house and approved an initiative entitled Proposition 13, amending Article XVIII A of the state constitution to limit property taxes. This was followed by the enactment of similar tax limitation laws in states across the country. The result in each is different, so each must be separately examined to answer the questions posed above. To minimize clutter in the text, Californians may find their answers in Endnote No. 86 at the end of this chapter.[86]

- **What About the Doctrine of Merger?** A legal doctrine is a rule, principle, theory or tenet of the law. The Doctrine of Merger derives from English trust law and, like the dry trust, is a mode of extinguishment. "Merger" is what takes place when the legal title (held by the trustee) and the equitable title (all remaining incidents of ownership held by the settlor and beneficiaries) are held by ("merged" in) one person. Extinguishment of the trust upon the merger of legal and equitable interests leaves that person as owner of the "fee title," or all the incidents of ownership. In order to enhance the uses of trusts and reduce the risk of merger from drafting error or unexpected developments, local law usually provides a safe harbor.

Here, for example, is that found in California at Probate Code Section 15209:

"Section 15209. Exception to Doctrine of Merger.

"If the trust provides for one or more successor beneficiaries after the death of the settlor, the trust is not invalid, merged, or terminated in either of the following circumstances:
(a) Where there is one settlor who is the sole trustee and the sole beneficiary during the settlor's lifetime.
(b) Where there are two or more settlors, one or more of whom are trustees, and the beneficial interest in the trust is in one or more of the settlors during the lifetime of the settlors."

With the land trust, our mind-set may be so oriented to ano-nymity and to the commercial functions of the trust that we risk drafting error leading to an invalid trust under the Doctrine of Merger; *e.g.*, providing for a single settlor, a single trustee, a single beneficiary and a reversion to the settlor upon expiration of the trust term or the settlor's estate on death, the settlor, trustee, beneficiary and holder of the reversion all being the same person. By providing in the trust agreement for remaindermen to take upon the death of the settlor-beneficiary, extinguishment under the Doctrine of Merger is avoided, even where the settlor, trustee and beneficiary are the same person.

Special Drafting Needs. Below are conclusions as to the special provisions of the trust agreement pertinent to asset protection and tax planning. Those applicable specifically to California land trusts are discussed at Endnote No. 87 at the end of this chapter.[87]

• Due to securities and tax law issues, transferability of beneficial interests in the trust should be restricted in some way, either by prior beneficiary approval of substituted status for assignees or by means of a right of first refusal.

• There are no securities law issues where only one person or entity establishes the land trust. Similarly, there are none where there are two or more settlor-beneficiaries and both or all of them participate in the management decisions. Securities law becomes a consideration only where there are two or more beneficiaries and one or more of them will depend on the efforts of others to manage the properties. In that circumstance, you must, on the one hand, either register or qualify the offering of beneficial interests as securities with the SEC or with your state regulatory agency, or on the other hand, you must bring the transaction within federal and state guidelines for exempt private placements of securities.

• Properly structured, the land trust should be taxed under the grantor trust rules. If so, all income and deductions flow through (proportionate to ownership) to the beneficiaries. The beneficiaries may be your tax haven trust, your family trust, individuals or a general or limited partnership, in which latter event the ultimate tax result is modified only by the terms of the partnership agreement. The beneficiary or beneficiaries may also hold their interests through a corporation, although that is generally unwise due to double taxation upon its liquidation. (The *General Utilities Doctrine* formerly used to avoid that result was repealed by Congress under the *Internal Revenue Code of 1986.*)

• Artfully tracking the provisions of Reg. 25.2511- 1 and 2 should avoid gift tax liability on transfers to an irrevocable land trust.

Section 1.5 Family Limited Partnerships

Background. A limited partnership is one having one or more general partners and one or more limited partners. So if you are unmarried, you will probably either bring in children as donee-limited partners or use a land trust and keep it all. If you are married, you may serve as the general partner with both your spouse and yourself as the limited partners. The latter, with possible gift interests to children, will serve as our working model.

Most states have adopted as their governing statute the *Uniform Limited Partnership Act* or the *Revised Uniform Limited Partnership Act*, the latter published by the National Conference of Commissioners on Uniform State Laws in 1976. Some have instead crafted their own.

California adopted the *California Revised Uniform Limited Partnership Act* which differs substantially from the *Revised Uniform Limited Partnership Act*. The California statute recognizes current securities market trends such as master limited partnerships by giving the limited partnership more corporate characteristics and by giving limited partners many of the advantages of corporate shareholders, without causing the partnership to be taxed as a corporation.

As general partner, except as provided by statute or by the partnership agreement, you have the same rights, powers and liabilities as a partner in a general partnership. As a limited partner with limited participation in partnership management, you are ordinarily free from liability for partnership obligations except to the extent of your capital contributions, except that you may be liable for the return of distributions received at a time when the partnership was insolvent. If you are both a general partner and a limited partner, of course, you have the liability of a general partner and the voting rights of each.

Pertinent Tax Issues. Whether a partnership is recognized as such for tax purposes turns on the same analysis described at Section 1.4 for land trusts. In addition, IRS will sometimes add requirements to those in the regulations when asked for an advance ruling on recognition. **Remember that these rules are used only for IRS determination of whether to consider a ruling request on tax classification of an organization. They are not substantive rules:**

• The combined interests of all general partners in each material item of partnership income, gain, loss, deduction or credit must be at least 1% of each such item. Under 1989 guidelines, the value of limited partnership interests owned by the general partners are considered for purposes of this test, and the 1% requirement need not be met at all if the limited partnership is capitalized for $50 million or more.[88] If the test must be satisfied (*i.e.*, where capitalization is less than $50 million), and if unless at least one general partner contributes substantial services as general partner, the general partners must maintain a minimum capital account balance equal to either 1% of total capital account balances for the partnership or $500,000, whichever is less.

• IRS issued new substantive rules in 1989 regarding classi-fication of business entities for tax purposes. When a limited partnership is formed in a state with a statute corresponding to the *Uniform Limited Partnership Act*[89] or the *Revised Uniform Lim-ited Partnership Act*,[90] IRS will concede that the partnership lacks continuity of life if the partnership agreement requires a majority in interest of the limited partners to remove an old general partner and to elect a new one to continue the partnership. IRS will also rule that the partnership lacks centralized management if limited partner interests, excluding those held by general partners, are less than 80% of the total interests in the partnership. IRS will, how-ever, consider all the facts and circumstances, including limited partner control of the general partners, in determining whether the partnership lacks centralized management. The partnership will generally be considered to lack limited liability if the net worth of corporate general partners, at the time of the ruling request, equals at least 10% of the total contributions to the limited partnership and that percentage is expected to continue throughout the life of the partnership.[91]

The partnership is not subject to income tax. Rather, you and each of the other partners report your respective share of income, gains, losses, deductions and credits on your individual income tax returns.[92] The Partnership Return of Income, Form 1065 (federal) filed by the partnership is an information return, not an income tax return. The character of most items of income, gain or credit included in your distributive share is passed through as though received directly.

Family Partnership Issues. You might consider a family limited partnership in your asset protection plan if sharing ownership with your children is of interest. It can be used to shift income within the family, given the right facts, although this is the area where most of the problems arise. The family partnership tax rules are found at IRC Section 704(e).

The Internal Revenue Code of 1986 fully restated *The Internal Revenue Code of 1954*, as amended. Among its provisions touching on family partnerships is Section 101, effectively eliminating tax bracket reduction from shifting income to children under 14 years of age. It is still available, given the right planning, for those over 13. The "family," for Section 704(e) purposes, includes you, your spouse, the ancestors of each, the lineal descendants of each and trusts created for their primary benefit.[93]

Intrafamily income shifting requires the satisfaction of numerous rules and tests imposed by IRS. I will summarize them here, but you should consult the regulations carefully before undertaking such an effort:

• The first test is whether the allocation of income is fair in relation to the partnership's capital and the services performed for the partnership.[94] Capital is a material income-producing factor if a substantial part of the partnership income is attributable to it.[95] If the income is primarily from fees, commissions or personal services, for example, capital is not a major factor.[96]

• The interests of the family members must be properly documented; if they came about by gift, it is prudent to make it for $100 or more above the $10,000 annual gift tax exclusion amount and file gift tax returns. That way a complete audit trail is established, the statute of limitation starts to run on the IRS' right to challenge the valuations used and the donee's status as a limited partner is more likely to be recognized.

After recognition is achieved, the donee partner's share of income is taxed to the donee rather than the donor if the donor is also paid reasonable compensation for any services rendered to the partnership, and if the share of income attributable to the donee's capital interest is not proportionately greater than that attributable to the donor's capital interest.[97] Sales of partnership interests by one family member to another are treated as gifts in applying this rule, in order to avoid circumvention.[98]

• Dominion and control tests are aimed at ferreting out those situations where the donor is the real owner.[99] It is determined from all the facts and circumstances, but IRS will look at proper execution of documents and the extent of any control given the donor under the partnership agreement. Among the more important controls is the power to decide when and to whom to distribute income.[100] This may be vitiated by requiring the consent of all partners in determining how much of the partnership earnings should be retained each year for its reasonable working capital needs. Another pertinent factor is the donee partner's freedom to transfer the partnership interest without penalty. A sensitive situation is one where the donor controls assets essential to the partnership operations or management powers inconsistent with normal partner relations. An arrangement where the donor is the managing general partner may not be seen as undue dominion and control if the donee partner is free to dispose of the gift interest without penalty. That freedom may not exist, however, if the donee is dependent on the donor.[101] Independence is sometimes difficult to prove, especially where control over the donee may be exercised indirectly through a separate business organization, estate, trust or other partnership. Where such indirect controls exist, IRS will look to the substance of the relationship.[102] Participation in management is strong evidence of a donee's control over the partnership interest; but such participation cannot exist if the donee is a limited partner, because of the minor management role required in order to preserve limited liability. Income distributions are good evidence of control over the donated partnership interest, unless they are loaned back or invested in such a way as to allow the donor to control the funds. Strict adherence to partnership formalities will help in close situations.

• A trust may be a partner.[103] With an independent trustee, recognition of the trust as a partner is usually given. Otherwise, recognition follows only if the trustee actively protects the interests of the trust beneficiaries.

• For tax purposes, a minor may be a partner if competent to manage his or her affairs and participate in partnership functions.[104] The question is determined by the opinion of disinterested persons. Absent such competence, the minor's interest must be controlled by a court-appointed guardian. Trouble often arises from giving partnership interests to minors who are not that capable or who are not represented by a guardian.

• All things considered, donees make the best limited partners in addressing the family partnership planning needs. Participation in management should not prove to be a problem, since it is beyond the scope of the limited partner function anyway.[105] The usual (right of first refusal) restrictions on transferability of partnership interests should not prove to be a problem in demonstrating dominion and control of the donee over the gift interest in the partnership.[106]

• One planning need requiring attention is related to your service as general partner; because you are risking your credit, IRS expects you to take a larger share of profits than your capital interest would provide;[107] but we have no cases providing guidance on how much.

• If the partnership agreement is drafted to address the issues described above, and if the partnership interests are properly documented, the motivation in undertaking the partnership venture is generally irrelevant. Tax motivation is ignored.

If you fail to compensate yourself reasonably for services rendered to the partnership, IRS may reallocate income and expenses in order to recognize them.[108] The same applies when allocations do not reflect capital interests where capital is a material income-producing factor.[109]

Enforcement of Judgments Against Limited Partnership

Interests. A wide-ranging discussion of enforcement of judgments law is found at Section 1.3. Here, we trace only that peculiar to partnership interests.

Two working definitions from Section 1.3 bear repeating here. "Levy" is the taking of property, including money, where the money is applied to satisfaction of the judgment but the property is either held by the levying officer or delivered to the creditor without sale. "Execution" is a levy that carries with it the right, without further court order, to sell the property and apply the proceeds to satisfaction of the judgment.

Local law may provide for *enforcement of judgment procedure other than execution.* If so, the court may construe that to authorize a court-ordered execution sale of otherwise exempt interests — like partnership interests. If so, the exemption for partnership interests does not apply to a court-ordered lien foreclosure.

Where there is no such statutory provision, partnership interests (both limited and general) are protected from execution sale. Rather, the creditor is given the right to seek a charging order against your partnership interest; and that is all!

A "charging order" is one imposing a judgment lien on the asset and requiring all distributions made on account of that asset to be delivered to the judgment creditor. The property remains in your possession and you retain your general partner management duties and all general and limited partner voting rights.

As general partner, you may put pressure on the creditor by withholding income distributions. Two results flow from that action: the creditor is deprived of funds from which to satisfy the judgment; and as assignee the creditor must pay from personal resources all income taxes on the liened share of partnership earnings. Of course, if other partners are involved, it can damage their interests as well; they are placed in the same position as the creditor. If the numbers work out and the others agree, however, your settlement posture should be enhanced.

Local law must be examined for both the result described above and for any exceptions created by case law. In California, for example, three cases create an exception to the rule that foreclosure of judgment liens on partnership interests are not permitted.[110] Under them, a court may order the sale of a debtor's partnership interest when three conditions are satisfied: the creditor has previously obtained a charging order; the judgment nevertheless remains unsatisfied; and the debtor does not render unique personal services critical to the success of the partnership enterprise. Sale is permitted (if the three conditions are satisfied) even when the partnership agreement prohibits sale, assignment or encumbrance. A partnership agreement provision reserving to the general partner the right to consent or refuse consent to an assignee-purchaser becoming a substituted limited partner, remains intact. That is of small comfort, though, when the creditor forecloses on both the limited and *general* partnership interests: The creditor holds the power. Worse yet, most of the time the limited partnership interest held by your spouse is the only other interest. In a community property state, *it* goes by the boards along with *your* interest, so the partnership no longer exists (the foreclosing creditor owns it all). That creditor may then sell the partnership assets and keep *all* the proceeds, even if they exceed the amount owed.

Conclusions. Properly structured and in a state with the right laws, the family limited partnership offers important benefits as an asset protection tool, whether or not you are interested in making gifts to your children. Income shifting is possible; if the assets placed in the partnership are business or investment holdings, it will be conventional enough to avoid being regarded as evidence of a fraudulent transfer; and major protection is provided under enforcement of judgments law.

Even there, though, there are two concerns: one is the trend of the law toward empowering the courts to order the execution sale of partnership interests; and the other is IRC Section 2036(c). The latter is discussed at length in Chapter 2 and deals with restraints on your right to make lifetime transfers to your lineal descendants.

Section 1.6 Tax Haven Trusts

The term "tax haven trust" is our little euphemism for a foreign trust designed for asset protection; more specifically, asset protection for the US person who desires to operate entirely within the law and with unfettered asset control.

First, a mundane memo. Chapter 3 serves as a primer on offshore business operations and investment activities relevant to your asset protection planning. There, we deal with proper selection of the foreign jurisdiction and the mechanics of how to use it for bank accounts, trusts and controlled foreign corporations. In this subsection of Chapter 1, we discuss only the purpose, form and content of a tax haven trust:

• **Purpose.** In the ordinary course of events, we begin to change our way of doing business as we approach retirement. We shift from high-risk to low-risk ventures, from illiquid to liquid assets, from concentrated to diversified investments. We need to liquidity so IRS can be paid its estate taxes on time. We need investment safety because there is no chance to replace the failures after we become too sick or too old to return to our business or profession. Use of a tax haven trust is consistent with this natural and logical shift in our affairs. The fact that it also insulates against the risks of litigation is mere serendipity.

For your investment and liquidity needs, the tax haven trust offers professional management for a portfolio of investment quality securities using the services of a major foreign bank of impeccable reputation. Costs are low: they are generally under the 1% to 1.2% we see with US corporate trustees, and you avoid custodial charges for American Depositary Receipts. US investments may be made through the trust with no withholding requirement on portfolio interest remitted to the haven. Even the withholding requirement does not have much of an impact when you consider that the typical dividend yield on a growth portfolio is around 1.5%; withholding amounts to less than one-half of one percent. You enjoy total tax neutrality because US taxation is exactly the same as if the funds were managed locally; there should also be no taxes imposed by the tax haven country.

As to serendipity, you will enjoy a sense of security. The prospect of a claimant discovering or successfully taking away your financial independence is remote indeed.

• **Form.** The terms "foreign" and "tax haven trust" are used in this book to indicate where the trust is established, not its tax status. As you might imagine, foreign trusts come in a variety of forms and are used for a variety of purposes. We are only concerned, however, with that form designed to manage a portfolio of investment securities and protect the assets of the US Target Defendant.

For the sake of clarity, here is how US tax law classifies trusts:

- If the trust is irrevocable, the country where the trustee is located, the nationality and residence of the trustee and the location of trust administration generally determine the domestic or foreign status of the trust.[111]
- If revocable, it is a "grantor trust"[112] and not considered to exist for tax purposes. Moreover, if it is recognizable for any purpose, its domicile is that of the grantor, making it a domestic trust as far as IRS is concerned. To buttress that conclusion, IRC contains the definition of a foreign estate or trust:[113]

> "The terms 'foreign estate' and 'foreign trust' mean an estate or trust, as the case may be, the income of which, from sources without the United States, is not effectively connected with the conduct of a trade or business within the United States, is not included in gross income under Subtitle A."

Subtitle A of the IRC contains a description of those categories of income subject to taxation, including that of individual US taxpayers.

- The form of trust we use for asset protection purposes is revocable. Hence, since its income is fully includable on your personal returns, it is not a foreign trust for tax purposes.

Under a grantor trust, it is not possible to shift the incidence of taxation to another person or to defer the timing of that taxation. Examples of other features that cause classification as a grantor trust include those where you hold a reversionary interest exceeding 5% in either principal or income,[114] revocable trusts, whether the power is held by the settlor, a nonadverse party or both,[115] trusts in which the income may be accumulated for the settlor or the settlor's spouse[116] and sales to trusts which may be construed as transfers with retained powers.[117] The tax status of the settlor determines US taxability, so if you are responsible for payment without the trust, you are still responsible for it with the trust. US citizens everywhere and resident aliens in the US are taxable on the income of their grantor trust, whether the trust is domiciled in the US or elsewhere.

We use the grantor trust form for asset protection because it provides direct control without engaging in a sham. The sham is the "irrevocable, discretionary trust" commonly promoted in the havens as an asset protection device. There, true control is provided by the side letter with which you instruct the trustee on distribution notwithstanding the discretions purportedly vested in the trustee.

Upon examination, IRS would cut through the form to the substance and classify it as a grantor trust.

• **Reporting Requirements.** Even though the tax haven trust does not exist for tax purposes, information returns of various kind are required. Schedule B at Part III on your Form 1040 federal income tax return calls for disclosure of all foreign-domiciled trusts in which you hold a beneficial interest, specifically referencing grantor trusts. Your first step is to procure a federal tax identification number for the trust. You use Form SS-4, Application for Employer Identification Number. IRS will respond with an assigned number in 10 or 15 working days.

The **trustee** must file Form 56 (Notice Concerning Fiduciary Relationship) and Form 1041 (the trust income tax information return). You, as **beneficiary**, must file Form 3520A (annual information return). Some writers assert that you must also file Form 90-22.1 for the trust bank accounts you indirectly control. I am not entirely certain about their conclusion; you may not have the information readily available, and certain discretions granted the trustee under the Ransom Clause in the trust agreement could call into question the extent to which you control the accounts.

As a practical matter, you will have the trustee's reporting forms prepared here and will tender them for execution, return and filing.

• **Penalties.** You may find the trustee unequipped to provide tax reporting service and surprised that you are doing so. That leads to consideration of penalties for failure to report.

In the absence of reasonable cause, failure to file the 3520A information return may lead to a civil penalty of 5% of the trust estate, maximum $1,000. If the failure is willful, it constitutes a misdemeanor punishable by a fine of up to $25,000, imprisonment for up to one year, or both. Of course, failure to report and pay the tax on trust income leads to a 5% per month penalty up to 25% of the tax due, plus interest.

• **Content.** Setting aside the Latin-laden terminology of English common law, the form of grantor trust I developed for asset protection use will seem familiar to American practitioners. It is called a Deed of Settlement and contains a trust name (which may be fictitious), a reference to the asset schedule with administrative provisions and property characterization as community or separate where appropriate, acceptance of trust by the trustee, amendment and revocation provisions, reserved investment direction powers, provisions for distribution during the life or joint lives of the settlor or settlors, distributions on the death of the settlor or either settlor, distributions on the death of the surviving settlor if appropriate, a perpetuities clause, provisions for life insurance and retirement plan benefits, general administrative provisions, investment powers granted to the trustee, provisions for payment of death taxes, accounting duties of the trustee, successor trustee provisions, expenses and compensation of the trustee, an incontestability clause, a special indemnity provision for the trustee, a special authorization for the trustee to employ the services of properly qualified affiliates, a special provision holding the trustee harmless for not asserting powers of ownership in business interests you place in the trust unless it actually becomes aware of dishonesty, a special provision permitting the trustee to appoint its officers and employees as officers and directors of companies the stock of which is included in the trust estate and to receive and retain reasonable compensation for their services, and authorization to use nominees and custodians where necessary to hold securities. Any time you become physically or mentally incapacitated, the trustee is authorized and directed to investigate and take whatever action is necessary to meet your support needs.

Not all trust companies are equipped to provide full-charge, worldwide portfolio management, but those that do usually achieve excellent results. Their services are priced competitively with those of US banks and trust companies for full-management trusts, and may be reduced by one-half or more if all you want the trustee to do is hold business interests and certificates of deposit at your direction and keep records.

To the extent you transfer assets to the trust and provide there for management and distribution after your death, the tax haven trust serves as a will substitute; there is no probate administration. You retain the right to alter, amend or revoke, as well as to replace the trustee. Because there is no probate, there is no will contest.

By using a corporate trustee, you have the assurance that your fiduciary will not die, lose interest or move away.

Under the choice of law provision, you decide what country's law will control the trust. In a related provision, called a "Cuba Clause," you may cause the trust to be moved to another country any time you feel threatened by changes in secrecy law, taxation or any other aspect of its operating environment.

In what may be described as a "Ransom Clause," the trustee may refuse to obey your instruction to pay money if it believes the instruction to be given under duress.

The trust must be drafted so as to protect the marital deduction for federal estate tax purposes, if it is otherwise available. This point may be addressed by either providing the surviving spouse a general power of appointment (automatic qualification) or a qualified terminable interest in the trust estate (qualification if elected by the trustee).

Some may dismiss the use of "self-settled trusts" for asset protection on the ground that "If *you* can reach the trust property, so can your *creditors.*" As an abstract principle of trust law, that is true. For 800 years, the law recognized that a person cannot create a trust for his or her own benefit that will protect that person's assets from the claims of creditors. Nothing has changed. Courts of equity still treat such trusts as void to the extent that it operates to defeat a creditor's claim. But to state the point is to beg the question. If the creditor cannot settle a foreign judgment as a judgment of the trust jurisdiction, or cannot secure a new one there, it matters little that the law provides for that creditor; the claim must be recognized at law to be enforceable against the trust; that means it must be reduced to a judgment enforceable in that jurisdiction.

As is considered in more detail at Chapter 3, you will select the tax haven after considering: its trust law; its political, economic and social stability; its reputation as an offshore financial center; its tax laws; its dominant language; its communications facilities; its ease of access; and the sophistication of its professional infrastructure (management companies and its accounting, legal and trust services). In addition, you will avoid a corporate trustee with a substantial US presence. If it has large holdings in the US and you fall into a dispute with a US government agency over some aspect of your affairs, that agency may gain access to your records by threatening the US office of the trustee with large financial sanctions.

Section 1.7 A Wealth of Wrong Information

Lest I mislead you with this caption, I hasten to say that there is a small but growing body of worthwhile published asset protection planning material. I have read much of the worthwhile and more — the good, the bad and the ugly — and include here a few reactions that may save you some time and mistakes.

The Complete Asset Protection Guide by attorney Arnold S. Goldstein was published in 1990 by Enterprise Publishing, Inc. It is a 216-page oversize paperback book in which Mr. Goldstein addresses the concerns of people in tax and financial difficulty generally. It is not geared to the special needs of the Target Defendant. He covers, for instance, how to fight off collection agencies and IRS seizures, but not estate planning and foreign trust. The discussion of each topic is succinct and accurate as far as it goes but may be too much of a summary to serve as more than a primer. Mr. Goldstein also edits an asset protection newsletter for the same publisher.

Lawsuit and Asset Protection by Vijay Fadia was published in 1989 by Homestead Publishing Company, Inc. No mention is made of his credentials. Like Mr. Goldstein's book, this is a general and cryptic overview of a wide range of topics in the asset protection planning area. It does, however, have one nine-page chapter on planning for professional persons. Notwithstanding its recent vintage, some of the material is out of date.

Both Fadia and Goldstein assume (perhaps with justification, given the self-help planning I see in the field) that the reader is disturbed enough to give away assets. I have largely ignored gifts as a planning tool because of the working assumptions stated at the beginning of this book.

Secrets of Offshore Tax Havens is not reliable as a reference piece. It was written by Robert Chappell and published in 1985 by ABM Publishing Co. Mr. Chappell is a former life insurance and securities salesman who was the subject of a 10-year IRS audit that left him outraged. He spent a few years after the audit experience developing a system he believed would avoid federal income tax liability and thwart IRS recovery attempts. Promotion of the system began about two years before publication of his book.

The Chappell system was promoted through "information officers" across the country. Unfortunately, the candor of one in Florida (who thought the IRS undercover agent was a hot prospect) brought about the downfall of both the information officer and Mr. Chappell. Both were subsequently convicted and imprisoned for mail fraud. Upon their departure, about 1,000 customers were left unattended. Since then, at least a dozen organizations using the same system have appeared and made themselves available to meet the needs of these customers and others.

The system features a proprietary creation called a "Contractual Company." This is an entity described with a hodgepodge of contract, trust and corporate labels in an attempt to give birth to an entirely new creature of the law. It is used in a Rube Goldberg arrangement of foreign trusts and domestic business trusts and implemented with a series of sham transactions by which the customer purportedly gives away the entire estate (with a wink, of course), living thereafter "tax-free" on money "borrowed" from one of the trusts.

It seems clear that Mr. Chappell would find few followers if they were permitted to seek the advice of their attorneys and accountants; they might learn that new forms of legal entities do not count; IRS (quite lawfully) analyzes the characteristics of the entity and classifies it using a form recognized at law for purposes of determining how to tax it, no matter what it is called. Because of the need to isolate the prospective customer from professional advisors, Mr. Chappell moves from his initial tirade against the IRS (which seems well-taken, based on his side of the story) to a bitter denunciation against attorneys and accountants of traditional training and experience. (We are engaged in "gluttonous racketeering.") The methodology is reminiscent of cult techniques and leaves the customer with no one to consult but Mr. Chappell and the attorney who prepared the caveat-riddled opinion letter on which he relies.

Almost every page contains incorrect assertions of fact and law. Each is the illogical extension of the false premises that precede it.

The latest of his customers to gain notoriety are Shirley and Richard Connelly of Las Vegas, Nevada. *The Wall Street Journal* reported on August 8, 1990 (page 1, column 5) as follows:

"TOO LATE TO DIG A MOAT? Fake a foreclosure to keep the IRS out.

"Richard L. and Shirley A. Connelly of Las Vegas, Nev., were consistent, at least. In 1986, they were convicted of not filing returns for two years and of filing a false refund claim for another. A judge sentenced them to a year in jail and $5000 fines, but released them on probation after six months on condition that they pay their taxes and cooperate with the IRS. Last year, they went back to jail; they had refused to cooperate and had paid only $17,134 of a $51,843 tax bill — through involuntary wage levies."

"The couple also tried to hide ownership of their one asset, their home: They said they mortgaged it for $65,000 to Nassau Life Insurance Co. [Chappell's company], trustee for Benco Management Co. of the Turks and Caicos Islands, and gave the cash to their children, who "blew it." Benco supposedly foreclosed upon default — then rented the house to the Connellys. But the IRS tied Benco to a well-known tax protester and showed the fraudulent deals were "self-serving fictions.""

"Shirley Connelly appealed the revocation of her probation. Now the 9th Circuit Court of Appeals has upheld it."

WFI Corporation is a Los Angeles organization run by Jerome Schneider. He is a nonlawyer who wrote and published several small books on offshore trusts and private international banks. The principal business of WFI is the sale of offshore bank charters and related consulting services. Business is promoted by means of direct mail and seminars. Although Mr. Schneider is occasionally in the news over some inquiry or another, he seems to run a clean operation. I attended his Los Angeles seminar October 3 and 4, 1989, and despite some gaps in coverage and incorrect tax advice by a couple of the invited panelists (not WFI employees), I found it both interesting and entertaining.

He closed his business late in 1991. The closing was attributed (*Los Angeles Times,* reported December 4, 1991) to increased tax haven regulation brought about by the *Bank of Credit & Commerce* scandal, and by tax changes stripping from the owners of private international banks many benefits previously enjoyed. The result was a 50% reduction in the number of bank charters sold in 1991 over 1990.

Laughlin Associates, Inc., like Chase Index Corporation from Riverside, California, is a corporate services organization in Carson City, Nevada. It promotes its services by direct mail, targeting people outside Nevada concerned with asset protection and state income taxes. It features a proposed operating business structure under which the preexisting home state operating corporation deals with a (apparently nonoperating) Nevada corporation that is under common ownership. The scheme is to divert all profits from the home state to Nevada, using nonstandard pricing and other mundane techniques, and loan back operating capital to the home state corporation using secured demand notes at high rates of interest until the home state corporation is rendered insolvent or nearly so. (Nevada has no income tax or usury law.)

The gleeful hyperbole with which the foregoing is described may easily cause the noncritical reader to forget asking a few important questions:

• What about the risk of a home state audit leading to reallocation of the income and deductions by which the profits were diverted? Many states adopt federal tax law as their own. IRC Section 482 permits the IRS to do such reallocations. The home state may have a large incentive (especially if you have followed a practice of accumulating profits in Nevada) to exercise its 482 powers to allocate profits to the operating corporation where they can be taxed.

• What about the risk of a fraudulent transfer judgment or conviction (yes, conviction — there are criminal penalties, too) for deliberately rendering the operating corporation unable to satisfy its obligations, thus defeating the claims of legitimate creditors?

• What about the fact that loan security taken by a shareholder is often set aside by the courts as a preference or as a fraudulent transfer?[118]

• What about the possibility that the corporate income tax saved may be offset in spades by the cost of the Nevada corporation and service package and the minimum franchise tax still payable in the home state?

• What about the fact that the home state personal income tax is still imposed on income from all sources — within and without the home state? California, for instance, has a top individual bracket of 9% and a top corporate bracket of 11%. As soon as the diverted profits are taken down as personal income, the savings drops to the 2% differential; it is that savings that must be measured against the cost (and risks) of implementing this plan.

That the Laughlin service package is rarely cost-effective begs the question; the point is that these major omissions from the promotional material may lead the uncritical reader into serious error. The promoter is in the business of selling services, of course, and takes no responsibility for the exercise of good business and legal judgment. That's your job.

Jay W. Mitton is an attorney from Utah and one of the early advocates of asset protection planning for Target Defendants. He uses intrafamily gifts with trusts and clusters of limited partnerships as his primary tools. I read an undated workbook from one of his seminars and attended the Arcadia, California presentation November 14, 1990. What I saw and heard troubled me. He overstates his opinions and, in a presentation best described as superficial, omits points of law any reasonable person needs for a principled analysis of his ideas. For example, he touted gifts of partnership interests to children to lower income taxes through their (presumably) lower tax brackets, without also saying that children under 14 are taxed at the highest bracket charged to the parent; no bracket leverage there. He disparaged the use of tax haven trusts by stating (as though by divine revelation) that US law is applied to the creditor's claim. True as far as it goes, but meaningless because US law is largely ignored when the creditor attempts to enforce the claim in the haven. Most of the Mitton seminar is devoted to whipping the audience to a fever pitch over lawsuits and lawyers to sell a $400 set of books. In the end, it is unclear whether he ignores land trusts, tax haven trusts and the evidentiary effect of overusing limited partnerships out of ignorance, or whether he panders to antilawyer bigotry and the "fortress America" mentality because it is easier to affirm conventional wisdom than to enlighten. Whatever the level of his sophistication in this area of the law, Mitton must be given his due for calling attention to asset protection planning needs and pioneering ways to deal with them.

Engel & Rudman is a small Colorado firm that in the mid-80s found its securities practice virtually uninsurable for professional negligence. The principals dealt with it successfully by developing a national practice, refining the ideas of Jay Mitton and supporting their promotion with sound marketing methods. They have advanced the state of the art materially, buttressing the weakest point in Mitton's approach, planning by which to avoid fraudulent transfer liability.

Even so, I fear his use of multiple limited partnerships to hold certain kinds of passive assets (in the Mitton style) will lead to trouble. It strikes me as too unconventional to hold bank accounts, certificates of deposit, personal residences and automobiles in such entities. The judge or jury in any fraudulent transfer claim is just too likely to conclude that no sound business justification exists for holding them that way, and that the only motivation for the transfer was to hinder, delay or defraud creditors.

Their earliest strategy was assigning the limited partnership interest to the tax haven trust. Their newest twist is providing for automatic dissolution of the partnership (with distribution to the trust) as soon as execution is attempted by a judgment creditor. This also gives me cause to pause. As noted at page 9 (Land Trusts), a corporate trustee cannot generally hold title to real estate outside the state where the trustee is domiciled. If the limited partnership holds local real estate, how does it convey title on to the offshore trust? While you are at it, think about standing before the judge with arms akimbo saying "I didn't do it. It happened automatically!" The judge or jury could rationally look through the form to the substance and say, "Yeah, but you set it up like a spring gun, so you might as well have pulled the trigger!" If so, you could face a fraudulent transfer conviction based on an agency theory (that the trustee acted as your agent in pulling the partnership assets away from the creditor).

Other. As to other published material in this field, most is tax-oriented and treat asset protection as a happy by-product of that pursuit. Much of the material is also incorrect, illogical, full of unkeepable promises and patent invitations to commit tax fraud. While examples of gross misinformation abound, the list is depressing and the lessons tedious. The purpose of raising the point at all is to serve notice that wrong information is the enemy. It robs you of correct legal advice and of the sense of confidence necessary to get started.

Endnotes

1. 1988 survey of its 2,700 members by the California Council of the American Association of Architects.

2. California Civil Code, Sec. 3439-3439.11

3. California Civil Code, Sec. 3439.05

4. California Civil Code, Sec. 3439.01; *Wright vs. Rohlffs* (1941) 48 CA2d 696, 702-708, 131 P2d 76; see also *Stearns vs. Los Angeles City School District* (1966) 244 CA2d 696, 737, 53 CR 482

5. *NLRB vs. Better Building Supply Corp.* (9th Cir Jan. 13, 1988), No. 87-7154

6. California Civil Code, Sec. 3439.04

7. *Hedden vs. Waldeck* (1937) 9 C2d 631, 636, 72 P2d 114; see also *Aggregates Associated, Inc. vs. Packwood* (1962) 58 C2d 580, 588, 25 CR 545

8. Specifically, 11 USC Sec. 548

9. Comment No. 6 to California Civil Code, Sec. 3439.04

10. Comment No. 7 to California Civil Code, Sec. 3439.04

11. California Civil Code, Sec. 3439.08

12. California Civil Code, Sec. 3439.03

13. Comment No. 3 to California Civil Code, Sec. 3439.03

14. California Civil Code, Sec. 3439.01(a)

15. California Civil Code, 3439.04(b)(2)

16. California Civil Code, 3439.02(a)

17. California Civil Code, 3439.02(c)

18. 629 F.Supp 175 (1985) p.187

19. 629 F.Supp at p. 184

20. California Civil Code, Sec. 3439.08(e)(2)

21. California Civil Code, Sec. 3439.09(a)

22. California Civil Code, Sec. 3439.09(b)

23. California Civil Code, Sec. 3439.09(c)

24. California Code of Civil Procedure, Sec. 481.010-493.660

25. California Civil Code, Sec. 3439.07

26. Comment No. 4 to California Civil Code, Sec. 3439.08

27. California Penal Code, Sec. 531

28. *Yokozeki vs. State Bar* (1974) 11 C3d 436, 521 P2d 858, cert. denied, 95 S.Ct 183, 419 US 900; see also *Allen vs. State Bar* (1977) 20 C3d 172, 141 CR 808

29. Underbill and Hayton, *Law of Trusts and Trustees* (14th ed.), p.225

30. Dicey and Morriss, *The Conflict of Laws* (11th ed.), Vol. 2, pp. 1115-1116

31. Uniform Commercial Code, Sec. 9301

32. For example, see California Code of Civil Procedure, Sec. 483.010 *et seq.*; see also *Advanced Transformer Co. vs. Superior Court of Los Angeles* (1974) 44 CA3d 127, 118 CR 350

33. *U.S. vs. Security Trust & Savings Bank* 340 U.S. 47, 71 F. Supp 111 (1950); *Calvin & Co. vs. U.S.* (1968) 264 CA2d 571, 574, 70 CR 578

34. *Farnum vs. Hefner* (1889) 79 C 575, —P —

35. Uniform Commercial Code, Sec. 9504-9506

36. *O'Conner vs. Blake* (1865) 29 C 312, 315; *Colver vs. W.B. Scarborough Co*, (1925) 73 CA 441, 443, 238 P 1104

37. *O'Dell vs. Cox* (1907) 151 C 70; *Haish vs. Hall* (1928) 90 CA 547, 265 P 1030; as to real property, see *Smith vs. Kessler* (1974) 43 CA3d 26, 117 CR 470

38. 11 USC 522 (d)

39. California Code of Civil Procedure, Sec. 703.130

40. Illinois Revised Statutes 1987, Sec. 110-12-1201

41. Majority: *In re Rauer's Collection Co.* (1948) 87 CA2d 248, 253-254, 196 P2d 803; *Daylin Medical & Surgical Supply, Inc. vs. Thomas* (1977) 69 CA3d Supp 37, 40-42, 138 CR 878; *Smith vs. Hume* (1937) 29 CA2d Supp 747, 749-751; *Medical Fin. Ass'n vs. Wood* (1936) 20 CA2d Supp 749, 63 P2d 1219
Minority: California Code of Civil Procedure, Sec. 703.050; *San Diego White Trust Co. vs. Swift* (1979) 96 CA3d 88, 157 CR 745; *National Collection Agency vs. Fabila* (1979) 93 CA3d Supp 1, 155 CR 356

42. California Code of Civil Procedure, Sec. 704.115(c)

43. California Code of Civil Procedure, Sec. 704.115(e)

44. Texas Property Code, c. 41

45. For example, see California Code of Civil Procedure, Sec. 704.710(b)

46. For example, see California Code of Civil Procedure, Sec.704.710(c)

47. Idaho Code 1947 Secs. 55-1907, 55-1008

48. For an exception, see Kentucky Revised Statutes 427.080-427.60; Texas Property Code, c. 41, *ibid.*

49. 15 USC 1673(a)

50. California Code of Civil Procedure, Sec. 708.160(b)-(c)

51. California Code of Civil Procedure, Sec. 708.320(a)-(b); on foreclosure following issuance of title charging order, see *Centurion Corporation vs. Crocker National Bank* (1989) 208 CA3d 1, 255 CR 794

52. California Code of Civil Procedure, Sec. 709.010

53. California Probate Code, Sec. 15300

54. California Probate Code, Sec. 18200

55. *Gray vs. Union Trust Company* (1915) 171 C 637, 643-644, 154 P 306

56. *Ringrose vs. Gleadall* (1911) 17 CA 664, 121 P 407

57. *Drennas Estate* (1956) 9 Ill.App.2d 324, 132 NE2d 599; *Rizzo vs. Rizzo* (1955) 3 Ill.2d 291, 120 NE2d 546

58. *Gallagher Speck vs. Chicago Title and Trust Co.* (1935) 238 Tll.App. 39

59. *Chicago Federal Savings & Loan Association vs. Cacciatore* (1962) 25 Ill.2d 535, 195 NE2d 670

60. The land trust survives this test in California under *Gray vs. Union Trust Co., supra, Craven vs. Dominguez Estate Co.* (1925) 72 CA 713, 237 P 821, *Botsford vs. Haskins & Sells* (1978) 81 CA3d 780, 146 CR 752 and California Probate Code, Sec. 15200-15210

61. The land trust interest may be recognized as a personal property interest in California under *Smith vs. Bank of America* (1936) 14 CA2d 78, 57 P2d 136. The *Smith* case deals with a form of land called a " subdivision trust." This is a trust in which developers anonymously acquire contiguous parcels of real property then rezone, subdivide and develop or resell. The court said that while it is true that words in a trust agreement do not create a conversion of real property to personal property, it throws some light upon the intention of the parties to the trust agreement, and the intention is the criterion. The trust agreement contained several provisions characterizing the beneficial interest as personal property, including this at Article TENTH:

> "...the interest under this trust and of each beneficiary is personal property and no such beneficiary has or shall have any right, title or interest in or to the property covered hereby."

Upon examination of the trust agreement, the court reached the following conclusion:

> "We are of the opinion that this clothes the trustee with all the indicia of ownership while carrying the burden of the trust exclusive of any ownership in the beneficiaries during the life of the trust, and while the beneficiaries are called upon by the trust to bear and pay all taxes, costs, fees, and expenses and all claims, liens, and encumbrances affecting the title to the property, this is nothing more than a condition exacted by the trustee before it will agree to assume the

trust burden and is not indicative of any reservation of title or vesting of title or estate in the beneficiaries....The interest of the appellant herein must be held to be personal property, and not an interest in realty."

Smith is regularly cited for recognition of the change in character from real to personal property, so it is settled law in California.

62. In California, the protection is afforded such an interest to the extent described in the discussion of charging and foreclosure orders at Section 1.3. See *Smith vs. Bank of America, supra, Houghton vs. Pacific Southwest Trust & Savings Bank* (1931) 111 CA 509, 295 P 1079 and California Code of Civil Procedure, Sec. 697.510. With no right or power to reach the land, the other beneficiaries are protected from interference with trust operations arising from judgment liens, foreclosure or partition proceedings. The creditor may only seek a charging order under which to receive distributions payable to the debtor-beneficiary under the trust interest or may (if a buyer can be found) seek an order permitting foreclosure and sale of the beneficial interest. There is every reason to believe the IRS would fare no better with a tax lien.

In order to fully appreciate the implications of this conclusion, these creditor rights must be read together with the discussion of irrevocability at Section 1.4. If the judgment debtor-beneficiary retains the right—acting alone—to alter, amend or revoke the land trust, the creditor may reach the underlying property to satisfy the judgment. Consequently, the California land trust should either be irrevocable or should have two or more beneficiaries who are not married to each other and all or a majority of whom must consent to any amendment or revocation.

63. Under California cases going back to 1909 and still cited as authority today, the beneficial interest is assignable. See *Title Insurance & Trust Company vs. Duffin* (1923) 191 C 629, 649, 218 P 14, and *Wright & Kimbrough vs. Carly* (1909) 11 CA 325, 104 P 1009.

64. Under California Probate Code, Sec. 18100, third parties are fully protected if they act in good faith, provide valuable consideration and have no actual knowledge that the trustee is exceeding its powers or improperly exercising them. Under Probate Code, Sec. 18102, the same protection is extended to third parties dealing with a former trustee in the belief that it is then still the trustee. Sec. 18104 provides a presumption affecting the burden of proof that a trustee holding title under a deed disclosing the existence of the trust but not the identity of the beneficiary holds the interest absolutely and free of trust. Thus, if challenged successfully, the trustee acts for the beneficiaries, and the judgment is binding on them. Otherwise, the transaction is conclusive as to a purchaser or encumbrancer in good faith and for valuable consideration.

65. California Civil Code, Secs. 5107-5108, 5110, 5118, 5119, 5126, 5105, 5125, in order of discussion

66. The '33 Act, Sec. 11; California Corporations Code, Sec. 25501

67. Under California law, see Corporations Code, Sec. 25102(f).

68. Rule 501(a)(1)-(8) of the '33 Act

69. The California rule is similar to Rule 501(a)(1)-(8) of the '33 Act but with a more liberal treatment of income in meeting the "wealthy investor" test. It also adds to the accredited investors category those who purchase interests of $150,000 or more and either have the capacity to protect their interests or are investing less than 10% of net worth. See Commissioner's Rule 206.102.1.

70. Rule 506(b)(2)(ii) of the '33 Act

71. The California "sophistication" requirements are similar. Corporations Code, Sec. 25102(f) allows as an alternate ground for the exemption a pre-existing relationship with the issuer (sponsoring beneficiaries).

72. *SEC vs. Ralston Purina* (1953) 346 US 119, 125

73. IRC, Sec. 677

74. Reg 301.7701-2

75. *Morrissey, et al vs. Commissioner* (1935) 296 US 344

76. Reg 301.7701-2(a)(2)

77. *ibid*

78. Reg 301.7701-2(a)(3)

79. Reg 301.7701-2(b)(3)

80. Reg 301.7701-2(c)(1)-(4)

81. Reg 301.7701-2(d)(1)

82. *In re Estate of Bork* (1986) 145 Ill.App.3d 920, 496 NE2d 329; *Dorman vs. Central National Bank in Chicago* (1981) 97 Ill.App.3d 429, 422 NE2d 1019

83. Reg. 25.2511-2(b)

84. Reg. 25.2511-2(c)

85. *ibid*

86. California's Proposition 13 added Article XVIII A to the California Constitution. This article provides for a limit on property tax rates, for an assessed value rollback to those values existing on March 1, 1975, for limitations on property tax rate increases, for limitations on alternate forms of taxation and for reassessment of new construction and upon change of ownership. Proposition 8 was adopted November 7, 1978, eliminating the apparent requirement that property damaged in a natural disaster then rebuilt must be reassessed at current market value. It also provides that property which declines in value may be reassessed downward for property tax purposes.

    "Change of Ownership" is defined at *Revenue & Taxation Code* (R&TC), Section 60 as "a transfer of a present interest in real property, including the beneficial use thereof, the value of which is substantially equal to the value of the fee interest." The most common transfers are addressed at Sections 61 to 67.

Under Sections 62(b), 62(c) and 63(a), transfers into an irrevocable trust where the settlor or the spouse of the settlor is the beneficiary, do not constitute a change in ownership permitting reassessment. Reassessment may follow death of a settlor and spouse, unless another exemption applies.

Where an undivided fractional interest in real property is conveyed to the trust, only that fraction will be reassessed where no exemption applies. (R&TC Sec. 65.1)

The land trust also qualifies as a " fictional entity" as contemplated at R&TC Sections 62(a) and 64. Here are the rules applicable to fictional entities:
- **General Rule**; Any transfer between fictional entities, or between one and any person (including a holder of beneficial interest) constitutes a change of ownership.

- **Exception No. 1:** A conveyance of real property to the land trust where the proportional ownership interests remain the same is not a change of ownership.

- **Exception No. 2:** Transfers of beneficial interest after a conveyance of real property to the land trust, or of ownership interests in an entity that is a trust beneficiary, do not constitute a change of ownership unless majority voting control of either also changes. If the voting control so changes after the conveyance in trust, it is deemed a change of ownership begetting reassessment.
Under R&TC Section 61(c), the creation or termination of a lease bearing a term of 35 years or more constitutes a change of ownership, leading to reassessment. Any transfer of a lease with a term balance of 35 years or more is a change of ownership requiring reassessment, but conveyance of the title to the property is not. On the other hand, transfer of a lease with a term balance of less than 35 years is not a change of ownership, but conveyance of the title to the property is a change leading to reassessment.

Beyond the scope of these remarks are transfers less likely to affect the land trust uses you are considering. They include transfers and grants of various " possessory interests," new construction, major rehabilitation, changes in use and construction date of completion.

87. Below are those conclusions peculiar to using land trusts in California:
- The duty of the trustee to perform all acts affecting title is sufficient in California to avoid trust termination as a dry, naked or passive trust.

- The express intent of the settlors to convert a real property interest in trust to a personal property interest is recognized in California.

- If the trust is irrevocable and the consent of all beneficiaries is required for trust distributions, a judgment creditor's practical ability to recover from the debtor-beneficiary should be limited to the beneficiary's right to trust distributions, insulating the trust property itself from those claims. It is possible, however, that a creditor could obtain an order for foreclosure and cause the sale of the beneficial interest. If so, the purchaser owns the entire beneficial interest, irrespective of the unsatisfied judgment balance. That purchaser need only wait until the term expires and take that interest in cash or in kind. See CCP Sec. 699.720, 708.310-320, 709.010(b)

- Purchasers for value without actual knowledge that the trustee is exceeding or misusing its powers are fully protected in dealing with the trustee (or former trustee).

- While a beneficiary as manager-spouse of the community property land trust interest may transact much of the business on a single signature, any such act must be taken with full recognition of the fiduciary duty owed to the nonmanager-spouse.

- The trust may be either revocable or irrevocable. Creditor protection in California, however, suggests that it be irrevocable, reserving only the right to order distributions of income with approval of all or a majority of the beneficiaries. Proceeds of sales and refinancings, along with net operating income, are ordinarily accumulated and reinvested during such time as a judgment creditor is holding a trust interest under a charging order or under an assignment from a foreclosure sale.

- Acquisition of property through the trust and from unrelated parties is a change of ownership which brings about reassessment for property tax purposes. The conveyance of property from the beneficiaries to the trust, where the beneficial interests are proportional to the preconveyance interests, are free from reassessment. The transfer of beneficial interests will not cause reassessment of the trust property unless direct or indirect voting control changes. Transfer of the beneficial interest to the beneficiary's grantor trust (the usual estate planning form) will not lead to reassessment. Leases with terms of 35 years or more are treated as a conveyance of title, thus may be a change of ownership for property tax reassessment purposes.

- Under the Probate Code, you are generally protected from the risk of trust invalidity under the Doctrine of Merger. The one way to lose the protection is to be the only settlor and beneficiary and to neglect to name one or more remainder beneficiaries.

- Predictability could be enhanced by means of special legislation, but for now, the land trust may be used with reasonable confidence in California.

88. Rev Proc 89-12, 1989-7 Int Rev Bull 22

89. 6 Uniform Laws Annotated, Secs. 1-30

90. 6 Uniform Laws Annotated, Secs. 101-1106

91. Rev Proc 89-12, 1989-7 Int Rev Bull 1

92. IRC Sec. 702(a)(5); Reg 1.70-1(a)

93. IRC Sec. 704(e)(3)

94. IRC Sec. 704(e)(1)

95. Reg 1.704-1(e)(1)(iv)

96. *ibid*

97. IRC Sec 704(e)(2)

98. IRC Sec. 704(e)(3)

99. Reg 1.704-1(e)(2)

100. *Driscoll vs. US* (CD Cal 1969) 69-2 USTC p. 9536, 24 AFTR2d p. 69-5249

101. Reg 1.704-1(e)(2)(ix)

102. Reg 1.704-1(e)(2)(iii)

103. Reg 1.704-1(e)(2)(viii); *Miller vs. Commissioner* (6th Cir 1953) 203 F2d 350, *Theodore D. Stern* (1959) 15 TC 521; but see *Hanson vs. Birmingham* (ND Iowa 1950) 92 F2d Supp 33

104. Reg 1.704-1(e)(2)(viii)

105. Reg 1.704-1(e)(2)(ix)

106. *ibid*

107. Reg 1.704-1(e)(3)(ii)(c)

108. Reg 1.704-1(e)(3)(ii)(b)

109. *Leo A. Woodbury* (1967) 49 TC 180, acq 1969-2 Cum Bull xxv

110. *Hellman vs. Anderson* (1991) 233 CA 3d 840, 284 CR 830, *Centurion Corp. vs. Crocker National Bank* (1989) 208 CA3d 1,255 CR 794; *Evans vs. Galardi* (1976) 16 C3d 300, 128 CR 25; see also Corporations Code, Secs. 15028, 15522, 15673

111. IRC Sec. 7701(a)(31); HR Rep. No. 658, 94th Cong., 2d Session 206 (1976); S. Rep. No. 938, 94th Cong., 2d Session 215 (1976)

112. As contemplated by IRC Secs. 673-678

113. IRC Sec. 7701(a)(31), *ibid.*

114. IRC Sec. 673(a)

115. IRC Sec. 674(a)

116. IRC Sec. 677(a)

117. IRC Sec. 678(a)

118. *Commons vs. Schine* (1973) 35 CA3d 141, 144, 110 CR 606

CHAPTER 2

Estate Planning

Summary. *Effective estate protection includes instructions to the survivors and durable powers of attorney. Consider your planning a team effort. Consider carefully the protection of your confidential communications. Be sensitive to conflicts of interest that may require your spouse or business associate to retain independent counsel. Remember to obtain documentation to support your tax deduction for tax-planning fees. You may lawfully dispose of only your separate property and your half of any community property. Property passes at death by title, contract or probate administration.*

Three areas are addressed in estate planning: transfer costs reduction, estate management for the surviving spouse and problems of guardianship. Various instruments are used to direct most of the estate into the family trust. The trust serves to preserve the marital deduction where available and provide a wide range of tools for effective estate management and distribution.

In Section 2.2 we examine basic estate planning concepts and techniques. In Section 2.3 we deal with the next step beyond the basic concepts, moving the life insurance out of the taxable estate and into a special irrevocable trust when it, combined with the remaining estate, exceeds the amount that may be passed free of death taxes. In Section 2.4 we review a series of additional tools, techniques and ideas that may be used or useful under certain circumstances.

The irrevocable life insurance trust, artfully drafted and carefully integrated with your estate plan, may be used to remove the death proceeds from your taxable estate at death, avoid gift taxes on the premiums paid during your life and keep the death proceeds available to your executor for payment of transfer costs.

The qualified terminable interest property trust ("QTIP") produces the same postmortem tax planning opportunities as the disclaimer, except that the planning decision is made by the executor or trustee instead of the surviving spouse. Plus it provides assurance that the interest of the first spouse to die will be preserved for preselected beneficiaries.

Usually as a last choice, installment payment of the federal estate tax is possible for up to 10 years on a showing of economic need, or 14 years if a closely-held business constitutes a large part of the estate. Installment payment of death taxes may not prove cost-effective when extended probate administration expenses are considered.

In order to avoid the breakup of family farms and businesses due to heavy death taxes, the real property involved may be valued at its actual use, rather than "highest and best" use.

Given the right circumstances, gifts may be used to reduce, shift or eliminate death and income taxes.

Selling some or all your interest in the family business remains the most popular means of generating cash for estate taxes.

Section 2.1 Rules of the Road

The Durable Power of Attorney. If you are a regular reader of Abigail VanBuren or Ann Landers, you are generally familiar with an instrument called a "living will." If not, you should quickly become so. Under legislation enacted by various states an adult may sign a paper directing his or her physicians not to use life-sustaining procedures if that adult is terminally ill. There are often specific requirements as to the form of the directive and how it is to be signed and witnessed. If you have seen or otherwise experienced the pointless prolonging of the life of someone close to you, and if you want to avoid the circumstance in your case, such a directive is a way to do it.

Your will is not the correct place to provide those instructions, because the will has no legal effect until after you die and it is admitted by the court for probate administration.

A similar device is the durable power of attorney for health care ("DPHC"). Although available for many years, it is still new to many lawyers and often confused with the living will.

Under the DPHC, you delegate to a family member or friend, authority to make your health care decisions during incapacity. Under the living will, you delegate that authority to a doctor, and only in life-threatening situations. In order for the doctor to exercise the authority so granted, the doctor must determine that your condition is "irreversible, incurable, terminal and imminent." This tends to frighten the doctor and chill its use.

Even given the willingness of the doctor to act, the absence of an authorizing statute renders it null and void if you are in a coma or otherwise incompetent at the time. A DPHC, however, remains in effect even though you become incompetent. At this writing, the living will is recognized in only eight states: Massachusetts, Michigan, Nebraska, New York, Ohio, Pennsylvania, Rhode Island and South Dakota.

A power of attorney is a written instrument executed before a Notary Public in which someone (the principal) appoints someone else (an attorney-in-fact) to perform certain functions for the principal under specified conditions.

As to effective use of the DPHC, new medical advances have added complexity to decisions on whether to accept, continue, reject or terminate medical treatment. Cardiopulmonary resuscitation ("CPR") is designed to prevent death by cardiac arrest. Because most cardiac arrest victims do not suffer heart muscle damage, they will respond to CPR. Resuscitation is not indicated for everyone, though. Reviving a dying person only delays the moment of death. The decision not to resuscitate may be proper and, if so, should be entered as a formal written order ("No-Code Orders"). Unless such an order is entered, the presumption remains that CPR will be started upon cardiac arrest. The generally accepted standard for entry of a No-Code Order is as follows, and is entered only with the consent of the patient or the holder of the patient's DPHC:

- The patient has a terminal condition.
- There is no reasonable possibility of recovery or long-term survival.
- There is no medical justification served by resuscitating the patient.

Historic definitions of death served us well when medical technology could not deliver oxygen to the brain to prevent damage while emergency treatment was provided. Now, of course, we can temporarily support circulation with CPR, a pacemaker and other mechanical means. Thus, we now focus on "brain death" (the irreversible cessation of all functions of the brain, including the brain stem). The determination requires application of accepted medical standards. Brain damage may leave the patient comatose but still able to breathe, due to partial function of the brain stem. Removal of life-support systems will either effect no change or bring about death, depending upon the brain stem function.

In the past, patients unable to eat could starve to death with artificial feeding. The stricken could be hydrated with intravenously administered fluids but could not get enough nutrients that way to maintain the body. Now, liquids can be taken by means of a needle in a vein, a tube inserted into the gastrointestinal tract or a catheter in a large vein. Cessation of artificial feeding presents a particularly difficult decision for patients and their families. Other developments include antibiotics, organ transplants, dialysis, angiography and open-heart surgery.

The inherent uncertainty in accurately predicting the moment of death—most physicians having experienced one or more "miracle recoveries"—leads to a continuing presumption favoring treatment. Those able to overcome that uncertainty may still apply the presumption from a fear of civil or criminal liability for removing life-support systems, food or both.

Often, the decision is influenced by the nurse who cares for the patient. The nurse may be the first to recognize the futility of further treatment. On the other hand, that nurse may grow attached to the patient and may feel a need to defend against those who would terminate treatment, life-support systems and feeding. A physician would be foolish indeed to ignore this, since that nurse could make an effective witness for the other side in any litigation arising from the medical choice made.

All this uncertainty (law, medicine and ethics) leads many physicians to seek protection and moral support for their decisions in ethics committees. Such committees do, in fact, provide a useful forum for resolving disputes between physicians, patients, families and other health care professionals.

The initial reaction of the health care community to the DPHC was skepticism, thus the DPHC was construed in a hypertechnical manner. More acceptance is usually accorded after adoption of enabling legislation, though. State legislation should recognize that the right to consent to medical treatment necessarily includes the right to refuse treatment, even if death is the likely or probable result. The statutory requirements as to form and content of DPHC are precise and inflexible, so careful review of forms presented to health care providers is still the order of the day.

Health care providers are usually delighted to be able to deal with an attorney-in-fact under a valid DPHC. They continue to be concerned about decisional disharmony in the patient's family (due to litigation risk), and influenced by the desires of the patient's spouse where that spouse is not the attorney-in-fact.

The attorney-in-fact should be aggressive in initiating discussions about treatment and prognosis. Otherwise, physicians tend to preempt that authority by not presenting the treatment options. (Based on a 1984 study at Boston's Beth Israel Hospital.)

Other problems arise from statements of desire in the DPHC that are vague or written too broadly. For example, artificial feeding and ventilator are often used for surgery, even minor surgery. So, a flat statement that "I never want to be artificially fed" or "a ventilator is never to be used" must be construed as not intended to apply to such routine care. To assist in this area, attorney-prepared forms and those provided by medical and hospital associations contain sample statements.

As you can see, careful drafting of the DPHC is critical. Just as important is care in choosing the attorney-in-fact. If that person feels unable to carry out your wishes, another person should be considered. You might even discuss the terms of and philosophy behind the DPHC in advance with your physician. You may find the physician has moral, medical, ethical or legal objections to your desires. If so, you must consider either changing your mind or changing your physician. The attorney-in-fact will have the option of changing physicians for the patient, and this option should always be considered when an impasse is reached as to treatment decisions.

The DPHC cannot solve all the issues that arise when considering the termination of life-sustaining treatment. It is, however, the best available means by which to plan ahead for that decision.

A memorandum and form of DPHC meeting the statutory requirements of California is set forth at the back of the book as Appendix A.

Funeral Instructions. Another item that should not be included in your will are your funeral instructions. These should be in a separate memorandum, placed where they can be easily found. In that same memorandum, you may wish to include other information that ease the survivors' tasks. That includes the following:

- The location of your will (and related papers, if any).
- A description of your financial situation.
- A list of your bank accounts, credit union accounts and certificates of deposit.
- Location and contents of your safe deposit box.
- Instructions regarding your credit cards.
- Description and account number for each stock brokerage account.
- The carrier, policy number, owner, beneficiary and purpose for each life insurance policy owned by you or insuring your life, along with its location.
- Description of any government and pension benefits.

- A list of club memberships for notification purposes.
- A list of organizations in which you may hold office at the time of your death, with instructions on the disposition of your files for them.
- How title is held to your home and what to do, if anything, about any existing loan or loans against it.
- Records of any stocks and bonds.
- The attorney and accountant to call for help with the probate administration proceeding and tax reporting.
- A reminder to pick up personal items from the office.
- A reminder to cancel unwanted subscriptions.
- A list of all debts and how to deal with them.
- Where to find the records the executor, attorney and surviving spouse will need.
- A list of other advisors such as the insurance agents, financial planner and trust advisor.

As a guide in preparing such a letter for the benefit of your surviving spouse, a detailed topical outline is set forth at the back of the book as Appendix B.

The Estate Planning Team. It almost goes without saying that estate planning is not a do-it-yourself project. The tools and abstract theory behind every effectively-made strategic decision are best made with thoughtful input from your attorney, accountant, insurance professional, financial planner and trust advisor (independent trust company or bank trust department). That is not to say you should convene a mass meeting every time a question arises, but remember that each team member plays a distinct and important role that should not be slighted in the well-developed plan. Generally, the attorney will obtain the information necessary to devise and propose a specific planning strategy. When you are comfortable with your understanding of the plan, its effectiveness in meeting your objectives and the trade-offs between costs or complexity on the one hand and the benefits derived on the other, then certain aspects may require scrutiny by the other estate planning team members. For example:

- Your accountant may advise on a proposed gift program,

stock redemption plan or business recapitalization.

• Your insurance professional should make certain that ownership and beneficiary arrangements are precisely correct for a separate irrevocable life insurance trust, or funded business continuation agreement, or a deferred compensation plan — qualified or nonqualified — or, for a split-dollar plan, that the split ownership or collateral assignment is properly documented.

• Your financial planner may execute an attorney recommendation that you skew your assets away from hard-to-sell real estate and closely-held business interests and toward publicly-traded securities where your estate faces substantial death taxes but your age or your health renders the purchase of life insurance for tax liquidity uneconomic.

• Your trust advisor may provide advice on specific trust services (real property management, custodial, escrow, as well as trust) as may be the case in which: your financial planner aids with asset planning and investment product sales, but is not equipped to provide ongoing securities portfolio management services; or you wish to observe the skill with which the trust advisor's organization functions while you are still alive and able to evaluate its capabilities (and change trustees if you don't like what you see); or if you simply want to engage the trust company or bank as trustee or custodian in order to relieve yourself from the burden of day-to-day asset management, record keeping and tax reporting.

For all this planning effort, you will pay fees to the attorney and the accountant, sometimes to the insurance professional, financial planner, as well as a "set-up" fee plus modest annual charges to the trust company or bank trust department. (More on fees below.) Any fees, however, are minuscule compared to the amount of taxes that may be saved and the peace of mind it produces.

We have experienced federal tax "reforms" every one to four years since 1969, with important "technical amendments" in the years between, so it is critical that you stay in regular contact with your attorney — at least every two or three years — to see if any such changes impact your plan. A good example is the definition of "maximum marital deduction" provided by the *Economic Re-*

covery Tax Act 1981 ("ERTA"), President Reagan's first major move to bring about death tax equity. If your will or trust was signed before September 12, 1982, and provides for a "maximum marital deduction," the old pre-ERTA, definition will be used. That definition limits the deduction to 50% of the estate otherwise subject to the federal estate tax. But if a trust amendment or will codicil was signed since that date using the phrase "maximum marital deduction," the estate tax marital deduction is unlimited! The difference can be the ability to defer payment of thousands of dollars in death taxes, or hundreds of thousands, leaving the surviving spouse able to enjoy the extra income generated by the funds that would otherwise be lost to taxes at the first death. Whether you always want to defer them is another question. See QTIP trusts at Section 2.4.

The Attorney-Client Privilege. The attorney will ordinarily suggest that third parties be excluded from the fact-gathering and strategy-development conference. The practical reason is that their presence may inhibit the free flow of expression; the legal reason is that the attorney-client privilege attaching to confidential communications may otherwise be lost. The choice, of course, is yours. But if the privilege is protected, the attorney may not be forced by the courts or anyone to divulge the confidential exchange of information. If the information is disclosed without your consent, it constitutes a serious breach of legal ethics for which you may hold the attorney fully responsible.

Keep in mind, however, that while sharing information of some previous or contemplated act is protected in this manner, advice on how to safely break the law is not. The attorney may lawfully advise only on ways and means of using or avoiding the law, not on how to safely engage in illegal conduct.

The privilege does not exist for confidential communications with your other advisors. As a consequence, do not say anything to them that you do not want to read in a deposition or trial transcript.

Dual Representation. In virtually all estate planning cases, a single attorney represents both the husband and the wife in developing the data and strategy, and in implementing the plan. There are certain instances, however, in which the attorney may be ethically bound to advise one or both of you to seek independent counsel or, where permitted by state law, procure a written, informed consent to the representation of adverse interests. Such instances may include interspousal gifts, the transmutation (meaning a change in character) of property from separate to community or vice versa, estate planning-related business agreements that may deprive a surviving spouse of control, or other transfers of property rights from one spouse to another that may seem useful in the estate planning strategy being developed.

The attorney will be hypersensitive to such issues and will usually raise them early in the discussion. Just understand that your interests may diverge at some point from that of your spouse, at which time an informed judgment must be made as to whether to rely on the existing relationship for fair treatment or seek independent counsel.

Deductibility of Fees. The fees you incur for legal, accounting, financial and trust advice in devising and implementing an effective estate plan pale into insignificance when compared with the saving and the asset-building results obtained. To perform a complete estate planning service, your advisors must consider death tax planning and estate liquidity, ownership and beneficiary designations for insurance and employee benefit plans, the character of the property involved and a whole host of related issues. It is more than simply drafting a few standard documents.

You should always discuss the nature and estimated charges at the initial conference. The professional who takes a businesslike approach will also require you to sign a fee agreement, even if the fee is only estimated.

Those fees attributable to tax advice are deductible for state and federal income tax purposes in the same manner as expenses incurred to maintain income-producing property, the production and collection of income or the determination of income taxes.[1] The fees incurred for document preparation (will, trust, community property agreement, etc.) are considered a personal expense, however, and are not deductible for income tax purposes.[2]

The apportionment between the deductible and nondeductible portions of the services rendered is highly subjective, but must be reduced to writing in order to support the deduction. The advisor should exhibit that apportionment on the statement for services.[3] As to the attorney fees, IRS will accept (if not clearly abusive) an allocation of 80% to tax planning (deductible) and 20% to testamentary planning (nondeductible), *Internal Revenue Code of 1986* imposes a 2% of adjusted gross income threshold on all such deductions. So now, only those income production and tax-planning charges exceeding that figure are deductible.

Character of Property. At the outset of the estate planning process, you establish the makeup and approximate value of the estate, then consider its character as community, quasi-community or separate property. Only at that point will you know the extent to which you have the legal right to dispose of the estate during your lifetime or at your death. Of the 50 states, eight are "community property" states (nine, if you count Wisconsin, which now has community property by another name), and the rest are "common law" states. The property rights of the spouses under the two legal concepts involved are fundamentally different. The spouse who is not employed outside the home is generally better protected in community property states. Community property states include Arizona, California, Idaho, Louisiana,[4] Nevada, New Mexico, Texas, Washington and Wisconsin. While the application of community property laws in these states vary, sometimes in material respects, the general rule is that each spouse has a present and existing ownership of an undivided one-half interest in the total community estate. It is that interest, together with your own separate property, of which you may dispose by gift, sale or will.

How Property Passes from a Decedent to the Beneficiaries. Another set of fundamental concepts to be kept clearly in mind is the manner in which property passes from a decedent to those entitled to it. (The legal phrase is "devolution of property.")

When someone dies, all the property in which the decedent held an interest at the time of death devolves upon those entitled to it in one of three ways: by title, by contract or by probate administration.

Probate administration is the catch-all dealing with property which does not pass by title or contract and is the only part controlled by the will. As a consequence, the will may control only a minor portion of the total estate if the various assets are largely in joint tenancy or contract form.

"Title" includes primarily joint tenancy and tenancy by the entirety assets. It also includes gifts with a reserved life estate. The decedent's interest goes immediately to the surviving tenant, tenants or remainder persons by operation of law and without a probate, no matter what the will provides.

"Contract assets" include such properties as life insurance policies, preretirement death benefits of a pension plan, annuity survivorship benefits, "Totten Trust" accounts at savings and loan associations and trusts. Such assets are paid to the named beneficiary, without a probate and no matter what the will provides.

As noted, only what is left is subject to probate administration. Those probate assets are the only assets affected by the will. Personal effects, furnishings and such, if of modest total value, may often pass in accord with the will using a statutory affidavit procedure instead of probate administration.

The most common mistake seen in estate planning is the failure of the client to fully consider and understand the manner in which the different assets will be delivered to the beneficiaries. For example, only one or two of several children are often joint tenants on a given bank account with the client (because mother wants them to have quick access to the money in case she gets sick or hurt and cannot pay her bills). Just as often, the husband's mother is found still the beneficiary under the $3,000 policy he owned when he married 28 years ago, because he forgot to change the designation. People often operate under some unfocused belief that the estate will be shared by the beneficiaries in the manner described in the will, even though virtually every asset is held in joint tenancy or contract form. Actual distribution is often grossly disproportionate, of course, and not at all in keeping with the desires of the decedent. Where state inheritance laws are in effect (*i.e.*, a death tax imposed on the beneficiary's right to survive and receive all or part of the estate), the attorney may be able to reduce the inheritance tax by persuading the state taxing agency that an oral trust existed under which the children were to receive the estate equally. If so, those taxes may be paid using the lowest possible rates. That will not help with an estate tax.

Probate administration is a legal proceeding by which those property interests of the decedent not passing by title or contract are ascertained, collected or secured, appraised as to date-of-death values, applied to the payment of approved creditor claims and taxes, and in which the remaining estate is distributed to those persons entitled to inherit. The proceeding generally requires nine months to a year to complete, although it often takes longer if difficulties are encountered in locating property, selling property, resolving the disposition of business interests, settling litigation, conducting ancillary probate administration proceedings for real property held in states outside the state of the decedent's last domicile or similar tasks.

The information relating to a probate administration proceeding is disclosed in a court file — a public record. Accordingly, any reporter, creditor, beneficiary, prospective contestant or nosy neighbor may gain access to that information by simply appearing at the courthouse and requesting the opportunity to examine the file contents.

The personal representative of the decedent is the person charged with the responsibility for collecting and securing the assets of the estate and performing all the nonlegal services in connection with its administration; *e.g.*, accounting for assets, income and disbursements, maintaining insurance on the properties and obtaining information on assets, liabilities and creditor claims. The attorney prepares all legal papers for the proceeding, advises the representative on the responsibilities involved, makes the legal judgments with respect to the estate liquidity needs, resulting property sales and tax planning, and interfaces with the probate court throughout the proceeding.

The general term "personal representative" includes within its ambit all the specific titles dictated by the circumstance under which that person or entity assumes those responsibilities. For example: an executor is the personal representative nominated in the will of the decedent; an administrator serves the same function for a decedent who died without a will; an administrator-with-the-will-annexed is one who serves in that capacity but who is not named as such in the decedent's will, assuming that role only because no executor was named or the chosen executor died before the decedent or declined to serve. References to the personal representative are determined by the existence of a will, specifically, "executor of the will" or "administrator of the estate." If the personal representative is female, the terms are "executrix" or "administratrix."

For the services provided, the personal representative receives compensation ("commissions"), as does the attorney ("fees"). The amounts and the manner of determination vary from state to state and are payable only upon approval by the probate court. Estate administration expenses for fees and court costs vary widely, and in some states may reach onerous levels.

In California, routine estate administration compensation for both the personal representative and the attorney is set by statute, at a regressive percentage. Each is paid from the same schedule: a sum equal to 4% of the first $15,000 of the gross value of the property subject to probate administration, 3% of the next $85,000, 2% of the next $900,000, 1% of the next $9 million, 1/2% of the next $15 million, and a reasonable amount as determined by the court for the amount exceeding $25 million.[5]

This statutory compensation schedule contemplates routine probate administration services but not extraordinary services. Extraordinary services might include will contests, the sale of real and personal property from the estate to raise funds for the payment of expenses, litigation, tax planning and tax return preparation. Such additional fee requests must be presented to the court in the final account, report and petition for fees and distribution, together with all supporting detail as to what was done, the attorney and support staff time required, the complexity of the task, the experience of the person performing the task and the benefit to the estate; the court decides whether the amount sought is fair and makes its order accordingly.[6]

If you reside in a state that maintains a modern judicial system imposing modest probate administration expenses, the prospect of a probate is no reason for great concern. While it deprives the beneficiaries of privacy and slows the process of distribution, it does not add materially to the cost of estate administration. Moreover, it may be the only way in which a surviving spouse is able to cut off the claims of certain creditors who could otherwise reach the nonprobate assets to satisfy their claims. In most states, a creditor claim time period (typically, four months) is provided in which the creditors of the decedent may present their claims in writing to the personal representative or file them with the probate court. With rare exceptions, claims not presented or filed in time are forever barred. Those claims approved by the personal representative and the court are paid in due course; those wholly or partially rejected are barred unless the claimant files suit on the rejected claim within a period described by statute.

Section 2.2 Take the Hard Questions First

Categories of Analysis. Your fundamental approach in virtually any estate planning strategy includes collecting the property in one place to manage it as a unified whole for simplicity of administration and for precision in its distribution. To do that, you establish a living (*inter vivos*) trust as the receptacle, change the beneficiary designations under the other contract assets (primarily life insurance) in order to cause the proceeds to be payable to the trust, direct in the will that the residue of the probate estate be distributed to the trust and terminate some or all of the remaining joint tenancies so as to render them subject to probate administration where the will may ultimately cause them to be distributed to the trust. The trust contains the provisions intended to minimize the death taxes and to hold, manage and distribute the trust estate with precision.

General estate planning considerations focus on three areas:

transfer costs, estate management for the surviving spouse and the problems of guardianship. The primary objectives are to secure the surviving spouse financially and to reduce, to the extent it can be done without present economic sacrifice, the costs of estate transfer (taxes, fees, etc.)

•   **Transfer Costs.** The term "transfer costs" for our purposes includes state and federal death taxes, commissions and fees (the latter two only for property subject to probate administration). There are two types of death taxes: an estate tax (the government's tax on the decedent's estate before distribution) and the inheritance tax (the government's tax on the beneficiary's right to survive the decedent and receive the inheritance). Many states have no inheritance tax, imposing only a "pickup tax" equal to the state death tax credit provided in calculating the federal estate tax. (If not taken by the state, it would be forfeited to the federal government, with no benefit to the decedent's estate.)

Others impose either an estate tax or an inheritance tax, sometimes at burdensome levels.

Under ERTA, the maximum estate tax rate was to be reduced in four 5% annual decrements from 70% to 50%. The 50% rate was to be reached in 1985, but was extended by Congress to 1988. Under *The Revenue Act of 1987*, Congress postponed that reduction for an additional five years, to 1993, setting the top brackets at 53% to 55% for estates between $2,500,000 and $3,000,000. Look for another extension in 1993. Perhaps the greater estate tax change wrought by that act was elimination of the unified transfer tax credit and of the graduated tax rate on estates over $10 million. For most, the unified transfer tax credit of $192,800 effectively exempts estate and gift taxes on the first $600,000 transferred by those means. Moreover, even though the top rate is 55%, the effective rate is less because of graduated tax brackets; they start at 18%. The tax savings provided by the credit and the rate gradations will now be recaptured by the government at the rate of 5% after the first $10 million. So estates between $10 million and $21,040,000 are now taxed at an effective rate of 60%. Congress used this act to launch an attack on not only large estates, but employee stock ownership plans, family partnerships and corporate recapitalizations, as well. The latter two are discussed later in this chapter.

Without planning, the portion of the estate exposed to taxation at the first death may be included in the estate of the surviving spouse on the subsequent death, aggravating the tax burden.

It is no great revelation that closely-held business interests and real property are illiquid. If an executor must sell such assets in order to fund transfer costs, it must be done within nine months following the date of death in order to avoid a late payment penalty. As a result, the selling price may be deeply discounted in order to meet the deadline. Thus, two costs are incurred: the tax and the discount resulting from forced sale.

As to future tax liabilities, if your estate grows at the rate of 15% after-tax, 10 years from now your present holdings will be worth 4.06 times its present net value, plus life insurance. The total transfer costs at that time may be greater than a proportionate increase in the present costs, due to the higher tax bracket.

• **Estate Management.** As to estate management for your spouse and children, you may either plan for steady liquidation of the principal in order to meet their living expenses, or you may plan for the estate to be or remain invested in income-producing securities or properties, retaining the principal and supporting your spouse and children with investment income plus government programs (social security, veterans' benefits, etc.) and any available pension income.

That second approach may be assured with life insurance and provides a measure of lifetime security for the family; the inevitable erosion of purchasing power by inflation will probably be offset by asset growth, generating a higher cash income. Of course, if the person handling the estate for the benefit of the family lacks experience and preparation for the task, using the principal retention approach could create problems. One of them is the likelihood that people would be pressing on your spouse ill-considered advice, or trying to borrow money. At such a time, the usual defenses are down because of the emotional loss felt throughout the first year or more after the death of a spouse.

In these enlightened times, we find wives more and better

educated and more often in a partnership role with respect to the family finances and major life choices than was the case a decade or two ago. Nonetheless, one spouse or the other is often unable to cope with all of the responsibilities alone during those months immediately following the death of the other spouse. That person should not be forced to deal immediately with issues of such magnitude, because the loss may render that spouse unable to make sound, long-term judgments for a period of time. The better plan is to have a mechanism in place that commences operation automatically when the critical event (the first death) occurs, but reserves to the surviving spouse the right to step in and retake control of the estate management at such time as that spouse feels able.

A classic example occurred in 1969. That summer, a commuter helicopter crashed in a California schoolyard with 29 aboard. There were no survivors. I was asked to counsel with the widow of the pilot a few weeks after the crash. At that meeting, I learned that: two or three relatives moved in with her temporarily the day of the funeral; a mutual funds salesman had already importuned her to invest in the go-go funds of the day, Enterprise and Commonwealth (mutual funds that specialized in unregistered securities, reporting huge annual rates of appreciation but with no market into which to sell the stock held by the fund); and one of the relatives had already requested a loan to finance a nephew through medical school. (From the advice she was getting, it reminded me of the time John Wayne, the actor, finally fired a business manager following his recommendation of an investment in a shrimp boat fleet in the Mediterranean.) When people smell money, they seem to come out of the woodwork. Here, everyone was aware that the widow had a $97,000 insurance check in the kitchen drawer and a $33,000 worker's compensation settlement on the way. The widow was left with four children; the oldest was already giving her "tortured teenager" problems at 14 years of age, and the youngest was a toddler still in diapers. The baby approached her twice during the conversation and tapped her on the elbow to ask when daddy would be home, a difficult conference as the widow frequently broke into tears. I recommended that she engage a local bank trust department to act as her trustee and, in that capacity, to invest her funds and distribute the income to her monthly; the combined investment income and social security survivorship benefits were sufficient to maintain a healthy measure of the previously-enjoyed standard of living. To my dismay, however, the mutual fund salesman persuaded her that the go-go funds could make her a millionairess by Christmas. I emphasized again that she lacked training in sophisticated investing (she did not know a convertible debenture from arbitrage), that she already held a full-time job — mother to those four children — and that it was too much for her to assume all those responsibilities. While acknowledging the logic of my arguments, she remained dazzled by the mutual fund prospects and conceded only that she would place $10,000 in a savings account. She lost $35,000 by Christmas.

The point is less that I understood the situation better than she, but rather that there was no longer a source of income from which to replace the loss. A widowed homemaker of either gender must assume a decidedly more conservative investment posture than is possible where mistakes may be remedied by earning more money.

• **Problems of Guardianship.** If a child is orphaned without prior estate planning, a guardian must be appointed by the probate court in order for that child to receive an interest in your estate. Such an appointment could result in the following situation:

• The guardian or guardians so selected may not be your first choice.

• Even if the court makes the best selection from the standpoint of care for the child, that person or those persons will also be responsible for management of the estate and may not be the wisest choice for that job.

• The guardian must invest the estate assets within strict and conservative boundaries set by the state, maintain a bond (paid for by the estate) and render periodic accountings to the court (with attendant legal expenses charged to the child's interest in the estate).

• In order to obtain authority to pay important nonsupport expenses (private schooling, educational summer trips abroad, an automobile, etc.) without personal risk of surcharge by the court, the guardian must petition in advance for authorization.

• All the estate assets for each child must be distributed at the age of majority (18 in some states, 21 in others), whether or not the child is mature enough to assume that responsibility.

I would like to believe that if I had received $1 million at age 18 I could have run it to $10 million by age 25; but if true, it would be the exception, not the rule. The more likely result is exemplified by an experience encountered back in the early sixties. I was invited by an insurance broker in Glendora, California to meet with him and a young family friend for some informal counseling. There I learned that this young man's parents died in an airplane crash a couple of years earlier, following which $250,000 wound up in a loosely-drafted testamentary trust for his benefit. The terms of the trust provided that he would receive the money at age 21 or upon his earlier marriage. His girlfriend learned of the trust terms, promptly became pregnant and they were married. He then dropped out of high school, regularly bankrolled the parties of all his friends and purchased and sold a series of motorcycles, automobiles and boats. His wife diverted $50,000 to an account of her own, went home to mother, and he "woke up to smell the coffee," as Ann Landers is wont to say, bending neon tubing for a living in a sign shop owned by his uncle.

The young man still had $100,000 in the bank, so in one sense it is hard to feel sorry for him; but he paid $150,000 for his lesson. It should not be necessary, and with proper planning it will not.

The Typical Estate Planning Strategy. The following documents are used to deal with the problems outlined and to mitigate deferred tax liabilities that grow with your net worth: a community property agreement (in community property states), two pourover wills, and a family trust.

• **Community Property Agreement.** Since property held in joint tenancy or tenancy by the entirety passes to the surviving joint tenant automatically by virtue of the title in which it is held, to get such property into the family trust (other than by direct transfer during life), a written declaration of change in title to community property is required. That makes it a probate asset, thus the will controls its disposition. It may be used to eliminate all joint tenancy titles (bank accounts, securities, residence, etc.), without separately dealing with the title to each asset.

Certain assets of a minor value but important utility immediately after death (the checking account and automobiles, for example) should be excluded from the scope of the agreement so they remain in joint tenancy. By that means, they are immediately and fully available to the surviving spouse without the complications of probate administration or dealing with the trustee. For different reasons, separate property may be excluded for reasons that range from the relative health of the spouses to the death tax implications of transmutation.

"Investment-type" assets should be transferred, assigned or conveyed directly to the trust during life in order to avoid probate administration. Other assets are usually left out (e.g., automobiles, personal effects, furniture, club memberships, etc.).

Your state law must be examined, of course, to see if this approach is equally effective in the state in which you reside. In California, the case law is such that the surviving spouse may simply say, "Your Honor, I know we held that million-dollar apartment house in joint tenancy, but we bought it with earnings during the marriage and intended for it to be held as community property, so I'd like to probate it." The judge will respond, "Fine, let's probate it." The written agreement simply goes one step further and makes a written record for the intent of the parties.

As you will see in the discussion of pourover wills below, one of the reasons for taking this step is to permit the property interests of both spouses to be probated and distributed to the trust at the first death.

• **Pourover Will.** "Pourover will" is a colloquial term describing a will in which the residue of the estate after transfer costs and specific bequests is "poured over" into the family trust. In the will, you may authorize the executor to obtain funds from the trustee for payment of transfer costs in the event needed (rather than force an executor to sell probate estate assets at a loss under pressure to raise cash). There, of course, you also deal with matters of special property dispositions, disinheritances, contests, the apportionment of transfer costs if not prorated among the beneficiaries, selection of guardians and nomination of a personal representative and an alternate.

- **Trust.** The family trust is designed to function as an estate management vehicle during your lifetime, or the joint lifetimes of you and your spouse, and to avoid, reduce or defer taxation.

The tax avoidance function is accomplished by technically leaving to the child or children (or other beneficiaries) up to $600,000 of the interest of the first spouse to die, but reserving a life income and power to invade principal to the surviving spouse so as to, in effect, give the survivor substantially all the economic benefits of outright ownership.

In some cases, primarily those in which the surviving spouse is not expected to survive for very long, it may be good strategy to level the transfer costs by paying part of them at each death instead of using the unlimited marital deduction to defer all such costs to the death of the surviving spouse. By that means, the applicable tax rates will be the lowest possible. The tool used for that purpose is a disclaimer provision — greatly liberalized by ERTA — or a qualifying terminable interest property subtrust (*infra*), both included in the trust agreement.

The trust goes into operation when it is funded by the transfer of assets during your joint lifetimes, or at the first death from the probate distribution, or both. During your joint lifetimes, the trust may be altered, amended or revoked at your pleasure. If you are already widowed, you may establish a simple trust; but of course you cannot have the benefit of the unlimited marital deduction without a spouse.

A trust provides flexibility in accomplishing the estate planning goals and removing the problems described. You may serve as your own trustee and may provide for various trusted (and, hopefully, competent) family members to serve as successor trustees at such time as you and other successors die, become legally disabled, resign or decline to serve. I suggest, however, that you name a bank trust department or independent trust company as the ultimate successor trustee. They do not get old, lose interest in the job or die.

In summary, a trust is simply a receptacle; something into which you put something. If it is a marital deduction trust, it is divided into at least two parts after the death of one spouse: the residuary trust (the part technically left to the children) and the marital deduction trust. Both are invested to produce income for the benefit of the surviving spouse. The surviving spouse may withdraw all or any part of the marital deduction trust at any time after its establishment. The surviving spouse may also reach the principal of the residuary trust on either or both of two bases:

• 5% of the principal or $5,000 per year, whichever is greater and whether or not it is needed. The surviving spouse need only request it.

• Invasion of principal to the extent that the estate income and marital deduction trust principal fail to cover the reasonable needs of the surviving spouse for care, support, education and maintenance, as determined by the trustee.

The residuary trust is the one left to the children (or others) with a life income to the surviving spouse. It is irrevocable so as to exclude it from the surviving spouse's estate for federal estate tax purposes.

Use of the trust provides the skilled, professional money management assistance of the trustee, as well as a ready defense when the surviving spouse is approached for speculative investments or loans. ("I'm sorry, it's all in trust.")

If you prefer to take or continue an active role in trust management at a policy level, you may reserve in the trust agreement the right to direct the trustee in specified areas. You are limited only by your fiduciary duties to your spouse in the way you exercise such powers, and the fact that you may not force unwanted administrative burdens on the trustee.

Use of the trust also provides an effective way of dealing with the problems of guardianship. It permits you to separate guardianship of the person from guardianship of the estate. In that way, the guardian best for the child need not be concerned with the estate. The guardian of the person may be selected on the basis of the relationship to the family, concern for the child, maturity of judgment, shared moral values and religious convictions or any other criteria you deem critical in the selection. It is not necessary for the guardian of the person to be sophisticated in financial matters, because that is the basis on which you will select a separate person or entity as guardian of the estate.

Of significant value is the right, when using a trust, to spread the ultimate distribution of the estate over a period of time, so as to minimize the chance that immaturity of a child will result in loss of money.

If the child is orphaned, social security benefits may be paid directly to the guardian of the person. The trustee may be directed under the declaration of trust to accumulate the trust income, paying out to the guardian only so much as is necessary to cover living expenses of the child, taking all other income (including social security) into account. That pattern precludes the accumulation of excess income outside the trust, thus minimizing the chance that the expense of a separate guardianship of the estate will be required to hold those excess funds. The will designates a guardian for the estate of a child only if one becomes necessary as, for example, when the child earns substantial income while a minor or inherits from a different source. The guardian of the estate so selected will ordinarily be the same person or entity serving as trustee.

When best to distribute to children (after you and your spouse are gone), depends on the age of the child, the maturity level, the quality of the child's marriage and any professional or career demands that may preclude spending the time necessary to effective estate management. The trust estate may be distributed:

• at the age of majority outright and the trust terminated; or
• the child may be given an income for life with the ultimate distribution going to your grandchildren; or
• income and principal may be distributed in any manner between these extremes.

If your children are presently minors, a typical pattern is for the trustee to distribute, beginning at the age of majority, all then-current trust income to the child and continuing to do so until the child reaches age 35, with principal distributions at ages 25, 30 and 35. The child may spend the first principal distribution unwisely but should learn enough from the experience to better manage the second and third. In any case, the trustee should be authorized to invade the principal of the child's share of the trust estate in order to meet special needs for support, medical care and education.

Unless a separate irrevocable life insurance trust is implemented for the purpose of removing life insurance from your taxable estate, personal life insurance should ordinarily be paid directly to the trustee. In that manner, your creditors may not be able to reach it — or all of it — and the proceeds will be available for payment of transfer costs and to generate investment income. For a discussion of irrevocable life insurance trusts, see Section 2.3.

The unified transfer tax credit provided under federal law is $192,800. You may use it as a tax credit for both lifetime gifts and for the federal estate tax at your death; but you may use it only once. If you make $300,000 in taxable gifts during your lifetime and use the credit to avoid paying the gift tax out of pocket, you will consume about $86,400 of the credit, leaving the balance for use in reducing the federal estate tax otherwise payable on your death. The credit produces an equivalent exemption of $600,000 for whichever purpose you choose; i.e., the gift or estate tax on $600,000 is $192,800, so a tax credit of $192,800 effectively avoids tax on $600,000. The residuary trust in the family trust described above is designed to preserve the equivalent exemption for each estate — yours and that of your spouse. For example, if you die leaving a surviving spouse, $1,400,000 and a simple will under which all goes to the spouse, there is no tax because the otherwise taxable estate is eliminated by the unlimited estate tax marital deduction. Then your spouse dies without remarrying. With no spouse, there is no marital deduction for that estate. The only tax help comes from the unified transfer tax credit — the equivalent exemption. That covers $600,000 of the $1,400,000 (assuming no taxable lifetime gifts) but leaves a $320,000 federal tax on the remaining $800,000. Compare that result to the $60,000 or $70,000 tax payable using the family trust described above, and you see why people engage in estate planning.

Section 2.3 Irrevocable Life Insurance Trust

Principal Characteristics. An unfunded irrevocable life insurance trust is one in which you and your spouse completely relinquish title to the property (life insurance policies and group life insurance certificates) and do not retain a right to alter, amend or revoke the trust. Its principal disadvantage is that you cannot, without the cooperation of the trustee and holders of certain rights, reclaim the trust property (the policies and certificates) if you later change your mind.

With the elimination in 1954 of the "premium payment test" for the inclusion of life insurance proceeds in the estate of a deceased insured, the irrevocable assignment of insurance policies to other members of the insured's family was greatly encouraged. The motive is to remove the life insurance from your estate for death tax purposes.

While such assignments are often outright gifts of insurance policies, two considerations should be weighed before using that method of removing the policy from your estate:

• Do you question the willingness of the donee-beneficiary to retain the policy proceeds and use them to meet the needs of your spouse?

• Are the death proceeds settlement options flexible enough to permit the life insurance to meet family needs which may exist at the time of your death?

The irrevocable life insurance trust is an attractive method of dealing with those issues.

There are two forms of insurance trust, each addressing different objectives and each useful in separate and distinct fact situations. The first is the "revocable insurance trust." It provides no savings in estate taxes apart from any included marital deduction provisions; the powers you retain during your lifetime keep the proceeds in your gross estate for death tax purposes. However, it provides a definite and flexible plan for the management of the proceeds after your death.

The second form of insurance trust is the "irrevocable insurance trust." With this form, estate tax savings are possible if both you and your spouse release all incidents of ownership in cash and policies transferred to it. While you may not be willing to take the irreversible step of turning over the insurance policy directly to your spouse or a child (for the reasons noted above), you may be entirely comfortable with giving the life insurance policy to a trustee to provide for the surviving spouse during the survival period and then your children. In that way, the policy proceeds may be preserved by a competent fiduciary.

All things considered, the simplest method of handling the distribution of principal and income on the death of the insured is to provide for cash advances from the trustee to the executor of the probate estate for transfer costs and hold, manage and distribute the remaining trust assets the same way as they are handled in your family trust.

Transfer for Value Rule. The sale or other transfer for value of an existing policy or any interest in the policy will, as a general rule, cause loss of the income tax exemption for the death proceeds.[7] As a result, care must be taken to characterize the policy assignments as gifts, not only in the language of the trust instrument but in that of the policy assignment forms involved; do not include the usual consideration recital ("For valuable consideration, receipt of which is hereby acknowledged.").

Federal Gift Tax. The irrevocable assignment of policy ownership to the trustee constitutes a "gift."[8]

As to the amount of the gift, the general rule is that the value of the policy transferred to an irrevocable life insurance trust is its "replacement cost."[9] More specifically, if the policy being transferred is a single premium or paid-up policy, its value will be the cost of buying a similar policy. If premiums are still being paid on the policy, then the amount of the gift will be the interpolated terminal reserve value (generally somewhat higher than its loan value) plus any unearned premium (that portion of the premium already paid for a period extending beyond the date of the gift), less any policy loan balance.[10] These figures are provided on request by the insurance company. If the policy transferred is term insurance, it will have a nominal value; basically the unearned premium.[11] With respect to the assignment of group life insurance, no gift tax is incurred because the benefits have no ascertainable value. However, the premiums subsequently paid by the employer are characterized as gifts by the insured employee to the trust.[12]

Generally, the donee takes the status of the donor with respect to the extent to which the death proceeds of the assigned policy or certificate are excluded from income taxation in the hands of the beneficiary. So, if the proceeds would be tax-free if owned by the donor and no "transfer for value" has occurred, the proceeds will be tax-free to the donee. In the context of this discussion, the donee and beneficiary are the same entity: the trust. Except for the situation in which the insured is the owner, the beneficiary and owner should always be the same person or entity. Otherwise at your death, the owner will be deemed to have made a "constructive gift" of the death proceeds to the beneficiary and will have to report and pay the required state and federal gift taxes thereon.[13]

The gift of policies to individual donees (as opposed to a trust) are gifts of a "present interest," thus qualifying for the annual gift tax exclusion of $10,000.00 per donee per year, or $20,000.00 per donee per year when both spouses join in making the gift.[14] Gift-splitting will require the filing of a gift tax return while, if the gift is limited to $10,000 per donee or less, no return is required.

When a trustee receives the policy subject to restrictions (through the declaration of trust) upon the right of the trust beneficiaries to receive benefits or to exercise ownership rights under the policies, the gift is one of a "future interest" and the $10,000 per donee annual gift tax exclusion is denied.[15] It is important to obtain the annual gift tax exclusion because:

• it reduces or eliminates the federal and any state gift taxes; and

• it avoids "unification" for federal estate and state inheritance tax purposes. That is, it keeps the premiums out of the estate for death tax purposes, and thus avoids pushing the estate remaining at death into higher tax brackets.

Accordingly, the trust agreement should contain a withdrawal provision based upon the holding of *Crummey v. Commissioner.*[16]

Such a provision is one in which beneficiaries other than your spouse (usually your children) are given the right during your lifetime to withdraw their share of your annual cash contributions to the trust, in an amount not to exceed $10,000 per child per year. Of course, while notifying the child of this right you should make it clear that your plan will be defeated if it is exercised; you want the money available to the trustee for use in paying life insurance premiums. The existence of the right provides "present interest" gift tax treatment for cash contributed to the trust, up to an aggregate amount equal to $10,000 per child per year.

When the child permits the withdrawal right to lapse, and when your annual contributions exceed the greater of 5% of the trust's fair market value or $5,000 (the "5&5 power"), that child is given a "continuing interest" in the trust to the extent of the excess.[17] If the contributions are less than that amount, there is no lapse of the withdrawal power and no continuing interest in the trust because of the *de minimis* rule[18] or "safe harbor" provided by IRC.[19]

If a child acquires a continuing trust interest in this manner, that interest is proportionate to the excess contribution in relation to the total value of the trust estate.[20] For example, you have two children, each with a $10,000 withdrawal right, and you contribute $18,000 to the trust each year to pay a $17,210 annual life insurance premium. 5% of $17,210 is $860.50, so $5,000 is greater. The continuing trust interest is then proportionate to $6,105 per child ($17,210 less $5,000 divided by two). If the policy values and cash on hand in the trust total $100,000, that proportionate interest is 6.105%. If either or both of those children predecease you, that continuing interest will be included in the child's gross estate for federal estate tax purposes.[21]

To avoid the consequences of a withdrawal right lapse in excess of the 5&5 power, you may employ a device popularly known as the "hanging power." The most commonly-used withdrawal right is in noncumulative form; if not timely exercised, it lapses; if a continuing interest comes into existence, you cannot get rid of it. The hanging power is a withdrawal right that is cumulative. Using it, the continuing interests of the children acquired each year due to contributions in excess of the 5&5 amount may be reduced by means of the continued right to withdraw after you stop making excess contributions. This presupposes, of course, that the trustee purchases a policy that eventually becomes paid up, requiring no further premiums, thus no further cash contributions to the trust. For example, you make an annual contribution of $10,000 to an irrevocable life insurance trust for eight years. The trust has one beneficiary who holds a $10,000 withdrawal right. After 10 years, the policy owned on your life by the trust becomes paid up. Each year's unexercised withdrawal right is $5,000 ($10,000 less the 5&5 power), so after the 10th year the aggregate continuing interests are $50,000. Starting with the 11th year, the aggregate continuing interests are allowed to lapse in the maximum amount allowed under the 5&5 rule, eliminating them within the next 10 years, along with the unhappy tax result for the estate of the child who predeceases you.

In this context, you should be aware of a Technical Advice Memorandum from IRS dealing with a perceived abuse of the withdrawal rights under *Crummey*.[22] IRS there addressed a case in which the irrevocable trust had 18 beneficiaries holding withdrawal rights. The primary beneficiaries were the two sons of the taxpayer; the others included one grandchild. The IRS ruled that the annual gift tax exclusion is available only for the two primary beneficiaries, deleting it for the others unless actually exercised. The rationale is original but strained; the premise of *Crummey* and its progeny is that an unrestricted right to demand a distribution is enough. IRS did not squarely address that fact, nor did it examine the notion that the holder of the withdrawal right could be deemed a transferor for generation skipping transfer tax purposes (*infra*), nor did it consider the withdrawal right as a power of appointment. But I digress. Suffice it to say, the line should not be pushed too far.

In a 1988 Private Letter Ruling,[23] IRS attempted to limit the use of hanging powers by declaring that it is "...a condition subsequent and deemed not valid as tending to discourage enforcement of federal gift tax provisions by either defeating the gift or rendering examination of the return ineffective." The case on which IRS relied, however,[24] turned on a saving clause (the gift would not be effective if subject to a gift tax) that (a) was intended to avoid any gift tax and (b) required adjudication by the federal courts as a last resort. It made the same attack on other similar saving or adjustment clauses since then, but all having the same two common denominators: total avoidance of gift tax as its aim and adjudication. The hanging power is distinguishable from the authority on which IRS relies, in that it does not avoid a gift tax to the extent trust contributions exceed the annual exclusion ($10,000 per donee per year) and it is not subject to judicial process. Here for illustration is a hanging power clause:[25]

"Notwithstanding the preceding provisions, if the lapse of any power of withdrawal would be deemed the release of a general power of appointment for federal estate tax purposes, such power shall continue in existence for the amount that would have constituted such a release except to the extent it is thereafter terminated as here provided. Such power shall lapse only upon and to the extent lapse does not result in the deemed release of a general power of appointment by the individual holding it."

The claim of IRS at this time is that any such right operating automatically and without judicial determination is to that extent invalid. Consequently, the present use of hanging powers may ultimately require litigation to prove that IRS stands on shifting sands. Bold tax planning is not for the faint of heart. So if this raises your pulse rate, the alternative is to keep the premium under $5,000 per year and use a noncumulative right of withdrawal.

Federal Estate Tax. As a general rule, a policy owned by and payable to the trustee of your irrevocable trust will not be included in your taxable estate as insured. However, the proceeds will be included if you retain any "incident of ownership" in the policy at the time of death, whether the ownership is exercisable by you alone or in conjunction with another person or entity.[26] Such incidents include the right to borrow the cash values, change settlement options, change the beneficiary, surrender the policy, change dividend options and assign the policy as collateral. The 5th Circuit Court of Appeals at one point decided[27] that an employee's power to select a settlement option under his employer's group life insurance plan was an "incident of ownership" for this purpose. However, the Third Circuit Court of Appeals took the opposite tack[28] involving the same employer and the same group plan, when it ruled that such a power was not an incident of ownership.

The present position of IRS on assigned group life insurance is that the death proceeds are not included in your estate if: you make a lifetime assignment, including all your incidents of ownership; both the group policy and state law permit such an absolute assignment, including any conversion rights; and the policy cost is funded entirely by the employer.[29]

On our assumed facts (gift by you as insured and your spouse of your respective interests in life insurance policies and group certificates to an irrevocable trust in which the life insurance proceeds are ultimately held, managed and distributed for the benefit of the surviving spouse for life, then to the children), there is one notable exception to the general rule noted above: the noninsured spouse is giving an interest in the policy to the trustee and is retaining a life estate therein. That will cause one-half of the proceeds (to the extent they remain unspent at the subsequent death of the surviving spouse) to be included in that spouse's estate for federal estate tax purposes as a retained life estate.[30] If, however, your assignment to the trust is preceded by the full and irrevocable assignment and release of all interests in the policies by your noninsured spouse to you as insured spouse, there is no "retained life estate." Thus, your noninsured spouse has a life estate in the policy proceeds and the policy was your separate property— not that of the beneficiary spouse — at the time assigned to the trust. By that means, it should be possible to avoid inclusion of the insurance proceeds in either taxable estate.

If the trustee is required by the terms of the trust to use the proceeds for the payment of your estate debts, taxes and other administration expenses as the insured decedent, the policy proceeds will be included in your taxable estate.[31] Accordingly, the trustee should be authorized but not required to so apply the policy proceeds. If the power of the trustee to so apply the proceeds is merely discretionary and the trust is for the benefit of named individuals, the proceeds are taxable in your estate only to the extent actually so applied.[32] Under the pattern described, liquidity for your estate is best introduced by authorizing the trustee to lend money to or purchase assets from the estate. Such powers should not subject the proceeds to taxation in your estate, nor is any part of the policy proceeds includable on any other basis; none is used for the direct payment of taxes, etc. Any receivables represented by such advances, or assets so purchased, will in turn be held in the life insurance trust as trust investments.

One final caveat: when you transfer ownership of the life insurance into the irrevocable life insurance trust, you must live three years beyond the assignment date in order to avoid the inclusion of those insurance proceeds in your taxable estate.[33] You may no longer avoid that result by claiming "living motives" for the gift of the insurance in trust.[34] The federal courts of appeal are in conflict regarding the inclusion of new life insurance purchased by the trustee.

Policies included are valued at their fair market value on the date of death, which is the maturity or face value. If included, of course, the substantial tax savings of the irrevocable life insurance trust is lost. Also includable is the amount of any gift tax paid on your transfers during the three years preceding death.

If the trust is the initial applicant and owner of the policy but you as insured pay the premiums directly to the carrier and die within three years after the policy is issued, the proceeds still will be includable in your gross estate, even though there is literally no transfer from you to the trust. That conclusion is based on several holdings that if the money the trustee uses to pay the premiums on the policy comes from the insured, it is as if the trustee was the agent of the insured in obtaining the policy, and therefore, there has been a constructive transfer of the policy from the insured to the trust.[35]

Even if the proceeds are not includable, the premiums paid

within three years of death will be includable.[36]

In order to posture your life insurance trust for estate tax exclusion, we take our planning steps from two recent cases in the 10th Circuit Court of Appeals:[37]

• In the first, the insured husband owned a corporation that loaned his wife money to pay premiums on a policy she purchased on his life as applicant, owner and beneficiary. She later assigned the policy to an irrevocable trust for the benefit of herself and their children. The husband died within three years following issuance of the policy. The court held the policy proceeds not includable in the estate of the husband because he never held any "incidents of ownership" in it. Without such incidents, there can be no "transfer."

• In the other case, the insured was a tax attorney, sophisticated in estate taxation. He established an irrevocable trust, appointing a bank as trustee, following which the trustee applied (as applicant, owner and beneficiary) for a life insurance policy on his life; the trustee paid the initial and each subsequent premium from cash contributed to the trust by the insured. All beneficiaries waived their (*Crummey*) withdrawal rights. The insured died in an automobile accident within three years following issuance of the policy. IRS argued that the proceeds should be included in the insured's estate because the trustee was the "agent" of the insured in procuring the policy. The court rejected the IRS argument, reasoning as follows:

> "The [thrust] of [the IRS argument] is that [the insured] indirectly paid the insurance premiums. However, under the terms of the trust agreement, the bank as trustee was permitted but not required to buy an insurance policy on [the insured's] life and to pay the periodic premiums [from cash] contributed by [the insured] or the income therefrom. We do not think this creates a [connection] sufficient to support a finding that [the insured] himself paid the life insurance premiums. The record as a whole supports a finding that [the trustee] did not act as [the insured's] agent in acquiring the policy."[38]

The court then concluded as follows:

"...the decedent, ..., never possessed any incidents of ownership in the policy on his life under [IRC] Section 2042,
consequently the proceeds therefrom are not includible in his
gross estate under [IRC] Section 2035(d)(1) and (2) and therefore are not includible under [IRC] Section 2035(a)."[39]

Given the conflicting court decisions and the guidance provided by the cases discussed above, we may infer the following
planning considerations in establishing your irrevocable life insurance trust in a way most likely to lead to estate tax exclusion:
  • The trust must be fully executed and funded before the
trustee applies for the policy.
  • The trustee must sign the application as applicant, owner
and beneficiary; you sign only as the proposed insured (that may
include the application, the medical or nonmedical form, the
medical authorization questionnaire and possibly a smoker's declaration).
  • The trustee must control the policy and proceeds at all
times; upon creation of the trust and continuing until it expires by
its own terms and the remaining trust estate is distributed.
  • You must never pay the life insurance premiums directly to
the insurance company.
  • You should use an independent third party as trustee to
avoid problems of income tax and agency relationship. You must
never serve as trustee of your own irrevocable life insurance trust.
  • Never transfer the exact amount of the premium to the trust;
it looks too much like the trustee has only one option in investing
the trust estate and serves to support an agency argument by IRS.
Round it up to the next thousand or two.
  • Each year in which you make contributions to the trust, the
beneficiaries holding withdrawal rights must waive them in writing. That means, of course, that you must advise them of those
rights, something you are expected to do anyway under an IRS
extension of the express findings of *Crummey vs. Commissioner.*[40]
  • In short, the form of the transaction should reflect an

arm's-length relationship between you and the trustee; you are just following instructions, not managing the transaction.

Federal Income Tax. The trustee takes your status as donor with respect to the extent to which death proceeds of an insurance policy are excluded from federal income taxation. Thus, if the proceeds are income tax-free to you (and no "transfer for value" occurred), they are income tax-free to the trustee.

If the cash surrender value of your policy at the time of the gift exceeds your cost basis, and if the trustee subsequently surrenders the policy, you must report as taxable income the gain existing at the time of the gift (the difference between the net premiums paid and the cash surrender value of the policy at the time of the gift). The proper year for you to include the subsequent gain as gross income is the year in which the policy is surrendered by the trustee.[41]

The funded life insurance trust (where you contribute income-producing property to the trust, the income of which is applied to the payment of premiums) is beyond the scope of this discussion, except for one passing note. If the income of a funded irrevocable life insurance trust is used to pay premiums on a policy insuring your life, the income so applied is taxable to you instead of the trust.[42] It is immaterial whether the insurance was procured before or after creation of the trust.[43] The rule applies to the investment portion of the premium as well as to that allocated to pure insurance protection.[44] The income is so taxed even if not so applied, so long as the trustee has the discretion to apply it to the payment of premiums for insurance on your life.[45]

You may wish to assign permanent "cash value" policies to the trust. In that event, you may choose not to lose access to those values. To avoid that result, procure a maximum policy loan and withdraw all the dividends prior to the assignment of the policy; after the assignment pay only the net premium remaining after application of the automatic premium loan provision and dividends, plus interest on the aggregate policy loan (usually referred to as "minimum deposit").

Prior to 1991, here is how you would have secured the interest deduction. First, you may not deduct interest for federal income tax purposes where the trustee is the owner of the policy. (The loan obligation is that of the trustee, not yours. You may deduct interest only on loans for which you are personally obligated.[46] In order to obtain a personal deduction for such interest payments, the trust must contain what is colloquially referred to as a "defective power" — a grantor trust power that makes you the owner of the policy for income tax but not for estate tax purposes. That may be accomplished as follows:

- IRC §671 provides that, when you are treated as owner of the trust estate, you are taxed on its income and get its deductions.

- IRC §675(2) provides that you are to be treated as the owner of the trust if a "nonadverse party" (see below) has the power to direct the trustee to lend money from the trust to you without adequate interest and security, unless the power extends to the public generally.

- IRC §672 provides that a nonadverse party is anyone not having a substantial beneficial interest in the trust adversely affected by exercise of the power.

Such a provision permitted you, prior to 1991, to finance permanent plans of insurance owned by the trust and perhaps gain a personal deduction for all or part of the interest thereon.

As to financed life insurance: interest paid or accrued on indebtedness incurred to purchase or continue in effect a life insurance, endowment or annuity policy, if purchased pursuant to a plan of purchase which contemplates the systematic direct or indirect borrowing of part or all of the increases in the policy cash values (either from the carrier or otherwise) is not deductible for federal income tax purposes.[47] This rule did not apply to policies purchased prior to August 7, 1963. As to post-August 7, 1963 purchases, there are four exceptions to this disallowance rule:[48]

- **The Seven-Year Exception.** Where four or more of the first seven annual premiums are paid without borrowing, the deduction was allowed on those and all subsequent policy loans. A new seven-year period does not begin upon transfer of the policy, whether for value or by gift.[49]

- **The $100-a-Year Exception.** Regardless of whether there is a systematic plan of borrowing, the interest deduction was allowed for any taxable year in which the interest did not exceed $100.00. Where such interest exceeded $100.00, the entire amount of interest (not just the excess amount) was subject to the general rule.[50]

• **Unforeseen Event Exception.** If the indebtedness was incurred because of an unforeseen substantial loss of income or unforeseen substantial increase in the taxpayer-insured's financial obligations, the deduction was allowed even though the loan was used to pay premiums on the policy. An event is not "unforeseen," however, if at the time the policy was purchased it could have been anticipated.[51]

• **Trade or Business Exception.** If the indebtedness was incurred in connection with the taxpayer's trade or business, the interest deduction was allowed. Thus, if an insurance policy is pledged as collateral for a loan, the interest deductions were allowed if you could show that the amounts borrowed were actually used to finance the expansion of inventory or other similar business needs. But borrowing to finance business life insurance (such as key person, split dollar or stock purchase plans) was not considered to be incurred in connection with the borrower's trade or business.[52]

All the foregoing rules on the interest deduction were rendered moot by the *Internal Revenue Code of 1986*, which classifies such policy loan interest as personal or consumer interest expense. The deductibility of personal interest was phased out over a four-year period beginning with 1987.[53]

Considering our loss of the policy loan interest income tax deduction, you may wonder why it is even discussed, or whether the defective power should still be included in the trust agreement. There are at least four reasons for keeping it in mind and including the defective power:

• Congress has a habit of tinkering with the tax law annually.

• The life insurance industry maintains a powerful presence in Washington, D.C.

• Like the capital gains tax provisions (the reduced rate of which was also eliminated by the *Internal Revenue Code of 1986*), the provisions for deductibility and nondeductibility of policy loan interest were left intact in the new code while being nullified by a new provision.

• The life insurance trust we here consider is irrevocable, so once you put it in place you have no further opportunity to correct or add features to it.

Congress would not have left the policy loan provisions in place unless it believed the deductibility issue would be reconsidered in due course (as will capital gains taxation). If deductible policy loan interest is in prospect, your ability to exploit it should be preserved.

Before leaving this subject, a simple illustration is in order. Assume for this purpose: that you are 60 years of age; that you are married with children; that you have a net worth of $10,000,000 growing at a consolidated rate of 7.5%; that you wish to take such planning steps as will reduce death taxes without impairing your standard of living; and that you and your spouse each have separate life insurance trusts, or that you have the only one but die first. (We could consider sharing one, using a last-to-die policy, but it does not quite fit the illustration.) We ignore for this purpose the stock redemption and installment payment opportunities afforded under the IRC, as well as deductions, state death taxes and probate administration costs.

Here is the result without estate planning:

• First death, all to the surviving spouse, maximum marital deduction = No tax.

• Death of the surviving spouse 10 years later, all to the children, estate growth at 7.5% per year = Estate of $21,120,000, tax of $11,064,000.

Here is the result with estate planning:

• First death, still held for the benefit of the surviving spouse, $5 million is allocated $600,000 to the residuary trust portion of the family trust and $4.4 million to the QTIP trust portion, using assets most likely to appreciate in both cases (15% growth rate), while $5 million is allocated to the marital deduction trust (-0-% growth rate) = No tax if the marital deduction is elected for the QTIP, otherwise it is $2,198,000.

• Death of the surviving spouse 10 years later, all to the

children:

> Residuary Trust (@ 15%) = Estate $2,664,000, tax -0-.

> QTIP Trust (@ 15%) = Estate $19,536,000, tax $10,385,600 if marital deduction elected at first death; -0- tax if not.

> Marital Deduction Trust (@ -0- %) = Estate $5 million, tax $2,198,000.

As some quick addition shows, without estate planning you will deliver a net estate to the children of about $10,056,000, while with it you will deliver between $13,044,880 and $14,616,400. The issue is, How does the estate deliver as much as $12.5 million cash for death tax payments with nine months' notice? That comes from the life insurance trust in the form of purchases by which to convert illiquid assets to cash without a forced sale.

Cash contributions to the life insurance trust are approximately 2.5% of the deferred tax liability each year for a period of six to eight years, after which the trust policy becomes paid up. A short-term 2.5% cost compared to payment from estate assets (dollar for dollar) and borrowing (dollar for dollar plus interest) makes life insurance funding of death taxes an impressive choice.

New legislation materially altering this analysis is always possible and cannot be reliably predicted. Accordingly, there is always an element of risk in this or any other tax-planning approach, although a determination to take no action leaves you facing the certainty of increased estate taxation to the extent life insurance is included in it.

Section 2.4 Sock It to the Tax Man! The Plan

The QTIP Trust. QTIP is an acronym for "qualified terminable interest property," a creature of the IRC used for postmortem tax planning. It is property in which the surviving spouse is given a life income (payable at least annually) and in which no other person has an interest during the lifetime of that surviving spouse.[54] It serves the same purpose as a disclaimer; the difference is in who makes the choices. Let us establish context by first examining the role of disclaimer provisions, then I will distinguish the QTIP trust.

Most family trusts intended to reduce death taxes for a married couple employ for that purpose a residuary trust and a marital deduction trust, each coming into existence as part of the family trust concurrently with the first death. Until then, there is only one trust, only one set of rules. At the first death, the assets of the trust estate are allocated between these two subtrusts. The residuary trust receives the maximum amount that will pass without a federal estate tax, but not exceeding one-half the total in community property states; i.e., $600,000 or less if the community estate is under $1.2 million, or if part of the unified transfer tax credit was used to satisfy taxes on lifetime gifts. Since the residuary trust will not be retaxed in the estate of the surviving spouse, property likely to appreciate in value is usually allocated to it. The marital deduction trust receives all the remaining trust estate. Disclaimer provisions in the trust permit the surviving spouse to reject all or part of the marital deduction trust with the result that the disclaimed portion returns to the residuary trust where it is included in the decedent's taxable estate, if any. An example may help:

Example 1: H & W have a community estate of $1.4 million. H dies. $600,000 goes into the residuary trust, $800,000 to the marital deduction trust. Because H's interest in the estate is $700,000 (one-half of $1.4 million), his estate would ordinarily pay approximately $30,000 in federal estate taxes on the $100,000 exposed to tax ($700,000 minus the $600,000 covered by the unified transfer tax credit leaves $100,000, ignoring deductions). But because W is given a life income and power to appoint under the marital deduction trust provisions, a deduction is claimed for that $100,000, producing these results: there is no federal estate tax to pay at the death of H; and the $100,000 covered by the marital deduction will be included in the estate of W if it is still there at her subsequent death. At her subsequent death, $200,000 is exposed to federal estate tax (ignoring any appreciation and accumulations from income, that is $800,000 minus the $600,000 covered by the unified transfer tax credit, leaving $200,000 exposed to tax) at a cost of approximately $70,000. During the survival period of W, she enjoys additional income produced by the amount that would otherwise have been paid in federal state taxes at the death of H.

Example 2: Same as Example 1, except that at the time of H's death, W is also terminally ill. She will probably "disclaim" the excess $100,000, causing the residuary trust, now $700,000, to pay approximately $30,000 in death taxes on the excess $100,000; her estate in the marital deduction trust, now also $700,000, will pay $30,000 on the amount exposed to tax, a total at both deaths of $60,000 and representing a savings of $10,000 because each tax was paid in the lowest possible bracket.

This is the tax-saving function of the residuary and marital deduction trusts as enhanced by a disclaimer clause. We now examine the QTIP trust. The QTIP trust is particularly useful for those circumstances in which the spouses have different ultimate beneficiaries in mind (children from prior marriages, etc.) or otherwise seek assurance that the surviving spouse will preserve the marital deduction trust for the mutual objects of their bounty (usually the children). Perhaps there is a fear that the surviving spouse may lose the estate to the blandishments of artful and designing persons as yet unseen (or perhaps already seen).

Under the QTIP trust provisions, the surviving spouse is given a life income (payable at least annually) and from which no one but the surviving spouse may benefit during the lifetime of the spouse. Thus, for example, the wife concerned about the growing senility of her husband, or about the threat posed by an avaricious relative may leave the $100,000 discussed in the preceding example to a QTIP trust (instead of his marital deduction trust) for the benefit of the husband for life, then to the children, without much fear of its dissipation or misuse. The executor (not the surviving spouse) may elect at the first death whether or not to claim a marital deduction for the $100,000, thus whether to defer the death tax or pay it at the first death from the estate of the first spouse to die. As you can see, the ultimate tax result is the same as is the case with the use of a disclaimer clause. The principal differences are that the surviving spouse does not make the decision whether or not to charge the estate tax to one side of the trust or the other (as that spouse would otherwise by means of the disclaimer) and that the surviving spouse may not spend more than one-half the total estate (the marital deduction trust) for the benefit of a new spouse, avaricious relatives, swindlers and hyperaggressive fund-raisers.

The QTIP trust is established at the first death, in exactly the same manner as are the residuary and marital deduction trusts. The surviving spouse then receives (as in our example) all the income for life from all three trusts. The trust will ordinarily provide for full access to the principal of the marital deduction trust and only limited access to the principal of the residuary and QTIP trusts. On special facts, however, limited access to principal of the latter two may be either included or withheld without changing the tax results.

On the death of the surviving spouse, such assets as remain in the marital deduction trust are ordinarily transferred and added to the residuary trust, as are those of the QTIP trust then remaining. The total is then distributed to the ultimate beneficiaries, usually your children. There are several variations, but this is the most common form.

Installment Payment of Tax. While actively pursuing your career, you often feel the day will never arrive when you will face no problems and have ample cash on hand. Unfortunately, death often heightens the liquidity problem. We have already addressed liquidity in passing terms and in connection with insurance funding of death taxes. Here, we touch on the financing options that may be available when all else fails.

Lest we lose sight of the fundamental verities, remember: that a tax dollar paid with borrowed funds costs $1.00 plus interest; that a tax dollar paid from the estate itself costs $1.00 plus, in many cases, a discount from a forced sale; and that a tax dollar paid from otherwise nontaxable life insurance proceeds will cost between 1% and 3% per year. The logic is obvious: first you plan your affairs so as to avoid the estate tax; if you still have too much, you try to fund the anticipated tax with life insurance; and if your health or age renders life insurance funding uneconomic, you reorder your holdings as quickly and efficiently as possible so as to favor publicly-traded securities that can be sold at fair market value within minutes. Only if all else fails, or if a cash flow analysis presents compelling logic for it, do you finance the payment of the federal estate tax. It is that last option we here address.

The tax itself is only one of many expenses for which the executor may be required to raise cash:

If you are a professional person in private practice, the value of that practice begins to diminish from the moment of death. So in addition to securing the prescription pads and drugs (doctor or dentist) and buying the "tail" on the professional liability insurance policy (a one-time premium that protects the estate from future professional negligence claims), the executor should raise the salaries of each office staff member so as to keep them on the job through the initial post-death period and obtain Special Letters of Administration along with the required authorization from the probate court so as to begin an immediate search for someone to purchase the practice. Those steps require quick, confident action and cash (all avoided, of course, if you have the foresight to enter into a buy-sell agreement with principals in the firm, employees or friendly competitors).

A cash allowance for the family may be required.

You may be a borrower or guarantor under bank loans containing default provisions accelerating the loan balance on your death.

As probate administration proceeds, cash will be required for filing fees, publication of required notices, appraisal fees, debt service during the period of administration on loans secured by estate assets, creditor claims for last illness expenses, funeral and burial costs, cash bequests, estate and inheritance taxes, and compensation for the personal representative and attorney.

The federal estate tax often represents the greatest cash need.

IRC (and usually state revenue statutes) provides for the deferred payment of death taxes under prescribed circumstances:

• **Reasonable Cause Deferral (10 Years).** If the executor (after analyzing the cash needs of the estate, the potential for generating cash from the sale of assets and the debt service impact on cash flow if the tax is paid in installments under the "reasonable cause" provision) concludes that tax deferral is a compelling economic need, the case must be presented to the IRS in writing and supported by evidence in order to procure the extension. The regulations provide several examples of reasonable cause, but a fact situation in which the estate consists largely of a closely-held business interest and lacks sufficient funds to pay the tax on time will be deemed reasonable cause for granting the extension. If approved, the tax may be deferred for as many as 10 one-year periods at rates of interest determined annually by the IRS (at approximately 90% of the then-current bank prime rate).[55]

If the executor uses the 10-year reasonable cause deferral, the more favorable 14-year provision discussed below will not be available.

• **Farm or Business Interest Deferral (14 Years).**[56] Federal estate tax deferral here does not require a showing of reasonable cause. It requires only that your estate include an interest in a farm or other closely-held business exceeding in value 35% of the adjusted gross estate. The term "adjusted gross estate" means all your property interests (whether or not part of the probate estate), less estate tax-deductible debts, expenses, claims and losses. Interests in farm property or other closely-held businesses are defined in a manner intended to preclude typical passive investment holdings; the social policy behind this provision is the preservation of family farms and businesses from forced sale to pay death taxes. If the tests are met, the federal estate tax attributable to that farm or business interest may be deferred for as long as 14 years, with the estate paying interest only for the first five years and thereafter paying 10 equal annual installments of principal and interest. (The reason the total payment period is 14 rather than 15 years is that the last due date for the interest installment coincides with the first installment payment of principal and interest on the tax.) The interest rate is 4% on the estate tax attributable to the first $1 million in value of the qualifying farm or business.

Any unpaid balance of the tax will become immediately due and payable upon disposition of one-third of the value of your interest in the qualifying farm or business, or upon aggregate withdrawals of one-third of your interest in money or other property, during the 14-year payment period.

One final note: Sometimes, in the arcane world of tax planning, something fundamental eludes us. One such fundamental is that during the period the estate tax payment is deferred, the probate estate must remain open. As long as it remains open, the executor must be compensated for continuing services rendered to the estate (accounting, fiduciary tax returns, property management, etc.), the attorney must be compensated for services rendered to the executor and to the estate (preparation of legal papers, court appearances, advising the personal representative, etc.), the fidelity bond premium (if bond is required) must be paid annually and a major part — if not all — of the estate must remain undistributed.

Special Use Valuation Property. In the same social policy mode discussed earlier, we have a limited measure of relief with respect to federal estate tax valuation of real property used in a closely-held farm or other active business.

Such property may often be converted to another use at a greater market value (highest and best use) than that for which it is employed. For example, a client of my former law firm was a third generation owner-operator of a large and successful lumber business in suburban Los Angeles. Competitive pressures began to impair profits, and he engaged an appraiser to place a value on the real property from which the business was conducted. He found, to his delight, that he could liquidate his equipment and inventory, sell the empty property to an apartment house developer, pay his resulting income taxes and enjoy from the invested net proceeds three times his former income with no management duties beyond reconciling his bank account each month.

The circumstances presenting an attractive opportunity for one property owner, however, may spell emotional disaster to another who prefers to continue operating the family farm or other business from those premises but is faced with a federal estate tax so immense — because it is based on highest and best use — that no choice remains but to sell the property.[57]

The thrust of the special use valuation provision is that the property used in the family farm or closely-held business may be valued for federal estate tax purposes at its actual current use, rather than its highest and best use; that will, in appropriate situations, produce a lower valuation, thus a lower tax. In no event may the reduction in value exceed $750,000. (Remember, Congress intends to benefit small family businesses, not large ones.) So, for example, if your estate includes qualifying property valued at $1 million at its highest and best use but the same property is valued at only $200,000 at its current use, the gross estate will be reduced by $750,000, although the difference in value is $800,000.

If you intend to utilize special use valuations to reduce the federal estate tax, two issues must be determined: first, the adjusted values of both the real and personal property used in the farm or business operation must exceed 50% of your adjusted gross estate; and second, the real property alone must exceed 25% of it. If there is time for pre-death planning, lifetime gifts of property may be used to bring the values within the qualification limits.

Another aspect is the effect on the property's basis for capital gains tax purposes. On your death, your property interests receive a step-up in basis (for purposes of computing the capital gain on later sale) to the value used in reporting the federal estate tax.[58] Using our example above, if the property is sold, the estate tax saving obtained from the reduction in appraised value will be offset to some extent by the additional capital gains tax on the subsequent sale. Both the calculation and the probabilities of future sale must be considered carefully.

This discussion of special use valuation summarizes its operation almost to the extent of being misleading. The rules regarding use of the property and by whom it may be used are complex in the extreme. If you ever find it appropriate to consider this tax reduction tool, be certain to obtain the advice of a practitioner who is intimately familiar with its operation, and be absolutely certain that your plans for the property involved are fully consistent with the statutory requirements for continued qualification. Otherwise, your heirs may find themselves facing an unexpected — and large — tax adjustment.

Noncharitable Lifetime Gifts. At the risk of stating the obvious, the purpose of lifetime giving is to reduce the estate of the donor — thus the estate tax — and to benefit the heirs. Before losing ourselves in the many ways by which to accomplish that noble end, however, certain nontax considerations must be evaluated.

A completed gift — the only kind that may be excluded from your estate — is one in which you give up all dominion and control over it. That may, depending on the property involved, present a psychological loss to be weighed against the benefit sought; *e.g.*, a gift of art, heirlooms, or residence.

Despite the value of lifetime gifts for medium-size estates, most gifts (except life insurance) are and will continue to be made only by persons of substantial wealth. There is a compelling nontax reason for that fact of life: none of us know what the future holds; and you may need that money or property someday. If there is a remote possibility that your financial security or standard of living may someday be jeopardized by having made the gift, it should not be made. You have heard one variation or another on the story of parents (often immigrants with an inordinate fear of IRS, and invariably without independent representation) who work hard to finance quality educations for their children, then deliver to them all or most of their remaining property to avoid the tax man, and usually based on an oral promise that the children will care for them in their old age. But the children then, if the money is not unwisely spent, adopt an attractive or even luxurious life-style, leave the parents to live on social security in modest quarters and are embarrassed to invite them into their homes, with their old-world accents, to meet their friends. Whether or not this old story is true, there is more truth than fiction to the old quip, "Money may not be everything, but it's a great way to keep the kids in touch!"

Having so disclosed my bias, let us move on to the question of how best to make these lifetime gifts.

The same unified transfer tax credit that is available to eliminate the federal estate tax on the first $600,000 at death, is available in the alternative to eliminate federal gift taxes. So to the extent it is applied to lifetime gifts, the amount left to apply later to the federal estate tax is reduced. (That is why they call it a "unified" credit. You can only use it once.) Fortunately, you may give $10,000 per donee per year (twice that amount if your spouse joins in making the gift) without gift tax, thus avoiding erosion of the credit. For that reason, noncharitable lifetime gifts are invariably planned around the maximum use of this annual exclusion. The $10,000 (or $20,000) annual exclusion is available only for gifts of a "present interest"; so it is of no help if you restrict the gift; e.g., "Here's the deed to my house for you to hold in trust for my grandson, but don't give it to him until he's 30."

Among the more commonly recognized advantages of lifetime giving are these:

• Any future appreciation in the value of the property is eliminated from your gross estate for federal estate tax purposes.

• Probate administration of the gift property is eliminated.

• Income earned on the gift property, after tax, is excluded from your gross estate.

• Estate death taxes (if any) are reduced.

• If the property is of a kind that generates tax preference income and causes you to incur alternative minimum tax liability, the transfer will avoid it.

• If the gift is to a family member age 14 or over who is in a lower income tax bracket than you, and if the gift is of income-producing property, it reduces your family's overall income taxes.

• The unlimited gift tax marital deduction,[59] permits spouses to transfer assets between themselves without tax liability. That frees you to, for example, adjust ownership of closely-held business interests in order to qualify for the tax deferral and special use valuation opportunities discussed earlier.

Among the disadvantages are these:

• Your heirs lose the stepped-up income tax basis, because

property they acquire from you by gift receives the same basis as yours in the property.

• Loss of control of the property without a corresponding transfer tax advantage. This can occur if, at death, your gross estate is not large enough to generate a death tax. It can also occur with respect to interspousal transfers in light of the unlimited estate tax marital deduction (which allows one spouse to make a transfer to the other at death, rather than during lifetime, usually without adverse transfer tax effects).

• Your liquidity needs at any age may render a gift impractical because you are unable to pay the gift tax. As a result, the net gift device may prove useful. A net gift is one made on the express or implied condition that the donee pay the gift tax.

• **Below-Market-Interest-Rate Loans.** The general rule is that any nonbusiness loan made at no interest or at less than market rate interest is considered a "gift loan," the gift being the amount of forgone interest. A below-market loan may generate both income tax (on interest imputed by the IRS) and gift tax liability.

All that notwithstanding, such loans may still prove helpful. There is no imputed interest for either income or gift tax purposes if on any given day during the tax year the total loan balance owed by the donee-borrower to the donor-lender does not exceed $10,000. This exception does not apply to loans made to acquire passive income-producing assets.

• **Gifts in Trust.** You will usually make a gift in trust for one or both of two reasons: you want to impose restrictions on the gift, or the gift property requires management attention that the donee is not equipped to provide. If restriction is the aim and the donee's inability to reach the gift is the result, the gift is of a "future interest." Such a gift does not qualify for the $10,000 (or $20,000 where your spouse joins) annual gift tax exclusion. That means you must report and pay the federal (and perhaps state) gift tax. If management is the aim and you are willing to let the donee take possession of the property, you will secure the annual exclusion; the trick is to persuasively present to the donee the advantages of qualified management.

A gift trust must be irrevocable. Otherwise, your ability to revoke it and retake the property makes it an incomplete gift; you must give up complete dominion and control in order to remove the property from your estate for tax purposes.

It is also prudent to avoid serving as trustee of the gift trust. The law on this issue has steadily narrowed over the years, so that too much control over the gift property or distribution of income can cause the property to be included in your estate or the income to be taxed to you, or both.

You may wish to give the stock in a business to your children without giving up control. A few years ago, a taxpayer accomplished that in a heavily-litigated case where he placed the stock in trust for his children but retained (as trustee) voting control of the gift stock. Congress responded with remedial legislation and the same attempt will now result in the stock going to the children on the donor's death, but its value being included in the donor's estate for federal estate tax purposes — an untidy consequence.

Here are the ground rules for gifts in trust to minors:[60]

"(c) TRANSFER FOR THE BENEFIT OF MINOR. — No part of a gift to an individual who has not attained the age of 21 years on the date of such transfer shall be considered a gift of a future interest in property for purposes of subsection (b) if the property and the income therefrom —

(1) may be expended by, or for the benefit of, the donee before his attaining the age of 21 years, and

(2) will to the extent not so expended —

(A) pass to the donee on his attaining the age of 21 years, and

(B) in the event the donee dies before attaining the age of 21 years, be payable to the estate of the donee or as he may appoint under a general power of appointment as defined in section 2514(c)."

One often-overlooked administrative aspect of such trusts relates to the legal duty of support owed to the minor donee. The trustee holds the discretion to accumulate or distribute the trust income. If that trustee is also the person charged with the duty to support the minor (*i.e.*, parents) and exercises the discretion as trustee to apply all or any part of the trust income to such expenses (food, education, clothes, rent, etc.), the trust income, to the extent so applied, will be taxed (for income tax purposes) to those owing the duty of support, rather than to the minor. The income is otherwise taxed to the trust if retained or to the minor if distributed.

You may feel that 21 is too young an age to receive substantial sums of money or property. The only effective technique for deferring distribution without also losing the annual gift tax exclusion (tied to "present interest" treatment) is to give the minor a general power of appointment (the power to withdraw the trust property) upon attaining age 21, but also providing that the trust estate will continue to be held for the benefit of the donee to the extent the power is not exercised. The rest is up to the parents' powers of persuasion.

• **Gifts of Life Insurance.** It requires only a moment's reflection to appreciate the utility of life insurance as a gift vehicle. We have already examined in detail its highly-structured use in trust as an estate liquidity tool. But here, we consider it simply as a means of gifting minor amounts of money annually (premium payments) that will mature (death proceeds) for much larger amounts of money.

Newly-purchased policies as to which the children are applicants, owners and beneficiaries may be used. You may also use existing policies, assuming the need for which they were originally purchased no longer exists. As to existing insurance, simply execute an absolute assignment of ownership and beneficiary change, on forms provided by the insurance company, and the children become the new owners and beneficiaries. Your spouse will also ordinarily be required to sign, so the carrier will not have to worry about a lawsuit claiming "asset diversion" if your marriage later fails.

In no way should you accept any consideration from the children for the policy or policies. To do so would provide IRS with an argument that the children "bought" them. If it can demonstrate a "transfer [of the policies] for value,"[61] the death benefits become partially taxable to the children for income tax purposes, whereas they are otherwise income tax-free.

Also, do not bother with the gift of life insurance if you know you will not survive three years following the date of the gift. The policy, at its death benefit value, will be included in your taxable estate if you die within three years after making the gift.[62] But the children will have the money. It may then take all the powers of persuasion your executor can muster to cause the children to advance funds to cover the estate tax attributable to those insurance proceeds.

Consider also the possibility that the gift may be subject to the generation skipping transfer tax. (Discussion *infra.*)

• **Estate "Freeze" Techniques.** The transaction form is limited only by the genius of man, but the central objective is to recharacterize an asset and make a tax-free gift or sale of an interest in it that has the effect of allocating all or most of the future appreciation in value to the donee. Following, from pre-1988 law, are some examples:

• You are age 60 and would like to spend more time traveling, playing golf and providing volunteer services (church work, civic work, appointive governmental position, etc.). You are the sole owner of a business. Your daughter has worked in the business for 15 years; she's bright, educated, enjoys the work and now carries many of the management responsibilities. Your two sons are married and not involved in the business. Your wife has a twinkle in her eye, a rose clenched in her teeth and her dancing shoes packed, waiting for you to make up your mind. Given those or similar facts, you may obtain an independent appraisal of the fair market value of the business (in order to defend yourself against any later IRS claim of a "bargain sale"); sell the business to your daughter for full fair market value, taking back a note and security agreement evidencing the purchase money loan. The results? Your daughter has maximum incentive to build the business, because it's all hers and she has to earn enough to service your note. You have "frozen" the value of your business interest, now evidenced by a note, thus shifting future appreciation to your daughter's estate. If she fails as the sole operator of the business, carefully crafted default provisions in the note can put you back in charge before the business seriously deteriorates in value. Your children will ultimately share equally in your estate as then constituted (including the note); any benefit the daughter receives from growth in value of the business constitutes a proper reward for her diligence and willingness to assume risk.

• Assume the same facts as above, except that the business is incorporated and you may, for a variety of tax and securities law reasons beyond the scope of this discussion, choose to accomplish the same end by changing the capital structure from simple to complex (from all common stock to common plus another form of security). A complex capital structure may include voting or non-voting preferred stock equal in value to the then-current appraised fair market value of the company, and voting or nonvoting common stock which, since all value is reflected in the preferred stock, has no value at that moment. Since the common stock has no value, you may make a gift of it to your daughter with no gift tax consequences. Since the income from the preferred stock is limited to the dividend coupon rate, it will not appreciate in value, thus all appreciation will be reflected in the common stock. So if the daughter builds a $1 million business into a $10 million business, $9 million of it is hers. You may allocate voting control between the two classes of stock in any manner that provides you comfort. For example: voting common and nonvoting cumulative preferred, but with all voting rights shifting from the common to the preferred 30 days following default on any dividend payment, thus placing you back in control of the company if your daughter cannot run it well enough to meet your dividend payments on time.

• Assume the same facts as before, but none of your children are interested in or able to operate the business successfully. You may recapitalize the business with common and preferred stock, keep the preferred and give perhaps 85% of the common to your children, selling (at a nominal price) 15% of the common to a key employee or professional manager brought in from the outside to take over management, and subjecting the manager's shares to a repurchase option. The repurchase option would be exercisable by your children at any time, whether the stock is held by the manager or by some subsequent transferee, and the exercise price would be based on a formula that tracks the one used in appraising the business at the time of the recapitalization transaction. By that means, you freeze the value of your business interest in your estate at the value of your preferred stock, your children receive 85% of all appreciation in value of the company (and will ultimately inherit your preferred stock) and your manager is given an important incentive to make the company as large and prosperous as possible.

These techniques somehow struck IRS as too good to be true. Following a novel — and unsuccessful — attempt to impose its interpretation of retained interests,[63] IRS fared better with a Congress desperate for increased revenue without political risk. It secured passage of IRC Section 2036(c), a statute that permits it to ignore these divisions of property rights.[64] 2036(c) is effective for transfer made after December 17, 1987 and provides essentially as follows:

Point	Comment
If a person	Or an entity in which that person has a direct or family interest.
"holds" a "substantial interest"	Direct or indirect ownership of 10% or more of the voting power, income stream or both.
in any "enterprise," and	A business or other property which may yield income or appreciation.
"in effect" transfers	Sells, assigns or conveys ownership to another by any means or in any manner, whether or not adequate consideration is paid.
property having a "disproportionately large share" of the potential appreciation,	Any share of appreciation in the enterprise greater than that retained by the transferor.

while retaining income, voting,
liquidation or conversion
rights in the enterprise,

| and if that retained interest is for the lifetime of that person, | Or of that person's spouse, or for a period ascertainable only by reference to that person's death, or for a period that does not end before the death of that person or that person's spouse. |

then the transferred interest
will be included in that person's estate for federal estate
purposes.

This tabular explanation is made necessary by the poor drafting of the statute, a statute rendered even more unintelligible by the accompanying brief and legislative committee reports. It was, of course, intended to eliminate the various "freeze" techniques, but its imprecision gave it a reach far beyond even that which IRS contemplated. 2036(c) was amended in 1988 and both narrowed and clarified by a 1989 Notice.[65]

At this point, here are our operational definitions:

• The "substantial interest" test: A substantial interest is 10% or more held by the transferor, directly or through family members. The family members include the spouse, lineal descendants of both the transferor and the spouse, parents and grandparents. Brothers and sisters are counted. It matters not whether you and your family hold the interests directly or through artificial entities (trusts, corporations, partnerships). You and your family must hold 10% or more of the entity's voting power, income stream, or both, for 2036(c) to apply. That voting power may arise or be evidenced by voting trusts, powers of attorney, stock pledges, proxies, stock voting right allocations, partnership agreement provisions or by fiduciary (trust) provisions. The term "enterprise" is not defined in the statute, but legislative history extends its ambit to include any property producing income or appreciation. If you hold a substantial interest under these rules, 2036(c) applies unless otherwise excepted.

• The "disproportionate transfer" test: There are two parts to this one, the transfer of a disproportionate share in future appreciation and retention of income or rights in the enterprise. As to the first, any variance of the rights and interests transferred and retained (*e.g.*, 100% of future appreciation transferred and 10% of income retained) is disproportionate. As to the last, "rights" include voting, conversion, etc. as noted in the tabular treatment above, and "income" may include any form of property interest (present or future), a promissory note, income for a period of time, employment arrangements, retirement arrangements or lease. The 1987 amendments included several exceptions to "retained interests." The primary insight afforded us by these exceptions is that 2036(c) is far-reaching and will continue to be so applied by IRS.

• The "safe harbor" exceptions: Five areas are provided by the 1987 amendments for planning latitude. They include grantor-retained income trusts (those in which you give property in trust, retaining an income from it for a period of years determined without reference to your death) and certain common business transactions IRS thought posed no opportunities for wealth transfer with retained interests. They are as follows:

• The grantor-retained income trust ("GRIT"): To avoid the reach of 2036(c), the GRIT must provide that only you (as the transferor) may be the income beneficiary, that your trust interest is limited to the trust income, that the trust term must not exceed 10 years and that neither you nor your spouse may be the trustee. If these requirements are satisfied, there will be no "deemed gift" on termination of the trust — only upon its creation. This way, you report and pay the gift tax at the time of the transfer and avoid inclusion of the appreciation in your estate. But there is a hitch; if you die during the trust term, the trust property is included in your estate at its date of death value, even though the estate is entitled to only the income.

• Start-up debt: Another safe harbor provided in 1987 is start-up debt. It is based on recognition of the fact that appreciation of a new enterprise is attributable to the effort of and risks assumed by the transferee, not to disguised wealth transfers. Your loan to the transferee must be unconditional and for a specified amount of money; the money must be used by the transferee to establish and operate an active trade or business; you cannot, before, during or after the loan transaction, transfer to the transferee any noncash assets (goodwill, customers, business opportunities), nor may you hold any interest in the business (including serving as officer, director or employee) other than qualified debt; the transferee must participate in the management decisions of the business; the loan must contain no voting rights, no conversion rights and no rights to acquire a prohibited interest otherwise. The 1989 Notice relaxed the third rule (transfers of noncash interests) by excluding transfers taking place more than three years before the start-up debt is incurred.

• Start-up preferred interests: This is a safe harbor created under the 1989 Notice. It is some form of preferred stock or special-class common stock given in exchange for cash and that otherwise satisfies the requirements of qualified start-up debt. It may be transacted either alone or in conjunction with qualified start-up debt.

• Agreements for sale or lease of goods or provision of services: Unless precluded by regulations (not yet issued), 2036(c) will not apply to the transfer with retained interest transaction solely because there is an agreement to sell or lease goods or other property used in the enterprise, or to provide services. In order to qualify for this safe harbor, the agreement must be made at arm's length and for fair market value, not involving any other change in interests in the enterprise. The agreement may not provide for payment in amounts determined in whole or in part by reference to gross receipts, income, profits or similar indicia of business operations.

• Options and other agreements to buy or sell property: This safe harbor was also created under the 1989 Notice. Here, you may enter into options to purchase or sell property to or from the object of your bounty as long as the purchase price is for fair market value on the date of exercise. A formula price determined on the date of the option (rather than date of exercise) is permitted if based on then-current valuation data and otherwise at arm's length.

Nothwithstanding the safe harbors provided under the 1989 Notice, IRS interprets 2036(c) so as to sweep within its scope intrafamily sales to children, redemptions of business interests from children, issuance of stock to children, nonqualified buy-sell agreements and options with children, installment sales to children, nonqualified start-ups, split purchases, irrevocable life insurance trusts (if and to the extent a covered enterprise is transferred to the trust), various shifting interests in appreciation, failure to exercise rights that have the effect of shifting appreciation, intrafamily private annuities and self-cancelling installment notes.

To appreciate the eye-popping result of 2036(c), an example is in order. You establish a business enterprise which in due course becomes profitable. One of your children shows special aptitude for the business. For the various reasons discussed earlier, you decide to deliver the business to that child, but in a way that gives equal treatment to the other children. You sell it to the child on liberal terms; say, no down and a $1 million secured note at market rate interest and based on an independent appraisal. This way, all the children share (when you and your spouse are gone) in the business value that existed on the date you parted with it, evidenced by the date of death balance of the note. The child turns out to be even better than you imagined, and runs the fair market value of the business to $11 million by the time you and your spouse are gone. Under the spousal unity rule,[66] and if 2036(c) is found to apply, IRS may add $10 million to either your gross estate or that of your spouse ($11 million less the $1 million paid for the business, plus or minus for minor adjustments), increasing the federal estate tax by as much as $5.5 million. Punitive hardly describes it.

The application of 2036(c) can be so subtle that you can be in trouble before you know it. Here are some fact situations that tell you that you may have a problem:

- A transfer with a retained interest.
- A lifetime transfer in which property is divided between your spouse and someone else.
- Fixed-price options to purchase. This includes purchase

agreements that amount to the same thing because the purchaser is not personally liable upon default.

- Any right, regardless of form, that entitles someone to compensation based on appreciation in the value of a business.
- Any agreement (*e.g.*, a disability buyout provision) where there is a right to purchase based on a formula price reflecting fair market value of the business interest.
- Any transfer of shares in a closely-held company having more than one class of stock or partnership interest. Examine with special care the possibility that debt may be classified as equity under prevailing IRS interpretation.
- A transfer to a spouse for life or for a term of years with a remainder over to some third person or persons. This may arise under innocuous, nontax circumstances; *e.g.*, a trust arrangement to provide security for a new spouse, transfers to carry out the terms of a prenuptial or postnuptial agreement, transfers attendant to a marital settlement agreement, etc.

If you see a fact situation like one of these, have the transaction checked carefully against 2036(c). If the statute appears to apply and you cannot rearrange the transaction to avoid that result, do not proceed unless you are certain the problem will be eliminated at least three years before your death. If you are already in trouble, get rid of the retained interest more that three years before your death.

Planning tools are available to you, but the best ones will be created by keeping pressure on Congress. At this writing, remedial legislation is under consideration. If passed, 2036(c) will be repealed and replacement provisions adopted in a new Chapter 14 of IRC. Under the proposed new provisions, the only tax will be a gift tax. It will be payable at the time of the transaction and based on the remainder interest of the gift or bargain sale. (The remainder interest is the gross value less your retained interest, using special gift valuation tables created by IRS just for these transactions.) These transactions will still be taxed more heavily than other gifts, but at least it will avoid the time bomb result of adding to your estate the appreciation of a business you gave away or sold years earlier. Since we do not yet know whether the new proposal will find its way into law, or its final form, be absolutely certain to get expert tax and legal advice before venturing into the intra-family sale or gift of business interests.

Charitable Gifts. A lengthy, detailed discussion of charitable giving methods (remainder trusts, unitrusts, lead trusts, gifts of appreciated property and the tax ramifications of each) is beyond the scope of this book. With that note, I will mention only two techniques beyond the obvious (naming the charity in your will).

   • **Tax Avoidance — No Children.** You may have no children or close relatives of any kind. If so, your estate planning concern is limited to your spouse and perhaps a few tokens of affection for friends. Given some compelling interest or concern beyond yourselves (church, youth, the poor, unwed mothers, an alma mater, etc.), you may wholly eliminate any taxes or probate expenses by establishing and funding a living trust for the benefit of the two of you and for the survivor for life, with the remaining trust estate going to charity upon the death of the survivor. The unified transfer tax credit and the unlimited marital deduction eliminate the tax at the first death, the ultimate charitable deduction eliminates any tax at the death of the survivor. Thus, the trust can be drafted without the restrictions of marital deduction provisions and with maximum flexibility for the two of you together and for the survivor.

   If some income tax shelter is desired as an added fillip, the trust may be established as an irrevocable charitable remainder or unitrust, either immediately or upon the first death. Such a trust is divided for tax reporting purposes into two segments: a life income and a remainder interest. Those two segments are based on the age of the surviving spouse at the first death (if that's when it begins) or on the ages of both of you (if it is to begin upon creation of the trust). A charitable deduction is provided for the income beneficiary or beneficiaries, based on the value of the remainder interest that will ultimately go to charity. For example: the estate is worth $400,000; the joint life income interest of the husband and wife is valued (using IRC tables) at $340,000, leaving the remainder interest valued at $60,000; the property is placed in an irrevocable trust that provides for distribution of 6% per year ($24,000) for as long as you, or either of you, live; the type of charitable beneficiary and the type of gift given determines whether the maximum income tax deduction is limited to 20%, 30% or 50% of adjusted gross income per year[67]; assuming it is a church (50%), you may eliminate from tax (via the charitable deduction attributable to the $60,000 remainder interest) $12,000 per year for five years (the maximum carryover period for deductions in excess of contribution limits).[68]

• **Meeting the Needs of Both Charity and Children.** A more common situation is this: suppose you are deeply involved in a church, charity or cause (the last presumably organized as a tax-exempt entity), but your estate is modest, to the point that a significant charitable gift — whether during life or by will — may upset the children. A life insurance policy may be used to accomplish the charitable end without alienating the family. Simply cause the charitable entity to apply for a life insurance policy on your life, name itself owner and beneficiary and you as premium payor. You pay the premiums each year and take a charitable income tax deduction for those payments. At your death, the organization receives the proceeds in cash, without the delay and loss of privacy of a probate administration proceeding, and neither your children nor your creditors will be in a position to challenge or claim any part of the insurance proceeds. If you wish to also designate the insurance proceeds for a particular use, it can usually be worked out informally with the organization. If you cannot do so, or if you choose not to rely on the assurances of the current board, the same end may be accomplished by creating a trust to own and receive the policy proceeds and apply them to the purpose intended as a separately-administered fund.

• **The Family Foundation.** Taking the foregoing a step further, you may wish to create now a formal structure for the specific application of your donated funds, but keep the family in control beyond your lifetime. Think about this:

• Establish a nonprofit corporation, tax-exempt for the selected charitable purposes under IRC §501(c)(3) ("The Family Foundation"). It has no members, so the board of directors constitutes the only control. Any board vacancies are filled by the remaining board members, so the board is essentially self-perpetuating. Once you appoint yourself and the family to the board, it should stay in control.

• Contribute to the Family Foundation the funds you would otherwise contribute each year directly to the church, charity or cause, and send them on as foundation grants. If you are presently contributing at or near the maximum income tax deduction limits, and if both religious and charitable causes are to be supported through the Family Foundation, some extra attention may be required in order to avoid losing deductions; it is nothing that cannot be resolved with a little thought.

• As your estate becomes more liquid, debts are satisfied and children leave home, you may find yourself with excess life insurance. Contribute it to the Family Foundation and keep it in force: the post-donation premiums are deductible as charitable gifts.

• As you consider the planning techniques discussed in this book, you may wish to direct that part of the estate otherwise subject to death taxes into the Family Foundation. The tax will be eliminated by the charitable deduction and the family may maintain control of its disposition, within the bounds of the Family Foundation corporate objectives. This is not an expensive option; just a few thousand dollars to form the corporation and obtain the exemptions plus professional fees to prepare one or two information returns each year. The real benefit is satisfaction; it tends to focus the attention of the family on joint action to deal with needs outside itself, and that can prove deeply rewarding.

Business Continuation Planning. Continuity of management for the family business must be carefully considered in the context of your death or disability as a key person. Without planning:

• the lenders may become anxious over the loss of your services (or your personal guarantees) and call their loans;

• employees may become concerned over their career prospects and leave;

• the business may require a year or more to locate and recruit a qualified replacement, with profits depressed during that period

due to the loss of your services;
- your surviving spouse will want — and usually demand — compensation equal to that which you now take (especially if that spouse has voting control), but will be unable or unwilling to provide skills and time on the job comparable to yours;
- the customers you hold to the business may leave;
- your estate may face unnecessary death tax problems, both because the IRS inflates the value of the business so as to inflate the federal estate tax and because the estate may not have the cash to pay the tax when due (nine months after date of death); and
- your surviving spouse is usually forced to rely on the skills, honesty and dedication of the employees and other shareholders for the continued success of the business.

The function of business continuation agreements is to buy out, for cash, the interest of a shareholder who is permanently disabled or deceased, and to do so at fair market value. Conceived and drafted properly, that will vest continuing control in the nondisabled or surviving shareholders, often with little or no purchase money debt, get the disabled shareholder or surviving spouse out of the business at fair market value, fix the value of the business interest for federal estate tax purposes and assuage the concerns of employees and lenders alike.

The value of your interest in the corporation is fixed for federal estate tax purposes only under two kinds of agreement. The first is one in which you agree that you will not sell your shares during life without giving the other principal the right to purchase, and if owned at the time of death, giving the other an option to purchase, at a price or valuation formula fixed by the agreement in either case.[69] Such an agreement fixes the price for federal estate tax purposes if fair at the time it is established, even if the survivor does not exercise the option.[70] The second is where you contract that upon death, your estate is bound to sell your shares and the survivor is bound to buy them at the [fair and] agreed price.[71]

In reviewing the effectiveness of a business continuation agreement to fix the business value for estate tax purposes, IRS cited *Estate of Seltzer v. Commissioner*,[72] in which the court stated:

To determine whether the buy-sell agreement in this case... fixes the value of the business for estate tax purposes, the following factors should be considered: (1) whether the price is determinable under the terms of the agreement; (2) whether the owner of the interest is obligated to sell at the contract price and the company or other interest holders are obligated to purchase at that price; (3) whether the obligation to sell at the contract price is binding upon the owner of the interest both during his lifetime, and upon his estate at his death; and (4) whether the agreement is a bona fide business arrangement and not a testamentary device.

• **Partial Stock Redemption.** If you are the sole owner and the business is incorporated, you may not wish the entire business sold on your death. If that is the case, you may arrange for the corporation to repurchase some of your stock upon your death so as to generate funds for the payment of estate taxes. That way you make the business liquid assets yours and your family maintains complete ownership. (They still own 100% of the remaining shares.) The trick here is to carry off the repurchase and redemption of the shares so as to avoid taxation of the proceeds as a constructive dividend.

In order to lawfully repurchase its own stock, the corporation must have at least as much surplus (usually expressed on the balance sheet as "accumulated earnings") as the amount to be paid for the shares.[73] Having the required balance sheet surplus on hand is only the first requirement, though. That surplus might be held largely in the form of inventory, equipment and receivables, not cash.

Another problem is the risk that the service may impose on your estate an inflated value for the company, increasing the amount of cash to be generated by the stock repurchase.

You may deal with the adequacy of cash surplus issue by causing the corporation to purchase and maintain key person life insurance on your life. You deal with the valuation problem by fixing the price (usually by formula) under a written agreement with the corporation, just as you would with business continuation agreements discussed above.

Partial stock redemptions must be qualified under IRC[74] in order to avoid characterization of the payment as a constructive dividend. Avoidance of that characterization is critical, since dividends are nondeductible to the corporation and fully taxable as ordinary income to the recipient. A redemption so qualified is still nondeductible to the corporation, but substantially avoids income tax to the recipient. The concern addressed by IRS is that business owners will issue large amounts of stock on formation or purchase of the corporation and cause it to repurchase and redeem small amounts each year for decades, effectively converting ordinary income into capital gains.

There is no preferential tax rate for capital gains under the *Internal Revenue Code of 1986*. The tax on your corporation is substantially eliminated, however, by virtue of the stepped-up income tax basis taken at your death.[75] Remember, that is the federal rule; state rules may not always comport with it.

Redemption of Shares Equal to Transfer Costs. Capital gains treatment (essentially no income tax, as discussed above) may be permitted for partial stock redemptions that do not exceed the sum of your estate's "estate, inheritance, legacy and succession taxes" plus "the amount of funeral and administration expenses allowable as deductions to the estate."[76]

Your estate may use this provision only if your business interest exceeds 35% of your adjusted gross estate. The adjusted gross estate includes separate property with your half of the community property, less estate tax deductions for losses, debts and administration expenses (whether or not those deductions are taken on the estate tax return). In applying the 35% test, your shares in two or more corporations may be treated as shares in a single corporation, so long as you own at least 20% of the stock in each of them at the time of your death.

The redemption must be completed after your death and before the expiration of three years and 90 days after the federal estate tax due date. If the estate pays the tax in installments under IRC §6166, the period may be extended.

Redemption of Shares Otherwise. If your estate does not

meet these criteria, a partial redemption is still possible. In order to establish a principled basis for determining whether the proceeds of a partial stock redemption constitute a disguised dividend, one or more tests must be satisfied.[77] They are:

- that the payment is not essentially equivalent to a dividend; or
- that it is substantially disproportionate with respect to the selling shareholder (as compared to other shareholders); or
- that it is in complete redemption of all the shares owned by the selling shareholder; or
- that it is in redemption of shares held by a noncorporate shareholder in partial liquidation of the corporation.

As to the second and third options, the method of computing whether a redemption is "substantially disproportionate" or is "complete" may be affected by the attribution to you of shares held by your family; specifically, by your spouse, parents, children and grandchildren.[78]

- **Cross-Purchase Plan Compared.** The most popular structure for a corporate buy-sell agreement is this full or partial stock redemption plan. It requires the corporation, as purchaser of the stock, to be owner and beneficiary of the life insurance used to fund the purchase. The alternative format is the cross-purchase plan, where the shareholders or partners agree between themselves and each owns a policy on the other or others, either directly or through a trust established for the purpose.

The stock redemption plan offers simplicity (fewer policies, two-party transaction upon repurchase of the stock), but contains two important flaws: the surviving or nondisabled shareholders receive no increase in basis for capital gains tax purposes (they are not the purchasers) and the life or disability insurance proceeds received by the corporation to fund the repurchase are subject to the alternative minimum tax, leaving (after the 24% tax) only 76% of those proceeds available for the intended purpose.[79] The trend now is to the cross-purchase plan.

The cross-purchase plan record-keeping can get complicated where there are several shareholders (five such principals requires 25 life and 25 disability policies), but the size of the problem can be reduced to manageable proportions by creating a trust to hold five life and five disability policies in the same aggregate face amount, with the principals as equitable policyowners and functioning otherwise much like a redemption plan. More importantly, the alternative minimum tax does not apply and each surviving shareholder receives an increase in basis equal to the price paid for the shares from the disabled shareholder or the estate of the deceased shareholder.

Remember, when you put a buy-sell plan in place, consider the likelihood of long-term disability (much greater than death before 65) along with the tax implications of the arrangement adopted.

The Generation Skipping Transfer Tax. The generation skipping transfer ("GST") tax[80] continues the US social policy of wealth redistribution. It does so by taxing certain transfers commonly made with the intent to compound family wealth by avoiding taxation at the skipped generation level. Typical transfers subject to it are those in which you provide a life income to your children with remainders over to your grandchildren. It also may reach those in which you leave your children enough property to provide them personal economic security and leave the rest of your estate directly to grandchildren. The tax can be a mind-numbing thing to contemplate, so careful planning is in order where your estate may be exposed. Except for outright gifts or bequests to surviving children and the grandchildren who survive them, the GST tax will be a consideration any time you give property (during your lifetime or at your death) to anyone — lineal descendant or not — who is more than 12.5 years younger than yourself.

GST taxation is a complex area of the IRC. Since this book is intended more for the use of sophisticated businesspersons than as a lawyer's reference tome, I have reduced it to its central elements. In that way, you may quickly determine whether or not you require guidance in planning around it.

The GST tax first came about in 1976 and was replaced with entirely new provisions in 1986. The new provisions introduce certain defined terms that must be understood in order to make sense of GST operations. The key ones are Skip Person, Non-Skip Person and Interest:

- **Skip Person.** A Skip Person is one assigned to a generation two or more below you where you are the transferor; *e.g.*, your grandchild is a Skip Person. A trust is a Skip Person if the only present interest beneficiaries are Skip Persons, or if there are no present interest beneficiaries and no distributions may be made to Non-Skip Persons.[81]
- **Non-Skip Person.** A Non-Skip Person is anyone (including a trust) who is not a Skip Person; *e.g.*, your child.[82]
- **Interest.** An individual has an Interest in a trust if that person has a present right to receive income or principal from it.[83]

IRC imposes a GST tax on three types of generation-skipping transfers. ("Taxable Events"). They are Direct Skips, Taxable Terminations and Taxable Distributions:

- **Direct Skip.** A Direct Skip is any transfer to a Skip Person that is subject to gift or estate tax.[84] Examples include a taxable gift or bequest to a grandchild, except for that portion of a gift exempt from gift tax by the ($10,000 per donee) annual exclusion.[85] A Direct Skip does not include gifts or bequests to your grandchild if the parent (your child) is predeceased.[86]
- **Taxable Termination.** A Taxable Termination is the termination of an Interest (in a trust, as above) if after termination all the remaining beneficiaries (if any) are Skip Persons; *e.g.*, a trust providing income for life to your child, remainders over to your grandchild.[87]
- **Taxable Distribution.** A Taxable Distribution is any trust distribution other than a Direct Skip or Taxable Termination (whether from income or principal) if the distributee is a Skip Person; *e.g.*, if you establish a sprinkling trust to benefit your children and grandchildren and a distribution is made to your grandchild, that is a Taxable Distribution.[88]

There are two principal exceptions to the Taxable Event rules:

- **Tuition and Medical Expenses Paid from a Trust.** If tuition and medical expenses paid from a trust would be a nontaxable gift if made by you during your lifetime,[89] it is not a Taxable Termination or a Taxable Distribution.[90]

- **Limited Gift or Estate Tax Exemption.** The GST tax does not apply to a Taxable Transfer or Taxable Distribution from a trust if and to the extent the transfer is subject to gift or estate tax to or in the estate of a person one generation below that of the transferor; *e.g.*, a trust providing your child a life income with a power to withdraw the trust funds at any time (a general power of appointment) and remainders over to your grandchild will be taxable in your child's estate, so there is no GST tax on distribution to your grandchild.[91]

The GST tax is imposed only once per generation. So, if your estate distributes to a Skip Person two or more generations below you (grandchild or great-grandchild), the transfer is subject to only one GST tax.[92]

The rule for avoiding double taxation (Taxable Termination and Taxable Distribution treatment of the same transfer) is as follows: in a GST after which the property is held in trust, the transferor is assigned to the first generation above the highest generation of any person who then holds an interest in the property.[93] Here is an example. You establish a trust to sprinkle income and principal for as long as the law allows to your child, grandchild and great-grandchild. Trust distributions to your child are not Taxable Distributions, because no generation is being skipped. On the death of your child with you surviving, there is a Taxable Termination. At that point, the highest generation with an Interest in the trust is your grandchild. For GST tax purposes, you drop into the place of your child so that subsequent trust distributions to your grandchild are not deemed Taxable Distributions.

The tax is calculated by multiplying the taxable amount by the applicable rate.[94] The taxable amount is determined as follows:

- **Direct Skip Amount.** The taxable amount of a Direct Skip is the amount received by the transferee.[95] The transferor is liable for the tax unless the Direct Skip is from a trust, in which case the trust is liable for the tax.[96] The tax is not included in the tax base, but is an added gift for purposes of the gift tax.[97]

- **Taxable Termination.** The taxable amount of a Taxable Termination is the amount or value of property in which the interest terminated.[98] The trust is liable for the tax.[99] The tax is included in the tax base.

- **Taxable Distribution.** The taxable amount of a Taxable Distribution is the amount received by the transferee.[100] The transferee is liable for the tax.[101] Any tax paid from other trust property is an additional Taxable Distribution. The tax is included in the tax base.

The tax rate is the maximum federal estate and gift tax rate in the year the GST occurs, multiplied by the Inclusion Ratio (*infra*):[102]

- The maximum rate is 55% until 1993 and 50% thereafter.[103]

- The Inclusion Ratio is 1 unless some GST Exemption (*infra*) is allocated to a transfer or the transfer qualifies for the annual exclusion.[104]

Therefore, if no GST Exemption is allocated and the transfer does not qualify for the annual exclusion, the rate is the maximum federal estate and gift tax rate. For example, assume you establish a trust paying income to your child for life, remainders over to your grandchild. No GST Exemption is allocated to the trust. Your child dies in 1994 and the trust value is $1 million. There is a Taxable Termination of the child's life estate in the amount of $1 million. The tax rate is 50% because that is the minimum federal estate and gift tax rate in 1994, multiplied by the Inclusion Ratio of 1. The GST tax is $500,000.

Each transferor has a $1 million GST Exemption. As with the unified transfer credit, this exemption may be used during life for gifts and the balance, if any, used in your estate for subsequent transfers to which the GST tax is otherwise applicable. If you predecease your spouse and a QTIP trust is created under the allocation provisions of your family trust or otherwise, a special election is available by which your trustee may use all or part of the GST Exemption to cover any GST tax arising from transfers and terminations after the death of your surviving spouse.[105] If you, your executor or your trustee do not make an allocation of the GST Exemption, IRS does it for you.[106]

The Inclusion Ratio is 1 minus the Applicable Fraction (*infra*), determined as follows:[107]

• The numerator is the GST Exemption amount allocated to the property transferred.[108]

• The denominator is the value of the property transferred (with adjustments for any charitable deduction pertaining to the property and death taxes payable from it[109]) and for gifts qualifying for certain gift tax exclusions.[110]

Here is an example. In 1994, you create a $2 million sprinkling trust for your children and grandchildren, allocating $500,000 of your GST Exemption to the transfer. The numerator of the Applicable Fraction is $500,000 (the GST Exemption amount), and the denominator is $2 million (the value of the property transferred). The Applicable Fraction is $500,000/$2 million or 1/4. Thus, the Inclusion Ratio is 3/4 (1 minus 1/4). The rate at which the GST is taxed is 50% x 3/4 or 37.5%. If there is a Taxable Termination or Distribution of $2 million, the tax imposed on the transfer is $750,000 ($2 million x 37.5%).

Viewed from another angle, a gift of $100,000 to a grandchild costs $400,000 when you account for all the taxes:

Funds needed to fund gift		$400,000
Less:		
Federal estate tax	$200,000	
on trust transfer		
GST tax	100,000	
Total		<300,000>
Amount distributed to grandchild		$100,000

The GST tax can spell destruction for the unwary. If these circumstances are in any way relevant to yours, secure the best advice you can find; you cannot afford to be wrong.

The Qualified Domestic Trust. If married, one of your most useful tools for deferring the federal estate tax is the unlimited marital deduction. But if either you or your spouse is not a US citizen, you could lose that tool.[111] The US abounds in resident aliens, so the need to plan around this problem is widespread.

• **The New Law.** The tax base for computing estate tax is the value of all of the decedent's property at the date of death.[112] Similar to income taxation, the estate tax base is reduced by allowable deductions.[113] In 1981, the marital deduction became unlimited, permitting full tax deferral if the decedent leaves all the property to the surviving spouse.[114] The property acquired by the surviving spouse is eventually included in the estate of that spouse.

If the surviving spouse is not a US citizen, however, the marital deduction is denied.[115] Congress' concern[116] is that the surviving spouse will return to the country of citizenship after the decedent spouse dies. The surviving spouse may thereby avoid the deferred tax by converting the decedent's property to non-US property.[117]

Although the logic is appealing, I doubt that this scheme is common enough to be abusive. The new law is unlikely to increase revenues since the estate tax is not a big US revenue source anyway.[118]

- **Persons subject to the law.** Oddly enough, non-citizens are not subject to the rule. Rather those **married** to a noncitizen must undertake some planning to avoid the restrictions. Remember, the law disallows the deduction to the estate of the **decedent** who transfers property to a noncitizen spouse. For practical purposes, however, the surviving spouse suffers the consequences of receiving the decedent spouse's estate only after a large estate tax is paid.

Thus, both of you should arrange your affairs to avoid the restrictions if either is a noncitizen. A green card, or other form of permanent residency, does not help. Similarly, no credit is given if you have lived in this country and paid taxes for years. Legally avoiding this unnecessary tax is achieved only by arranging your affairs to fall within one of the exceptions to the rule.

- **The Exceptions.** The easiest way to avoid the restrictions is to become a US citizen. If the recipient spouse becomes a citizen by the time the decedent's estate tax return is due, the marital deduction is allowed.[119]

A person who was not born in the US or to US parents acquires citizenship by applying for naturalization with the Immigration and Naturalization Service at the Department of Justice.[120] To qualify for naturalization, an individual must be a US resident for five years and show "good moral character."[121]

Many countries require a person to renounce their original citizenship if the person adopts the citizenship of another country. Before applying for US citizenship, see if dual citizenship is permissible under the laws of your home country or under any applicable treaty with the US.

• **The Qualified Domestic Trust.** If obtaining United States citizenship is undesirable, or if ineligible for citizenship, the marital deduction may be preserved only if the decedent transfers the estate to a Qualified Domestic Trust.[122] ("QDT") The noncitizen surviving spouse may be the beneficiary as long as the trust document contains four terms:[123] (1) the trustee must be a US citizen or a domestic corporation, (2) all trust income must be payable to the surviving spouse annually or at more frequent intervals, (3) the trust must meet the requirements of IRS regulations, and (4) the executor must make the proper election on the estate tax return.

In addition, the QDT must meet the requirements for the marital deduction if disallowance is to be avoided.[124] Thus, a transfer of a life estate to a spouse must satisfy the Qualified Terminable Interest Property rules if the martial deduction is to be allowed.[125]

If a trustee of a QDT distributes more than trust income to the noncitizen surviving spouse, the transfer of principal is taxed in a particular manner. First, the amount of principal distributed is added to the decedent spouse's estate and the estate tax is recomputed. The QDT tax is then measured by the difference between the amount of tax as recomputed less the estate tax paid on the death of the first spouse to die.[126] Confusing? Confusing enough to avoid, if possible.

• **Jointly Held Property.** Generally, the value of the surviving spouse's share of jointly held property is excluded from the gross estate of the decedent spouse.[127] Under the new rules, the entire value of the property is included in the decedent's gross estate if the surviving tenant is an alien spouse.[128] The marital deduction can be salvaged if the property which passes from the decedent to the noncitizen spouse is either transferred or irrevocably assigned to a QDT before the decedent's tax return is filed.[129] Nonetheless, considering loss of the stepped-up basis available for community property,[130] holding property as joint tenants may be impractical for international couples.

• **Lifetime Gifts.** A gift tax is imposed on transfers of property that exceed $10,000 per donee, per year.[131] The unlimited marital deduction generally permits a tax-free transfer of any amount of property to a spouse.[132] As of July 14, 1988, the marital deduction is denied for gifts between spouses if the recipient spouse is not a US citizen, but the amount of the annual exclusion in such circumstances is increased to $100,000.[133]

• **Conclusion.** Whether the cost of avoiding the QDT requirements will be less than the potential tax consequences depends on the circumstances of each couple. International couples without an estate plan should consider some planning if they own a home, hold good jobs, and own some life insurance. Ordinarily, any couple with an estate in the range of $600,000 to $1.2 million is able to avoid entirely the estate tax by using the marital deduction and taking full advantage of the unified transfer tax credit.

An international couple who arranged their estate before 1989 should review the estate plan. In plans that use a living trust, the surviving spouse is often named the sole trustee upon the death of the first spouse; that could result in an otherwise avoidable estate tax. This defect is easily cured by making transfers to the marital deduction trust conditioned upon the surviving spouse obtaining citizenship before the due date for the return. In the alternative, the transfer must be made to a QDT and the essential terms should be provided in the amendment to the trust.

If you have combined asset protection planning and estate planning, you should review those as well, since asset protection planning involves the use of a foreign bank as trustee; that violates a key requirement of the QDT. You should amend your plan so that a US trustee succeeds the foreign bank upon the death of the spouse who is seeking protection.

The new law is not widely known; that makes it a trap for the unwary. Do not let yourself be caught unaware if the law applies to you.

The Special Needs Trust. The widespread abuse of alcohol and drugs in modern society is producing increasing numbers of disabled persons, both adults and children. If you have a child among them, you must consider the special needs trust. It may be either incorporated into your family trust or established separately.

Two needs drive the design of the Special Needs Trust: the need for competent asset management, and the need to preserve qualification of the child for state and federal medical and mental health programs. Its most popular use today is in meeting the needs of disabled adults requiring long-term nursing home care (available under Medicaid but not under Medicare), but it serves your purpose just as well.

The objective in drafting the Special Needs Trust is to avoid it being "deemed available" to your child under the eligibility requirements of various state and federal programs, particularly Medicaid; if not "available," it is not a resource considered in determined eligibility.

The state agencies administering Medicaid and mental health programs may bring an action against the trustee to force the exercise of its discretion to distribute funds to or for the benefit of your child, if the trust language commits the trustee to pay for support needs. If the government is successful in that effort, the trust estate held for the benefit of your child will be exhausted before the government is required to pay anything. The purpose of the Special Needs Trust is to permit the child to enjoy the best opportunities and standard of living possible under the circumstances. That cannot be provided if the trust is consumed by the costs of special care.

A substantial body of case law on Special Needs Trusts now exists, as attorneys work to develop trust language that will withstand judicial scrutiny. The trend of legislative policy, however, is to remove artificial means of protecting assets in this arena. Accordingly, such trusts must be crafted with great care.

In order to make clear the distinguishing features of the Special Needs Trust, let us compare it with its cousin, the support trust. It is characterization of our Special Needs Trust as a support trust that we fervently wish to avoid. As its name implies, the support trust is intended to pay for the care, support and maintenance needs of the beneficiary. The trustee of the support trust is directed to accumulate the income of the trust and to distribute from the common fund such amounts as the trustee deems necessary to meet the reasonable support needs of the beneficiary, taking into consideration the beneficiary's accustomed standard of living and income from other sources.

The difference between the support trust and the Special Needs Trust is the extent of the discretion given the trustee in making distributions. Under the Special Needs Trust, the trustee shares that discretion with no one, and is expressly prohibited from making such distributions if and to the extent the needs can be satisfied from other sources, specifically referencing state and federal medical and mental health programs. Some such trusts (including mine) go one step further and give the trustee the power to terminate the trust and distribute to persons other than the beneficiary if a court ever determines that it is "available" in the manner contemplated by such programs for eligibility determination; the objective is to chill the desire of the program administrators to force distributions.

You may wish to establish a separate Special Needs Trust for a disabled child during your lifetime, leaving that child out of the family trust. In the alternative, you may incorporate the Special Needs Trust provisions into your family trust to govern only the share ultimately established for the disabled child. Your other children will ordinarily be named remainder beneficiaries of the share held for the disabled child. If established as a separate living trust, you and your spouse may take back the property if you survive the child or otherwise cause it to go to the other children.

If established separately during your lifetime, the Special Needs Trust may be either revocable or irrevocable. If revocable, no gift tax issues are presented, since the gift is not complete until you give up "all dominion and control" over the property.[134] You will, of course, provide for the trust to become irrevocable upon the death of either you or your spouse, or that of both you and your spouse, depending upon the desired control and estate tax result. If you make the trust irrevocable, but provide for the property to come back to you if you survive the child, the trust will be included in your gross estate for federal estate tax purposes if the survival probability exceeds 5%.[135] If you wish to remove the gift from your taxable estate, then make the trust irrevocable, have the remainder interest go to the other children and use an independent trustee. You should avoid serving as trustee because the powers given that person permit skewing of benefits between the child and siblings; that may cause the remaining trust estate to be included in your gross estate for federal estate tax purposes.[136]

The Special Needs Trust is a powerful tool in meeting with precision and fairness the needs of disabled persons.

Endnotes

1. IRC Sec. 212

2. IRC Sec. 262; see also *Estate of Helen S. Pennel* (1926) 4 BTA 1039

3. *Sidney Marians* (1973) 60 TC 187, ACQ, 1973-2 CB 2, supporting 20% of fee for estate planning services and 80% as deductible portion of fee attributable to tax advice.

4. Although Louisiana is more affected by French law than the Spanish law from which community concepts are derived.

5. California Probate Code, Secs. 901.910

6. California Probate Code, Secs. 902.910

7. IRC Sec. 101(a)(2)

8. Reg 25.2511-11(h)(8)

9. *Guggenheim vs. Rasquin* (1941) 312 US 254

10. Reg 25.2512-6

11. *ibid*

12. Rev Rul 76-490

13. *Goodman vs. Commissioner* 156 F2d 218

14. IRC Sec. 2513

15. Reg 25.2503-2; *Commissioner vs. Bowing* 123 F2d 86

16. 9th Cir (1968) 397 F2d 82

17. IRC Sec. 2041(b)(2)

18. *De minimis non curat lex.* "The law does not concern itself with trifles."

19. IRC Sec. 2514(e)

20. IRC Sec. 2041(b)(2); see also Reg 20.2041-3(d)(3)

21. Reg 20.2041-3(d)(5)

22. IRS Ltr Rul 8727003

23. 8901004, issued Sept. 16, 1988

24. *Commissioner vs. Procter* 142 F2d 824 (4th Cir 1944)

25. Paraphrased from *Crummey Rules Have Changed,* Journal of the American Society of CLU & ChFC, Sept. 1989, Vol. XLIII, No. 5, p. 37, by Edward H. Stone, JD. This example is predicated on the assumption that the power holder is the only beneficiary to whom the trustee may pay income or principal, and has a limited power of appointment over the trust estate.

26. IRC Sec. 2042; Reg 20.2042-1(c)(4); *Farwell vs. US*, 243 F2d 373; *In re Rhodes*, 174 F2d 548; *Seward's Estate vs. Commissioner*, 164 F2d 434

27. *Estate of Lumpkin vs. Commissioner*, 474 F2d 1092 (5th Cir 1973)

28. *Estate of Connelly vs. US*, 551 F2d 545 (3d Cir 1977)

29. Rev Rul 69-54, 1969-1 CB 221; see also Rev Rul 72-307, 1972-1 CB 307

30. IRC Sec. 2036(a)(1)

31. IRC Sec. 2042; Reg 20.2042-1(b)(1); *Mathilde B. Hooper*, 41 BTA 114; *Pacific National Bank of Seattle (Morgan Hill)*, 40 BTA 128; *Estate of Rohnert*, 40 BTA 1319; *Estate of Logan*, 23 BTA 236

32. *Estate of Charles H. Wade*, 47 BTA 21; *Old Colony Trust Company (Flye's Estate)*, 37 BTA 871, acq.

33. IRC Sec. 2035

34. *ibid*

35. *Bel vs. US*, 452 F2d 683 (5th Cir 1971), cert. denied, 406 US 919; *Detroit Bank & Trust Co. vs. US*, 469 F2d 964 (6th Cir 1972), cert. den., 410 F2d 929 (1973); *First National Bank of Oregon vs. US*, 488 F2d 575 (9th Cir 1973)

36. Rev Rul 71-497, 1971-2 CB 329

37. *Estate of Leder vs. Commissioner*, 89 TC 235 (1987) and *Estate of Headrick vs. Commissioner*, 93 TC 171 (1989); see also *Estate of Chapman vs. Commissioner*, TCM 105 (1989)

38. *Estate of Headrick, ibid*

39. *ibid* at p. 180

40. Rev Rul 81-7, 1981-1 CB 474; 83-108, 1983-2 CB 167; Ltr Ruls 7947006, 8007080, 8014078, 8433024, 8701007; Rev Rul 73-405, 1973-2 CB 321

41. Rev Rul 69-102, 1969-1 CB 32

42. IRC Sec. 677(a)(3); Reg 1.677(a)-1; *Burnet vs. Wells*, 289 US 670

43. *Arthur Stockstrom*, 3 TC 664

44. *Heffelfinger vs. Commissioner*, 87 F2d 991

45. *Reick vs. Commissioner*, 118 F2d 110

46. 41 BTA 111

47. IRC Sec. 264(a)(3)

48. IRC 264(c)

49. Rev Rul 71-309, 1971-2 CB 168

50. Reg 1.264-4(d)(2)

51. Reg 1.264-4(d)(3)

52. Reg 1.264-4(d)(4); *American Body & Equipment Company vs. US*, 751 US 87 (5th Cir 1975)

53. IRC Sec. 163(h)(1)

54. IRC Sec. 2056(b)(7)(B)

55. IRC Sec. 6161(a)(2)

56. IRC Sec. 6166

57. That dilemma is addressed by Congress in IRC Sec. 2032A.

58. IRC Sec. 1014

59. IRC Sec. 2523

60. IRC Sec. 2503

61. IRC Sec. 101(a)(2)

62. IRC Sec. 2035

63. *Estate of John G. Boykin*, TCM 1987-134

64. The Revenue Act of 1987

65. The Technical and Miscellaneous Revenue Act of 1988; Advance Notice 89-99, IRB 1989-38, 4

66. IRC Sec. 2036(c)(3)(C)

67. IRC Sec. 170(b)

68. IRC Sec. 170(d)

69. *Broderick vs. Gore*, 224 F2d 892; *May vs. McGowan*, 194 F2d 396; *Lomb vs. Sugden*, 82 F2d 166; *Wilson vs. Bowers*, 57 F2d 682; *Salt*, 17 CT 92

70. *Wilson vs. Bowers, supra*

71. *Third National Bank vs. US*, 64 F Supp 198; *Weil*, 22 TC 1267; *Reicher*, 3 TCM 1294; *Mitchell*, 37 BTA 1; *Newman*, 31 BTA 772

72. TCM 1986-519, AU 85-5

73. In California, for example, Corporations Code, Sec. 500

74. IRC Secs. 302 or 303

75. IRC Sec. 1014

76. IRC Sec. 303

77. IRC Sec. 302

78. IRC Sec. 318

79. The alternative minimum tax provisions of the code and regulations contain no specific reference to life insurance. This conclusion is based on the book and tax income differences caused by the income tax exclusion for death proceeds. The Temporary Regulations under 1.56-OT and 1.56-1T relate to the corporate book income issue.

80. IRC Ch 13

81. IRC Sec. 2613(a)

82. IRC Sec. 2613(b)

83. IRC Sec. 2613(c)

84. IRC Sec. 2612(c)

85. IRC Secs. 2612(c)(1), 2641(c)(1)

86. IRC Sec. 2612(c)(2)

87. IRC Sec. 2612(a)

88. IRC Sec. 2612(b)

89. IRC Sec. 2503(e)

90. IRC Sec. 2611(b)(2)

91. IRC Sec. 2611(b)(1)

92. IRC Sec. 2612

93. IRC Sec. 2653(a)

94. IRC Sec. 2604

95. IRC Sec. 2623

96. IRC Sec. 2603(a)(2)(3)

97. IRC Sec. 2515

98. IRC Sec. 2622

99. IRC Sec. 2603(a)(2)

100. IRC Sec. 2621

101. IRC Sec. 2603(a)(1)

102. IRC Sec. 2641

103. IRC Sec. 2001(c)

104. IRC Sec. 2631(a)

105. IRC Sec. 3652(a)(3)

106. IRC Sec. 2631(b), (c)

107. IRC Sec. 2642(a)

108. IRC Sec. 2642(a)(2)(A)

109. IRC Sec. 2642(a)(2)(B)
110. IRC Sec. 2642(c)(2)(A), referring to exclusions at Sec. 2503(b) and (c)
111. IRC Sec. 2056(d)
112. IRC Sec. 2031. Taxable property includes property that is real or personal, tangible or intangible, wherever situated.
113. IRC Secs. 2051-2057
114. IRC Sec. 2056(a)
115. IRC Sec. 2056(d) became effective October 11, 1988.
116. The legislative history is silent as to what factors prompted it to restrict the marital deduction.
117. The estate of a resident includes worldwide property. Nonresidents are subject to estate tax only on property located in the US. (IRC Sec. 2103)
118. Because of the large unified transfer tax credit, only a small percentage of estates are subject to tax.
119. IRC Sec. 2056(d)(4). The surviving spouse must remain a US resident at all times after the decedent's death and before becoming a citizen.
120. US Constitution, Article 1, Sec. 8, Cl. 4
121. 8 USC Sec. 1427
122. IRC Sec. 2056(d)(2)(A)
123. IRC Sec. 2056(a)
124. The newly-enacted rules do not specifically so provide, but common sense dictates as much.
125. IRC Sec. 2056(b)(7)
126. IRC Sec. 2056A(b)(2)
127. IRC Sec. 2040(b)
128. IRC Sec. 2040(b) is inapplicable if the surviving spouse is not a US citizen. (IRC Sec.(d)(1)(B)
129. IRC Sec. 2056(d)(2)(B). This special rule was amended to apply to both probate and nonprobate property.
130. IRC Sec. 1014(b)(6)
131. IRC Secs. 2501, 2503(h)
132. IRC Sec. 2523
133. IRC Sec. 2523(i). In addition, the previously-repealed provisions relating to holding real and personal property in tenancy by the entirety are made applicable to such transfers. (IRC Secs. 2515, 2515A as repealed in 1981 by ERTA.)

134. IRC Sec. 2038; Reg 25.2511(b)
135. IRC Sec. 2037(a)(2)
136. IRC Sec. 2036(a)(2)

Chapter 3

The Artful Use of Offshore Tax Havens

Summary. *One purpose of this chapter is to present a principled argument for global investment diversification. In order to physically hold title to offshore investments, trusts and controlled foreign corporations domiciled in tax havens provide the greatest utility. Tax havens may serve as tax shelters, but they are not always the same. People really invest outside the United States, in very large numbers. Among the reasons for going offshore with part of your holdings are risk diversification, investment opportunities, privacy, relief from domestic economic chaos, relief from overregulation, and protection of assets from divorce, family disputes and lawsuits. One more reason is to prepare for a dignified, low-cost retirement abroad. Right now, moving funds offshore is still legal, but that may not last long. Act now!*

The odds of getting away with tax evasion are pretty good, but can you afford the price if you become a statistic?

Fraudulent transfer claims may arise from the timing and manner of your movement of funds offshore.

If you choose a tax haven bank that maintains one or more

offices in the US, you may open your account in person without leaving the country, or you may do so by mail or by traveling to the haven. If the bank does not maintain US offices, you are left with the second and third options. The types of accounts are similar to those with which we are familiar, except for generally lower rates of interest and less liquidity. Major Swiss banks are much like those here in the US. The amount you place offshore is dictated primarily by your reasons for doing so. Reporting requirements include declaring amounts over $10,000 when entering the US, declaring financial accounts, trusts and stock in foreign corporations on your tax returns and transaction reports by your bank.

The trust most useful for the purposes here considered will be established in a common law jurisdiction, will be for the benefit of you and your family and will be subject to your right to change or cancel it at your pleasure. You will use it to purchase and hold title to investments in various foreign countries, wherever attractive opportunities are present. You can do it without a lawyer, but not well and not safely. In selecting a tax haven, consider political stability, cost, secrecy practices, the legal system, the primary language, communication facilities and the quality of local services.

Your trust is operated, in terms of transferring funds in and out, much like a foreign bank account. Reporting foreign grantor trust income is, apart from Schedule B disclosure and annual information return Form 3520A, simply a matter of adding it to your personal tax return in the same manner as if US-source income.

To invest offshore through a controlled, foreign corporation requires that you conduct an active business enterprise through it; otherwise, the tax burdens eliminate the benefits. Among those active offshore business enterprises that will lead to nontaxation of corporate income are sales companies doing business only with "unrelated persons," those manufacturing or assembling offshore (even where material is purchased from a "related person") and sold into foreign markets to "unrelated persons," offshore service companies (construction supervision, engineering, consulting, etc.) operating without "substantial assistance" from the US "related person," captive insurance companies insuring foreign risks, private merchant banks and Foreign Sales Corporations.

Privacy needs or the desire for simplicity in your affairs may dictate investment in those property forms not required to be reported to the US Government, rather than through a foreign trust or corporation. Such investment properties include: foreign bank or securities accounts with aggregate values less than $10,000; precious metals and stones stored in safe deposit boxes; Canadian, British or Swiss equity-based life insurance and annuity policies; and offshore public securities purchased through a US broker. Bank reporting may be avoided by means of periodic trips to Mexico or Canada and wiring funds from those countries.

If you invest offshore, either limit the investments to a business with which you have a history of success, or hire an expert.

Section 3.1 Why Invest Outside the US?

While researching for this book, I found dozens of reasons advanced by others for investing offshore—reasons that range from the legal and logical to the illegal and inane. This chapter serves as a conceptual and substantive guide in considering and acting upon utterly legal methods of offshore investment and business activities. You will find a discussion of tax haven abuse, but the purpose in doing so is to variously define for you the limits of legality or to put you on notice of the swindles to which you may otherwise fall victim.

What is a "Tax Haven"? Definitions of a tax haven vary widely, but one broad enough to cover them all is a jurisdiction providing either low tax rates or no tax at all, usually with either banking or commercial secrecy. (The latter includes banking secrecy.) That definition places more than 80 countries around the world in the tax haven category.

It is important that you not confuse tax haven with tax shelter. Under certain circumstances, you may combine the two, but they are separate and distinct functions.

Do People Really Do It? The US Treasury Department is intensely interested in measuring the extent to which US taxpayers actually conduct business offshore. Their interest, of course, is to quantify the levels of tax evasion and other forms of criminal activity. Unfortunately, the bank and commercial secrecy characteristics of tax havens render accuracy an impossible task. It is clear from available data, however, that as recently as 1982, deposits of nonresidents in Caribbean banks (both domestic and foreign branches) exceeded $465 billion, up from $175 billion four years earlier.[1]

A Litany of Reasons. The reasons for diversifying your holdings geographically range from the desire to exploit investment opportunities globally to the imminent threat of major economic dislocations at home.

Let's examine the more prosaic reasons for diversifying part of your holdings offshore:

• **Diversification.** Risk is reduced by diversification, usually geographically, by industry, by number of issues and by properties. Inevitably, a certain number of your investments prove unsuccessful, but if your holdings are diversified, those losses should be more than offset by your successes. It is for that reason that small investors purchase mutual funds and the *Employee Retirement Income Security Act of 1974* ("ERISA") imposes the duty of diversification as a standard of care on pension plan managers. ERISA, by expressly requiring diversification, effectively imposes liability for negligence on plan managers who fail to diversify and are unlucky enough to lose money because of it.

You may consider foreign investments risky, but the opposite is more true. Risk reduction is the reason for international diversification: it spreads risk across several markets to limit political and economic exposure; it insulates you from unfavorable economic conditions at home; and historical comparisons between global and US portfolios demonstrate that it decreases risk by more than 50%.[2]

Performance may be superior, as well. During the 1980s, US markets averaged consolidated returns of 13.9% while France was

15.6%, Britain was 18%, Hong Kong was 19.7% and Japan was 26.5%.[3] The US economy is now in difficult straits, leaving most major markets of the world growing at a faster pace. This is likely to continue, and perhaps accelerate.

International diversification enables you to protect against a decline in the dollar's exchange rate, even to profit from it. When Britain conceded its "monetary sovereignty" (read "option to influence its economies through inflation") by entry into the Common Market's Exchange Rate Mechanism ("ERM") October 5, 1990, the last block fell into place for an integrated European economy. The US economy is still the larger, but prospects for the ERM block appear brighter. ERM is solidly based on the deutsche mark, providing it with a strong, stable monetary system, unlike the US which is still wallowing in soft money. Consolidation of the nine ERM nations' currency will insulate it from exported US inflation, leading to the conclusion that the dollar will continue its exchange rate decline against the major European currencies throughout at least the mid-1990s.

While rapid growth in foreign markets since 1980 brought dramatic profit opportunities, it also reduced the role of the US market on the world stage. At the end of 1987, the US share of world stock market capitalization was only 31%, down from 66% in 1970, and bonds denominated in US dollars represented only 51.5% of all outstanding world bonds.[4] Restricting your selection of securities to the US markets alone eliminates 50% to 70% of the opportunities.

While you may invest internationally through American Depositary Receipts, specialty mutual funds and single-country "closed-end" funds, the services of your own portfolio manager through a tax haven trust is more flexible, lower in cost and likely to produce better results.

• **Privacy.** Privacy is a relative thing. As in most aspects of life (religion, politics, family, beauty, art) it is of little consequence to some, but an end in itself for others. Most of us fall somewhere between.

Test your true level of concern for your privacy by reviewing the information in this section. If you decide it is more important than you first believed, take comfort in the fact that a high degree of confidentiality for your personal and financial affairs is possible through the judicious use of offshore strategies and otherwise being aware of your rights.

In an earlier day, privacy was sought and respected, and few intrusive institutions existed. That is no longer true.

Heightened concern by the US government about the drug trade led to stiff new regulations under the *Bank Secrecy Act of 1988*. Under it your bank must verify and record your identity any time you purchase cashier's checks, traveler's checks or money orders for $3,000 or more in cash. The record includes your account number, your name, identifying records (driver's license, etc.) and details of the transaction.

The government's use of this and other such data reflects less and less concern for your privacy. Under the *Right to Privacy Act of 1978*, federal agencies cannot exchange your bank information with each other without prior notice to you and opportunity for you to object. There is an exception to this law for suspected drug dealers who are referred to the US Justice Department for prosecution.[5] Additional inroads are being sought in order to assist the Financial Crimes Enforcement Network in its investigation and prosecution of financial crimes. The stance of the government is that the notice requirement is "cumbersome and does not serve any legitimate privacy interest."[6] Permitting such incursions would, of course, aid materially in efficiently organizing a case for prosecution before the guilty target knows enough to hide evidence. Consider, however, that free access by each federal agency may lead to the information being sought without concern for your right to constitutional due process, including probable cause. "This is the electronic equivalent of a general search."[7]

As to foreign banking privacy, a 1988 case is particularly disturbing.[8] There, the US Supreme Court affirmed a 5th Circuit opinion holding that a US resident there under investigation for tax evasion may be compelled to "consent" to the disclosure of foreign bank records. The US Treasury Department knows few limits when pursuing tax haven records. It has arranged for the seduction of a foreign banker travelling in the US, using the moment of reverie to purloin documents from his briefcase, documents which led to numerous US taxpayer investigations.[9] It has sought production of bank records from the US branches of foreign banks and financial sanctions for the banks' refusal to produce them, notwithstanding the fact that doing so would subject bank personnel to criminal penalties in the tax haven country.[10]

Credit-reporting agencies are less abusive than was the case before passage of the federal *Fair Credit Reporting Act.* Now, if your credit application is denied because of a credit report, the organization must tell you so and provide the name and address of the credit-reporting agency involved, along with the derogatory material on which the credit decision was based. On written demand, the credit reporting agency must disclose to you the content of your credit file. If you find it incomplete or inaccurate, you are entitled to either have it corrected or have your own explanatory statement included in their file, to be provided along with all other credit information to those subscribers of the agency requesting it. In addition, the credit-reporting agency must provide a corrected or supplemental report to every subscriber who requested and received the uncorrected or unexplained report.

Life insurance companies support and utilize an organization called the Medical Information Bureau. It serves the same purpose for underwriting policies that credit-reporting agencies do for organizations granting credit, and is almost as susceptible to error.

All in all, information may be collected on you from dozens of sources:

- Driver's license
- Motor vehicle licenses and registrations
- Professional licenses
- Social Security
- Welfare payments
- Tax returns
- Medical histories
- School records
- Unemployment compensation
- Birth, marriage and death certificates
- Military and veterans' benefits

- Law enforcement organization records
- Court records
- Deeds
- Recorded contracts and powers of attorney
- Passports
- Census records
- Insurance companies
- Employment agencies
- Doctors
- Credit bureaus
- Banks and financial institutions
- Brokerage houses and investment funds
- Various service companies with which you do business
- Clubs and organizations to which you now or have in the past belonged

There is no way to avoid having records made of your life. But since you are usually the one providing the information, it is within your power to limit its effect.

- **Protection from Economic Chaos.** As a general proposition, the road to riches is travelled by avoiding loss, not speculation against long odds. We avoid commodities and bear markets. A troubled economy is a bear market in macrocosm. When deprived of economic predictability, we must seek more secure shores.

Economic turmoil is nothing new to this century, nor to the US. We, though, have assumed since World War II that the US economic engine is so powerful no adversity can long restrain it. Look again.

The enormous and chronic budget and trade deficits of the US are sapping the vitality of its economic engine, and no saviour is in sight. In 1985, the US joined the ranks of the world's debtor nations, owing foreigners more than they owe us for the first time in 70 years.

Several consequences flow from being a debtor nation. One is that dividend and interest payments leaving the country may exceed those received. As long as foreign investors reinvest their receipts here, our domestic living standards will not suffer in the near term. But if they decide to repatriate that income, it reduces our living standards. A debtor nation must also devote an increasing part of its economic output to its foreign obligations leading, in the case of the US, to the need for trade surpluses in order to service our external debts. That is difficult to accomplish when you realize that trade deficits helped put us in this position in the first place.

In 1989, it happened; investment earnings sent from the US to foreign investors exceeded the foreign investment earnings of US investors for the first time since the 1950s. Do you want to wait and pray? Or do you want to anticipate the natural consequences and protect yourself?

As a debtor nation, we are more dependent on foreign investors to finance our budget deficits by purchasing US government bonds. If they decide to withdraw those funds, we will face entirely new problems. For example, the dollar exchange rate will drop dramatically. That may encourage export-oriented US business owners, but 15% (and growing) of US businesses are now owned by foreigners. It will also raise interest rates if the US Federal Reserve Bank (as might be expected) steps in to soften the effect. That, in turn, could produce a recession. Higher interest rates could just as easily come about from foreign investors shifting new investment attention to other countries, even without withdrawing funds from the US. If that happens, the US government must either eliminate its deficits or turn to domestic credit markets, putting upward pressure on interest rates.

In 1990, it happened; foreign new investment in the US dropped 72% and US investments abroad increased 16%, both against 1989 figures. Consistent with the economic consequences described above, this contributed to the dollar's decline against the major currencies of the world; it dropped 20% against the mark, 18% against the pound and 14% against the yen. This represents an acceleration of the 50% overall erosion between 1985 and 1990.

Can we depend on statesmanlike leadership from Washington? From 1980 to 1990, federal tax revenue grew 8% annually, US government spending grew 11% annually, the federal deficit accelerated past $3 trillion and Congress looks only at "soak the rich" tax increases to bring our fiscal problems under control. Consid-

ering that a 100% tax on all untaxed 1990 personal incomes above
$100,000 per year would operate the federal government for only
19 days, that 90% of all taxable income is in brackets of $45,000
or less and that Congress shows little concern for eliminating the
massive US government waste found by The Grace Commission,
we can reasonably assume that Congress is more concerned with
pursuing special interest agenda than with statesmanlike action.

The US is in relative decline as a global economic power. The
social fabric of America is deteriorating hand-in-hand with living
standards for most of the population. Unless you are in a position
to take control of Congress, your only real option is to protect
yourself as best you can. To preserve and enhance our economic
security and that of our children requires that we loose the shackles
of conventional wisdom and consider opportunities beyond our
shores.

  • **To Gain Regulatory Relief.** A developed country, almost
by definition, maintains a regulatory system that in view of the
regulator, deters abuse and fraud, while in the view of the regulated
is regarded as an expensive strait jacket on creative business
operations.

In his empirical study of offshore financial centers,[11] R.A.
Johns calls regulatory systems "national economic friction struc-
tures," and the process of attracting operations to offshore centers
as "competitive frictioneering."

Congress uncritically acknowledges the process in a staff
report:

> "...The offshore financial market has many advantages for
> rational economic operations. The Euromarket efficiently
> serves national governments, semi-public agencies, private
> corporations and individuals. The reasonable expectation,
> when one learns that an entity is engaged in offshore, is that it
> is there for honest economic reasons, buttressed by whatever
> advantages privacy holds. The major categories for offshore
> use are to profit from higher interest rates when lending, to
> enjoy lower interest rates when borrowing, to escape taxation,
> to enjoy greater business flexibility by avoiding regulation in

an efficient market, to enjoy the protections of confidentiality when engaged in activities, which if known to others in advance might hazard business success or profit margins, and, through the confidentiality mechanisms, to hedge and enjoy other risk-allaying methods through offshore diversification, liquidity, forward speculations and the like."[12]

The US serves as a classic example of rational, but intense regulation. Here, a commercial bank, for instance, is responsible to most of the governmental agencies listed below, in addition to a long line of industry-specific laws:

- A state banking commission (if state chartered).
- The Federal Deposit Insurance Corporation.
- The Federal Reserve Board.
- The Comptroller of the Currency.
- The Securities Exchange Commission.
- The Fair Trade Commission.
- The Equal Employment Opportunity Commission.

The nature and scope of regulation in general and US regulation in particular intensified in the early sixties, while a need developed in all the advanced economies and especially in the US for the geographical extension of regulatory activities to match the growth and influence of multinational corporations. That trend was key to the early development of offshore financial centers. US banks responded by expanding their branch operations, while European banks, except for the British, preferred to do so by consortia; the preference for consortia rose primarily from the fact that the European banks had far fewer multinational corporations as customers, and secondarily from the fact that it more comfortably fitted the syndicated Euroloan market. Eurocurrency business and syndicated international loans were attracted to both traditional tax havens (Luxembourg and Switzerland) and to certain of the island states; many of the latter were newly independent and actively seeking development opportunities. Subsequent to the 1973 oil crisis, certain of those island states were ideally located to benefit from the huge tide of petro dollars flowing from the OPEC-member countries, resulting in a significant shift throughout that decade in syndicated Eurocurrency bank credits. More recently, the tax havens of Latin America and the Far East have made their presence felt in a major way.

During the seventies, the Eurocurrency markets emerged, international wealth shifted and political independence spread to former colonial areas, leading to a network of offshore financial centers and to the transformation of many into major players. US regulatory and monetary pressures in the sixties (and to a lesser extent from other advanced countries) created a need for regulatory relief in international business and banking. Tax havens were ready and anxious to compete seriously with each other to meet that need. They provided little or no regulation, imposed little or no taxes, little or no production conditions and a generally permissive business attitude.

Given geographical proximity to onshore capital markets and the time zone implications for communications, four primary regions of activity developed: the Caribbean area and Central America for serving North and South America; European enclave countries and island states for the European markets; the Gulf area for the Middle East; and Hong Kong for the Asian-Pacific region.

Within each region, continued business activities depend on the active cooperation (or at least the continued tolerance) of the regional capital markets being served. That continues to be the case.

In each region, at least one tax haven dominates: Cayman, Switzerland, Bahrain and Hong Kong. Around each such dominant haven is a cluster of second-level financial centers, both regionally and inter-regionally. The main secondary havens for the Caribbean and Central American area are Bermuda, the Bahamas and the Netherlands Antilles; those for the European region are Luxembourg, Liechtenstein, the Isle of Man, Jersey and Guernsey; those for the Middle East are the United Arab Emirates; and in the Far East, Singapore and Vanuatu (formerly the New Hebrides). A few havens may yet emerge as strong players; they include Barbados and the Turks and Caicos Islands. On the periphery, but still contributing are Andorra, Anguilla, Gibraltar, Monaco, Nauru, Puerto Rico, St. Vincent, Montserrat, the Phillipines and the Virgin

Islands (both British and American). Additional centers that may develop in the decade to come include Mexico, Cypress, Campione, Costa Rica, Tunisia, Egypt, Malta and Jordan.

• **Various Personal Reasons.** Reasons for diversifying which should be mentioned, but on which reasonable people may differ from an ethical perspective, include protection from losses related to divorce, family disputes and lawsuits.

Divorce actions ("marital termination proceedings," in more genteel states), often degenerate into all-out war. It does no good for one spouse to offer to divide the property equally and provide ample support if the other's objective is to destroy. It does no good for one to make the same offer if bent on secreting assets from the other spouse and the court so as to adopt a less wealthy posture for purposes of minimizing property division and support awards. Given such vindictive and irrational conduct (and believe me, it is routine in domestic relations law), you should be aware of the tools available, so at least so you can figure out how your spouse is using them.

Character strength is the willingness to act ethically and speak truthfully, even when done at personal sacrifice. In human beings, that characteristic ranges from nonexistent to the price of life itself. Unfortunately, even those with no character strength belong to a family. If you have one or more such persons in yours and the circumstances otherwise call for it, having funds offshore may avoid much grief.

Holding funds offshore places you in a relatively low-profile position financially. That, in turn, will often prove advantageous in settling lawsuits. Put yourself in the position of the plaintiff's attorney in a malpractice lawsuit against a doctor: the value of your client's claim exceeds the face amount of his professional liability policy by perhaps $300,000; so you order an asset investigation of the doctor; you find that he lives in a nice home with a large loan against it, has plenty of furnishings, two cars, a low five-figure aggregate bank balance, perhaps a pension plan and his medical practice. Not disclosed by the credit report is the money the doctor moved offshore into commercial property and securities. As plaintiff's attorney, you are simply evaluating your settlement options in the medical malpractice case, so you are unlikely to probe too deeply. Grounds for punitive damages (gross negligence, fraud or malice) must be established through the litigation discovery process before plaintiff's counsel has the right to place the defendant under oath and inquire into his financial affairs. The doctor's home equity is mostly or fully covered by the homestead. Exemptions from the claims of judgment creditors cover the furnishings, the pension plan, a part of the savings and part of the value of one car. The medical practice has little market value without the active coop- eration of the doctor involved. Consequently, going to trial with its attendant delays, costs and risk of loss in order to seek a judgment that exceeds the policy limits by $300,000, when the (apparent) assets available for satisfaction of that excess amount do not exceed $50,000, is not promising. As a prudent plaintiff's attorney, you will probably recommend that a settlement be sought for some figure at or within the policy limits, leaving the doctor with no material financial loss and no judgment against him.

• **A Dignified Low-Cost Retirement Abroad.** Retired American citizens face increasing demands on limited incomes for housing and medicine. There is, however, a remedy. A comfortable life-style on a limited budget may be achieved by living abroad. Hundreds of thousands of Americans live, and live well, in such diverse places as Costa Rica, Portugal, Mexico, Poland, Germany and Ireland.

The possibilities are virtually endless. In Appendix C at page 305, **Survey of the Major Havens,** you will find some information on those of the havens actively promoting themselves as retirement locations. More information may be obtained from the consulate of those countries in which you are interested. General information (which I do not warrant as entirely correct) may be gleaned from back issues of *International Living* magazine. Mail your inquiry to 824 East Baltimore Street, Baltimore, MD 21202.

• **Opportunity to Act.** The US is among only 20 industrial- ized countries with no exchange controls. Even though you must disclose whether you are bringing into the country more than $10,000, it is perfectly legal to do so. But the US has restricted or blocked the transfer of funds out of the country before, and the mechanism by which to reimpose such restrictions on a moment's notice remains in place. The mechanisms are your required currency declarations, the requirement that all banks operating in the US report any transfer out of the country in excess of $10,000, the requirement that the banks record cash purchases of negotiable instruments for $3,000 or more and the requirement that you disclose on your tax return all foreign financial accounts, trusts and corporate interests. Any number of circumstances could reintroduce such controls, including but not limited to something as simple (and likely) as a massive outflow of dollars to low-tax or low-inflation jurisdictions. The time to act is now.

Section 3.2 Evasion and Tax Haven Scams

Tax Evasion. Tax evasion is a national pastime in most of the industrialized nations of the world. The US is unique with respect to the level at which taxes are paid voluntarily, forthrightly and without widespread evasion. In recent decades, however, inflation moved a large part of the population steadily into higher income tax brackets, brackets found by the taxpayer to be burdensome at best. One of the results of increasing incomes is that skilled and semi-skilled workers improved their social and political self-perception as they came to enjoy job security, large suburban homes, two automobiles, long vacations, boats, motor homes, etc.; they begin to believe that the cost of huge social welfare programs, created at their behest and for their benefit in an earlier day, falls unfairly on their own shoulders today. Another result is the spreading notion that the IRS is a paper tiger, and that its ranks are spread too thin to permit effective policing. Statistically, the paper tiger notion is not far off target: clearly, most tax evaders are successful. That is small consolation, however, to the evading taxpayer who is caught. The consequences may be enormous in terms of financial penalties, loss of reputation and self-esteem. In considering some of the easy abuses of offshore investing, count the cost: ask if you can afford to be wrong.

Tax Haven Scams. When you purchase a new automobile, it is amazing how many of the same model you see on the highway. Similarly, once you broaden your horizons to contemplate worldwide opportunities, you will notice ads and direct mail solicitations for tax haven services, dual passports, mail drop services and 35% certificates of deposit in brass plate banks located in obscure island countries. Go slow. It takes a little time to mature as an international man or woman, and with maturity comes a healthy skepticism of such things. Fraudulent international investment scams cost Americans more than $1.1 billion in 1988-89, according to the North American Securities Administrators Association in a report prepared for the House Commerce, Consumer and Monetary Affairs Subcommittee. Most were operated by US promoters falsely claiming to be engaged in overseas investment programs in precious metals, currencies, bonds and banking instruments.

This discussion serves to acquaint you with the more common swindles operating through the tax havens:

• **Money Circle.** The US taxpayer conspires with a tax shelter promoter in a fraudulent "money circle" scheme in which a tax haven bank controlled by the promoter loans funds to the US taxpayer who adds funds of his own (which serve as the fee for the promoter) to purchase a commodity interest or to finance a deductible business expense. The commodity or expense is, in fact, nonexistent. To conceal the true nature of the transaction, a circle of entities controlled by the promoter simultaneously negotiates a series of checks. All entities maintain bank accounts at the same offshore bank. None of the accounts contains sufficient funds to cover the checks, but since all are negotiated on the same day, debits and credits through each account balance. With the money circle complete, the Promoter can produce documentation to corroborate substantial expenditures. For a modest fee, the US taxpayer has obtained a large and apparently legitimate business deduction.

• **Telemarketed Investments.** A high-pressure telephone salesperson calls, excitedly extolling the virtues of precious metals, currency speculation, bonds and "no-risk" certificates of deposit paying rates of 35% or more. The victim gets caught up in the story and sends money, only to eventually learn that the investment product (or bank) does not exist. Bogus offshore banks in the Pacific and Caribbean, and sales operations in Costa Rica and Panama are the major fraud centers. Special areas of concern are Nauru, Vanuatu, Tonga, Marshall Islands and the Northern Mariana Islands. Nauru allows people to establish banks by mail.

- **Advance Fee Scam.** The advance fee scam is old, but still effective in parting victims from their money. In its simplest form, the confidence person approaches someone who wishes to finance the purchase of property or a business, and either cannot qualify for conventional financing or prefers not to pay the market rate. The contact is usually through a small ad in a newspaper offering business loans, perhaps through an introduction. The "money broker" explains that he has money available, frequently from abroad, and that the lender must invest outside his own country due to political concerns. The rate is below market and the broker presents original correspondence showing that a bank or law firm stands ready to receive and disburse the loan funds as escrow agent. Names of bankers and lawyers are mentioned with familiarity, and business cards are displayed. However, a "Nondisclosure" or "Noncircumvention Agreement" must first be signed, and the funds cannot be sent until a broker's commission or some part of it is paid. Payment is made, and the victim proceeds with the purchase. At the closing, the loan funds do not arrive. The purchase cannot be completed, and neither the broker nor the lender can be found.

- **Another Advance Fee Scam.** A variation on the advance fee scam is one in which the broker makes collateral available, instead of loan funds. The idea is that the conventional lender will provide better terms if the loan is fully secured.

- **Still Another Advance Fee Scam.** A more sophisticated variation on the advance fee scam is the self-liquidating loan. Its superficial attraction can persuade even participating brokers that the proposal has merit. The loan pays for the collateral and liquidates itself. The broker only facilitates the transaction. Here are the usual elements: the victim is promised principal without a duty to repay; loan proceeds exceed the victim's borrowing needs; the lender makes a secured loan; a third party provides the collateral; the loan is interest-only for a term of 6 to 10 years; and the size of the transaction must be large enough to make the broker's advance fee worthwhile.

Here is how it might be sold. The victim needs $500,000. A domestic lender is asked to loan $900,000 interest-only for 10 years and fully secured by a $900,000 letter of credit from another bank. The broker "finds" a bank to provide the letter of credit. The issuer bank is usually, but not always, domiciled offshore. The letter of credit is issued, payable upon default by the borrower, but in no event before expiration of the loan. The domestic bank, believing it is fully secured, funds the loan through a loan escrow. The loan escrow proceeds are allocated $400,000 to the bank issuing the letter of credit and $500,000 to the victim, the latter net of broker's commission. The broker explains that the bank issuing the letter of credit can invest its $400,000 at 10% compounded for the 10-year period, accumulating a fund of $1,037,496. This provides an assured source if called upon to make good on the letter of credit, plus a profit of $103,750. The domestic lender is attracted by the assured source of repayment of its principal. The victim gets the $500,000 sought and never has to pay back the principal (anticipating a default at the end of 10 years).

The logic breaks down on the most superficial analysis. A thoughtful lender will decline such a proposition because even if the issuer bank is creditworthy, a default before the term expires (failure to pay the interest installments) will reduce the collateral value of the letter of credit (the then-present value of $400,000 due at the end of the term) to near zero; and the victim must pay interest on $900,000, a sum well in excess of the debt service on a $500,000 loan.

The volume of international investing by private investors is huge and growing: $150 billion in 1988, up from $18 billion in 1980. That attracts confidence people like flies. Protect yourself by going slow, keeping your objectivity and seeking qualified advice from people not involved in the proposed transaction.

Section 3.3 Foreign Bank Accounts

Establishing the Account. Opening an offshore or tax haven bank account is a simple task. You may do it by mail, by personal appointment with a bank officer at a US branch or representative office or by going personally to the tax haven in which you are interested. If you choose to open it by mail, simply go to your local library and copy the bank names and addresses for the jurisdiction in which you are interested, using the American Bankers Association's *Directory of Foreign Banks.* Type (don't write longhand, ever, since it only increases the chances of misunderstanding) and mail to each bank a short letter requesting information on available services and current rates; nothing more. On receipt of the responses, compare and decide. Then send the selected bank another short, typed letter with a cashier's check or money order for your initial deposit, along the following lines:

Dear Sir or Madam:

Enclosed is my money order for US$10,000. Please open a Swiss Franc deposit account for me, using the enclosed funds. Send all correspondence to me at the address above.

Very truly yours,

In the normal course of business, you will receive a deposit receipt, a statement of bank policies and procedures to sign and return, a form by which you provide for deposit and withdrawal authority over the account and an application. The bank will assign an account number, just as do American banks. The assignment of an account number will not, however, make it one of those famous "numbered Swiss bank accounts." Such an account is still avail able, but may rarely be opened by mail. Responsible bankers want to first meet you personally and investigate your background to be certain you're not a racketeer. Some tax haven banks will not offer numbered accounts to Americans at all; some will, but require you to first sign a waiver of privacy that permits US authorities access to the original bank records if procedures are properly followed.

You can always depend on being able to repatriate your money at any time. The US is unlikely to block funds from being brought onshore; it is the rules permitting you to get it out of the country that could change at any moment.

Three of the five largest Swiss banks maintain branch or representative offices in major cities of the US. Union Bank of Switzerland, for example, maintains offices in New York, Chicago, San Francisco, Los Angeles and Houston. If you wish to open your account personally but without going to the head office, simply look in the Yellow Pages of your nearest large city under "Banks." Call and make an appointment with the designated officer. Of course, there's nothing wrong with taking a vacation to a beautiful part of the world and keeping an appointment to open the account at the headquarters office, either.

The kinds of accounts available to you are similar to, but often not quite the same as, those to which you are accustomed. Here are the types you will find in Switzerland and Mexico:

• **Current Account.** What we call a checking account is generally referred to by tax haven banks as a "current account." Unlike American banks, they do not issue checkbooks. That should not pose any great problem, however, since you do not ordinarily pay your routine monthly living expenses from a tax haven bank account. You will usually send a letter or wire by which to instruct the bank as to deposits and withdrawals. They are usually non-interest-bearing accounts, although some Swiss banks do pay low rates of interest on current accounts if the balance remains high and the number of transactions low. Always keep in mind that if the account balance is denominated in non-US currency, changes in the exchange rate will raise or lower the value of any repatriated funds.

• **Deposit Account.** A "deposit account" is similar in many respects to the savings account to which you are accustomed. The difference is in the amount that may be withdrawn. The bank will ordinarily permit the withdrawal of a certain amount each month without advance notice (on the order of $5,000), but to withdraw more you may be required to provide 90 days' notice. The Swiss bank will pay a modest rate of interest if the account is held in Swiss francs, and a slightly higher rate if held in some other currency.

- **Savings Account.** The account producing the next higher level of interest is a "savings account," generally paying one or two percent more than a deposit account. The restriction on the savings account is that the amount you may withdraw without notice is less than a deposit account, and the notice requirement for withdrawing more is much longer; usually six months.
- **Investment Savings Account.** The "investment savings account" pays yet more interest and provides less liquidity. You may still withdraw, but the amount that may be withdrawn without notice is nominal. This is obviously not the account for someone who may have a sudden need for the money.
- **Fixed Deposit Account.** With the "fixed deposit account," you have no option to withdraw without notice at all. You agree to place a certain amount of money in the account and leave it there for a predetermined period (three months, six months or a year). It, of course, pays the highest rate of interest among any of the time deposit accounts.
- **Cash Bond.** An account that is more a security than an account is the "cash bond." It is similar to a fixed deposit account, in that your funds are committed for long periods of time with no interim withdrawal options, and are evidenced by bonds issued by the bank with interest rates approximating the fixed deposit account.
- **Custodial Account.** A "custodial account" is a safe deposit box (or vault). The contents of the "account"—like the safe deposit box in the US—are not assets of the bank, so the insolvency of the bank will not result in loss of the account contents. That is the place to put your diamonds, gold bullion or coin collection.
- **Trust Account.** In similar fashion, "trust accounts" are not really "accounts" as much as they are managed portfolios of securities. Your return is whatever investment return is generated from the management activities of the bank serving as portfolio manager. I suggest that you keep the role of banker and portfolio manager separate in your mind; they require entirely different

skills and attitudes. If you need a money manager, look for a money manager, not a reconstructed banker.

• **Eurocurrency Account.** The "Eurocurrency account" is used to buy and sell currency in any country other than the country issuing it. The bank acts as a broker in, for example, the purchase of 20,000 Dutch guilders, and has no risk if you guess wrong with your exchange rate predictions. Currency exchange speculation is one of the highest-risk forms of investing and should be undertaken only by a well-trained specialist who has plenty of financial staying power.

• **Certificates of Deposit.** "Certificates of Deposit" may be purchased in a way similar to funds through a Eurocurrency account, with the bank acting as your broker. There is no withholding tax and no negative interest tax, and interest can be quite attractive.

• **Mexico.** If your target jurisdiction is Mexico, you will find that the peso-denominated accounts pay considerably higher interest than do the US dollar-denominated accounts. That, of course, takes into account the risk of devaluation, along with continuing inflation in that country. You have to compare the premium to the inflation rate and the risk of devaluation in order to make a determination as to whether the risk is worth it. If you are interested in monitoring finance and business activity in Mexico, write for a complimentary subscription to the Banamex publication, *Financing Business in Mexico.* Send it to Press Department, Banco Nacional de Mexico, S.A., P.O. Box 229, Mexico 1, D.F. For the Bancomer publication, *Economic Panorama*, write to Banco Information Center, Avenida Universidad, 1200, Mexico, D. F.

One caution: not all banks in Mexico are fully conversant with the right of survivorship aspect of joint tenancy accounts. As a consequence, you may think you have a joint tenancy account — or tenancy by the entirety — but find on the death of a tenant that the account is tied up in probate for ten years. If joint tenancy — or tenancy by the entirety — is what you want, get in writing when you open the account that the balance may be transferred to the surviving joint tenant without a probate administration proceeding.

Aside from the foregoing, the principal difference between banking practice in Mexico and those in the US and Canada is that Mexican banks do not impose a service charge on checking accounts, but they do charge a commission of about one-tenth of 1% on all foreign checks deposited. That charge will be waived for a substantial depositor who presses the issue. Postdated checks are illegal in Mexico. The banks also keep your cancelled checks, although they will provide copies of them when requested. Because the copies are neither cheap nor quickly provided, most people insist on obtaining receipts.

Fund transfers from the US to Mexico are usually slower than with other haven countries. They will usually assure you a 24 to 48-hour transfer by telex, bank-to-bank, but it invariably takes much longer. Be careful not to place yourself in a position where you depend upon the rapid transfer of funds. They can take up to a month because of misplaced or misdirected documents.

•   **Switzerland.** Switzerland is similar to other, less substantial offshore financial centers in that there is a small group of large, modern, full-service banks, a larger group of private banks that are both more personal and more selective in choosing their customers, and all the others, a category that includes offshore branches of US banks, most of which are positioned to serve the citizens of specific countries.

In Switzerland, five banks fall into the first category: the Swiss Credit Bank, the Union Bank, the Swiss Volksbank, Bank Leu and the Swiss Bank Corporation. They are by far the largest banks in Switzerland. The appearance of their offices makes dealing with them much like dealing with a US bank. All of them are prepared to answer your questions and otherwise make it easier for you to open and operate your account, but some authorities feel that Bank Leu may be more responsive to the needs of the small account holder (under US$100,000).

The private banks of Switzerland are much like the nineteenth-century American merchant banks (which are, incidentally, enjoying a modest revival). Each is a general partnership of individual bankers, so each partner is liable for bank losses to the full extent of his or her net worth. That makes them especially cautious. Under

Swiss law, banks that advertise must publish their financial statements. Private banks are loathe to disclose this information, so they preserve their confidentiality by declining to advertise. Finding and approaching one is generally done on the basis of a referral from an existing account holder or another banker.

In this context, the revival of private banking by large commercial US and European banks presents confusion in the meaning of the term, confusion that must be sorted out for perspective. Since the 1980s, "private banking" means specialist banking for the rich: the commercial bank just lumps its richest customers together and sells them portfolio management services, estate planning and trust services, and unsecured credit lines. "Rich" usually means $1 million in liquid assets, although the bank will not refuse a $50,000 deposit from a customer known to be worth millions. While large commercial loans must be tightly priced because of competition, the banks are usually able to obtain spreads (large by comparison) of 1% to 2% from private banking customers. For this reason, most such customers wisely maintain relationships with several banks. The US commercial banks emphasize lending services, while the European banks—still the capital of international private banking—is almost entirely concerned with investment management. The confusion in terms arises from the name being placed on these contemporary practices. While some of the traditional private banks now provide trust and loan services, the historically accurate meaning of "private banking" is a bank owned by partners who share unlimited liability for operating losses. This imposes real discipline in banking practices, since the bankers are in effect lending their own money. Among this diminishing breed are C. Hoare & Co. (London) founded in 1672, Brown Brothers Harriman & Co. (New York) founded in 1882, and two in Switzerland, Pictet & Cie and Lombard, Odier & Cie (both in Geneva). Considering that there is little private about the private banking programs of the US and European commercial banks, their claim to that title is a remarkable conceit. They are not risking their own money (else, why the billions lent to Latin America) and in the US, banking risks are effectively socialized by means of government deposit guarantees. The reduced numbers of private bankers, using the historical definition, demonstrates one aspect of deteriorating credit standards. Another is the comparative performance mentality now prevailing: a portfolio loss of 20% is viewed by the manager with delight if the competition lost 30%, rather than with chagrin because the manager failed to protect the customer's capital after allowing for inflation. The private banking fad is most extreme in its expression by US commercial banks, a result far removed from the historically-accepted meaning of the term. Traditional private bankers understand the distinctions and address proven customer needs in a time-honored fashion. They will continue in business a century after the current fad passes.

As indicated, the remaining banks are mostly offshore branches of nonhaven banks. Generally, if privacy is of value to the diversification decision, you avoid using offshore branches of banks doing a major amount of their business in the US. That is because the regulatory authorities here may have enough leverage (by threatening its US operations) to force records production. Some have anticipated the problem by establishing and working through "affiliates" over which they have no legal control, thus no power to require the production of documents in violation of local (tax haven) law.

Operating the Account. The process of depositing and withdrawing funds, reconciling account balances, etc. will be explained when you open your account and may be handled by mail or in person, at your option.

If your diversification decision is based primarily on fear (economic or political instability, etc.), you may wish to place offshore only enough funds to permit you to leave the country and make a new start, or to permit you to leave the country and retire with dignity if not panache. If based on the need to appear judgment-proof, the amount placed offshore will be whatever you own in excess of available state or federal exemptions from the claims of judgment creditors plus known present or contingent claims. If based on investment opportunities abroad, it's whatever risk-reward level provides you comfort.

Reporting on the Account. The first report involved may be the US Customs Form 6059B form you will be required to complete upon reentering the US. On it, you must respond "yes" or "no" to the statement, "I am/We are carrying currency or monetary instruments over $10,000 U.S., or the foreign equivalent." On the reverse side of the declaration form, note that transporting currency or monetary instruments is legal regardless of the amount, but that bringing into the US more than the designated amount requires filing Customs Form 4790 with the US Customs Service. That form provides on the back:

"Failure to file the required report or false statements on the report may lead to seizure of the currency or instruments and to civil penalties and/or criminal prosecution."

"Monetary instruments" includes coins or currency of any country, traveler's checks and money orders. The term also includes shares of stock and other securities if they are in bearer form, or any other form that permits title to pass upon physical delivery of the instrument. We can probably conclude that bearer form includes publicly-traded securities with an executed stock power attached, permitting the transferee to immediately liquidate it. The term, of course, also includes bank checks, traveler's checks or money orders payable or endorsed "to order." Transfers of funds through normal banking channels, or course, need not be reported by the taxpayer.

The first report involved, if you open your account without leaving the US, will be Form 4789 filed by the bank under the *Bank Secrecy Act of 1988* ("Act") if your initial or any subsequent deposit is for $10,000 or more. The Act requires financial institutions to establish and maintain records disclosing the identification of each customer, copies of checks and similar instruments used in connection with the account along with certain other records, and to report certain foreign and domestic transactions used and useful in tax investigations. If $10,000 or more is transferred from another bank account on its way to your offshore account, the remitting bank reports it. If you bank through a local US office of your tax haven bank, and it concedes that it is subject to the Act, it must report the transfer of funds. Whether or not it makes that concession, if you make your deposit in cash, it must be reported by the branch.[13] Similarly, if you take a suitcase full of cash (more than $10,000) to your attorney to deposit in trust and forward to your haven bank, the attorney must report the transaction.

The next report you are likely to face will be in connection with the next federal income tax return you file. Schedule B (Form 1040) at part III provides as follows:

"11. At any time during the tax year, did you have an interest in or signature or other authority over a bank account, securities account, or other financial account in a foreign country?"

(See Page 23 of the Instructions for Exceptions and Filing Requirements for Form TD F 90-22.1.)

The Privacy Act Notification at the bottom of Form TD F 90-22.1 provides in relevant part as follows:

"Disclosure of this information is mandatory. Civil and criminal penalties, including under certain circumstances, a fine of not more than $500,000 and imprisonment of not more than five years, are provided for failure to file a report, supply information, and for filing a false or fraudulent report."

Notwithstanding the foregoing, no response of any kind is provided to the two Schedule B (Form 1040) questions in approximately two-thirds of the US returns filed. That fact seems to generate no great excitement on the part of IRS, overwhelmed as they are in meeting their day-to-day work processing requirements.

It almost goes without saying that the interest or dividend income from your account, as well as any earned profits on currency transactions are reportable income in the same manner as would be the case if earned within the US.

Section 3.4 Tax Haven Trusts

Establishing the Trust. Assets placed in trust are "contract assets" payable on your death to named beneficiaries without a probate and no matter what your will provides. Your tax haven trust may stand alone as a will substitute (as to the assets placed in the trust), or it may be (and usually is) carefully coordinated with your domestic family trust. You might use a tax haven trust as the sole or primary estate management vehicle if you travel frequently to the haven in which it is domiciled and plan to retire there. Otherwise, it exists simply to hold and manage offshore investments while the rest of the estate is held in the domestic trust.

Most of the havens you will consider are common law jurisdictions; the law is or evolves from English law. Common law jurisdictions provide a centuries-old body of trust law, permitting more confidence and predictability as to the legal effect of the strategy employed than might be the case if you establish the trust in a civil law jurisdiction. Historically, civil law jurisdictions do not recognize the trust concept. In those which have enacted trust laws, of course, the supporting case law (construing the statutes) is limited, providing less certainty that a rule or provision legally accepted now will remain so well into the future.

A common law trust is an obligation binding the trustee to deal with the property delivered by the settlor for the benefit of designated beneficiaries or classes of beneficiaries (which beneficiaries may include the settlor). You, as creator of the trust, are the settlor; the trustee is designated by you, as are the trust beneficiaries. The obligation imposed on the trustee may be oral, but is usually written. Any act or neglect by the trustee not authorized or excused, either within the terms of the trust instruments or by applicable law, is a breach of trust for which the settlor or any beneficiary may recover damages.

The tax haven trust generally: is created by you as settlor in a country other than the one where you reside; has a corporate trustee (bank or trust company) located in the selected tax haven country; is a living (not a testamentary) trust; accumulates and reinvests earnings until you or other designated beneficiaries need or want them; permits you as the settlor to alter, amend or revoke the trust, including the right to change trustees; provides a Cuba Clause for automatic shift of the trust domicile to another tax haven country upon the occurrence of one or more specified events (*e.g.*, any change or reduction in existing commercial secrecy laws); and remains in effect for no longer than 21 years following the death of the last survivor of a named class of persons.

Typical Patterns of Trust Use. A typical pattern for a US citizen using a tax haven trust would be a Bahamian trust (with automatic shift in domicile to the Cayman Islands if commercial secrecy in the Bahamas is ever seriously eroded), which in turn holds securities and bank accounts in Great Britain and continental Europe and which may employ a Swiss portfolio management firm to manage European securities and Eurocurrency investments. The offshore holdings are accumulated until needed, usually being augmented or reduced from time to time as the dollar exchange rate rises and falls. Aside from that, the genius of man knows few limits when it comes to structuring arrangements of tax haven trusts and corporations.

Do You Need a Lawyer? In the interests of objective analysis, I have tried without success to uncover or imagine a circumstance in which you may safely and legally place funds offshore through any legal entity, including a trust, without competent domestic and offshore legal counsel: there are none. I acknowledge the appearance of bias — my being a lawyer — but I can reach no other conclusion in light of the reporting, legal analysis and drafting requirements of the task.

Those who publish handbooks on tax evasion as promotional pieces for their presigned, printed-form bearer-certificate, fill-in-the-blanks tax haven trust "damn attorneys with faint praise" while effectively killing interest in their use by reference to the purportedly large fees involved. In fact, even the uninitiated are fully aware that attorneys in the US are ethically and legally prohibited from advising clients how to violate the law with impunity; we may only advise as to ways to fulfill client objectives while fully complying with the law. It is therefore clear that trust form publishers and shell bank brokers appealing to tax evaders must keep attorneys out of the process without being too obvious; hence the fees ploy.

Assuming you wish to operate offshore in a manner that will withstand IRS scrutiny and leave you sleeping nights, the cost of using competent legal counsel in structuring the transaction and in providing continuing legal advice is a modest expense, especially compared to the amount of funds typically involved. Using an attorney: questions will be raised in developing a strategy that may never have occurred to you on your own; you will be able to examine several reasonable methods for accomplishing your objectives along with the tax implications of each, their cost effectiveness and psychological comfort level; you will wind up with legal instruments and documents custom-drafted to meet your individual needs; and the copious, checklist-oriented approach of the attorney will provide reasonable assurance that no significant opportunity or risk is overlooked. Usually, two attorneys will be involved: US counsel to develop the strategy with you and draft the documents and instruments; and local counsel in the tax haven country to assure compliance with jurisdictional requirements as to law, form, content and procedure. You have no other option that does not place you at substantial legal risk.

Which Haven? Characteristics of the major (and some minor) havens are discussed at more length in Appendix C. But here are a few thoughts on those that may prove most (and least) attractive for tax haven trusts:

• **Political Stability.** Certain of the Caribbean havens may be politically unstable, now and in the foreseeable future. If your tolerance for business risk nonetheless leads you there, you should be certain to include the Cuba Clause.

• **Costs.** Variances in legal fees and costs for US counsel are minor, impacted principally by the client conference time and the complexity of the plan, although they will be noticeably higher if US counsel finds it necessary to travel to the haven in order to interface with local counsel, handle trust funding, deal with a local problem requiring client input or lacks skill in offshore planning matters. As to fees and costs for haven trustees and local counsel, they vary according to the haven used and according to the complexity of the matter. Various organizations have published comparisons from time to time, all constantly changing, of course. Those currently prevailing are found in Appendix C.

• **Confidentiality.** While bank secrecy at some level is provided by all tax havens, and commercial secrecy (a broader term that includes bank secrecy along with other records used in offshore transactions) by most, there is no substitute for quality and discretion with respect to local counsel, accountants and public officials. Some tax haven countries are so poorly staffed (in terms of trained, disciplined and well-paid public officials) that a bribe can still work wonders. Some have no system of legal ethics worthy of the name, leaving the confidentiality of your communications in jeopardy. If privacy is of concern, you should consider those factors and should discuss offshore investment activity only on a "need to know" basis.

• **Legal System.** Except for Panama and the Netherlands Antilles, most of the havens of the Caribbean are former crown colonies, thus English common law jurisdictions. Civil law or the Napoleonic Code applies in most European havens. Jersey and Guernsey (the Channel Islands) are an admixture of English common and French feudal law. As was suggested earlier, you will usually be more comfortable with the familiar legal concepts of a common law jurisdiction.

• **Miscellaneous.** Using an English-speaking tax haven country (unless your primary language is different) will raise the efficiency of your dealings, as well as your confidence in the documents involved. If you want to establish a trust, be sure the country is at least as interested in attracting that business as it is in attracting banks, insurance companies and shipping companies. Be certain it has a good telex, telephone and mail communications system. See that it is well-supplied with local accountants, attorneys and bankers who are trained and knowledgeable in facilitating offshore investments. Fees for transferring and exchanging currency should be reasonable, otherwise your transaction costs may

be unacceptably high. In the same vein, local reporting requirements and filing fee costs for share transfers, trust amendments,
passport control, etc. should be modest. The haven need not be
easily accessible, but it helps. If you intend to retire in the haven,
consider spending enough time there to be sure you will enjoy it.

Operating the Trust. As with foreign bank accounts, additions to
or withdrawals from the trust may be accomplished by wire, mail
or in person. The question of which revolves around issues of
convenience, expense and privacy. As to the last, the IRS uses
passport and air travel information to identify people (for their
investigations list) traveling regularly to and from tax haven countries. You may ignore that fact, especially if the haven is also a
tourist area, or you may go to extremes to cover your trail if it is
important to you (wiring funds from Mexico or Canada to avoid
bank reporting requirements, a post office box or mail drop, etc.).

Periodic reports and accountings from the trustee will be
required in any well-drafted trust instrument. Those, as well, may
be delivered in person or by mail.

Since the mechanisms for deploying funds in trusts are more
complex than for bank accounts, thus more expensive, the minimum amount required to make the whole trust transaction cost-effective is much higher, perhaps on the order of $100,000.

Reporting on the Trust. The reports for the declaration of funds
upon returning to the US and for bank transfers apply with equal
force to depositing and withdrawing funds to and from your trust.
Schedule B of Form 1040 provides for disclosure of foreign trusts,
including foreign grantor trusts, as follows:

"12. Were you the grantor of, or transferor to, a foreign trust
which existed during the current tax year, whether or not you
have any beneficial interest in it? If 'Yes,' you may have to file
Forms 3520, 3520A, or 926..."

An annual information return for the trust is required on Form
3520A.[14] Failure to file may subject you to a civil penalty equal

to 5% of the trust estate, not to exceed $1,000.[15]

Taxation. Until 1988, a 35% nondeductible excise tax was applicable to the transfer of appreciated property to a foreign trust, even foreign grantor trusts (where the tax obligations of the taxpayer are unchanged). The only way to avoid this result was to procure an IRS letter ruling that the transfer was not made for the purpose of avoiding federal income taxation. Since tax avoidance is not the purpose of such transfers, there was no problem obtaining such a ruling, but it took time and legal fees to get the ruling. In 1988, *Revenue Ruling 69-450*, on which this bizarre requirement rested, was revoked. You may now freely fund the trust with anything from cash to securities. In the absence of open reciprocity from the state or states in which you own real property, however, the tax haven trust may not hold title to your real property.

The Treasury Enforcement Communications System ("TECS") is controlled by the Customs Service, not the IRS. It is a computer-based information storage and retrieval system which collects and maintains information from several nontax reporting forms (including the customs declaration you complete upon entering and exiting the country) and is made available to various federal government personnel for their law enforcement functions. It is separated from tax information because IRC §6103 provides that tax returns and information returns are confidential.

Tax return information includes the taxpayer's identity, detailed information on income and deductions as well as assets, liabilities and net worth. Such information may not be disclosed except as authorized under the IRC. The IRC permits disclosure, with specific approval for federal estate tax administration and to US treaty partners. In certain cases, pursuant to a court order, disclosure may also be made to officers and employees of a federal agency engaged in a judicial or administrative proceeding by which to enforce a federal nontax criminal statute. Major penalties exist for unauthorized disclosure.

There was a day, prior to the *Tax Reform Act of 1976*, when the creation of virtually all offshore trusts was tax-driven. It was then possible to avoid US income tax on foreign-source income and capital gains, permitting the tax-free accumulation of funds off-shore until repatriated to the US.

Under the 1976 Tax Reform Act, Congress sought to nullify those benefits by: taxing the US grantor on all the foreign trust's income for life; imposing a nondeductible 6% per year interest charge on taxes due under the throwback rules from trusts created prior to the *Tax Reform Act of 1976*; increasing the excise tax on transfers of appreciated securities to a foreign trust to 35% and broadened in its application; and converting capital gains from offshore holdings to ordinary income, typically taxable at a much higher rate. As a result of those changes, the tax reasons for moving funds offshore became less attractive, substantially reducing activity in that area.

It is important for you, however, to consider the tax aspect as just part of the total picture, not as the sole reason for going offshore. By that means, you will not be easily led to an unsupportable conclusion.

Historical matters aside, the general rules of US taxation are as follows:

• The US taxes its citizens, residents and corporations on their worldwide income.

• The US taxes nonresident alien individuals and foreign corporations on their US-source income if not effectively connected with the conduct of a trade or business in the US. They are also taxed on that income which is effectively connected with the conduct of a trade or business in the US, whether or not that income is US-source or foreign-source.

• Worldwide taxation can result in double taxation of foreign-source income. The US mitigates this double taxation by permitting a dollar-for-dollar credit for foreign taxes paid. In doing so, all income taxes paid to all foreign countries are combined to offset US taxes on all foreign income. An exception to that general statement should be mentioned. Controlled foreign corporations must, under the *Internal Revenue Code of 1986*, distinguish between operating income and passive income, taking credit for taxes paid only on the former. A credit is also provided for resident aliens, but only for certain foreign taxes imposed on foreign effectively-connected income.

The trust estate, since we are assuming grantor trust status, will be included in your taxable estate at your death. In fact, even if you choose to avoid that result by avoiding the grantor trust rules altogether, you may render that trust subject to taxation in your estate if a prohibited transfer occurs or if a prohibited power over the transferred property is retained. Inclusion in your taxable estate is not necessarily inconsistent with all the other objectives (privacy, investment diversification, etc.) satisfied by the use of the foreign trust.

Because we are assuming grantor trust status, there will be no gift tax imposed on your transfer in trust.

Section 3.5 Controlled Foreign Corporations

Establishing the Corporation. For purposes of examining the use of a foreign corporation as an offshore investment vehicle, we will assume it to be wholly-owned by you. As such, it will be classified under the IRC as a "controlled foreign corporation" ("CFC"). To assume otherwise would broaden the discussion into joint ventures, partnerships, nonprofit corporations and widely-held corporations, areas providing little of use to your asset protection needs.

Because the shares in the corporation constitute personal property subject to probate in the US, it is common practice to have the shares issued to the tax haven trust. The shares then become a "contract" asset not subject to probate administration. That technique, of course, should be considered irrespective of the jurisdiction used for the corporation.

The Tax Issues that Narrow the Choices. The general tax pattern for domestic corporations is that taxes on corporate earnings are paid by the corporation and shareholders are taxed only on cash dividends actually received. A foreign corporation is taxed by the US only on certain kinds of income from US sources and on foreign income effectively connected with US business operations. US shareholders of the CFC are taxed only on dividends actually received, irrespective of the source of income providing those dividends, unless the CFC income is covered by IRC subpart F or is effectively connected with a US trade or business.

Unless prevented by anti-avoidance provisions in the law, you may transfer assets to a corporation located in a no-tax jurisdiction, conduct an active business and accumulate the income tax-free unless and until repatriated. If you sell the stock of the foreign corporation, you may receive capital gains treatment. If you hold the stock until your death, it receives a basis for capital gains tax purposes (in the hands of your heirs) "stepped-up" to the date of death value, permitting either its tax-free liquidation and repatriation to the US or continued offshore accumulation of earnings.

Accumulated Earnings Tax. The first anti-abuse measure was enacted in 1913, the year the personal income tax system began operations. It was the "accumulated earnings tax." ("AET") The original form of the AET was to ratably tax to the shareholders the retained earnings of the corporation to the extent those retained earnings exceeded the reasonable capital needs of the corporation. It was amended in 1921 to add a penalty tax on the corporation itself, the form that continues in use today.[16] The penalty tax is made expressly applicable to accumulations of US-source income of a foreign corporation, as well as the worldwide retained income of the domestic corporation.[17] The AET is imposed in addition to any other corporate income tax and is due at the rate of 27 1/2% on the first $100,000 of excess accumulations and 38 1/2% of the remainder,[18] both subject to a deduction of $250,000 plus a dividends-paid deduction.[19]

The AET is not applied to personal holding companies, foreign personal holding companies or non-profit corporations.[20] That is because other, more onerous, sanctions are applied to the same effect.

Personal Holding Company. A domestic corporation is a "personal holding company" ("PHC") if: more than 50% of the stock value is owned directly or indirectly by no more than five people after applying special family attribution rules,[21] and 60% or more of its gross income is passive (rents, royalties, dividends, interest, etc.)[22] PHCs are taxed at the corporate level at a flat 50% of undistributed income. The legislative purpose, of course, is to encourage the distribution of corporate earnings. The PHC surtax is objective; *i.e.*, the tax avoidance motive need not be shown in order to impose it. The AET, on the other hand, may be avoided if sufficient business needs can be shown for the excess accumulations (capital expansion requirements, etc.).

Once liability for the PHC surtax is determined, the corporation may reduce the liability by paying a "deficiency dividend."[23] The shareholders are, of course, taxed on that distribution.

Just as the AET and PHC surtax are mutually exclusive, so are the PHC and "foreign personal holding company" ("FPHC") surtax rules. If a corporation is classified as a FPHC, it will not also be classified as a PHC.[24]

Foreign Personal Holding Company. A FPHC is a foreign corporation of which more than 50% of the stock value is owned, directly or indirectly (and applying those same family attribution rules) by no more than five US persons, and 60% or more of its gross income is passive.[25] The FPHC rules are designed to address issues unmet by the PHC rules; specifically, undistributed foreign-source income.

The first remedial legislation was enacted in 1937, in response to a request by President Roosevelt and The Report of the Joint Committee on Tax Evasion and Avoidance by the Congress.[26] Unlike PHC treatment in which the surtax is imposed only on passive income, the FPHC penalty, once found to apply, is imposed on retained operating profits as well.[27] Also unlike the PHC provisions, the tax is imposed proportionately on the US shareholders, not the corporation. (That is logical, since the corporation is beyond US jurisdiction.)

As noted, both the stock ownership and gross income tests must be met in order for the foreign corporation to be classified as a FPHC. Unless you are willing to share ownership with five unrelated people (an assumption beyond the scope of this discussion on the ground that it is an unattractive option), you must control the results solely by means of the gross income test. You might consider holding the stock with five other relatives, but you are unlikely to avoid FPHC treatment because the attribution rules treat all stock held by closely-related people (parents, grandparents, children, grandchildren, brothers and sisters) and controlled or related entities (corporations, partnerships and trusts) as being held by one person.[28] As to the gross income test, the source rules are ignored; worldwide income irrespective of US or foreign source is used in classifying the foreign corporation.[29]

The next logical extension of congressional attempts to narrow the use of foreign corporations by US persons is evidenced by the CFC provisions.[30] They were enacted on the recommendation of President Kennedy in 1962. The policy behind them is similar to, but much broader than, that applicable to FPHCs. Under the CFC provisions, Congress seeks to tax operating income as well as passive income, preventing its shelter within a foreign corporation. The approach follows that of the FPHC provisions: tainted income of the corporation is imputed and taxed to the US shareholders.

Controlled Foreign Corporation. A CFC is so classified if "...more than 50% of the total combined voting power or value of all classes of stock entitled to vote is owned...by United States shareholders on any day during the taxable year of such foreign corporation."[31] A US shareholder is defined as a "US person"[32] who owns 10% or more of the foreign corporation's voting stock.

While classification as a PHC or FPHC is based on a two-part test (ownership and gross income), classification as a CFC is based solely on ownership. As with the FPHC test, ownership may be actual or constructive. Constructive ownership rules apply not only at the level of testing stock ownership, but at the level of status as a "US person."[33] So it is of no value that your spouse may be a nonresident, non-US citizen and owns the stock.

US tax on the foreign-source income—assuming that the CFC is not also an FPHC—may be deferred until repatriated if it is neither tainted "Subpart F Income"[34] nor "effectively connected" with a US trade or business.

To recapitulate: your strategy must be directed toward accepting the CFC classification, but avoiding both FPHC taxation and CFC taxation; the FPHC surtax is avoided by keeping passive income at a level lower than 60% of gross income, and CFC taxation is avoided by conducting an active offshore business that avoids those areas of business expressly made subject to US taxation (Subpart F of the IRC and "effectively connected" with a US trade or business). Any other choice is simply too costly in terms of the regulatory and tax burdens. If you are unable to conduct an active offshore business, you should rely on direct and trust ownership of your offshore passive investments and pay the income taxes as they accrue.

Subpart F. A brief examination of Subpart F income, an "effectively connected" trade or business and some collateral regulatory tools available to IRS will round out your understanding of the task, before proceeding to funding the CFC and some qualifying business activities.

The IRC subjects "foreign-base company income" to current taxation under Subpart F. That term comprises FPHC income, sales income from property purchased from or sold to a related person if the property is manufactured and sold for use, consumption or disposition outside the country of the corporation's domicile, service income from services also performed outside the country of the corporation's domicile for or on behalf of any related person and certain shipping income. This provision is designed to prevent tax avoidance by the diversion of sales or other types of income to a related foreign corporation which is incorporated in a country imposing little or no tax on such income. In the same part, the IRC also provides for the current taxation of any income derived by a CFC from the insurance of certain US shareholders' risks. Foreign base company income, income from the insurance of certain US shareholders' risks and certain other income are collectively referred to as "Subpart F income."

In 1976, Subpart F income was expanded to include boycott-generated income, together with illegal bribes or other payments paid by or on behalf of the CFC directly or indirectly to a governmental official. Neither of those items, of course, necessarily involves tax havens. Subpart F expressly excludes from foreign-base company income that arising from the use of ships in foreign commerce, to the extent that the income is reinvested in shipping assets. Foreign-base company income also does not include any CFC income if the Commissioner of Internal Revenue is persuaded that neither its creation nor the specific transaction giving rise to the income has as one of its significant purposes the substantial reduction of income taxes. Needless to say, that exception is rarely advanced.

Subpart F also contains a *de minimis* provision: if foreign-base company income is less than 5% of gross income or $1 million, whichever is less, then none of the gross income is taxed as foreign-base company income. By the same token, if more than 70% of its gross income is foreign-base company income, then its entire gross income is treated as foreign-base company income. If the percentage is between 5% and 70%, then the actual amount of foreign-base company income is identified and taxed as such.

Income derived from the insurance or reinsurance of US risks is Subpart F income if the CFC receives premiums in respect of or reinsurance in excess of 5% of the total premiums and other considerations received during the taxable year. For purposes of applying the insurance of US risks rules, a CFC in certain cases includes a corporation in which more than 25% of the total combined voting power of all classes of voting stock is owned by US shareholders. While a fair amount of syndication activity takes place in organizing offshore reinsurance companies for major employers, it is not the kind of endeavor lending itself to asset protection planning. Hence, it is beyond the scope of this discussion.

In the *Revenue Act of 1962*, Congress requires a US shareholder who disposes of shares in a CFC to report any gains on the disposition as a dividend, to the extent of the earnings and profits of the CFC accumulated after 1962.[35] That, at first blush, has the appearance of a penalty, since dividends are taxed as ordinary income. However, the rule may be beneficial due to the fact that foreign taxes paid or accrued by the corporation may be credited against any US taxes of a domestic corporation which owns and disposes of shares of the CFC. Logically also, the 85% intercorporate dividend exclusion should be available to a domestic parent corporation.

The *Revenue Act of 1962* also includes a provision requiring that any gain from the sale or exchange of patents, copyrights, secret formulas or processes or similar property rights to a foreign corporation by a person controlling that corporation is to be treated as ordinary income rather than capital gain.[36]

Related Person. A "related person" for purposes of determining whether a specific transaction is brought within the ambit of Subpart F is anyone who directly or indirectly controls the CFC, and any person or entity controlled by the person who controls the CFC.[37] You, then, as well as any trust, partnership or corporation you control, are "related persons."

Subpart F income includes CFC profits from the resale of any products sold to it by a related person. It also includes CFC profits from the sale of anything to a related person. It does not include CFC profits from the sale of products that are "created, fabricated, manufactured, extracted, processed, cured or aged" by the CFC from parts or raw materials either purchased from or sold to a related person.[38]

Effectively Connected with a US Trade or Business. A CFC is conducting a business that is "effectively connected with a US trade or business" if management decisions involving discretion and judgment are provided in or from the US.[39] This, however, is a general proposition requiring much explanation.

Neither the IRC nor the accompanying Treasury Regulations contain a complete definition of what constitutes "engaging in a US trade or business." The IRC does provide that the term includes "performance of personal services within the US," but excludes certain temporary personal services performed for a foreign employer, as well as certain stock, security and commodities transactions. IRS attempts no substantial elaboration in the regulations.

The inquiry must begin with the facts and circumstances of

each case. Borderline facts lead at best to a reasonable guess. "As a general rule, the more deeply a foreign corporation becomes enmeshed in the economic and commercial structure of [the US], the more likely it will be found to have established a business nexus [with it]."[40] Thus, to some extent, extrapolation from known principles is necessary.

The existence or nonexistence of a US trade or business is determined anew for each taxable year. Your CFC is considered engaged in a US trade or business for a full taxable year if so engaged at any time during it.[41]

As a general proposition, the quantity and quality of a CFC's US business activities determine whether a nexus exists sufficient to impose US income tax. Historically, continuity, regularity and substantiality of the CFC's US activities, together with their nature (*e.g.*, whether passive investment or active business) are considered in making the determination.[42] To find the US connection, the CFC business activities must be those for which it was established.[43]

The greatest weight is given to the location from which the CFC management decisions are made. This "management situs" test was described by one commentator as follows:[44]

"The 'management situs' test appears to be of great importance in determining where the activities of the corporation will be deemed to have taken place. Thus, it may not be enough merely to incorporate in a foreign country and have certain minimum contact therein, with all decisions and policy making emanating from within the United States. For if the test of where the business is conducted revolves around the factor of management activity, the courts will look at the substance of the entire operation in deciding whether the corporation is engaged in a United States trade or business."

Where the US office of a CFC performs mere clerical or routine services, it appears that the foreign corporation is not engaged in a trade or business in the US. Thus, one deeply-divided Tax Court[45] found a Scottish company not engaged in a US trade or business. That entity collected and deposited interest and dividends on its US investments, checked the accuracy of the amounts, remitted them to the home office in Scotland, maintained records, prepared reports to the home office and US tax returns, leased US offices and paid related expenses. All major policy decisions, however, were made at the home office in Scotland. The Tax Court stated:

"We are not convinced that the services of this local office, quantitatively extensive and useful as they may have been, approached that quality which is necessary in order that petitioners can be characterized as having engaged in business in the United States."

On the other hand, the opposite result could come about from the regular exercise of management discretion from the US by either the CFC owner or by some agent.[46]

If the CFC business you contemplate will require some services in the US, they should be provided through an independent contractor. They will be attributed to the CFC only if the relationship between the contractor and the CFC is both regular and exclusive. If it is casual, or if the contractor represents itself as a provider of such services for itself, others or both, no attribution should result. Even if attribution follows, services of a clerical or administrative nature should not be sufficient to characterize the CFC as being engaged in a US trade or business.

Apart from independent contractors, if an officer, employee or "dependent agent" of the CFC is located in the US and provides services of the required quantity and quality, the CFC will be considered engaged in a US trade or business.[47] If you own the CFC through a domestic corporation, you are considered the "dependent agent" of the CFC. Consequently, senior management personnel should be located outside the US.

All the foregoing notwithstanding, your CFC will not be considered to have a US office for purposes of an "effectively connected" finding merely because it makes use of the US office of another person or business, whether or not that office belongs to a "related person," so long as the CFC business is "relatively sporadic or infrequent, taking into account the overall needs and conduct of...[its business]."[48]

It also will not be considered to have a US office for that purpose merely because its controlling shareholder uses one to exercise "general supervision and control over the policies [of the CFC]."[49]

In fact, your CFC will not be considered to have a US office for this purpose unless it is staffed with an agent who has "the authority to negotiate and conclude contracts in the name of the [CFC] and regularly exercises that authority, or...has a stock of merchandise belonging to the [CFC] from which orders are regularly filled [on its behalf]."[50] Avoid the authority and the inventory and you avoid the problem.

To keep this matter in perspective, the "effectively connected" issue arises primarily when the CFC conducts some or all of its business in the US. If its business is conducted entirely outside the US, the need for concern is much reduced.

Where the "effectively connected" issue must be addressed, arrange for all significant day-to-day management functions to be performed outside the US. Those non-US services should be carefully documented in the corporate files and minute book so as to be prepared for any tax audit. Taking such precautions does not guarantee that IRS will never assert the "effectively connected" argument, but it does minimize the risk.

Funding the CFC. A major concern of Congress, beginning with enactment of the first income tax law, concerned the potential for abuse in avoiding taxes through recapitalizations and liquidations using foreign corporations. In the Revenue Act of 1932, it gave this example:

> "A, an American Citizen, owns 100,000 shares of stock in Corporation X, a domestic corporation, which originally cost him $1,000,000 but now has a market value of $10,000,000. Instead of selling the stock outright, A organizes a corporation under the laws of Canada to which he transfers the 100,000

shares of stock in exchange for the entire capital stock of the Canadian company. This transaction is a nontaxable exchange. The Canadian corporation sells the stock of Corporation X for $10,000,000 cash. The latter transaction is exempt from tax under the Canadian law and is not taxable as United States income under present law. The Canadian corporation organizes Corporation Y under the laws of the United States and transfers the $10,000,000 cash received upon the sale of Corporation X's stock exchange for the entire capital stock of Y. The Canadian corporation then distributes the stock of Y and A in connection with a reorganization. By this series of transactions, A has had the stock of X converted into cash and now has it in complete control."[51]

Congress addressed this risk by limiting the extent to which a foreign corporation may claim nonrecognition.[52] Any recapitalization of a domestic corporation involving a foreign corporation must be approved by the Commissioner of Internal Revenue within 183 days following the first transfer on the ground that the transaction does not have as one of its principal purposes the avoidance of federal income taxes.

Also in 1932, Congress addressed a second aspect of the transfer problem by enacting the predecessor to today's IRC §1491. Under that section, a nondeductible excise tax of 35% is imposed on the transfer of appreciated property by a US citizen to a foreign corporation (whether as paid-in surplus or in exchange for newly-issued shares), or to a foreign estate, trust or partnership, unless the taxpayer chooses[53] to recognize and pay the capital gains tax at that time. The nondeductible excise tax, if applied, is calculated on the full appreciation in value.

A nondeductible 35% excise tax is imposed on the transfer of appreciated property to your CFC.[54] The tax is calculated on the difference between your basis and its fair market value. Your choices are to pay the excise tax, recognize and pay the capital gains tax or attempt to obtain a letter ruling from IRS exempting the transfer on the basis that it is not intended to avoid federal income taxation (a monumental task).[55] As to your likelihood of securing a favorable letter ruling, the determination is made on the facts and circumstances of each case.[56] As to your choice of options, remember that recognition and payment of the capital gains tax leads to a step-up in basis, where payment of the excise tax does not.

Creating the CFC. The trust company you appoint as trustee for the tax haven trust ordinarily provides a range of services that includes the formation of tax exempt CFCs. It will have a volume discount arrangement with local counsel that leaves you paying the same amount whether you go directly to the attorney or use the trust company. Both the law firm and the trust company will provide continuing services in timely renewal of the franchise, filing of reports and payment of government fees. In Cayman, for example, the total costs for formation of the corporation (service fees, filing fees and corporate records) are on the order of $2,700; the annual renewal costs are about $1,900. Included in those figures are trust company/legal fees of about $1,500 first year and $1,000 in each renewal year.

You will often see small classified ads in the international press offering low-cost trust and corporate formations. Just remember that these service agents, like the tax haven trust companies and attorneys, cannot properly advise you on the US law applicable to asset protection planning. Without qualified advice, you use them at great personal risk.

Active Businesses that Operate Outside Subpart F. Virtually every major international corporation today conducts activities in and through tax havens. When Congress considered the *1972 Revenue Act*, IRS described certain categories of tax avoidance devices used by taxpayers doing business overseas. Today some of those uses are substantially eliminated, but others continue to be used, some in a substantial way. Corporations continue to divert income to foreign subsidiaries which engage in no real activity abroad. They continue to organize foreign subsidiaries to carry on the same type of business activity previously conducted by the domestic parent, and to divert income through special pricing arrangements and the transfer of valuable income-producing assets, both tangible and intangible. Diversion of income through generous expensing continues, as do foreign transportation and reinsurance.

Certain industries operate in predictable patterns. For example, the petroleum industry makes significant use of tax havens by forming companies there to carry out the traditional functions of shipping, refining and selling petroleum, as well as transshipping.

The insurance industry continues to make extensive use of tax havens. Foreign insurance companies doing business in the US often have a Bermuda or Cayman subsidiary through which they reinsure those US risks. US multinational companies form tax haven captives for the insurance of offshore subsidiaries. The *Internal Revenue Code of 1986* extends the coverage of Subpart F so that its provisions apply to any US shareholder of a foreign insurance company which is 25% or more owned by US shareholders to the extent that the company insures risks of those shareholders or any party related to them. Any such insurance company may elect to be taxed at the corporate level as if its income were effectively connected with a US trade or business.

The growth and use of tax havens by the construction industry has outstripped the growth of any other industry group.

The shipping industry uses tax havens almost exclusively, including US shipping companies. The favorites are Liberia and Panama.

Virtually every major bank has extensive operations in tax havens, usually through branches, although some operate through subsidiaries or affiliates. Bank use of the havens has grown enormously in recent years.

Finally, the heavy equipment industry utilizes sales companies located at the tax havens. Sometimes manufacturing or assembly operations are conducted there. Generally, however, manufacturing and assembly operations are conducted in low-cost areas offering tax incentives to attract industry; *e.g.*, Taiwan, Korea, the Philippines, Ireland and Puerto Rico. Sometimes, a tax haven corporation is formed for the purpose of investing in a manufacturing business located in those low-cost areas.

Following are a series of business activities which should produce tax-free or low-tax (depending on the haven jurisdiction) income from your offshore business activities by avoiding the application of Subpart F and the FPHC rules, and by complying with IRS pricing regulations.[57]

• **Illustration 1.** A CFC may be used as a sales company. The sales company may not buy from or sell to related persons; it may only engage in sales with unrelated persons.

You will recall that foreign-base company sales income as contemplated by Subpart F (the type we are trying to avoid) is CFC income derived from the sale of property purchased from a related person, or the purchase of personal property for sale to a related person, if the property is produced outside the country under the laws of which the CFC is created or organized and the property is sold for use outside of that country.[58] Commission income from such sales is included, as well.

The crucial element in foreign-base company sales income is the purchase from or the sale to a party related to the CFC. If the transactions are with unrelated parties, there is no foreign-base company income, hence no tax to the US shareholders.

In the petroleum industry, trading companies are often formed by major integrated companies as well as by small oil companies; those trading companies are commonly referred to as oil resellers and do not have production capabilities of their own. The majors will often use the trading companies for dealing with unrelated parties. In many cases, however, all of the decisions regarding the purchases and sales by the trading company are made in the US. In some cases, the business functions of the parent are duplicated by the foreign subsidiary. There may be two buying and selling organizations, one engaging in domestic business and the other in foreign business with respect to the same oil. It is difficult for IRS to determine which company is really doing what for whom. Similar patterns exist in the grain industry.

Just so you know enough about the clearly illegal schemes to avoid their taint, here is how some operate. The perpetrators hold themselves out as trading companies. They organize in offshore tax haven jurisdictions in order to obtain commercial secrecy in the tax havens. Transactions are occasionally arranged with friendly third parties to avoid purchases and sales with a related party. For example, oil company X forms subsidiary corporation Y in a tax haven. Y is to engage only in the purchase and sale of foreign oil. Usually Y buys foreign oil from an unrelated party and sells that oil to an unrelated third party. It is believed, however, that at times swapping arrangements are entered into under which Y buys from an unrelated party and sells to an unrelated friend at a high price. The friend then sells to X, the US parent, at its cost or at cost plus a small profit. In reality, Y has sold oil to X at a price which is too high. If the facts were known, the IRS would reallocate the income to X, and Y would have Subpart F income. Because of the frequency of transactions, the fungibility of oil and the lack of adequate records, it is difficult for IRS to establish the substance of the transaction in order to prove fraud.

• **Illustration 2.** Foreign-base company sales income treatment may be avoided also by structuring a CFC as an assembly operation rather than as a sales company. Foreign-base company sales income does not include income from the sale of property manufactured, produced, grown or constructed by the CFC in whole or in part from property which it purchased.[59] Property is considered manufactured, produced, grown or constructed by the CFC if it is substantially transformed prior to sale or if the property purchased is used as a component of the property sold.[60] The "substantial transformation" test is subjective. The "component" test in the regulations may be met through a cost test or a subjective test. Purchased property is used as a component if the operations conducted by the CFC in connection with the property purchased and sold are substantial in nature, as are manufacturing, production or construction of property.[61] In addition, the operations of the CFC in connection with the use of the purchased property as a component part of the personal property sold is considered the manufacture of a product if, in connection with the property, conversion costs of the corporation are 20% or more of the total cost of the goods sold.[62]

So, you may form a CFC in a tax haven and sell components to it, have the CFC assemble the components and take the position that no foreign-base company sales income is earned on the sale of the property that includes the components.

The assembly operations may be subject to scrutiny under the intercompany pricing rules. IRS may reallocate income from sales between the haven subsidiary and a related person.[63] In addition, allocations may be made on the ground that a related person is performing services for the CFC, or that it has licensed intangibles (such as a trademark) to the CFC without adequate compensation.[64]

- **Illustration 3.** Another item included in foreign-base company sales income is income of a branch of the CFC operating outside the country in which the CFC is domiciled, if the use of the branch has substantially the same tax effect as if the branch were a wholly-owned subsidiary of the CFC.[65] The regulations assume a "substantially similar tax effect" if the branch is taxed at a lower rate than would have been the case in the country where the CFC is domiciled.[66] Under this rule, if a tax haven CFC is organized in Panama, and has a selling branch in the Cayman Islands, the branch rule will operate because Panama imposes a corporation tax on business income from Panamanian sources. If, however, the base company is formed in the Cayman Islands (which has no tax), it may establish a branch in a second country and not be subject to the branch rule. (Of course, if the second country is a high tax country, there may be no overall tax avoidance.)

An increasingly popular pattern is to take advantage of the branch rule and the 5% or $1 million (whichever is less) foreign-base company sales income *de minimis* rule. A US company taking advantage of a tax holiday offered by a country seeking manufacturing investment, forms a CFC in a tax haven with which the United States has a tax treaty and transfers to it the required capital and technology. The tax haven company constructs the manufacturing plant in the tax holiday country and its production is exported and sold to unrelated persons. Assuming the initial transfer qualifies,[67] a favorable[68] IRS ruling would ordinarily be issued because the property will be used in the active conduct of a trade or business.[69] The manufacturing profits are not taxed to the US parent because they are not foreign-base company income. The sales profits are not foreign-base company sales income because of the local manufacturing test. In addition, the passive income of the CFC may be reinvested in the tax haven free or substantially free of tax if less than the lower of 5% or $1 million of the CFC's gross income.[70] The tax haven entity is used because, while the tax holiday country does not tax the export manufacturing profits, it may tax the passive income earned on retained earnings at a high rate. The tax haven may tax those earnings (depending on the haven chosen), but if so it would be at a low rate. The retained earnings of the tax haven CFC might also be reinvested in active business assets, free of tax. The tax effect is avoidance of the tax holiday country tax, the haven tax and the US tax.

• **Illustration 4.** The service and construction industries make extensive use of tax haven entities. That growth is despite the application of Subpart F to services and the existence of allocation regulations.

Subpart F income includes foreign-base company services income. Foreign-base company services income is defined as income from the performance of technical, managerial, engineering, architectural or like services outside of the country of incorporation of the CFC, if such services are performed for, or on behalf of, a related person.[71] Such services include: direct or indirect compensation paid to a CFC by a related person for performing services; performance of services by a CFC which a related person is obligated to perform; performance of services with respect to properties sold by a related person where the performance of services constitutes a condition of sale; and substantial assistance from a related person or persons contributing to performance of the services by the CFC.[72] A related party provides "substantial assistance" to a CFC if the assistance furnished provides the CFC with "skills" that constitute a principal element in producing income from the performance of the services, or the cost of the assistance to the CFC is 50% or more of the total costs of performing the services. Assistance is not taken into account unless it assists the CFC "directly" in the performance of the services.[73]

Despite those provisions, IRS garners almost no income taxes from the service or construction industry tax haven operations.

Congress had manufacturing-related services in mind when it passed the foreign-base company services income provisions. It states that "as in the case of sales income, the purpose here is to deny tax deferral where a service subsidiary is separated from manufacturing or similar activities of a related corporation and organized in another country primarily to obtain a lower rate of tax for the service income."[74] Today, independent construction, natural resource exploration and high-technology services, none of which are related to manufacturing, are the services most often provided through the tax havens. Part of the business which is conducted in the US may simply be excised from the US business and transplanted to a tax haven. The services are not performed for a related party, but rather for unrelated parties. The income is being accumulated free of tax.

The service rules problems are generally due to the approach taken by Congress; it mandates regulations requiring difficult decision-making. IRS finds itself unable to clearly discern the facts and circumstances necessary to prove that substantial assistance was rendered to the CFC. Only two examples are available from the regulations, neither of which is particularly helpful. In one, if a contract for services is supervised by employees of the US parent corporation who are temporarily on loan to the subsidiary, and substantial assistance is rendered to the subsidiary by the related person, then the income from the performance of the contract is foreign-base company income. If, however, the contract is supervised by permanent employees of the subsidiary and the US parent only provides clerical assistance, then such assistance is not "substantial." Of course, if permanent employees of a CFC oversee a contract with no assistance rendered by a related person, then no foreign-base company services income arises from the performance of the contract, thus there is no taxation on it to the US parent.

The determination of whether an employee is permanent or temporary also presents a difficult factual issue. By characterizing employees as permanent employees of the CFC, a US shareholder may take the position that the transactions in question do not produce foreign-base company services income. A classic illustration is the US parent that establishes a tax haven CFC to conduct offshore drilling operations outside the tax haven. The officers of the parent may negotiate the drilling contracts and then enter into an agreement with third parties as officers of the CFC. The parent corporation is not liable on the contracts and does not guarantee their performance. The parent corporation may lease the equipment necessary to conduct the drilling operation at the safe harbor "arm's-length" charge.[75] The day-to-day drilling operations are managed and performed by on-site employees of the CFC, who are characterized as permanent employees. The joint officers of the parent and the CFC perform various managerial services for the CFC. In many cases, there will be little or no tax imposed on the income by the country in which the services are performed.

The parent corporation of the CFC will take the position that it renders minimal, rather than substantial, assistance to it; therefore, income from the drilling operations is not foreign-base company services income. IRS may challenge the characterization on its facts, but the issue is difficult to resolve.

A construction company will often form a CFC in a tax haven to conduct its construction projects abroad. A construction project will consist of three phases: a conceptual phase in which the project plans are developed; a planning phase during which detailed plans are prepared; and a construction phase during which a construction manager is placed on-site to supervise construction.

The initial conceptual phase will often be handled by a US company. If the company is successful in obtaining the contract, the contract will be signed by officers of the CFC, who may also be officers of the US parent. Supervision of the construction will be conducted by the CFC through an on-site manager employed by the CFC, an on-site manager who at one time may have been an employee of the US parent.

As with the drilling operation, it may be difficult for IRS to establish that the services were performed for or on behalf of a related person. Once the CFC develops financial and managerial substance overseas, so fewer of its services are being performed by the US parent, it becomes even more difficult for IRS to make the "substantial assistance" case.

While finding itself unable to support its conclusions, IRS feels that certain of these cases are abusive. Their notion of "abusive," however, is something like the timing of the contract execution (negotiated by the parent and signed by the CFC officers).

Some companies have accumulated significant retained earnings offshore by leasing equipment to a tax haven CFC to be used in a service business. By manipulating the rental safe harbor rule[76] and the fair market value of the equipment, significant income may be accumulated in the tax haven CFC. As substance is created in the tax haven CFC, the arrangement between the two companies becomes even more difficult to challenge.

• **Illustration 5.** Captive insurance and reinsurance companies operate by the hundreds from those few tax havens that maintain an attractive regulatory environment and where qualified local management may be found. The captives are usually formed by multinational corporations in order to insure or reinsure their own operations. Although self-insurance reserve deposits are rarely tax-deductible, a deduction for insurance premiums paid to a related corporation may be permitted in some countries. There are both tax and nontax reasons for forming a captive.

The term "captive" includes those formed by a group of multinational corporations to insure offshore subsidiaries of the members of that group, and those formed by a single multinational corporation to insure its offshore subsidiaries. The insurance may be provided directly with all or part of the risk assumed by larger insurance companies under reinsurance agreements, or the insurance may be provided by an unrelated carrier then reinsured with the captive, or the risks may be self-insured with a stop-loss form of coverage provided by the captive. Because of the capitalization and management costs involved, it is rarely cost-effective to establish a captive insurance company unless you are presently paying more than $500,000 per year in property damage and liability premiums. Ordinarily, such risks would be self-insured by the large multinational corporation. But as noted earlier, deposits into a self-insurance reserve are not usually deductible, and the movement of funds is often limited by exchange control restrictions. A captive insurance company may solve both problems: some, perhaps most, countries permit an income tax deduction for insurance premiums paid to an affiliated carrier, and such insurance premiums may be exempt from exchange controls.

Commercial carriers labor to some extent under market-driven product restrictions. The captive, however, may provide substantially any form of coverage used or useful in the operation of its parent's business.

The "float" is an important profit producer for the captive that "fronts" coverage for a commercial reinsurer. The parent-insured pays the premium at the beginning of the policy term, but the captive need not pay the reinsurance premium until the policy term expires. In the meantime, the reinsurance premium is invested to produce interest or dividends.

Premiums attributable to the insurance of US risks are tainted Subpart F income, taxable to the US shareholder.[77] As a consequence, relatively few US-owned captives are used to insure US risks. Under certain circumstances, offsetting benefits may change that conclusion. It requires close analysis of premium payment timing, characterizing some or all of the Subpart F income as foreign-source income in order to use excess foreign tax credits, and any excise taxes to be paid on the premiums involved.

Historically, the insurance of solely foreign risks by captives did not produce Subpart F income; nor was investment income attributable to invested insurance premiums and reserves, to the extent received from unrelated persons.[78] In 1972, however, IRS adopted the position that insurance through a captive amounts to nothing more than nondeductible self-insurance. That led to a 1977 ruling to the effect that there is no shift in the risk when it is transferred from the parent to the captive.[79] The multinationals responded by either transforming the captives into commercial insurance companies insuring the risks of unaffiliated companies, or forming consortia to own the captives so as to shift risk among the various owner-insured corporations. Most take an aggressive stance regarding any IRS audit threat and are prepared to fully litigate any disallowance of deductions where the disallowance is based on the idea that there is no risk-shifting.

The first such case to arise was won by IRS.[80] Carnation Company, a large dairy products firm, insured a foreign subsidiary through an unaffiliated domestic insurer, which then reinsured 90% of the risk with a Carnation-owned Bermuda captive. The deduction was disallowed. Carnation challenged it. The tax court ruled in favor of IRS, the 9th Circuit Court of Appeals affirmed the tax court, and the United States Supreme Court refused to hear and review the case.

Because the loss of the Carnation case barely slowed aggressive insurance tax planning by multinational corporations, Congress included in the *Tax Reform Act of 1984* a provision that the insurance of "related persons" not located in the same jurisdiction as the captive itself constitutes Subpart F income, taxable to 10%-or-more US shareholders. Note two aspects of this provision: the geographic location of the risks insured and the fact that a "related person" is any person or entity holding 10% or more of the captive's stock. Thus, IRS moved in the direction of challenging consortia-owned captives and did not concede its right to challenge the deductibility of premiums for the insurance of affiliates within the jurisdiction where the captive is domiciled. Syndicators of offshore, consortia-owned captives responded by simply increasing the size of the shareholder groups to reduce each interest below the 10% level.

Finally, the *Internal Revenue Code of 1986* extended the coverage of Subpart F so that it applies to any US shareholder of an offshore insurance company in which US shareholders all together own more than 25% of its stock, to the extent that the insurance company insures the risks of those US shareholders or of any person or entity related to them. The company may elect to pay the US tax at the corporate level as if its income is effectively connected with a US trade or business.

Assuming that, through trade association activities, you are able to and interested in syndicating an offshore insurance company through which to insure the foreign properties and business operations of the consortia owners, Bermuda is probably the best tax haven for the purpose. It has a modern, but not onerous, system of laws regulating insurance.[81] The minimum paid-in capital requirement is $120,000 and the annual fee to the government is $1,500. Several full-charge management companies for captive insurance carriers are located in Bermuda. Total costs, including management fees, range upward from $15,000 per year.

Another attractive location for a captive is the Bahama Islands. It, too, has effective but nonburdensome insurance regulations.[82] Although it imposes a 1% premium tax, the tax is waived for captives that insure only risks outside the Bahamas.[83] You must file audited accounts each year, but need not publish them.

In similar fashion, Cayman established a modern regulatory scheme for insurance in 1979.[84] It was rewarded by the establishment of several hundred captives since that date. You may operate the captive with either a restricted or non-restricted license; the latter requires a net book value of at least $120,000. Annual government and management fees are about one-third less than those you may expect in Bermuda (although the amount thereof representing government fees is higher).

On balance, the decision-weighing may tip toward Bermuda because of its excellent London reinsurance connections and because the quality of the local management companies seems noticeably higher than that available in the other jurisdictions.

• **Illustration 6.** Tax havens serve as the domicile for large numbers of banks, most of them established within this past decade.

Multinational corporations use captive banks and finance companies as a conduit for private Eurodollar loans. If such loans are made directly from, for example, France to the US, the outbound interest payments (US to France) are subject to US income tax withholding at the rate of 30%, but if routed through a country with a favorable US tax treaty via a subsidiary bank or finance company, the withholding rate may be reduced. That is a much more satisfactory arrangement from the standpoint of the European lender, and the US borrower may establish an interest rate differential in the low-tax country that leaves 1% to 5% accumulating offshore.

US, Canadian and British banks establish subsidiary banks and trust companies in havens so as to be able to pay interest to foreign depositors without tax or at a low withholding rate, to underwrite or participate in the underwriting of securities, assist US customers in obtaining Eurodollar loans and assist customers (both foreign and domestic) in establishing offshore corporations, trusts and related financing arrangements.

Wealthy families often establish offshore banks for both privacy and economic reasons. Large lines of credit may be obtained from Canadian, British or European banks for the benefit of the offshore private bank, permitting the family to borrow competitively with total privacy, and accumulating any interest rate differential offshore.

Often, the private banks established by multinational corporations are staffed with unusually talented and experienced people who function as private merchant bankers. This is a much wider scope of activity than simply accepting deposits and making loans. Because of the business relationships of the parent, the captive bank often enjoys enormous borrowing resources and, by specializing in the banking needs of the parent, is often more efficient in executing foreign exchange transactions than would be a commercial bank.

Prior to 1965, a bank could be established in a major tax haven jurisdiction by simply incorporating a CFC with banking power; no application to any banking authority was required because no such authority existed, thus the bank was free to operate without regulations or capital or reserve requirements. As the word spread, people without banking experience established large numbers of offshore banks, often as a facade behind which to conduct swindles of one kind or another. "Shell banks" became popular and remain so today. A shell bank is one formed without paid-in capital; it is still possible to establish one in Anguilla, St. Vincent and several Pacific Rim countries. Promoters establish and resell shell banks at a substantial markup to buyers who believe they are receiving a valuable banking license; in fact, the lack of standing in the banking community renders such franchises of no material value. Anguilla has terminated most of its shell banks, usually because the annual fees are not paid, and St. Vincent now requires a license from the Governor and approval of the St. Vincent Trust Authority.[85] Although the law in St. Vincent now imposes minimum capital and reserve requirements, the Trust Authority does not appear serious about compliance. The current version of the shell bank is one formed by a bank promoter with perhaps $5,000 paid-in capital and resold for as much as $30,000.

In 1965, the Bahamas led the way to legitimacy as an offshore financial center by passing the *Bahamas Islands Banks and Trust Companies Regulation Act.*[86] Existing as well as new banks are required to comply with reasonable banking standards. Passage of the bank regulations produced a quick remedy for an embarrassing situation, eventually establishing the Bahamas as an important offshore financial center. Today, it serves as the domicile for more than 350 banks and trust companies established by major international banks and multinational corporations from all over the world.

In 1966, the Cayman Islands followed suit, enacting banking regulations virtually identical to those of the Bahamas. It is now a major offshore financial center, hosting more than 400 banks and trust companies.

Only three banks are domiciled in Bermuda, and an offshore bank is not permitted. It is possible, however, to establish a finance company there that performs many of the important functions of a bank.

The *Turks and Caicos Banking Ordinance*[87] deals only with banks. Thus, trust companies in the Turks and Caicos Islands may be organized without regulation or restriction of any kind.

In all cases, regulated offshore banks are divided into two groups: those that conduct business within the tax haven jurisdiction, with its citizens, and those that conduct solely offshore—non-haven—banking business. The latter are referred to as "exempt" banks and are subject to less stringent capital, reserve and reporting requirements than nonexempt banks.

Anyone, including an individual, may establish an exempt bank in Vanuatu.[88] The license fee is about V100,000 (approximately US$1,000) and minimum capital V12,500,000 (US$125,000).

Although Switzerland, Jersey and Guernsey all host quite a few offshore banks, the regulatory attitude toward permitting new ones is decidedly chilly. Restrictive legislation is now in place, making it difficult to establish a new bank in those havens.

In Luxembourg, a new bank must be sponsored by two established banks and must have at least LFr 350 million (approximately US$10.5 million) paid-in capital. It is a major international banking center, working hand-in-glove with Swiss banks, and regulation by its Banking Control Commission is as close as any in the world.

Panama is the conduit for enormous amounts of flight capital from Latin America. Under its banking law, three classes of license are provided: local, offshore and representative offices. To obtain an offshore license, you must capitalize your bank for at least US$250,000, and the capital must be maintained on deposit in Panama. Licenses today are restricted to major bank applicants. More than 100 banks, including branches and subsidiaries of international banks, now operate in Panama.

Unlike other financial centers, the Netherlands Antilles imposes an income tax on exempt banks domiciled there; it is 3% on interest and dividends and 6% on all other banking income (loan origination fees, etc.). Banks domiciled in the Antilles must have authorized capital of at least NAF1,00,000 (about US$550,000), and paid-in capital must equal or exceed 20% of authorized capital.

As is the case in Vanuatu, an individual with a good reputation may establish a private, exempt bank in Nauru. In fact, it reportedly may be done by mail. Nauru is an island country in the Central Pacific. Licenses are issued by the Minister of Island Development & Industry. Annual fees are modest.

The same shell bank problem that plagued the Bahamas dogged the British Virgin Islands for years. It passed a banking law in 1973 that substantially resolved the problem by imposing high standards on new entrants and providing a transition period within which existing banks must either meet the new capital and reserve requirements or lose their licenses. Today, only reputable banks operate out of the British Virgin Islands.

In choosing a financial center within which to establish an exempt bank, consider first the Bahamas and the Cayman Islands. They are close, they have the most effective banking regulations and they have stood the test of time in terms of banking standards. In either one, the application is custom-prepared in response to a list of questions propounded by the banking authority, often exceeding 100 pages in order to deal adequately with the information required; they require prior banking experience among the directors, as well as references for every officer, director and shareholder. You must file audited financial statements each year that demonstrate, among other data, that the minimum paid-in capital requirements were and continue to be satisfied. Plan on funding the bank with at least $250,000 plus start-up costs. It will take several months to get the application approved and the license issued. The bank license costs about US$9,000. A Bahamian bank must be owned by no fewer than three persons and entities.

In terms of annual fees, an offshore bank license ("class B") in the Cayman Islands costs CI$8,500 (approximately US$10,980), and, as an exempt company, the bank receives a 20-year guarantee against taxes. The bank may be owned by one person.

It is not necessary to open a local office in either the Cayman or the Bahama Islands. You may engage another bank to manage your operations at an annual cost ranging from US$15,000 to $25,000, depending on the range of services involved.

The critical issue is, "How does the US tax offshore banks?" Here are the key rules:

• A CFC does not have tainted (FPHC or Subpart F) income on dividends, interest and profits from securities trading arising from the conduct of banking business with unrelated persons.[89]

• As a US shareholder, you may, if the CFC becomes an FPHC by virtue of its passive income, avoid current US taxation of its undistributed income by obtaining an annual certification from IRS that you did not establish or use the bank principally for avoiding US income taxes.[90]

• Your bank may be subject to US taxation on its foreign-source income if you cause it to both engage in business with the US and maintain an office here.[91]

In applying those rules, your use of a CFC bank as a medium for international diversification of your holdings requires that you: cause the bank to invest so much of its paid-in capital in the foreign holdings you would otherwise purchase directly so as to avoid FPHC classification (less than 60% passive income); look for ways to conduct quasi-banking functions with the rest (such as loaning 40% to 50% of the bank funds to individuals and commercial borrowers in carefully underwritten loan transactions, or having the bank originate loans for borrowers through other banks for a 2% to 5% origination fee); obtain your annual certification from IRS for any year in which your bank becomes a FPHC by virtue of failing to keep at least 41% of its income in a "bank operating income" category; and do not open an office in the US for the conduct of your offshore banking business. Under the *Internal Revenue Code of 1986*, protection from FPHC status is withdrawn as to CFC bank passive income earnings unless that income is earned from financing US exports. That leaves you relying even more on annual certification as noted above.

Foreign Sales Corporations. Let us now turn to an entirely different CFC, the "foreign sales corporation" ("FSC"). It is an export incentive that in 1985 replaced the former Domestic International Sales Corporation.[92] At bottom, it earns commissions on foreign sales made by a US business, and some or all of the commission income is exempt from US taxation. Thus, a CFC that is carefully steered through the straits of the FPHC and Subpart F rules will generate income not taxed currently by the US (but fully taxed upon repatriation), while a FSC may be currently taxed to some extent (but exempt profits are never taxed upon repatriation). On particular facts, the planning and operation of a CFC may carry higher risk of error—thus current taxation—than the well-defined and officially-sanctioned FSC.

Unlike the CFC that, in negotiating the straits between the FPHC and Subpart F, must do business only with unrelated persons, the FSC is typically a subsidiary of a US manufacturer selling the parent's products to foreign customers. In order to become and continue to qualify as an FSC, it must meet the following requirements throughout each year for which FSC status is claimed:
- It must be incorporated in a qualified jurisdiction.
- It may not have more than 25 shareholders.

- It may not authorize the issuance of preferred stock.
- It must maintain a business office in a qualifying jurisdiction, although not necessarily the one in which it is incorporated. The office may be that of a local (to the qualifying jurisdiction) management company, and the books, records and invoice copies must be maintained there.
- Certain records must remain within the US.
- At least one director must be an individual and a nonresident of the US.
- The FSC status must be elected 90 days prior to the fiscal year for which that status is sought.
- It may not be a member of any controlled group that includes an "interest charge" Domestic International Sales Corporation.

Four US possessions are among the qualifying jurisdictions. They are the American Virgin Islands, Guam, American Samoa and the Northern Mariana Islands. A foreign country may qualify by entering into a program for the exchange of information with the US Treasury and obtaining Treasury Department certification.[93] Barbados is now qualified by virtue of signing a Caribbean Basin Initiative exchange of information agreement essentially waving commercial secrecy laws as to agencies of the US government. It followed certification by enacting legislation by which to attract FSC business.

Along with the four US possessions and the Caribbean Basin Initiative participant, the US certified[94] other US tax treaty partners that maintain acceptable exchange of information programs:

Australia
Austria
Belgium
Canada
Denmark
Egypt
Finland
France
Germany
Iceland

Ireland
Jamaica
Korea
Malta
Morocco
Netherlands (but not the Netherlands Antilles)
New Zealand
Norway
Pakistan
Philippines
South Africa
Sweden
Trinidad and Tobago

The US possessions and certain of the treaty partners are especially aggressive in pursuing FSC business. The American Virgin Islands is the most successful, with probably two-thirds of all the FSCs established to date. Among the others enjoying notable success with more than 100 each are Guam, American Samoa, Northern Mariana Islands, Barbados, Belgium, Jamaica and the Netherlands.

By way of cost illustration, an FSC incorporated in the American Virgin Islands pays an incorporation fee of $400 and an annual license fee of $100. In addition, a franchise tax ranging from $400 to $25,000 is imposed. The franchise tax is a function of gross receipts, less a tax credit for local payroll.

The General Agreement on Tariffs and Trade requires the FSC to maintain an adequate foreign presence, hence the requirement of at least one nonresident individual director. The nonresident director may be a US citizen.[95] You have 30 days in which to replace that director on death or resignation, but there are no guidelines as to what happens if nonresidency status is lost due to excessive time spent within the US or loss of a green card. As a result, it is prudent to have two or three US nonresidents on the FSC board.

If you produce foreign sales through the FSC exceeding $5 million and choose FSC treatment for the entire amount, the FSC must comply with four management restrictions:

- All shareholders' and directors' meetings must be held outside the US. They need not, however, be held in a qualifying jurisdiction. Shareholders' meetings may be held through proxies. Avoid holding directors' meetings in a country using a managed-and-controlled test for purposes of determining whether a corporation is resident there for tax purposes (for obvious reasons).
- For the moment, at least, the bank account must be maintained in a qualifying jurisdiction, though not necessarily the one in which the FSC is incorporated.
- All disbursements for dividends, legal and accounting fees, directors' fees and officers' salaries must be made from the bank account noted above, providing IRS a ready audit trail.
- An FSC must produce "foreign trading gross receipts" by selling products made in the US by a company other than the FSC into one or more foreign markets. The exporter is typically the parent corporation of the FSC. If you produce through the FSC foreign sales exceeding $5 million and choose FSC treatment for the entire amount, the FSC must execute its transactions so as to meet "foreign economic process tests." The requirements are as follows: the FSC or its agent must participate in at least one of three sales activities (direct solicitation, negotiation or entering into a sales contract), which activities must take place outside the US, though not necessarily in a qualifying jurisdiction; the FSC must spend specific percentages of its direct costs of operation outside the US for advertising and sales promotion, order processing and delivery arrangements, transportation, invoicing and collecting receivables and the assumption of credit risk.

Given full compliance, the FSC escapes US taxation on its "exempt foreign trade income." In order to segregate and identify "exempt foreign trade income," whichever of three available transfer-pricing methods[96] produces the best result for the FSC is applied. The transfer-pricing rule purportedly brings about an "arm's-length" pricing arrangement between the manufacturer-parent and the FSC, leaving taxable the portion attributable to the manufacturer and substantially exempt the portion attributable to the FSC.

No tax is imposed on exempt FSC income repatriated to the

US, nor are credits allowed for foreign taxes paid. As to the latter, several qualifying jurisdictions (including all four US possessions) impose no income taxes on FSCs.

The fiscal year of the FSC and that of its parent must be the same.

An FSC may not enjoy any of the benefits of a US income tax treaty. It is a creature of statute, and its benefits are conferred solely pursuant to the IRC.

A "small" FSC need not meet the foreign management requirements. Thus, it need not hold its shareholders' and directors' meetings outside the US or maintain its principal bank account in a qualified jurisdiction. It also need not meet the foreign economic process tests. It qualifies as a small FSC by limiting its sales to $5 million per year, either in the aggregate or by picking the most profitable $5 million to report as "foreign trading gross receipts."

If you are not now exporting, the conservative approach would be to contact an export manager's trade association, identify your product and ask for referrals to export managers specializing in the sale of that product in foreign markets. If you have a particular market in mind, ask for referrals to export managers specializing in sales development in that particular country. Interview, evaluate and qualify the prospective export managers. They can provide a wide range of services, the extent of which is a function of your needs for education in foreign sales development versus your willingness to share your profits. After hiring an export manager, travel to the qualifying jurisdiction most directly accessible to the US in the direction of the target market, contact and interview local FSC management companies and select one to manage yours. The management company can undoubtedly refer you to local counsel through whom to establish the FSC.

Reporting for the CFC. You must provide IRS with certain information each year regarding the CFC and its connection with you. The information is provided on IRS Form 5471 and accompanying schedules. Form 5471 is filed as an attachment to your personal federal income tax return (or your corporate return, if the CFC is formed as a subsidiary of your domestic corporation) for the year the CFC was organized and for each subsequent year. Procedurally, you note on the face of the federal income tax return that Form 5471 is attached and file it as usual; then send a copy of each to the IRS Philadelphia Service Center. (See the instructions for the address.) The first year, you attach Schedule O to the Form 5471 to report the organization of the CFC.

Because you will have a "financial interest" in the CFC's bank accounts by virtue of your ownership of the corporation, you must also file Form TD F 90-22.1 to make the required disclosures for each account. It must be filed each year before June 30, at the Detroit address shown on the form.

Section 3.6 Foreign Investments

Foreign Investments, Disclosure of Which is Not Required. If either privacy or the desire for simplicity in offshore investing is of paramount importance and you are willing to accept a limited range of investment choices, you may lawfully avoid all US reporting requirements until such time as your funds are brought back to the US at a profit. The requirement is to simply avoid using the vehicles described on Schedule "B" (Form 1040), as well as the CFC. You are required at Schedule "B" to disclose any "bank account, securities account, ...other financial account in a foreign country" (No. 11) and any "foreign trust" (No. 12). Owning a CFC, or course, requires that you file disclosure Forms 5471 and TD F 90-22.1. What's left? More than you might imagine:

- **Small Foreign Account.** For the small account, note that the instructions for Schedule "B" (Form 1040) No. 11 (foreign accounts) directs you to answer "No" if "the combined amount of all the [foreign] accounts was $10,000 or less during the whole year." You may thus maintain one or more foreign accounts with an aggregate balance of less than $10,000 at all times. While that does not represent a serious attempt at diversification, it does establish the mechanism by which to transfer and report larger amounts on short notice, should circumstances require it.
- **Safe Deposit Box.** A safe deposit box is arguably not a

financial account. You simply purchase gold, silver, platinum or precious stones from time to time and place them in the box.

• **Life Insurance.** A life insurance policy is a private contract between the insured, applicant and carrier, not a financial account. Since the Securities Exchange Commission asserts no regulatory right over life insurance other than variable life, such policies are not deemed "securities." Accordingly, no reporting requirement is triggered by the purchase of a foreign currency-denominated equity-based policy. "Universal Life Insurance" is the most popular form of cash value policy being sold in the US today. It is a flexible policy in which the cash values accumulate at a rate based on the actual investment experience of the carrier, subject to a minimum guarantee. By assuming investment risk, the policy owner may enjoy cash value accumulation at rates as high as 11.25%, less mortality, administration and profit charges. British and Swiss life insurance companies were selling equity-based policies for decades before it became popular in the US. Moreover, those companies are able to denominate benefits in the currency of your choice. You may also cross our northern border and purchase Canadian dollar-denominated policies. If you prefer to conduct one transaction at a time, rather than obligate yourself to an annual premium commitment, simply purchase a single premium life insurance or annuity policy in each transaction; the initial cash value is about 96% of the premium and grows from there at the rate provided. Since the cash value accumulations are not taxable until you surrender the policy at a profit (or take the funds as a life annuity after the cash values grow to a value greater than the aggregate premiums), there is nothing to report during the holding period.

• **Use US Broker.** Although the records are not protected from governmental inquiry, you may purchase publicly-traded foreign securities and gold through your US broker, thus obtaining at least semiprivate diversification.

Currency Declaration and Bank Reporting. In funding the purchase, whatever form it may take, remember the currency declaration and transaction requirements. If you wish total secrecy, you must either transfer less than $10,000 out of the country at a time, or periodically travel into Canada or Mexico with any amount of money and wire the funds overseas. International bank transfers that pass momentarily through a US correspondent bank are not reportable under the *Bank Secrecy Act of 1988* or the *Bank Privacy Act of 1970*, although both Canada and Mexico have US tax exchange agreements. You may repatriate funds in the same way (wired into Canada or Mexico and carried back across the border), bearing in mind that repatriated funds may represent reportable profits.

Section 3.7 US Remedial Action, Present and Proposed

Periodically, from 1913 to the present, the US government has acted to stem the uses of tax havens in ways deemed abusive of our taxing system.

Since 1980, the attention of the US Treasury Department has, if anything, heightened. In 1979, Richard A. Gordon, Special Counsel for International Taxation to the Internal Revenue Service, was directed by the Oversight Committee of the House Ways and Means Committee to prepare and submit a report identifying tax havens, reviewing and quantifying their use and proposing options by which to deal with perceived abuses. A comprehensive 235-page report *(The Gordon Report)* was presented in January 1981; that report was quickly adopted by the Congress and the Treasury Department as the master plan by which to ultimately eradicate the use of tax havens by US taxpayers.

Even the Treasury Department and the Congress acknowledge that most business conducted through tax havens is perfectly legitimate and in full or substantial compliance with US law. Governmental frustration arises from bank and commercial secrecy laws. They effectively prevent it from quantifying legal and illegal tax haven use so as to permit an informed judgment about whether and how much of its investigative resources to commit to enforcement. They also prevent it from obtaining the bank and beneficial ownership records for tax haven transactions, accounts, trusts and corporations crucial to the task of tracing back to their source funds surfacing in the US.

The harsh remedial tactics proposed in *The Gordon Report* caused an uproar of protest among certain of the Caribbean tax havens, notably Bermuda. Those tactics include administrative, legislative and treaty actions.

Among the administrative options proposed were: to impose upon the US taxpayer a duty to obtain and produce the records of foreign subsidiaries, notwithstanding any secrecy laws governing those subsidiaries in the offshore jurisdiction; to increase the burden on taxpayers to substantiate deductions, valuations and pricing, together with better instruction by IRS to its agents on methods for determining when the burden of proof is satisfied; to clarify and simplify the transfer pricing rules; to withhold the income tax on all funds remitted offshore, subject to refund upon the filing of tax returns; to simplify tax reporting by combining certain aspects; to enhance coordination among the various US government departments engaged in investigating crimes that involve tax havens; to expand IRS's International Examination Program and give examiners additional training; and to establish a department-wide network by which to collect information on international transactions, directed through ombudsmen located in the National Office of the Chief Counsel.

Among the legislative options proposed were: to expand Subpart F to add jurisdictional tests under which US shareholders of the CFC are taxed on all its income; to add (to the shareholder control test) a "management and control" test for subjecting CFCs to US taxation; to simplify and rationalize the taxation of tax haven income by combining FPHC provision with Subpart F; to emphasize the burden of proof by providing for disallowance of a tax haven-related deduction unless the taxpayer establishes by clear and convincing evidence that the underlying transaction, in fact, took place, along with the substance of the transaction and the reasonableness of the deduction amount; and to discourage bold tax planning by imposing a no-fault penalty resulting from a tax haven transaction that is disallowed.

Among the treaty options proposed were: to terminate the

existing income tax treaties extended to the Netherlands Antilles by the Netherlands and to the United Kingdom colonies and territories by the United Kingdom, then deal directly with all countries in negotiating new treaties; to be more selective in negotiating income tax treaties with countries where the US has no significant trade or investment relationship, and refuse to enter into income tax treaties with known tax havens, or alternatively, to enter into limited treaties with tax havens that include nondiscrimination provisions, competent authority mechanisms and an exchange of information provision overriding secrecy laws and practices; to insure adequate access to information in criminal tax investigations by insisting upon a strong exchange of information provisions in all US income tax treaties, a provision that would override foreign secrecy laws and practices; to periodically review treaties to determine whether abuse is taking place or is invited by changes in local laws and practices, and whether the treaty is serving the function for which it was initially negotiated; to pursue mutual assistance treaties with the more important tax havens; to threaten increased taxes on payments to those havens which decline to adopt measures discouraging US taxpayers from investing there; and to incorporate strong treaty provisions by which to limit their use to residents of the treaty country itself, so as to avoid treaty shopping by citizens of countries not a party to that treaty.

As a major first step in implementing *The Gordon Report* proposals, President Reagan announced to the Organization of American States on February 24, 1982 the "significant tax incentives" that later found formal expression in the Caribbean Basin Initiative ("CBI"). Seventeen months passed before CBI was passed by the Congress, due to delays in reconciling several competing factors: tax benefits given to designated beneficiary countries of the Caribbean undercut existing incentives to transfer business to Puerto Rico and the US Virgin Islands; CBI benefits had to be carefully structured to avoid permitting tax haven investments to benefit from the investment tax credit; a policy position had to be developed by which to respond to any requests for similar benefits from less developed nations; technical problems had to be resolved regarding the investment tax credit for US firms that, to comply with foreign law, are required to invest in the Caribbean through CFCs; benefits had to be structured to avoid a windfall to US mineral producers already conducting mining operations in the Caribbean; the cost in terms of revenue loss attributable to the CBI had to be minimized; and finally, Congress had to be certain that the real benefits go to the beneficiary nation, not just US investors.

On July 14, 1983, the House of Representatives passed the CBI as H.R. 2769 by a largely bipartisan vote of 289-129. The Senate quickly passed its version and the House-Senate Conference cleared it before the month was out. Certain amendments delayed implementation, however; notably the requirement of a report better quantifying the then-current use of tax havens for tax evasion, on the effect of implementing the CBI on US tax revenues, comments on the CBI's impact on drug trafficking and related criminal enterprises and on the Department of the Treasury's then-current tax haven investigation efforts. The report was submitted January 6, 1984.

The CBI basically offers selected Caribbean nations certain limited tax incentives in exchange for an agreement under which the US Treasury Department may gain access to its commercial records for criminal and tax investigations.

The incentives are a five-year extension of the investment tax credit (now repealed) with which to attract US industry, and the allowance of tax deductions for business conventions held in the tax haven with which to attract US tourist trade. As it develops, the incentives are too modest and too speculative to prove interesting to the island-states of the Caribbean; 21 have come under the plan to date but the lack of investment funds for adequate infrastructure (water, roads, communications, etc.) continues to discourage meaningful business investment.

The CBI Exchange of Information Agreement must be signed before a US President-designated "beneficiary country" may receive the benefit of the incentives. That agreement was described in Treasury Department News Release R-2780, July 24, 1984. The model agreement contains a number of provisions that may not apply to particular beneficiary countries, others that are negotiable and still others that constitute the non-negotiable core of the US's minimum expectations and without which there will be no agreement. Among the provisions to be sought by the Treasury Department are the following:

• To provide methods for the exchange of information that will assist the contracting states to enforce their tax laws, the exchange to be without regard to the residence or nationality of the person under investigation or of the person in possession of the information.

• The taxes subject to the agreement are those on wealth or capital, inheritances, real property, and general consumption (such as value-added and sales taxes). No information will be sought as to a claim that is barred by the statute of limitations. No exchange of information is provided for the investigation of unpaid state, county or municipal taxes.

• There is no requirement that the matter under investigation be a tax matter or proceeding; it may be a purely criminal matter in which tax evasion is the means of bringing about a successful prosecution.

• In addition to formal application for access to information, provision is made for spontaneous exchanges when information comes to the attention of the tax authorities in one state that is likely to be relevant to a tax matter in the other state.

• If the information available in its tax files is not sufficient to satisfy the request, the requested state must take all appropriate steps, including compulsory measures, to provide the applicant state with the information requested.

• The production of information for exchange is not to be limited by laws or practices of the requested state pertaining to the disclosure of information by banks, nominees, or persons acting in an agency or fiduciary capacity. Similarly, the attorney-client evidentiary privilege protecting confidential communications is to be ignored by the requested state, but "preserved for resolution by the applicant state." The purpose is to avoid permitting courts of the requested state to rule on the privilege; the US wants that prerogative.

- Provision is made for receiving the information in a form admissible in a US court of law. That will have the effect of shifting the burden of proof, or at least the burden of going forward with the evidence, to the person contesting authenticity or trustworthiness of the information.

- Restrictions are included which avoid the need: to take measures that do not comply with the law of the contracting states; or require either to supply information not lawfully obtainable in either state; or to supply information that would disclose a trade secret; to violate public policy; or to take any action that would result in discrimination against a national of a requested state.

- The applicant state may enter the requested state to interview individuals and examine records with the consent of the individual contacted. That permits direct participation in the information-gathering process within the requested state. Officials of the applicant state would have no authority to compel disclosure, but their presence may be helpful in obtaining the specific information most useful in the pending prosecution.

- Information exchanged under the agreement would be subject to the same laws as is tax information generally in the contracting states; it is to be disclosed only to individuals or authorities involved in the determination assessment, collection and administration of the recovery and collection of claims and enforcement or prosecution. A US grand jury is one such authority.

To date, the advanced nations of the world have pursued their provincial interests to the near-total exclusion of any coordinated effort to address either the problems presented by tax havens or the tax and regulatory burdens that provide their *raison d'etre*. Although that is unlikely to change soon, the actions contemplated by the US Treasury Department may further limit offshore investing and business activities in the years and decades to come. For now, however, the proper use of tax havens is perfectly legal, not seriously limited by law or practice and not philosophically opposed by the US government.

Section 3.8 The Action Plan

This book is limited to guiding you in pursuing asset protection planning through investment diversification internationally. You may accomplish that end with privacy from all but IRS by means of direct offshore investments or by a tax haven trust through which to hold those investments. If you are in a position to do so, you may add tax deferral or tax avoidance benefits to the plan by engaging in an active offshore business conducted through a CFC.

I will add only one more suggestion, one born of many years experience as businessman and attorney: Play to your strong suit, not your weak one. In the late 1950s, I met D. Paul Fansler, one of the nation's leading life insurance salesmen. Paul invested $200,000 in a venture—a chain of weight-training studios—and lost it all. His reaction? "Most people make it in their own business, and lose it in someone else's." He knew the life insurance business, but not the gym business, so he lacked the experience needed to properly evaluate the venture proposal.

In planning hundreds of estates over the years, I see a recurring pattern: the client who takes risks and works hard to achieve financial independence, only to become conservative and attempt to limit risk by becoming a full-time investor as soon as that level of independence is reached. This tactic not only fails to produce the same results, but often a large part of the accumulated wealth is lost.

In a study by Srully Blotnick, Ph.D., a research psychologist and widely-read author on the psychological aspects of investing, Dr. Blotnick states that those who stay with the business or investment pursuits that produced their first million dollars are nearly four times as likely to earn a second million within five years after earning the first as are those who sell their businesses or quit their jobs to become full-time investors.[97] Your "strong suit" is the business you know. Your "weak suit" is the other person's business.

The point? If your offshore investments are going to be in currencies and securities and you have no demonstrated training, experience and success in those media, hire a professional. Watch closely, of course, but don't try it yourself unless you can afford to lose it all. If your offshore investments will take the form of an active business through a CFC, make it a business in which you have training, experience and a history of success. You may still lose, but the odds are infinitely better.

Endnotes

1. *Staff Study, Crime and Secrecy: The Use of Offshore Banks and Companies*, made by the Permanent Subcommittee on Investigations of the Committee on Governmental Affairs, United States Senate, February 1983, p. 44

2. B. Solnik, *International Investments*, Addison-Wesley Publishing Co., Inc., 1988

3. *Morgan Stanley Capital International Perspective, 1990*

4. *ibid*

5. The Anti-Drug Abuse Act of 1988

6. Testimony of Peter K. Nunez, Assistant Secretary of the Treasury for Enforcement, before the United States Senate Banking Committee, 1990

7. Marc Rotenberg, Director, Computer Professionals for Social Responsibility, Washington, D.C. Office, International Herald Tribune, May 29, 1990, p. 17, col. 6

8. *Doe vs. US*, 88-2 USTC, 108 SCt 2341 (1988) affirming an unreported decision by the 5th Circuit.

9. *US vs. Payner*, 80-2 USTC, 447 US 727 (1980 pp.730-34.) The Supreme Court held that the US taxpayers had no constitutional right of privacy in the bank records, so they had no standing to challenge IRS's conduct. It did not, however, condone such conduct. (pp.737-38)

10. *US vs. Bank of Nova Scotia*, 691 F2d 1384 (11th Cir 1982), cert. denied, 462 US 1119 (1983); *In re Grand Jury Proceedings*, 740 F2d 817 (11th Cir 1984), cert. denied, 105 SCt 778 (1985); *US vs. Chase Manhattan Bank*, 84-1 USTC, 584 F Supp 1080 (SDNY 1984); *SEC vs. Banca Della Svizzerra Italiana*, 92 F2d I11 (SDNY 1981)

11. *Tax Havens and Offshore Finance*, St. Martin's Press, New York, 1979

12. *Staff Study, Crime and Secrecy: The Use of Offshore Banks and Companies, ibid*

13. IRC Sec. 6050 I

14. IRC Sec. 6048(c); Reg. 404.6048-1

15. IRC Secs. 6048(d), 6677(a)

16. IRC Secs. 531-537

17. IRC Sec. 532A

18. IRC Sec. 531

19. IRC Secs. 531, 535(c), 561. The deduction is reduced under Section 535(c)(2) to $150,000 for personal service corporations operating in the areas of health, law, engineering, architecture, accounting, actuarial science, performing arts and consulting.

20. IRC Sec. 535(c)(2)(B)

21. IRC Sec. 554

22. IRC Secs. 541-547

23. IRC Sec. 547

24. IRC Sec. 542(a)(5)

25. IRC Secs. 551-558

26. H.R. Doc. No. 337, 75th Cong., 1st Session

27. IRC Secs. 551(a), 553

28. IRC Sec. 554, *ibid*

29. IRC Sec. 555(a)

30. IRC Secs. 951-964

31. IRC Sec. 957(a)

32. IRC Secs. 957(d), 7701(a)(30)

33. IRC Sec. 958(b)

34. Income described at IRC Secs. 951-964, which is Subpart F of Part III of Subchapter N of Chapter I of Subchapters, Subtitle A, of the IRC.

35. IRC Sec. 1248

36. IRC Sec. 1259

37. IRC Sec. 954(d)(3)

38. IRC Sec. 864(a), 954(d)(1)(A), noting that (A) and (B) are expressed in the conjunctive.

39. IRC Sec. 864

40. See generally, Garelik, *What Constitutes Doing Business Within the United States by a Nonresident Alien Individual or a Foreign Corporation,* 18 Tax Law Rev. 423 (1962), and Bittker and Eustis, *Federal Income Taxation of Corporations and Shareholders* (4th Ed), pp. 17-14

41. IRC Sec. 864(b)

42. *Commissioner vs. Spermacet Whaling & Shipping Co.,* 281 F2d 646 (6th Cir 1960); *Consolidated Premium Iron Ores, Ltd.,* 265 F2d 320 (6th Cir 1959); Rev Rul 55-182, 1955-1 CB 77; Rev Rul 62-31, 1962-1 CB 367; Rev Rul 65-263, 1965-2 CB 561

43. *Scottish American Investment Co., Ltd.,* 12 TC 49 (1949)

44. Garelik, *ibid*

45. *Scottish American Investment Co., Ltd., supra*

46. *Commissioner vs. Nubar,* 185 F2d 584 (4th Cir 1950), cert. denied, 341 US 925 (1951); Rev Rul 55-282, 1955-1 CB 634

47. *Helvering vs. Boekman*, 107 F2d 388 (2d Cir 1939)

48. Reg 1.864-7(b)(2)

49. Reg 1.864-7(c)

50. Reg 1.864-7(d)

51. H.R. No. 708, 72d Cong., 1st Session 20 (1932)

52. IRC Secs. 332, 351, 354-356, 361, 367

53. IRC Sec. 1057

54. IRC Sec. 1491

55. IRC Secs. 1057, 1492(2)

56. Reg 1.1491-1(b)

57. As to the pricing regulations, see IRC Sec. 482 and applicable Treasury regulations.

58. IRC Sec. 954(d)(1)

59. Reg 1.954-3(a)(4)

60. Reg 1.954-3(a)(4)(ii) and (iii)

61. Reg 1.954-3(a)(4)(iii)

62. *Dave Fischbein Manufacturing Co. vs. Commissioner*, 59 TC 338 (1972), acq. 1973-2 CB 2

63. IRC Sec. 482

64. Reg 1.482-2(d)

65. IRC Sec. 954(d)(2)

66. Reg 1.954-3(b)(1)

67. IRC Sec. 351

68. IRC Sec. 367

69. Rev Proc 68-23, 1968-1 CB 821, 823

70. IRC Sec. 954(b)(3)

71. *ibid*

72. Reg 1.954-4(b)(1)

73. Reg 1.954-4(h)(2)(ii)(b) and (c)

74. H.R. No. 1881, at 84, 1962-3 CB 703, 790

75. Reg 1.482-1 *et seq.*

76. Reg 1.482-2(c)

77. IRC Secs. 953, 957(b)

78. IRC Sec. 954(c)(3)(B)

79. Rev Rul 77-316, 1977-2 CB 53

80. *Carnation vs. Commissioner*, 71 TC 400 (1978), aff. 640 F2d 1010 (9th Cir 1981), cert. denied, 454 US 965 (1981)

81. Bermuda Insurance Act of 1978

82. Bahama Islands Insurance Act, No. 3 of 1969

83. Bahama Islands Nonresident Insurer (Exemption) Regulations

84. Cayman Islands Insurance Law of 1979, No. 24 of 1979, as last amended by Law 9 of 1980

85. St. Vincent Trust Authority Act, No. 31 of 1976; St. Vincent International Companies Act, No. 32 of 1976

86. No. 64 of 1965

87. No. 1 of 1979

88. Formerly New Hebrides, made famous by Michener in his book, *South Pacific*; Vanuatu Bank Regulation No. 4 of 1970, as amended

89. IRC Sec. 954(c)(3); Reg 1.954-2(d)(2)(ii)

90. IRC Sec. 552(b)(2); Regs 1.552-4, 1.552-5

91. IRC Sec. 864(c)(4)

92. IRC Secs. 921-927

93. IRC Sec. 927(e)(3)

94. In Notice 84-15, 1984-2 CB 474

95. Senate Print 98-169, Vol. I at 637, 1984

96. IRC Sec. 482

97. Forbes, October 28, 1985

CHAPTER 4

Conclusion: A Case Study

The front door opened slowly, as the lean, sixtyish man stepped out, carefully balancing a mug of steaming black coffee. He placed it on the porch table, yawned, stretched mightily, scratched his ribs through the bulky Irish knit sweater and eased himself slowly into the well-worn rattan armchair.

The house is large and comfortable, whitewashed stucco with large windows and an Italian tile roof, unusual for the area. Jim Goldsmith squinted pensively into the bright morning sunlight, slowly sipping his coffee. He ran his fingers casually through his wavy white hair, thinking he may be a few weeks overdue for a trim.

It is springtime in the Isle of Man. The warm Gulf Stream sweeping through the Irish Sea keeps the weather temperate all year around, and today is no exception.

The house is a tiny speck of white against the emerald-green mountain slope set in a colorful riot of gorse and heather. At the foot of the slope, a jagged, rocky beach holds back a shimmering, azure-blue ocean, stretching as far as the eye can see.

The rattan chair squeaked comfortably as Jim leaned forward, peering eastward. He saw a glimmer of silver against the powder-blue sky. Manx Airlines' morning flight is on time and preparing to land at nearby Ronaldsway Airport. "Hon, the plane's on time. You'd better put on another pot. Sean'll have Ray up here in 20 minutes or so."

"I wonder why Ray's in such an all-fired hurry," he muses. "Aw, Ray's always in a hurry. He couldn't even save a few bucks by waiting for the Heysham ferry — had to fly. It's good to have a partner like that, though; someone willing to work the extra hours on practice development and administration that made ours one of the most successful medical clinics in Palo Alto."

Like clockwork, 20 minutes after the coffee was put on the stove, the worn 1952 Morris Minor lurched into view, chugging slowly up the gravel drive from the main road to the house. At the wheel is Sean Corcoran, a wizened old Gaelic-speaking handyman who Jim keeps busy with fence repairs and other odd jobs around the place. Stuffed into the tiny automobile beside Sean is Ray Hotchkiss, a large man in his fifties with black, crew-cut hair and a serious, businesslike demeanor.

Jim rose to his feet and stepped off the porch to welcome his guest. Ray slowly extricated himself from the tiny vehicle, clearly relieved to be free of it, and turned to grab Jim in a huge bear hug. "You son of a gun, it's great to see you!"

"You too, Ray. It's been too long."

"Sean, will you take these bags to the guest room, please? Ray, put away that briefcase and get into some jeans. Whatever brought you halfway around the world can wait until you can relax, breathe deep, sip some good Irish coffee and take in this gorgeous view."

"You got it, babe," said Ray as he disappeared into the house.

As he waited, Jim reflected on the years he and Ray worked together. Jim had joined an old general practitioner in Palo Alto shortly after completing his residency in pediatrics, bought the practice a year later and soon, partly because of his personal charm and partly because he is an excellent and caring doctor, found himself with a large and prosperous practice. His wife, Martha, however, began to chide him about working too many hours and neglecting his own health, not to mention his family, so he spread the word that he needed a major talent to help. Pete Hoyt, a buddy from his Stanford days, put him onto Ray. He called Ray, who was soon to finish his residency at Children's Hospital in Los Angeles, and invited him up for a visit. The chemistry was right, and Ray joined him a few months later. Even though Ray had no prior local medical community contacts, his natural bent for business brought about referral networks with three local hospitals that, when combined with his solid medical talents and prodigious appetite for work, soon had them looking for more help. They stopped adding doctors at eight and began limiting the number of patients instead. It worked well: a real sense of collegiality, a well-paced practice environment supported by state-of-the-art equipment, good earnings and good people to cover for you when you needed a few weeks off.

Then came that slip-up by the anesthesiologist, and the little girl who never recovered consciousness.

Jim's brow furrowed and his teeth clenched as he recalled it, but he pushed it aside as Ray stepped onto the porch looking like an NFL tackle in his yellow jumpsuit and jogging shoes.

"Pull up a chair, Tiger," Jim said, pointing to the other rattan chair. "The coffee's here, and Martha's on her way with some of her special muffins."

"That's great," he said, sinking into the chair and picking up the steaming mug. "Those muffins I remember. This is gorgeous, Jim. You look like you have a good life," Ray said whimsically.

"Not bad," Jim responded. "We have time and opportunity to read and travel, I fill in for the local doctors on occasion, we either bring the kids here or go back to see them in California several times a year and I'm working on another book. But never mind that, how's the practice going?"

"Well, Ed retired and moved to Palm Springs, where he's practicing part-time. We brought in a whiz kid from Rochester who's goin' day and night. We turned down an offer to merge with the Carlyle Group to form a full-service clinic; I was afraid we'd lose the referral support of the local GPs if they thought they might lose patients by sending them to us there."

"Smart move, I think," mumbled Jim.

"Financially, though," said Ray, "things are getting tight because of the overhead."

"More to the point, we're having problems renewing our malpractice insurance. May have to cut the limits and raise the deductible so much it would send us to the bank if we're ever sued; might even have to go bare."

"Now you probably know why I'm personally delivering your last check from the practice buyout instead of mailing it to you," Ray said with a sidelong glance.

"Yeah," Jim replied with a wry grin spreading over his tanned face. "I'll bet you want to know how I avoided all that, right?"

"Bingo!" Ray said, matching Jim's grin.

"Well, you know 'necessity is the mother of invention,' to coin a phrase. When old Joe screwed up on the Carter girl's operation, the insurance company trial lawyer warned me that the family might win and win big. That meant that even though I did my job perfectly, I might get tagged for a million dollars more than our policy limit!

"Well, that made me glad I had reordered my affairs a few years earlier with an eye toward reducing record evidence of personal wealth. I had nosed around and found a tax attorney who understood international estate planning. He brought me up to speed on how to reshuffle assets to use exemptions from the claims of judgment creditors. Then he suggested I move the rest of my holdings offshore. Well, that was a novel notion, for me. I'd always been too busy practicing medicine to do much more than put the money in the bank; we were talking about international finance, fer cryin' out loud!"

"He'd been through it enough times that he was able to break it down so I could understand it. Basically, it's perfectly legal for a US taxpayer to transfer assets out of the country as long as the transfer is disclosed to the government. I had to report the foreign income and pay the taxes, although a credit is available for taxes paid to foreign governments. But taxes weren't my concern — it was asset preservation.

"Checking some of the 'offshore financial centers,' as they call themselves, I looked for a supportive local attitude, a stable government, a low tax structure and a nice place to live in case I decided to retire there. There are several havens that fill the bill, but I picked the Isle of Man, right here in the middle of the Irish Sea, with Scotland on the north, Wales on the south, Ireland on the west, England on the east, Europe just a short plane ride away, great summer weather, modern facilities, a large and beautiful island country and honest, hardworking people who speak my language.

"The attorney established a trust for me here, using a major English bank as trustee. I put some money in it and bought this house on 20 acres and four industrial buildings here on the island, then placed the rest of it in a portfolio of managed securities.

"It was after going through that whole exercise that the malpractice case came up. The claim was eventually settled with the insurance company picking up the whole tab. Long before then, though, my horizons were expanded by this process. You know, tax havens began when Switzerland enacted commercial secrecy laws back in the thirties because people in Germany were nervous about the rise of fascism; it's all that saved the ones smart enough to plan ahead. In the non-US world, people routinely diversify their holdings geographically due to the risks of political, religious and racial persecution, oppressive governments, confiscatory taxes, war, often an unstable home economy ravaged by inflation and, of course, people like me who first thought of it because of potential lawsuits. All things considered, though, just the opportunity to invest where the opportunities exist throughout the world is reason enough.

"Basically, Ray, it makes sense to diversify assets geographically, just as you diversify between real estate and corporate securities. It reduces risk, increases opportunity and gives you a way to start over if things go to pot at home. But you have to plan ahead. It wasn't raining when Noah built the ark.''

Durable Power of Attorney (Health) California Requirements

As the person executing a durable power of attorney, you are the "principal." The person to whom you give the authority is the "attorney-in-fact." That attorney-in-fact may also be called the "agent" or "proxy." The power is "durable" if it becomes or continues to be of legal effect after the principal becomes legally incompetent.

The durable power of attorney for health care ("DPAHC") authorizes the agent to make those health care decisions that the principal would make if competent and to give or withhold consent to specific treatment. Any California resident at least 18 years old and of sound mind may execute a DPAHC.

A DPAHC must be witnessed by two persons who declare the principal apparently of sound mind and under no duress. At least one of the two witnesses must also declare that he or she is not related to the principal and, as far as is known, not entitled to a share in the principal's estate. Those who cannot serve as witnesses include: a health care provider, an employee of a health care provider, the attorney-in-fact, the operator of a community care facility, and an employee of a community care facility. Alternatively, the document may be acknowledged before a notary public who declares the principal apparently of sound mind and under no duress. When the statutory form is used without the advice of an attorney, only the two-witness acknowledgment procedure may be used.

Neither treating health care providers nor their employees may serve as attorney-in-fact. A limited exception is provided for employees related to the principal by blood, marriage, or adoption. If the statutory form is utilized, it must include numerous warnings in boldface type, including the warning that the agent may withdraw or withhold "treatment necessary to keep you alive." The warnings, however, must also provide that no treatment may be given to the principal over his or her objection and that health care necessary to keep the principal alive may not be stopped if the principal objects. The health care provider must ascertain the principal's capacity to give an informed consent. If the principal is capable of doing so, his or her wishes must be followed regardless of the prior execution of a DPAHC.

The agent may not authorize placement in a mental health facility, convulsive treatment, psychosurgery, sterilization or abortion, or anything "illegal." Further, the DPAHC expires seven years after execution unless at that time the principal is incompetent, in which event it continues in force until death or restoration of competence. While competent, the principal may revoke the authority granted at any time, either orally or in writing, by giving actual notice to the attorney-in-fact. Once the health care provider is notified of the revocation, it must note the revocation in the patient's chart.

The statute imposes several requirements on the health care provider. The provider must believe in good faith that the agent is authorized to make the treatment decision and that the proposed treatment is not inconsistent with any express desires of the principal, whether or not those desires are described in the DPAHC. When the decision is to withhold or withdraw life-sustaining treatment, the health care provider must first make a good faith effort to determine the desires of the principal and note the results of that effort in the medical chart.

The statute provides expressly that it is not to be construed as condoning or authorizing "mercy killing." Its authorization is limited to withholding or withdrawal of treatment "so as to permit the natural process of dying."

A successor agent may be appointed if desired. The principal may nominate a conservator of the person or estate or both for consideration by the courts should later conservatorship proceedings be commenced.

The Statutory Form

The pre-printed statutory form of DPAHC contains warnings to the principal in boldface type. There are then eleven designated paragraphs. At paragraph 1, the health care agent is designated. At paragraph 2, the principal's intention to create a durable power of attorney for health care is provided. Paragraph 3 contains a broad grant of authority for the agent to make all health care decisions that the principal could make if capable of doing so. It further provides that the agent shall make those decisions in a manner consistent with the desires of the principal as set forth in the document itself or as otherwise made known to the agent.

The most important part of the statutory form is paragraph 4, entitled Statement of Desires, Special Provisions and Limitations. There, the principal may include a statement of desires concerning life-prolonging care with blank lines following it to be filled in entirely at his or her discretion. There is also an "additional statement of desires, special provisions, and limitations," which is similarly followed by blank lines to be filled in by the principal as appropriate.

At paragraph 5, the agent is authorized to obtain medical records and verbal or written health information, and to execute the necessary releases or consents on behalf of the principal. At paragraph 6, the agent is authorized to execute waivers or liability release forms.

At paragraph 7, the agent is authorized to make a disposition of the principal's body parts under the *Uniform Anatomical Gift Act*, Health & WC §§7150-7157. The principal is advised that if any limitations on the agent's discretion are desired concerning anatomic gifts, those limitations should be set forth in paragraph 4. Paragraph 8 provides that the power of attorney will be in force for no more than seven years unless a shorter time is specified by the principal or unless the principal lacks capacity when it expires.

Paragraph 9 provides for the appointment of an alternate agent in the event the designated agent is unable or unwilling to serve. Paragraph 10 contains a nomination of conservator of the person if that becomes necessary. The court will ordinarily appoint the person nominated unless it is contrary to the best interests of the principal. Finally, paragraph 11 serves to revoke any prior durable power of attorney for health care.

Ethical Considerations and Conclusions

The DPAHC presents an opportunity to establish decision-making control over your health care, regardless of later incompetence. It also presents several ethical considerations:

• The agent you name for asset management may not support the decisions of the one you name for health care decision-making. Health care and asset preservation objectives may conflict. Insurance may minimize this conflict, but might not eliminate it.

• When your health care agent is also a beneficiary of your estate, an obvious conflict of interest is present. What role should the attorney play when the agent is an existing client? Under such circumstances, the DPAHC should, at a minimum, contain a disclosure that the agent is a beneficiary of the principal's estate.

• The DPAHC should be fully discussed with your attorney, and your desires candidly expressed. In accomplishing this, the lawyer is providing a valuable and needed function for you, one not met by the unadvised use of the statutory form. Copies of the instrument should be provided to the family physician and to the attorney drafting the DPAHC. The agent should keep the original in a safe but accessible place. You may wish to indicate on a card carried in your wallet or purse the location of the original and the name of the agent.

Drafting a personalized and easily-understood DPAHC is not an easy task. But it is too important for you to just fill in a stationery store form.

Sample Form

The sample form is submitted for illustrative purposes. You should tailor the form to your particular wishes.

Durable Power of Attorney for Health Care

WARNING TO PERSON EXECUTING THIS DOCUMENT:
THIS IS AN IMPORTANT LEGAL DOCUMENT. IT CREATES A DURABLE POWER OF ATTORNEY FOR HEALTH CARE. BEFORE EXECUTING THIS DOCUMENT, YOU SHOULD KNOW THESE IMPORTANT FACTS:
  • THIS DOCUMENT GIVES THE PERSON YOU DESIGNATE AS YOUR ATTORNEY-IN-FACT THE POWER TO MAKE HEALTH CARE DECISIONS FOR YOU, SUBJECT TO ANY LIMITATIONS OR STATEMENTS OF YOUR DESIRES THAT YOU INCLUDE IN THIS DOCUMENT. THE POWER TO MAKE HEALTH CARE DECISIONS FOR YOU MAY INCLUDE CONSENT, REFUSAL OF CONSENT, OR WITHDRAWAL OF CONSENT TO ANY CARE, TREATMENT, SERVICE, OR PROCEDURE TO MAINTAIN, DIAGNOSE OR TREAT A PHYSICAL OR MENTAL CONDITION. YOU MAY STATE IN THIS DOCUMENT ANY TYPES OF TREATMENT OR PLACEMENTS THAT YOU DO NOT DESIRE.
  • THE PERSON YOU DESIGNATE IN THIS DOCUMENT HAS A DUTY TO ACT CONSISTENTLY WITH YOUR DESIRES AS STATED IN THIS DOCUMENT OR OTHERWISE MADE KNOWN OR, IF YOUR DESIRES ARE UNKNOWN, TO ACT IN YOUR BEST INTERESTS.
  • EXCEPT AS YOU OTHERWISE SPECIFY IN THIS DOCUMENT, THE POWER OF THE PERSON YOU DESIGNATE TO MAKE HEALTII CARE DECISIONS FOR YOU MAY INCLUDE THE POWER TO CONSENT TO YOUR DOCTOR NOT GIVING TREATMENT OR STOPPING TREATMENT WHICH WOULD KEEP YOU ALIVE.
  • UNLESS YOU SPECIFY A SHORTER PERIOD IN THIS DOCUMENT, THIS POWER WILL EXIST FOR SEVEN YEARS FROM THE DATE YOU EXECUTE THIS DOCUMENT AND, IF YOU ARE UNABLE TO

MAKE HEALTH CARE DECISIONS FOR YOURSELF AT THE TIME WHEN THIS SEVEN-YEAR PERIOD ENDS, THIS POWER WILL CONTINUE TO EXIST UNTIL THE TIME WHEN YOU BECOME ABLE TO MAKE HEALTH CARE DECISIONS FOR YOURSELF.

• NOTWITHSTANDING THIS DOCUMENT, YOU HAVE THE RIGHT TO MAKE MEDICAL AND OTHER HEALTH CARE DECISIONS FOR YOURSELF SO LONG AS YOU CAN GIVE INFORMED CONSENT WITH RESPECT TO THE PARTICULAR DECISION. IN ADDITION, NO TREATMENT MAY BE GIVEN TO YOU OVER YOUR OBJECTION, AND HEALTH CARE NECESSARY TO KEEP YOU ALIVE MAY NOT BE STOPPED IF YOU OBJECT.

• YOU HAVE THE RIGHT TO REVOKE THE AUTHORITY GRANTED TO THE PERSON DESIGNATED IN THIS DOCUMENT TO MAKE HEALTH CARE DECISIONS FOR YOU BY NOTIFYING THE TREATING PHYSICIAN, HOSPITAL, OR OTHER HEALTH CARE PROVIDER ORALLY OR IN WRITING.

• THE PERSON DESIGNATED IN THIS DOCUMENT TO MAKE HEALTH CARE DECISIONS FOR YOU HAS THE RIGHT TO EXAMINE YOUR MEDICAL RECORDS AND TO CONSENT TO THEIR DISCLOSURE UNLESS YOU LIMIT THAT RIGHT IN THIS DOCUMENT.

• IF THERE IS ANYTHING IN THIS DOCUMENT THAT YOU DO NOT UNDERSTAND, YOU SHOULD ASK YOUR LAWYER TO EXPLAIN IT TO YOU.

1. **Designation of Agent.** I [1. principal's full name] of [2. address], California, age [3. age], being of sound mind, hereby designate and appoint [4. agent's full name], [5. address and telephone number], as my agent to make health care decisions authorized in this document.

2. **Creation of Durable Power of Attorney for Health Care.** By this document I intend to create a durable power of attorney for health care as authorized by the California Civil Code. This power of attorney shall remain in force despite my subsequent incapacity.

3. **General Statement of Authority.** In the event I become incapable of giving an informed consent to any health care decision

and to the same extent that I could if I were competent to do so, I hereby grant to my agent full power and authority to consent, refuse consent, or withdraw consent to any type of health care procedure (including any procedure to maintain, diagnose, or treat any physical or mental condition), or to make any other health care decision, subject to the terms of this instrument. My agent shall exercise this power and authority in accordance with my expressed desires, known to my agent, whether contained in this document or not. Before acting, my agent shall attempt to communicate with me regarding my desires unless such attempt would be futile. If my desires are unknown, then my agent should decide for me, having my best interests in mind.

[A Statement of Desires and Special Provisions is recommended but not required. Use either paragraph 4 (with or without its optional provisions) or paragraph 4-1.]

4. **Statement of Desires and Special Provisions.** I declare that I wish to live as long as I can enjoy life, but I do not wish to receive medical treatment which is futile and will provide no benefit to me. [Add the following subparagraphs as desired.]

☐   If I am in a coma (and have been for at least [6. number of days] days, which two (2) qualified physicians familiar with my condition have diagnosed as irreversible so that there is no reasonable possibility that I will ever regain consciousness, then I desire that all life-sustaining treatment be withdrawn or withheld, even if my death will result.

[If the preceding subparagraph is used, it may be concluded with a statement of wishes regarding food and water.] However, please continue to give me food and water in any way you can.
[Alternatively or continuing]
[However, if/If] I have been in such an irreversible coma for [7. number of days] days, do not continue to give me food and water by any artificial means, unless I can be fed or given water manually by mouth, or unless stopping food or water will cause

me to experience pain as a result.
[Continuing — Optional]

☐   I do not wish to receive treatment which will not improve
    my living conditions or my health if I am incurably and ter-
    minally ill. When two (2) qualified physicians who are fa-
    miliar with my condition have made such a diagnosis, then
    I only want treatment, including life-sustaining treatment,
    that offers benefits to me greater than the burdens it will
    impose. My agent should consider whether the treatment
    will relieve suffering or improve my prognosis, what intru-
    siveness, risks and side effects it involves, whether it will
    extend my life and, if so, what quality of life or enjoyment
    of life I will retain.

[Continuing — Optional]

☐   When two (2) qualified physicians who are familiar with
    my condition have diagnosed that I am incurably and ter-
    minally ill, I wish to receive treatment necessary for my
    comfort and relief of pain, even if its unintended but un-
    avoidable side effect is to hasten the moment of my death.

[Alternative to all of the foregoing options]

4. Statement of Desires and Special Provisions. I desire that my
life be sustained and prolonged to the greatest extent possible,
regardless of prognosis, pain or cost of treatment.
[Continuing — Optional]

☐   Other Desires or Special Provisions. [8. Specify particular
    treatments desired or prohibited, whether life-sustaining or
    not, and particular circumstances in which you want spe-
    cific things done (*e.g.*, dietary and blood transfusion limita-
    tions based on religious beliefs).]

5. Contribution of My Body Parts.
[One of the following]
I do not wish to donate my body or any of its parts for any purpose.
[Or]

I wish to donate any needed organ or body parts, under the Uniform Anatomical Gift Act, for any scientific, educational, therapeutic, or transplant purpose.
[Or]
I wish to donate the following organ(s) or body part(s), under the Uniform Anatomical Gift Act, for any scientific, educational, therapeutic or transplant purpose:
[Continuing — Optional]

6. Designation of Alternate Agent.

If the person designated as my agent in paragraph 1 is unable or unwilling to act as such, or if I revoke that person's appointment as my agent, then the first alternative agent named below shall become my agent with the power and authority conferred by this instrument; and if the first alternative agent shall be unable or unwilling to act as my agent or if I revoke that person's appointment as such, then the second alternative agent named below shall become my agent with the power and authority conferred by this instrument:
A. First alternative agent (name, address, and telephone number):
B. Second alternative agent (name, address, and telephone number):
[Continuing — Optional]

7. Nomination of Conservator of Person.

If it becomes necessary to appoint a conservator of my person, I nominate the following individuals to serve as conservator of my person, to serve alone in the order named (name, address, and telephone number):
    [Continue]

8. Authority Concerning Medical Information and Records.

    Subject to any limitations set forth elsewhere in this instrument, my agent shall have the power and authority to do all of the following:
A. Request, review, and receive any information, verbal or written, regarding my physical or mental health, including but not limited to, medical and hospital records.

B. Execute on my behalf any releases or other documents that may be required in order to obtain information.

C. Consent to the disclosure of medical information.

D. Execute documents such as Refusal to Permit Treatment, Leaving Hospital Against Medical Advice, or any necessary waiver or release from liability required by hospital or physician.

9. Duration.

This power of attorney is effective immediately and shall remain in force for [seven years] unless I am incapable of making health care decisions when this power otherwise expires, in which case it will continue in force until I regain the capacity to make health care decisions for myself.

10. Declaration of Principal.

I declare that my lawyer has explained to me my rights in connection with this instrument, and the consequences of signing it and not signing it, and that I have read the warnings contained herein. Executed this ___ day of _____, 19___, at _____, California.

_____
[Name of Principal]
Certificate of Acknowledgment of Notary Public
STATE OF CALIFORNIA   )
COUNTY OF LOS ANGELES)ss.
On this ___ day of _____, 19___, before me, [Name of Notary Public], personally appeared [Name of Principal], personally known to me or proved to me on the basis of satisfactory evidence, to be the person whose name is subscribed to this instrument, and acknowledged that he or she executed it. I declare under penalty of perjury that the person whose name is subscribed to this instrument appears to be of sound mind and under no duress, fraud, or undue influence.

_____
Signature of Notary Public
Statement of Witness
[If form not notarized]

I declare under penalty of perjury under the laws of California that the principal is personally known to me, that the principal signed or acknowledged this durable power of attorney in my presence, that the principal appears to be of sound mind and under no duress, fraud, or undue influence, that I am not the person appointed as attorney-in-fact by this document, and that I am not a health care provider, an employee of a health care provider, the operator of a community health care facility, nor an employee of an operator of a community care facility; further, I am not related to the principal by blood, marriage, or adoption, and to the best of my knowledge I am not entitled to any part of the estate of the principal upon the death of the principal under a will now existing or by operation of law.

Signature:

Print Name:

Residence Address:

Date:

Signature:

Print Name:

Residence Address:

Date:

Guide for Preparing a Letter of Instruction on Estate Matters

[Date]
My dearest [wife/husband]:

As we have discussed from time to time, this letter (which, incidentally, is not to be construed as my will) should be opened upon my death and serve as a reminder of some of the matters which we have talked about over the years. A copy has been furnished to [attorney] and [accountant]. They will advise you as to certain matters you will be facing in the first several months.

Funeral Arrangements
As we discussed, I would like a simple funeral and burial. Flowers should be kept to a minimum. You decide on the location; [City] or [City].
Estate Plan
[For example: Our original wills, trust and community property agreement, as well as the life insurance policy and certificate are in the den file cabinet marked ''Estate Documents'' and ''Life/Health Insurance'' respectively. I have named you as Executrix of my Will. See [attorney] and [accountant]: they will guide you through the probate administration.]

Location of Records:
[For example: File folders at home; den file cabinet.]

Summary of Estate Plan:
[For example: You have a simple will that leaves all your estate
to me. If I predecease you, your estate goes at your subsequent
death into the family trust for the children.]

[I have a pourover will that leaves the cars and furnishings to
you and the rest of the estate to the family trust for your benefit
and after you, the children.]

[The trust provides you with an income for life, together with
limited powers to invade principal. [Name of bank] will serve as
trustee. You can replace the trustee at any time. The trustee will
take care of all financial matters except paying your monthly living expenses for you; it will do that if requested, but it shouldn't
be necessary unless you become disabled.]

[The (amount) life insurance policy from Occidental is payable
to the trust. The (amount) group term life insurance policy from
Travelers is payable to you directly. If a disability precedes my
death, a total benefit of (amount) per month may be payable under two disability income policies from Occidental.]

[The encumbrance on the house is (amount). The interest rate is
at (percentage); it is so low it should not be paid off.]

[At this writing, there is no debt, other than that noted above
and current monthly charge accounts.]

[I think your income will be more than adequate to continue that
standard of living we have enjoyed during the past several
years. It seems to me that the children are equipped both voca-
tionally and emotionally to take care of themselves, so you
should not feel it necessary to skimp for their benefit.]

Bank Accounts

[For example: You may write checks on our joint bank account then, just as you can now. In addition, the checking account has a sizable line of credit which you may use in case there is a delay in starting income distributions from the Trust.]

[The money market account at [name of bank] is in my name as trustee of the family trust. The bank successor trustee will take over.]

[The various accounts for the [family business] will also wind up in the trust, since I expect [attorney] to sell or dissolve the company.]

Safe Deposit Box

[For example: I have a safe deposit box in the [name of bank] branch downstairs from the office. It is No. [number] and in the name of the company. Duplicate keys are on my key chain and in the center drawer of my desk. It is accessible only to me, so you will have to be appointed executrix before you can enter it. The box contains primarily original securities and notes receivable of ours.]

Credit Cards

[For example: Notify companies in which I have credit cards (department stores, oil companies, etc.). Also destroy or mutilate the cards in my wallet and in the third drawer of the highboy. If you desire, you can usually get the cards re-issued in your name.]

Brokerage House

[For example: Notify each brokerage firm in writing and cancel any standing or special instructions I have given them. At this writing, I have accounts at [names of brokerage firms], but only the [name] account is active. It is in the name of the trust. The broker is [name/phone number].]

Life Insurance
[For example: Ask [name] Insurance Company to send a death claim form. The local general agent is [name/phone number]. The group insurance file at the office should contain all the necessary claim forms for the group life insurance. If not, call the broker, [name/phone number].]

Government Death Benefits
[For example: When you are 60 or older, you should be entitled to a widow's retirement benefit. It is tax-free and could be fairly sizable if the Social Security system doesn't go broke.]

Offices Held
[For example: Return to the various church and trade organizations all files and other records in connection with the offices I held.]

Home
[For example: Our home is held in community property title, making it a probate asset. As a consequence, it will ultimately be distributed from the probate estate to the trust. If you ever decide to sell it, you have the power to direct the trustee to do so. The proceeds will be allocated to both your side and my side of the trust, but you can similarly direct the trustee to purchase a new home (in the name of the trust) from either or both sides.]

First Steps to be Taken
[For example: Call [attorney name/phone number] to commence the probate administration proceeding. Special Letters of Administration will be required to vote the stock of the company.]

[If the company is to be dissolved: meet with key staff; increase their salaries, and give them time to look for new jobs in order to gain their cooperation for the wind-down of the business. Move fast — close the office as soon as the files can be transferred and receivables collected.]

[Again, if the company is to be dissolved: prepare a letter report to customers notifying them of my death, suggesting that they obtain new representation so their file can be forwarded and offering them a discount for early payment of their account balance, if any. Press the collection of receivables hard so the office can be closed within thirty days, cutting off continuing overhead expenses.]

[Contact the broker on the company's general liability and errors and omissions insurance and "buy the tail" (a one-time payment to cover future liability claims).]

Miscellaneous
[For example: Contact my secretary and ask her to send home the various pictures, portraits and other mementos, as well as any personal correspondence files.]

[Cancel all of my subscriptions to publications in which you have no interest. You may be entitled to refunds for the unexpired portion of the subscription price.]

[We presently have no outstanding debts other than current monthly charge accounts and the loan against our home. As far as I know, we are not owed any money other than that mentioned in this letter.]

[A list should be made of all checks you receive. [Attorney name] will tell you which go in the probate accounts and which you can keep. Generally, checks made out to you alone may be deposited or cashed as before.]
[Keep a record of all bills, whether paid or not.]

Assets
[For example: Generally, there is the family business, the house, bank accounts at [name of bank] and [name of bank], a few notes receivable, judgment lien, and the stock of [name]. The company, in turn, holds: [etc.]. Apart from these holdings, there

is only an assortment of personal property items: two cars, one boat, household furnishings, etc.]

[The company is incorporated with only cash, receivables, pre-paid expenses, a small telephone system and work in process as assets. Except for the telephone system, the furniture, fixtures and equipment are all held personally and rented to the company at [amount] per month. The rental agreement is in writing at the office. Exhibit "A" attached to it describes every item involved, its purchase price and date of purchase.]

Business Relationships
[For example: [Name of passive business interest] is owned equally with [name]. It has independent management, requiring only policy direction and long-range planning assistance from the owners. There is no buy/sell agreement between [name] and me. The stock should probably be held to produce income. You and [name] should take out 5% per month of gross revenues, then split the net profit at the end of each year, after reserving adequate working capital. Accounting is provided by [name of accountant]. Corporate records are at the office.]

Income, Estate and Other Taxes
[For example: Contact [accountant] and [attorney] regarding the necessary tax planning and forms to be filed. Copies of personal tax returns are in the den file and also in [accountant's] office. Copies of all financial statements are in a black binder on the credenza in my office, and also in [accountant's] office.]

[A federal Estate Tax Return may be required, although the marital deduction should eliminate any tax. Decedent's final income tax returns must be filed; withholding and quarterly estimates already paid should cover any tax due.]

[You will have to file tax returns for your trust income and any family allowance you receive from the probate estate (excluding capital distributions contained therein). See [accountant] for help in organizing for that job. The life insurance proceeds are income tax-free.]

[Titles to the cars are in the files in the den under ''Cars.'']

[I have attached a listing of names, addresses and telephone numbers for your ready reference. Also attached is a copy of the last personal financial statement I prepared.]

[As questions come up, you may wish to call [attorney] or [accountant].]

Personal Message...

APPENDIX C

Survey of the Major Havens

An Overview

In order to select a tax haven through which to invest internationally, you must first assess the personal importance of tax and privacy issues, as well as the feasibility of conducting an active offshore business. You then examine the specific characteristics of those havens most closely meeting your needs and make your selection based on location, culture, legal system, political stability and specific laws addressing those needs.

To aid in that regard, more than 20 of the most popular or promising havens are discussed in Appendix C. This discussion provides enough information to permit you to materially narrow your search, perhaps to make a final choice.

Various tax havens are discussed elsewhere in the book in the context of specific transactions. Here, we separately collect information about each haven, addressing generally its location, culture, political system, legal system, local support services, currency, bank or commercial secrecy, general corporate and trust law, special business entities, cost comparisons and prospects for continued viability as a tax haven.

A loose definition for the term "tax haven" is "any country having a low or zero rate of tax on all or certain categories of income, with or without banking or commercial secrecy." Applied literally, that definition would include in its sweep many of the industrialized countries of the world, countries not typically regarded as tax havens.

The term may also be defined by the "smell" test; that is, a country is a tax haven if it takes steps to attract offshore business and is considered to be a tax haven by those who care.

As a rule, all jurisdictions regarded as tax havens impose low or no taxes on some category of income and, with or without specific secrecy laws, a high level of confidentiality as to banking transactions.

Certain tax havens specialize by establishing laws that encourage particular kinds of business, such as insurance, banking, finance companies, trusts, etc. Certain tax havens design their tax system around a treaty network, permitting pockets of opportunity for specific industries.

Often the haven is a poor, underdeveloped country with a small population rendering an income tax system impractical. Tax haven status permits it to establish a license or fee system for generating revenue from offshore business entities and individuals. Administration costs for collecting such revenues are minimal.

In other tax havens, the local population is more heavily taxed but the jurisdiction imposes low rates or no tax on certain income from foreign sources. That permits a local corporation conducting only offshore business to be formed and managed in the tax haven at little or no cost other than its annual governmental license fees.

The secrecy with which commercial transactions in general and banking transactions in particular may be conducted through tax havens has its origin in either the common law or in local statutory law. Common law secrecy is found in those jurisdictions which were or still are part of the British Commonwealth. It is based on an implied contract between a banker and customer that the banker will treat all of the customer's affairs as confidential. If the confidentiality is breached, the customer may sue the banker and recover all consequential damages. Certain jurisdictions have extended the common law rules by statute, sometimes adding criminal sanctions for their breach. Among the newer tax havens, such laws constitute the central marketing feature of the jurisdiction as a tax haven; they are enacted for purely competitive reasons. Secrecy at some level is common to all countries, tax and nontax havens alike. Most, however, will not protect information from a proper inquiry by a foreign government, especially where the inquiry is based on the authority of a treaty. The posture of tax havens, however, is to decline to respond even where the inquiring jurisdiction demonstrates a violation of its laws. The friction between haven and nonhaven countries arises from the place that line is drawn: toward the legitimate rights of countries to enforce their laws on the one hand, and the rights of individuals to privacy on the other. Notwithstanding substantial advances in recent years in obtaining disclosure from traditional tax havens where US law violations are under investigation, disclosure continues to be a substantial problem as to most havens and to all of them with respect to tax evasion investigation.

Offshore banking is a critically important endeavor for most tax haven countries; the magnitude of the transactions is large, permitting higher annual fees than may be imposed upon other private corporations or personal trusts. The laws encouraging offshore banking involve placing it in a separate category from domestic banking activity, imposing little or no reserve requirements as well as low or zero tax rates and no foreign exchange controls.

Key to the success of a country promoting itself as a tax haven is modern communications facilities; particularly telephone, cable and telex services linking them to other countries. Almost as important are good airline service and convenient location.

Another key feature is the absence of currency controls. Often, a currency control system regulates the affairs of the tax haven residents, but exempts nonresidents, including corporations domiciled there but formed to conduct offshore business. That freedom relieves you from concerns that your resources may be trapped within the jurisdiction by a hostile local government.

Most tax havens have few, if any, tax treaties with other countries. Others have numerous treaties but use them artfully in order to position themselves for the particular kinds of business activities in which they are interested.

The archetypal modern tax haven is Switzerland. Actually, Switzerland began as a haven for capital — not a haven from tax — for the persecuted citizens of Russia, Germany, South America, Spain and the Balkans. Today, most tax havens regard themselves as "offshore financial centers" — centers for international borrowing and lending in nonlocal currency.

The Netherlands Antilles

Summary. *Until terminated effective January 1, 1988, the US-Netherlands tax treaty made the Netherlands Antilles a major offshore financial center for Eurodollar loans to US multinational corporations. It has little left to distinguish it from a dozen other havens.*

Location. The Netherlands Antilles is a group of four islands and part of a fifth located near the coast of Venezuela. The principal city is Willemstad on the island of Curacao. Access to the Antilles is by nonstop jet flights to Curacao from New York (about 4 1/2 hours) and from Miami (about 2 1/2 hours). It has adequate telephone and telex facilities. To dial direct from the United States to Curacao, use country code 599 and city code 9. A sixth island, Aruba, seceded January 1, 1986.

Culture. The Netherlands Antilles has about 200,000 in population, primarily black. Most of the people live on Curacao. Unemployment is high (about 30%) due to automation of the local oil refineries.

The official language is Dutch, although the local population speaks Papiamento, a mixture of several languages. Most of the population also speaks both English and Spanish. On St. Maarten, the primary language is English.

Political System. The Netherlands would like to see the Antilles become independent, although the Antilles is reluctant to sever its association. Most viewers conclude that independence is likely. It should not, however, rupture the close links of the Antilles with the Netherlands; Antilles is likely to remain a major offshore financial center.

Legal System. The Netherlands Antilles operates under a civil law system. It is a signatory to the 1961 Hague Convention. Accordingly, documents executed in the Netherlands Antilles are authenticated by an Apostille, the standard certificate provided by the convention. The Apostille should be signed by the Lt. Governor.

Local Support Services. The number of lawyers, tax consultants and accountants available is adequate. The documents by which corporations are formed must be executed by a notary; Notaries Public, under the civil law system, are better-trained and have more authority than is the case in the US.

Currency. The Netherlands Antilles guilder or guilder florin equals approximately US$.56. Although the Antilles has exchange control rules, corporations formed by nonresidents are exempted from them.

Secrecy. The Netherlands Antilles has no specific secrecy law. Corporation information is available to the public from the Commercial Register of the Chamber of Commerce. It is not a signatory to the Tax Information Exchange Agreement with the US.

General Corporate Law. *Netherlands Antilles Commercial Code* §§33-155 governs the formation and operation of corporations. Those provisions are substantially unchanged since the time they went into effect in the mid-forties. There are several published English translations available, but they differ enough that it is problematic whether a particular point may be resolved without recourse to a bilingual lawyer who understands Dutch.

In the US, we are familiar with Articles of Incorporation and Bylaws as separate documents. In the Netherlands Antilles, the Bylaws are included in the Articles of Incorporation. The form and content of the incorporating documents must be approved by the Minister of Justice. The minister may do so either before the fact, when the articles are in draft form, or after they have been executed before the Notary Public. In either event, formation does not take place until both approval and execution. Forming a Netherlands Antilles corporation may take several weeks, due to delays in obtaining approval by the Minister of Justice. The Articles of Incorporation and the Minister of Justice's Decree of No Objection must be published in the Official Gazette and registered in the Commercial Register. Every corporation name must either begin with or end with the words *naamloze venootschap* or the letters "N.V." That corresponds to "Ltd." "S.A." or "Inc." in other jurisdictions.

In the US, directors set policy and supervise operating officers, whereas operating officers execute policy and manage the day-to-day affairs of the corporation. In the Netherlands Antilles, the affairs of a corporation are managed on a day-to-day basis by "managing directors." At least one of the managing directors must be a resident in the Netherlands Antilles, and any one may bind the company as to third parties unless the Articles of Incorporation provide otherwise. The resident director is typically a local management company providing that particular service. In order to maintain control over the corporation, you would ordinarily require three managing directors and empower any two of them to bind the corporation as to third parties, elect one the resident director and two as nonresident directors and provide in the Articles of Incorporation that the action of two of the three is required in order to bind the corporation as to any third party. Local counsel often criticize that approach because of its inefficiency in carrying out corporate actions; nonetheless, you will feel more secure if you are able to control the affairs of the corporation in that manner.

The shares of the Netherlands Antilles corporation may be either registered or issued to bearer. Shares must have a par value, and all shares must have voting rights. At least 20% of the authorized capital must be subscribed initially. If the corporation is formed using local nominees, they will ordinarily demand proof that the subscribed capital was paid in; otherwise they become jointly liable for all claims against the corporation before payment of the subscribed capital. Shares that are issued and outstanding may be redeemed by the corporation at any time, so long as at least 20% of the authorized capital remains issued and outstanding. Shareholder meetings must be convened in the Netherlands Antilles at least once each year. If the corporation issues only registered shares, however, the shareholders may authorize having the meeting outside that jurisdiction.

If the power to redeem shares is important in your planning, the *Netherlands Antilles Commercial Code* permits a complex capital structure (both common and preferred stock with varying rights) with fairly flexible redemption rights.

It may be important to transfer the domicile of your corporation from one jurisdiction to another if tax or secrecy law changes, or if political or economic unrest cause you to lose confidence in the jurisdiction. The *Netherlands Antilles Commercial Code* permits the transfer of the corporate domicile to the Netherlands in Europe, but only in case of emergency (revolution or threat of war).[1] A new law now under consideration would permit the domicile to be transferred to any other country that has legislation authorizing it to receive foreign corporations.[2]

Every Netherlands Antilles corporation must pay a tax on its worldwide income, except as otherwise provided by law or by treaty.[3]

Both the type and the nature of the taxes on corporations vary widely, but the tax on those suitable for tax haven operations are, for the most part, nominal.

The tax rate for investment companies is in a range of 2.4 to 3%.[4] There is no corporate profits tax on capital gains, nor are municipal surtaxes imposed. Current rates are guaranteed until at least 1999.

The tax rate of 3% or less applies as well to holding companies, including those that hold patents, trademarks, copyrights, motion picture distribution rights or real estate. Shipping companies are taxed at a maximum rate of 10%.

There is no withholding tax on either dividends or interest paid by a Netherlands Antilles corporation to its nonresident shareholders or payees. Nonresidents are also exempt from personal income tax on dividends and interest received from Netherlands Antilles investment companies, holding companies or other corporations that are entitled to special rates of tax under the *Profits Tax Ordinance of 1940*. Capital gains derived from selling the shares of such corporations are also exempt.

There is no Netherlands Antilles estate or inheritance tax on the shares of a Netherlands Antilles corporation owned by a nonresident decedent.

Until repealed by the US in 1987, the US-Netherlands tax treaty was extended to the Netherlands Antilles and (combined with a lower corporate tax rate than that of the Netherlands) made it a major haven for use in facilitating the borrowing of US dollars held by European institutions ("Eurodollars"). The usual pattern routed the funds through a finance company established in the Netherlands Antilles by a US multinational corporation parent. The finance company borrowed the money and relent it to its parent, with income tax withholding from interest payments by the parent-borrower dramatically reduced from the usual 30%. No replacement treaty is yet in place for either the Netherlands Antilles or Aruba, and none is in prospect. That leaves the Netherlands Antilles without a competitive edge, compared to no-tax havens.

Thus, its US-source passive income is taxed just like other nontreaty countries; *i.e.,* a 30% withholding tax on the gross amount, except for "portfolio interest" income. "Portfolio interest" is interest on any obligation which is not in registered form provided: there are arrangements reasonably designed to insure that the obligation will be sold or resold only to non-US persons; the interest is payable only outside the US and its possessions; and the face of the certificate evidencing the obligation bears a statement that any US person who holds it "will be subject to limitations under US income tax laws."[5] Interest on registered obligations is also tax-free portfolio interest provided that it represents US Treasury obligations or that the US person who would otherwise be required to withhold the US tax receives a statement that the beneficial owner is not a "US person." (A "US person" is a US citizen, resident, partnership, corporation, estate or trust.)[6] Portfolio interest treatment is not recognized, though, where the foreign person or entity receiving it is a 10%-or-more owner of the borrower. Nor does it include either routine borrowing by a US corporation from a foreign bank, or borrowing by a US person from a CFC where the two are "related persons."[7] Repeal of the 30% withholding tax on qualified portfolio interest permits US multinational corporations to issue bonds directly to the foreign lenders. That effectively eliminates the Netherlands Antilles' reason for existence. It remains to be seen whether it will effectively reposition itself.

Special Corporations. The Netherlands Antilles is home to several mutual funds and a large number of private family investment companies.

Trusts. As a civil law jurisdiction, the Netherlands Antilles has no enabling law permitting the formation and operation of trusts. It is considering establishing such law, but the absence of a substantial body of case law on trusts makes the Netherlands Antilles useful primarily, if not entirely, for corporations.

Cost Comparisons. If you purchase a "shelf" company to reduce the lead time in forming a corporation in the Netherlands Antilles, it may cost you between US$2,000 and $3,000. Taking it step-by-step would be less, since a premium is charged for the convenience of a shelf corporation. Maintenance costs (local tax return, local office and a local managing director) run approximately $1,200 per year.

Prospects. To protect its monopoly on Eurobonds, the Netherlands Antilles actively lobbied against the *Tax Reform Act of 1984* that eliminated the 30% withholding tax on portfolio interest paid to foreign persons. In spite of congressional complaints about alleged abuses under the existing treaty, and in spite of continuing negotiations between the US and the Netherlands Antilles, no new income tax treaty seems in the offing. Consequently, its future as an offshore financial center turns on the alacrity with which it repositions itself to compete without the tax treaty monopoly it so long enjoyed.

Endnotes

1. National Act Governing the Voluntary Transfer of Seats of Legal Entities, as amended

2. Proposed Ordinance re Transfer of Corporate Seats of Netherlands Antilles Corporations

3. Profits Tax Ordinance of 1940, as amended

4. Profits Tax Ordinance, Secs. 14, 14A

5. IRC Secs. 871(h), 881(c)

6. IRC Sec. 7701(a)(3)

7. IRC Secs. 864(d)(4), 881(c)

Bermuda

Summary. *Bermuda is a highly-regarded, low-profile tax haven. It imposes no direct taxation and it is not a party to any tax treaties. Its exempted companies receive long-term guarantees against future taxes on income and capital gains. The initial and annual fees imposed on exempt companies by the government are higher than most other tax haven jurisdictions. It is probably your first choice in establishing a captive foreign insurance company, as well as an excellent place to establish a holding company if tax treaty benefits are irrelevant to your needs. With its well-established body of common law precedent, it is an excellent place to establish your trust. You cannot establish an offshore bank there.*

If any local business is conducted, that business must be at least 60% owned by Bermuda citizens. Exempt (offshore) companies may not conduct business in Bermuda except to maintain an office through which to conduct their offshore activities.

Bermudians prefer that their country not be called a "tax haven," particularly if it carries any hint of impropriety. It carefully screens those persons who seek to form an exempted company, relying on its network of contacts and bank references.

Location. Bermuda is located in the Atlantic Ocean, approximately 775 miles southeast of New York City. It is reached by nonstop jet flights from London, Canada and New York, as well as other east coast cities. It has excellent telephone and telex service. For direct-dialed calls, use area code 809, plus local prefix 29. Bermuda time is one hour later than that of New York throughout the year. The capital is Hamilton, located eight miles from the Bermuda airport.

Culture. The language of Bermuda is English. The population is approximately 55,000, about 40% white and the rest black. Although the government is biracial, local blacks feel that it is dominated politically and economically by the white minority. A number of significant training and career opportunities are available to young Bermudians, programs particularly helpful to upgrading the career opportunities and aspirations of the indigenous black population. Per capita income is high and unemployment low. It enjoys a low crime rate by any modern standard and no notable public corruption. As a nation, Bermudians are proud of their heritage and intent on shaping their future. The US Navy maintains a base for its anti-submarine defense which occupies 10% of the Bermuda land mass. Hence, the American influence comes from more than its simple proximity 600 miles to the west.

Political System. As part of the United Kingdom, the Governor of Bermuda is appointed by the British Government. England retains control over the external affairs, defense, internal security and the public policies of Bermuda. Politically and economically, Bermuda is stable, although it had some disturbances and riots by black dissidents in 1973 and again in 1977.

Legal System. The legal system is based on English common law, as modified by local statute. Final appeals from Bermuda courts go to the Privy Council in England.

It is a signatory to the 1961 Hague Convention. Accordingly, documents executed in Bermuda are authenticated by an Apostille, the standard certificate provided by the Convention. The Apostille should be signed by the Governor of Bermuda or any member of his staff signing on his behalf and using his official seal.

Qualified Bermudians are given a priority in filling any available positions, although work permits are generally available for foreign managers and executives of offshore companies. Special permission from the Governor-in-Counsel is required for non-Bermudians to acquire improved real property. You will be encouraged to purchase a condominium rather than a house. You may purchase a condominium if it has an annual rental value of as little as US$6,000, whereas you may not buy a house unless its minimum annual rental value is at least $12,000. In purchasing improved real property, you must pay a fee to the government equal to 10% of the purchase price. You will not be permitted to purchase unimproved land.

Exempted companies are encouraged by exemption from import and export duties and by guarantees against taxes on income and capital gains to carry on light manufacturing, processing and warehousing in Freeport on Ireland, about 10 miles from Hamilton.[1]

Local Support Services. The professional facilities of Bermuda, including banks, attorneys, accountants and management companies, are excellent.

Bermuda has only three banks, a cartel that effectively keeps out any competition from foreign international banks. As a consequence, the local banks enjoy operating profits reportedly in excess of 30% per year on invested capital. That presumed effect notwithstanding, there are reports (now dated) that the absence of effective bank regulation over the cartel has resulted in imprudent banking practices that present serious risks of insolvency.[2] Bermuda would clearly benefit from the presence of major international banks on the island. The local population would also benefit by elimination of the local cartel; it depresses interest income available to depositors while loaning at a spread rate often exceeding 10%.

The two oldest and largest banks have assets exceeding US$1 billion each and are owned almost entirely by Bermuda citizens. The newest bank is affiliated with a major international bank.

Offshore banks owned by nonresidents are not permitted. Nonresidents may, however, use an exempted Bermuda finance company to carry on limited banking services from Bermuda; they are restricted to financial services for affiliated companies.

Currency. The Bermuda dollar is maintained in parity with the US dollar, a practice that is likely to continue. While exchange-control regulations exist, they are imposed only upon individuals and corporations resident and doing business in Bermuda; exempted companies and trusts formed by nonresidents operate freely in any currency other than the Bermuda dollar.

Secrecy. Common law, rather than specific legislation, provides the basis for commercial secrecy. Such protections are carefully observed, making it difficult for foreign governments to obtain any information about Bermuda companies, trusts and bank accounts in the absence of civil fraud or criminal activity recognized under Bermuda law.

Since the register of shareholders for exempted companies is a public record maintained at the registered office of the company, shareholders desiring anonymity should use nominees. The Memorandum of Association (Articles of Incorporation) of an exempted company is a public record maintained at the office of the Registrar of Companies. Other corporate records are not open to public inspection. But see the last paragraph under General Corporate Law, *infra*.

General Corporate Law. Formation of a new exempt company requires the prior approval of the Minister of Finance or his delegate. The Minister may withhold approval without providing any reason. The Controller of Foreign Exchange, an official of the Bermuda Monetary Authority, is the official delegate of the Minister of Finance for this purpose. It usually takes about one month to organize a Bermuda company, because of the approval process.

The Companies Act 1981, which took effect in 1983,[3] controls the formation and operation of Bermuda corporations. Under it: a company must publish and file a prospectus before offering shares of debt instruments to the public; it may not buy its own shares or those of its holding company; what we term "paid-in surplus" is allocated to a "share premium account," treated as capital and available for limited purposes; liens are given no priority unless and until registered with the Registrar of Companies; unless waived by all shareholders and directors, audited financial statements are required annually; and exempted companies may incorporate by reference all of the purposes and powers set out in *The Bermuda Companies Act 1981*, thereby shortening and simplifying the Articles of Incorporation.

An exempted company is excused from the requirement that it be at least 60% owned by Bermudians. It can also obtain a guarantee against taxes on income and capital gains until the year 2016. About 20% of the 6,000 exempted companies now operating out of Bermuda are insurance companies.

Minimum capitalization is US$12,000. The issued shares need

not be fully paid, but if not, each shareholder is liable for the unpaid balance.

As is the case with the Netherlands Antilles, the law demonstrates little concern for separating the policy-making responsibilities of the board of directors from the policy-executing responsibilities of the officers. Each company must have at least three directors, of whom two must live in Bermuda. Directors' meetings may be held within or without the colony. The board elects a president and vice president, both of whom must be directors, and a secretary, who need not be either a director or shareholder. Each director must hold at least one qualifying share, which share is customarily endorsed and held in trust for the beneficial owner.

All stock must be registered in the name of the shareholder of record, no provision being made for bearer shares. Only par value stock is permitted. Each corporation must have three or more shareholders. Although a shareholder may attend a meeting by proxy, only another shareholder may hold that proxy.

Bermuda has no law permitting a corporation to move its domicile into or out of that jurisdiction, nor any prohibiting it. Thus, there is a risk that doing so may be treated as a constructive dissolution for tax purposes. Because of the recent move of a major Hong Kong trading company to Bermuda, however, it is reported that redomiciliation provisions may soon be enacted.

Except for a modest payroll tax based on salaries and other income paid to local employees and on self-employment income, Bermuda has no tax on personal income, no tax on corporate income and no tax on capital gains. There are no gift, estate or inheritance taxes, although Bermuda does impose a modest probate fee covering real and personal property of the decedent located in Bermuda.

This general 5% payroll tax is not imposed on employees of exempted companies. In 1976, however, Bermuda passed a new, separate 4% hospital levy on all persons working there, including the employees of exempted companies.[4] The books and records of exempted companies are not open for inspection, so the salaries on which to impose this tax are presumed to be $35,660 per year, leading to an annual tax of $1,426 on each employee. This willingness to legislate a gross income tax does not well serve the reputation of Bermuda as a stable tax haven.

Historically, Bermuda avoided tax treaties with other nations. Because of the importance of its insurance industry, however, the United Kingdom acted on its behalf to enter into a treaty with the US in July 1986, limiting US taxation of Bermuda insurance companies. The treaty includes provisions for the exchange of tax information between Bermuda and the US. Following passage of enabling legislation in Bermuda and approval by the US Senate, the treaty became effective in December 1988.

Special Corporations. While it is virtually impossible to establish a new bank or trust company in Bermuda, that country serves as an important base for several other types of special companies. The most important are insurance companies, shipping companies and mutual funds. It is also an important base for personal trusts.

The Bermuda Insurance Act of 1978 and related regulations became fully effective in 1981 with the blessing of the local insurance industry. It provides limited regulation for captive insurance companies, regulation that the industry finds nonburdensome. Bermuda insurance companies require authorized capital of at least US$120,000, all of which must be paid-in. Local insurance personnel are highly trained, and excellent relationships exist between the local industry and reinsurance markets in London and Switzerland. It is developing its own reinsurance market, as well.

Bermuda is a popular domicile for shipping companies. Any ship owned by a Bermuda exempted company must be a British ship, meeting British crew requirements. It, however, may charter or subcharter ships of any nationality. Consequently, Liberian or Panamanian flagships are often chartered by Bermuda shipping companies.

Mutual funds and unit trusts find Bermuda an important base. They are typically organized by special acts of the legislature authorizing the redemption of shares, a practice historically prohibited in British Commonwealth territories.

At least one automated commodities futures exchange opened in Bermuda in October 1984, Intex. Whether that is a harbinger of things to come is not yet known.

Trusts. As a common law jurisdiction with political stability and high-quality local services, Bermuda is a good choice as the domicile for personal trusts. There are no restrictions under local law on accumulation of trust income. Any of the three Bermuda banks may act as trustee, either directly or through a local subsidiary. A 1/4 of 1% stamp tax is payable on the value of trust assets.[5]

A Bermuda trust may authorize the transfer of its domicile to a different jurisdiction, either on the occurrence of a specific event or in the discretion of the trustee. Thus, a back-up position is preserved in the event of any change in law or loss of political or economic stability.

Cost Comparisons. It costs about $4,000 to form a tax-exempt corporation in Bermuda, including the $1,600 government franchise fee, publication charges and local counsel. Thereafter, the annual maintenance costs are on the order of $3,400 to 3,900, including the franchise fee plus fees for local directors and local counsel. An insurance company will cost substantially more to form and operate, due to the minimum capitalization requirements, the more comprehensive vetting process and the need to use a specialized management company in the haven in order to avoid an IRS finding that the company is "effectively connected" with a US trade or business; annual government fees and operational costs for the local management company may run $30,000 to $50,000 per year.

The only substantial cost for establishing a Bermuda trust is securing initial approval of its form and content from local counsel for the trust company. This cost is included in the trust company's setup fee and is typically $1,000 to $2,500, depending on the negotiating time required. Thereafter, the costs include a modest government franchise fee plus a trustee fee of less than 1% of trust assets, minimum $1,000 to $2,500 per year.

Prospects. The future of Bermuda as a tax haven is impacted by the probability that the black majority will eventually acquire full political control. Judging by the history of the country, however, they are likely to do so by constitutional means. The payroll tax on exempt company employees gives cause to pause; but on balance the future portends continued stability, both in the law and politically.

Endnotes

1. Exempted Undertakings Tax Protection Act, Bermuda Act 41 of 1966, as amended

2. *Staff Study, Crime and Secrecy: The Use of Offshore Banks and Companies*, February 1983, Permanent Subcommittee on Investigations of the Committee on Governmental Affairs, United States Senate

3. Bermuda Companies Act of 1981, No. 59 of 1981, as amended, and related rules and regulations

4. Bermuda Miscellaneous Taxes Act of 1976, No. 17 of 1976, and Miscellaneous Taxes (Rates) Act 1976, No. 18 of 1976, both as amended

5. Bermuda Trust Act, No. 2 of 1975, governs trusts in Bermuda

The Cayman Islands

Summary. *The Cayman Islands ("Cayman") is today one of the world's fastest-growing and most substantial tax havens. It grew to that status in less than two decades. More than 2,000 new corporations are created there every year as political instability in other tax havens forces investors to move their corporations and trusts.*

Cayman imposes no direct taxation, is not a party to any tax treaties and provides long-term guarantees against taxation to its exempted companies and trusts. Its governmental fees on companies, however, are noticeably higher than is the case in the Bahamas.

Cayman was once regarded by US tax authorities as a haven for criminal and tax evasion funds. One IRS official estimated in 1983 an annual flow of funds amounting to $3 billion from traditional criminal activity and an additional $3 billion in unreported income; a US Justice Department official asserts a higher figure, $10 billion annually. While such figures are unsubstantiated, Cayman was regarded as presenting a near-crisis criminal tax evasion condition, one justifying "severe sanctions."[1]

Location. Cayman is an island country, located south of Cuba in the Caribbean Sea. It is 475 miles south of Miami, a one-hour flight. There are regular nonstop jet flights to Grand Cayman from Miami, Memphis and Houston. No visa is necessary, just your US passport or birth certificate.

The capital is George Town, Grand Cayman, one mile from Owen Roberts Airport. A 10-minute drive from George Town is Seven Mile Beach, where you will find several hotels.

Cayman's telephone system and telex facilities are modern, and include direct-dial service. To call Grand Cayman, use area code 809, plus the prefix 94. Cayman is on Eastern Standard Time and does not employ daylight savings time, so its time is the same as New York in winter and Chicago in summer.

Be certain to send any mail to Grand Cayman, B.W.I.; mail addressed to "George Town, Grand Cayman" may wind up in Guyana or Exuma.

Culture. The population of Cayman is about 22,000, racially mixed and fully integrated. Color is considered immaterial in the context of social and economic relations and opportunities. Consequently, Cayman has fewer ethnic stresses than most of the other Caribbean and Atlantic island-states.

English is the language of Cayman.

Political System. As is the case with most British colonies, Cayman is partially self-governing. The governor is appointed by the Queen of England. England is responsible for finance, defense, foreign affairs, internal security and civil service. The elected legislative assembly governs other matters under its 1972 constitution. While the trend is toward more internal self-government, there is little likelihood of independence from Britain in the foreseeable future. Cayman is politically and economically stable.

Legal System. Cayman has an English common law system, as amended by local statute. It has its own court of appeals and any appeals therefrom go the Privy Council in England.

It is a signatory to the 1961 Hague Convention. Accordingly, documents executed in Cayman are authenticated by an Apostille, the standard certificate provided by the convention. The Apostille should be signed by the Governor of the Cayman Islands.

Non-Caymanians, including British citizens, may not work there without permits. The number of permits are limited, but not difficult to obtain. The government encourages the use of local people by means of the work permit license fees; the permit for a senior executive now costs US$2,400 per year. Non-Caymanians may own land in Cayman, but approval is required for a non-Caymanian to own more than 40% of a company doing local business.[2]

In an effort to diversify the local economy, Cayman provides concessions to encourage development.[3]

Local Support Services. The law and accounting firms found in Cayman are excellent, as are the banks, trust and management companies.

Currency. All exchange controls were eliminated by Cayman in 1980[4] and the Cayman dollar is now tied to the US dollar. The current exchange rate is one Cayman Islands dollar to US$1.20.

Secrecy. In a report to the Committee on Governmental Affairs for the United States Senate in 1983, the committee staff made the following observations about Cayman's commercial secrecy laws and attitude:

> "A reading of the Cayman law shows that provisions do exist, on application, for information to be provided in criminal matters. Furthermore, Cayman authorities occasionally indicate a desire for proper relations with the US and other countries in matters of information exchange, and investigations which are not 'fishing expeditions.'

> "Whatever the status of current negotiations, and there has been a series of meetings, some quite recent, US officials consider the Caymans fundamentally uncooperative. Given present political realities on the Islands, they are deemed incapable of effective cooperation, since public pressure tends to influence decisions of the all-important Executive Council, which decides on information requests.

> "Under the conditions of tension in the Caymans, that is, forces for and against cooperation with the US, an informal agreement might be preferred, one not publicly polarizing Cayman internal dissent or jeopardizing in a showdown the position of pro-cooperation groups. One problem with such a solution is inevitable US pessimism which has been generated over the years. Caymanian resistance to American efforts — even where proper procedures are followed — has been substantial. A recent Jamaican court decision has created an important precedent in the Caymans, however, insofar as disclosure of records and depositions are concerned.

> "This decision overrules a Cayman court and required a

Cayman bank to disclose its records for a US criminal case (*US vs. Joseph LeMire, et al.*). The Kingston court emphasized that it was not the intention of Cayman confidentiality statutes to shield criminals."

These past two decades have seen several serious efforts to penetrate commercial secrecy within Cayman, including those IRS investigations designated *Operation Tradewinds* and *Project Haven*.

In response to the 1976 jailing of Cayman banker Anthony Field, when he refused to testify about the bank and its customers and was held in contempt of court, Cayman enacted the *Confidential Relations (Preservation) Law*.[5] The legislative commentary attendant to that legislation, points out that preceding secrecy laws proved inadequate and subject to misinterpretation. The new law added substantial sanctions and broadened the scope of matters subject to commercial secrecy. The intent is to leave no doubt as to the passion of Cayman for commercial secrecy by imposing criminal sanctions on all breaches of confidential information. It covers not only acts committed within Cayman, but those committed outside Cayman in relation to Caymanian subject matter. Anyone who divulges confidential information may be punished by a fine of up to US$6,100, imprisonment for up to two years, or both. The penalties may be doubled and redoubled under certain circumstances. The ambit of the matters protected by the secrecy law includes all details involved in business of a professional nature arising in or brought into Cayman. There is only one exception: disclosure may be made upon prior approval by the Cayman Grand Court or by its designated governmental officials, or with the express or implied consent of the principal acting through a professional representative.

The secrecy law is not without its side effects. Some banks now require all customers to sign form waivers because they fear inadvertent disclosure (such as responding to a credit reference request) or sanctions if they are compelled by US regulatory authorities to divulge information. Because the new law purports to cover all professional persons and is not limited to those based in Cayman, if a US lawyer assisting a client in forming a Cayman company is compelled to disclose information concerning the company to a federal grand jury, the attorney may be deemed to have violated the new secrecy law without ever setting foot in Cayman.

The public position of the Cayman government is that a foreign government (such as the US) investigating a crime that also constitutes an offense under Cayman law if committed in Cayman, may obtain necessary information by applying through official Cayman channels. Assistance will be denied for investigations of tax crimes, however, since they are not criminal offenses under Cayman law.[6]

Similarly, a Cayman court may be asked for permission to disclose confidential information before a foreign court. The Cayman court may either authorize or refuse to authorize the disclosure, subject to any conditions it may impose. On rare occasions, such permission has been granted. For example, in 1982 it was permitted in *United States v. Carver*, a nontax criminal fraud investigation. In July 1984, the US and the United Kingdom, acting on behalf of Cayman, entered into an agreement that provides the US Attorney General access to Cayman records in investigating narcotics cases, in exchange for US agreement to refrain from the subpoena of bank records. That agreement was the forerunner of a wider disclosure agreement approved by the Treasury Department, Cayman and England, ratified by the US Senate and signed in July 1986. In addition, a Cayman-US mutual assistance treaty was approved by the US Senate Foreign Relations Committee in July 1989, to aid in prosecuting criminals other than tax evaders.

While an exempted company is required to maintain a register of its directors and officers, its mortgages and charges and its shareholders, the information is available only to the Cayman government. There is no public disclosure of the directors, officers or shareholders.

General Corporate Law. As with other jurisdictions in the British mode, a "local company" is one that conducts business within the jurisdiction, and an "exempted" company is one that conducts solely offshore business. An exempted company may use a local

328   Appendix C

office from which to conduct its offshore business and may be formed within a day or two. What we know as the Articles of Incorporation and Bylaws are described as the Memorandum of Association and the Articles of Association, respectively. Standard bylaws regulations in Table A of the Companies Law may be adopted by reference, materially shortening the Articles of Association.

Of the 250 new companies incorporated each month in Cayman, about two-thirds are exempted companies. More than 20,000 corporations are now domiciled in Cayman, a country with a population of only 22,000 persons; it has one of the highest per capita number of corporations in the world.

Under the Cayman Islands' *Tax Concessions Law (revised)*, an exempted company is usually given a 20-year guarantee against taxes. An exempted company may issue shares without par value and may issue them either in registered or in bearer form. Although local law does not require anything in its name to indicate limited liability status of its exempted company principals, it is prudent to do so; the failure to so notify those doing business with the corporation may, in certain jurisdictions, open the shareholders to personal liability for corporate obligations. Unlike certain other tax haven jurisdictions, the exempted company Memorandum of Association may be amended freely.

Although at least one directors' meeting annually must be held in Cayman, alternate directors may be used in order to avoid the trip. Table A of the enabling law requires that each director hold one qualifying share, but that requirement may be deleted under the Articles of Association. Aside from the foregoing, directors may meet anywhere in the world, and there are no nationality or residence requirements for either directors or officers.

If you cease doing business through the Cayman Islands exempted company, you may save the costs of a formal liquidation by requesting the Registrar of Companies to strike the company from the register on the ground that it is no longer carrying on business. The company may be reinstated if assets are later discovered. Doing so, however, requires the assistance of local counsel and, on particular facts, may require as much as four months' time to complete.

Since 1989, a corporation may move its domicile into or out of that jurisdiction. Thus, corporations may be moved almost as freely as are trusts.

The only Cayman taxes are import duties and stamp duties required on deeds conveying local land, loans secured by real property, leases and on most documents. There is no personal income tax, no corporate income tax, no capital gains tax, no employment tax, no withholding tax, no gift tax, no estate or inheritance tax, no probate fees, no sales tax and no property tax. The substantial revenue of Cayman arises from annual fees imposed on companies — primarily exempted corporations — and on banks and insurance carriers.

Cayman has had no tax treaties since losing its status as a Jamaican dependency in 1969.

As noted, a 20-year guarantee against income taxes is provided all exempted corporations. An exempted trust is similarly guaranteed against taxes for 50 years. Based on the present attitude and the terms of the guarantees, it is likely that no income taxes will be imposed in the foreseeable future.

Special Corporations. Cayman has enacted special legislation under which to attract certain specific kinds of business. Among them are banks, trust companies, insurance companies, mutual funds and shipping companies. As a stable, nearby common law jurisdiction, it is also popular and widely used for trusts.

More than 500 banks and trust companies are now licensed in Cayman. Approximately 35 conduct local business and the remainder conduct only offshore business.

Bank and trust company licenses are issued by the Governor and by the Executive Council.[7] Class A licenses permit operations both locally and abroad; Class B licenses permit operations only offshore. The minimum capital requirement for a Class B banking license is US$400,000, paid-in or guaranteed.

As to continuing expenses, a Class A banking license now costs US$36,000 per year; an unrestricted Class B license costs $10,800 per year. The total costs of legal services and governmental fees (excluding capitalization) to set up a Class B (offshore) bank in

Cayman should be about $35,000 and annual maintenance costs should run approximately $20,000. You must file quarterly financial statements with the Inspector of Banks and Trust Companies, along with annual financial statements. The statements, while they must be audited, need not be published.

Since enacting its insurance regulations in 1979,[8] Cayman attracted several hundred captive insurance companies. All license applications and annual returns are reviewed by the Superintendent of Insurance. Although restricted Class B insurer's licenses are available, most applicants seek and obtain unrestricted Class B offshore licenses requiring a minimum capitalization of US$120,000. Cayman is rapidly closing on the expertise of Bermuda in attracting and supporting offshore captive insurance companies. The cost of incorporating the carrier and the initial license fee is approximately $12,000, and are about the same amount each year thereafter.

Cayman is not yet ready, but has designs on, the development of foreign-owned shipping business. When preparations are complete, it will market its facilities to foreign-owned shipping companies for ship registrations, including the Cayman registry for British ships.

Mutual funds operating from a Cayman base generally are given a restricted offshore bank license — restricted to mutual fund management. It is possible to organize a mutual fund as a trust in Cayman, but doing so precludes the right to redeem shares. Hence, it is an unlikely vehicle except for closed-in mutual funds.

Trusts. Under the Cayman trust law,[9] Cayman is a popular jurisdiction for the establishment of common law trusts. Two types of trusts are sanctioned by local law. An "ordinary trust" is similar to that established under most British Commonwealth jurisdictions. But an "exempted trust" is unique to Cayman.

The distinction of an exempted trust is its guarantee against possible future Cayman taxes, a guarantee that runs for 50 years following the date of the trust. It is also exempted from the rule against perpetuities if the alternate provision of a 100-year term is elected. Because the proposed trust declaration must be approved by the Registrar of Trusts, it may take several weeks to establish an exempted trust. The Registrar must be satisfied that no beneficiary is likely to become a Cayman resident. If any beneficiary does, in fact, become a Cayman resident, he or she will not be able to enforce the guarantee against taxes. Either an ordinary trust or an exempted trust may authorize the transfer of its domicile to a different jurisdiction (the so-called "Cuba Clause"). The transfer may be brought about automatically upon the happening of a specific event, or may take place at the discretion of the trustee or some other designated person.

Cost Comparisons. An exempted corporation pays a minimum incorporation fee to the Cayman government of US$1,307, a fee that has been increased several times in recent years. In addition, the exempted company pays a minimum annual government fee of $580 each January. Because of the long-term guarantees against taxation, these higher-than-usual governmental fees may be regarded as, in part, insurance premiums against future taxes.

If an exempted company is capitalized for more than $900,000, the initial and annual fees are higher. The cost of forming an exempt company is now approximately $4,000, including the current governmental fees, local lawyers and a law firm or trust company serving as corporate secretary, alternate director and registered agent. Total maintenance costs, including the annual government fee and fees for local maintenance and local directors or alternates, is now in a range of $1,500 to $2,000 per year.

While the exempted trust is similar to the ordinary common law trust, its initial and annual fees are higher. A stamp duty of $49 is payable upon the formation of each Cayman trust, whether ordinary or exempted. An exempted trust, however, requires a registration fee of $244 and an annual fee of $122 thereafter, neither of which is payable by an ordinary Cayman trust. Given the protection afforded by a Cuba Clause against future imposition of tax, it may be cost-effective to use an ordinary Cayman trust and move the domicile if circumstances later dictate it.

Prospects. Cayman stands alone in its aggressive pace of fee increases. It is a matter that bears watching, since the unrestrained continuance of the practice could cause Cayman to price itself out of the market. We saw a drastic decline in new company formations after the last increase took effect in 1982, although the rate is now approaching 1981 levels: from a high of 3,052 in 1981, new company formations declined to 2,089 in 1984. In short, it is expensive, but its political stability provides a material advantage over many of the other havens and offshore financial centers.

Endnotes

1. *Staff Study, Crime and Secrecy: The Use of Offshore Banks and Companies*, Permanent Subcommittee on Investigations of the Committee on Governmental Affairs, United States Senate, February 1983

2. Cayman Islands Local Companies (Control) Law, revised

3. Tax Concessions Law and Hotel Aids Law

4. Cayman Islands Exchange Control Law No. 5 of 1980, repealed

5. Cayman Islands Confidential Relations (Preservation) Law, No. 16 of 1976, amended by No. 26 of 1979

6. Budget address of the Financial Secretary, March 1977

7. Cayman Islands Banks and Trust Companies Law 1989 (No. 4 of 1989)

8. Cayman Islands Insurance Law 1979, No. 24 of 1979, amended by Law No. 9 of 1980

9. Cayman Islands Trust (Foreign Elements) Law 1987 (No. 17 of 1987)

The Bahama Islands

Summary. *The Bahama Islands ("Bahama") is one of the world's best-known tax havens, domicile to thousands of companies. It imposes no direct taxes and government fees are modest. Local law does not provide for exempted companies or offer guarantees against future taxes. It has no tax treaties.*

Relations between the US and Bahama are troubled, due to the US perception of Bahama as a haven for criminals and tax evaders. The Bahamian government takes great umbrage to the US position, claiming that the US is unable to support its contentions with any credible evidence. While the US is intent upon extending Caribbean Basin Initiative benefits to Bahama in exchange for information-sharing agreements, Bahama is flatly opposed to providing any such information.

Location. The nearest of the Bahama Islands is a mere 50 miles off the Florida coast. The country has excellent airline, telephone and telex service. Direct-dial service is available; to call Nassau, use area code 809 plus local prefix 32. Bahama time is the same as New York throughout the year.

The 700 islands of Bahama lie between Florida and Haiti; only 22 are inhabited. The capital is Nassau on New Providence Island, about 12 miles from Nassau International Airport. Nassau may be reached by nonstop jet in two and one-half hours from New York, and in much less time from Miami which is only 200 miles away.

Culture. About one-half of the 230,000 residents of Bahama live on New Providence Island. Recent years have brought rapid population growth, and with it a 27% unemployment rate. English is the official language.

Political System. In the late 70s, the black majority took full political control from the white minority, entirely by constitutional means. Independence from Great Britain was later granted. Although independent since 1973, Bahama remains a member of the British Commonwealth.

An underlying and growing level of unrest is observable, attributable in large part to the high aspiration level of its younger people, an aspiration level that cannot be met under current economic circumstances. Bahama lacks certain key elements required for a robust economy: natural resources, agriculture and a motivated work force. Its wage standards are high, making attraction of foreign industry difficult. Because there is no local market economy, $6 of every $7 are spent on US imports. Tourism contributes about 70% of the gross national product, and tourists pay most of the special taxes assessed.

Because of the foregoing, the socio-economic conditions in Bahama are volatile. Concern is often expressed that the current government may be replaced by a socialist or Marxist government if the economic situation does not improve. Complicating the current economic situation is maldistribution of income: high per capita earnings in and around Nassau are contrasted with pervasive poverty in the outlying islands. There is a large criminal economy, leading to high levels of violence, from piracy to street crime. That, of course, negatively impacts tourism.

Bay Street is the center of the main Nassau business district. A hill lies to one side of it. It is said that if you go "over the hill," you may never return; the muggers routinely kill their victims. The houses all have bars on the doors and windows, and burglaries of entire apartment houses, room-by-room, are common.

Legal System. The legal system of Bahama is based on English common law, as amended by local statute. The Privy Council in England continues to serve as the court of final appeal for the Bahama justice system.

It is a signatory to the 1961 Hague Convention. Accordingly, documents executed in Bahama are authenticated by an Apostille, the standard certificate provided by the convention. The Apostille should be signed by the Permanent Secretary of the Ministry of External Affairs.

Work permits are granted to qualified foreigners if the employer can demonstrate that there is no Bahamian available to do the job. Most foreigners remain in Bahama for only three to five years, due to continuous training of Bahamians to fill available positions. Bahama now boasts a substantial number of qualified clerical and sub-management people from its indigenous population.

In order to encourage the existing trend, the annual cost of work permits is fairly expensive; a permit for a senior officer of a company now costs US$5,000 per year, and permits for other key employees range from $2,500 to $3,500 per year, depending on the position held. In a serious effort to attract retirees, Bahama enacted legislation in 1975[1] providing for a Certificate of Permanent Residence. While the issuance of the certificate is discretionary and the $5,000 one-time fee is not insubstantial, Bahama presents an attractive low-cost place to retire. The certificate covers the applicant, a spouse and all dependent children. The retiree, of course, may not engage in any gainful occupation without also obtaining and paying for a work permit. In order to get the certificate, the retiree must demonstrate to the satisfaction of the Bahamian government that he or she is self-supporting without employment, and must commit to remitting at least $25,000 of foreign-source income into Bahama each year and to invest at least $150,000 in the country within two years after receiving the Permanent Residence Certificate. It is the hope of the Bahamian government to attract 500 new permanent residents to the islands each year.

Other legislation[2] is intended to attract manufacturing enterprises to Bahama by offering no-tax guarantees. Its effect to date is nil.

Local Support Services. Numerous law and accounting firms are located in Bahama, along with a large number of banks and trust companies. It is alleged by the US[3] that as much as 20% of the local lawyers knowingly advise and represent criminals in laundering funds and in related criminal enterprises. While there is no formal ethics structure for imposing professional responsibility on accountants and attorneys, it is believed that the vast majority function under recognized standards of professional ethics.

Currency. The Bahama dollar is maintained in parity with the US dollar, and the prospect is for that to continue. Exchange-control regulations protect the Bahamian dollar, a matter of some concern because of an extraordinary outflow of funds just prior to a crucial 1972 election. Much of the outflow was converted Bahamian dollars. Bank deposits maintained in Bahama by local residents and foreigners with work permits are automatically converted by the exchange control regulations into Bahamian dollars, but foreigners may keep deposits in the currency of their country of domicile.

There is some concern that foreign currency deposits maintained by nonresidents might be automatically converted to Bahamian dollars then devalued. That seems unlikely, however, because foreign currency deposits do not adversely affect the Bahamian dollar.

Secrecy. Bahama imposes commercial secrecy by virtue of its common law tradition, and banking secrecy by statute.[4] Its bank secrecy law is identical to the old secrecy law in Cayman.

As to information to be maintained and filed, banks and insurance companies must prepare financial statements and either publish or file them. Other companies file annual statements with the Registrar General disclosing shareholders and directors, but no financial information. Local companies are required to maintain books and records in connection with the business turnover tax.

The success of the US in covert operations designated *Operation Tradewinds* and *Project Haven* brought strong protests from the Bahamian government, alleging illegal acts committed by IRS agents in Bahama. Those projects aggravated the relationship of the two countries to the point where cooperation is now virtually nonexistent.

The Bahamian government claims that the US is disinterested in cooperation and treats them in a high-handed manner, pointing to a period of almost two years in which they were provided no US Ambassador. For a number of years, the Bahamian chief of state was not invited officially to the US. The US grants tourism convention tax favoritism to Jamaica, but not to Bahama, even though the latter is more dependent on tourism income and has been a steadier ally of the US in recent decades.

IRS projects are perceived by the Bahamians as overly aggressive, threatening both the sovereignty and the economic well-being of that country. The Bahamian government threatened to lift the work permits of all Americans there if such operations are repeated. Moreover, *The* (1981) *Gordon Report*, proposing heavy sanctions for failure to cooperate, exacerbatcd the outrage of the Bahamian government. Much of the argument comes down to which country should accept blame for allegedly drug trafficking conducted from and through Bahama; whether Bahama is to be blamed for accepting it, or the US for exporting it.

The bank secrecy law provides a procedure by which foreign governments may obtain a court order permitting disclosure of banking information for purposes of proving criminal fraud of a nontax nature. It is asserted, justifiably, that much of the failure to cooperate arises from US failure to idcntify and follow the procedure provided by Bahamian law. Acknowledging its own failure to request disclosure and follow procedure, the US argument shifts to the conscious imposition of impediments to any such court order. Specifically, Bahamian law requires that the petitioning foreign government show that a crime was committed or is suspected, the proof of which bears on the requested documents. The dilemma is that the prosecutor needs an indictment and, if enough evidence to indict exists, does not need the Bahamian records. The court decisions consistently hold that criminal proceedings of some sort must be underway at the time the disclosure is sought.

Notwithstanding all the foregoing, no one has ever claimed that the Bahama court system is tainted. The same may not be said for its elected and appointed officials.

General Corporate Law. The law governing corporations was enacted in 1866 and remains, despite numerous amendments, a throwback to the nineteenth century.[5]

Although the incorporation documents are lengthy, a Bahamian corporation may be formed within a few days. The estimated number of corporations registered in Bahama is about 25,000 although at one time it was considerably higher. Following a four-fold increase in the annual fee payable to the government by foreign-owned companies, a large number of corporations were voluntarily liquidated or involuntarily stricken from the register for nonpayment.

There is a minimum shareholder requirement of five, although no citizenship or residence requirements are imposed for directors, officers or shareholders. That renders it unnecessary to use local directors and saves the management fees for that service. Meetings of directors and shareholders may be held within or without the country. Bahama does not authorize bearer stock corporations, but one can issue share warrants to bearer if authorized by the Articles of Association (Bylaws).

Bahama has no law permitting a corporation to move its domicile into or out of that jurisdiction, nor any prohibiting it. Thus, there is a risk that doing so may be treated as a constructive dissolution for tax purposes.

Bahama imposes no personal income, corporate income, capital gains, withholding, employment, gift, estate or inheritance taxes. It does impose property taxes on both developed and undeveloped real estate, as well as stamp duties on the sale of property and a gross premium tax on insurance companies. Most documents require stamp duties, and it imposes duties on imports. The largest single source of revenue for Bahama is from annual fees imposed on banks, corporations and those charged for work permits.

A few years ago, at the behest of the World Bank and the International Monetary Fund, Bahama considered introducing an income tax on residents. It concluded, however, that the low average income of the indigenous population would not produce enough revenue to offset the political cost; it instead enacted a business turnover tax.

The business turnover tax is imposed solely on local businesses and professions and looks very much like a corporate income tax. It is based on gross receipts from local sources, although the amount payable depends in part on profitability. Businesses and professionals must maintain books and records disclosing both turnover and profit margins in order to permit calculation of the tax.

Bahama is a party to no tax treaties, although rumors surface from time to time that it is negotiating a tax treaty with the US. Invariably, such rumors are denied by the Bahamian government out of concern for its reputation as a stable tax haven jurisdiction.

Clearly, the US would like to have a tax treaty with Bahama, as well as other tax havens, providing for an exchange of tax information. It would be an important tool in prosecuting US tax evaders who presently hide behind the cloak of bank or commercial secrecy. It is unlikely to occur, however, in the absence of additional pressure or substantial economic benefit. A mutual assistance treaty was approved by the US Senate Foreign Relations Committee in July 1989. When enacted, it will open the door to effective nontax criminal investigations.

Under the *Caribbean Basin Initiative*, the US extends a number of important tax benefits and subsidies to Caribbean Basin nations that enter into agreements for the exchange of information and mutual assistance. To date, only Jamaica, Barbados, Dominica and Granada have entered into such agreements with the US, but efforts continue in that direction. It is under consideration by Trinidad and Tobago, Costa Rica, St. Lucia and Belize.

Although Bahama does not provide exempted companies with guarantees against future taxes, special long-term guarantees are provided to licensees of the Grand Bahama Port Authority who operate businesses at Freeport on Grand Bahama Island.

Special Corporations. Banking law[6] and regulations provide several different categories of licenses, along with annual fees which vary considerably from category to category. The fees range from US$2,500 per year for a restricted trust license to as much as $160,000 per year for an authorized dealer in foreign currency and gold. Required paid-in capital is at least $1 million. The annual cost of operating an unrestricted offshore bank, using local trust company management services, is on the order of $35,000 to $50,000, including an annual government license fee of $25,000.

Every bank must publish its audited statements annually in the official gazette.

Insurance law,[7] much like the banking law passed in the mid-1970s, was designed to upgrade the image of Bahama as a legitimate offshore financial center, rather than a haven for criminals. In doing so, however, Bahama may have priced itself out of business. Strictly offshore carriers file audited financial statements annually, but are exempt from other filings.

Bahama hosts a large number of offshore mutual funds, subject to no apparent regulation. In 1971, it enacted a securities act designed to control mutual funds and all offerings of securities made from the Bahamas, but since a proclamation putting the law into effect was never issued, it is inferred that the government is untroubled by the manner in which the mutual funds have conducted their affairs.

Bahama has a comprehensive statutory law for merchant shipping,[8] containing 288 sections and running 124 printed pages, but its success in competing for such business is marginal. The law permits foreign-owned vessels to register under the Bahamian flag, using Bahama as a flag of convenience. Each ship must be at least 1,600 net registered tons, engaged in foreign trade and not more than 12 years old.

Trusts. Bahama boasts a large number of well-established and efficient trust companies, along with a well-developed body of trust law. The trust law is archaic by comparison to certain other jurisdictions, but provides the benefits of no limit on accumulations. The Rule Against Perpetuities (limiting the term of private trusts), however, applies. As is the case with corporations, there is no law permitting a trust to move its domicile into or out of that jurisdiction nor any prohibiting it. Local trust companies, however, routinely include automatic or discretionary change-of-domicile provisions in their trust documents.

Cost Comparisons. In 1976, the Bahamian government surprised everyone with a quadrupling of the annual fee imposed on Bahamian corporations not locally controlled; the annual charge rose from US$250 to $1,000. A locally-controlled corporation still pays only $250 per year.[9]

When that happened, a large number of exempt corporations were abandoned or liquidated, and others were transferred to the Turks and Caicos Islands or elsewhere, using directors, officers and managers based in Nassau. By that means, local management facilities could still be used without paying the higher Bahamian governmental charge. Although banks and trust companies registered in Bahama are exempted from the annual corporation fee, bank license fees were increased after 1976.

The cost of forming an exempt Bahama corporation is approximately US$2,500; it is approximately $2,000 each year thereafter to maintain it in good standing. Those figures include stamp duties and governmental fees, as well as legal fees and administrative charges for local management of an exempt corporation with minimum capital. Trusts incur no registration or annual governmental fees other than a nominal stamp duty.

Prospects. The black majority has assumed full political control by peaceful means and without changing the image of Bahama as a tax haven. The political stability bears continued watching, however, due to the high level of unemployment and the limited success in attracting labor-intensive industry. Bahama will probably continue to enforce its strict work-permit policy.

Endnotes

1. Bahamas Immigration (Amendment) Act (No. 26 of 1975)

2. The Industries Encouragement Act (Act 10 of 1970)

3. *Staff Study, Crime and Secrecy: The Use of Offshore Banks and Trust Companies*, Permanent Subcommittee on Investigations of the Committee on Governmental Affairs of the United States Senate, February 1983

4. Bahamas Banks and Trust Companies Regulation Act 1965, Sec. 10 (No. 64 of 1965)

5. The Companies Act 1965, Ch. 184 of 1965, Bahamas Revised Statutes, as amended

6. Banks and Trust Companies Regulation Act 1965 (No. 64 of 1965), as amended

7. The Insurance Act 1969 (No. 3 of 1969)

8. The Merchant Shipping Act (No. 16 of 1976)

9. Bahamas Companies Amendment Act 1975 (No. 35 of 1975)

The Turks and Caicos Islands

Summary. *The Turks and Caicos Islands ("Turks and Caicos") is a new player in the tax haven ranks. It made the decision to establish itself as such, conducted its homework for the task, passed the enabling legislation and aggressively (and successfully) markets itself. It is a British colony located on a group of islands approximately two hours flying time from Miami. It features, under its 1981 Companies Ordinance the right of a company incorporated elsewhere to move its domicile to Turks and Caicos, and for a Turks and Caicos corporation to move its domicile elsewhere. The redomiciliation provision is a major advantage in attracting the favorable attention of offshore investors who live with a continuing concern about governmental attitude and political stability. Turks and Caicos buttresses this feature by means of a stand-by permit authorizing the transfer of a company's domicile into Turks and Caicos at any time within three years following issuance of the permit.*

Turks and Caicos has no income tax and none is likely to be enacted. It is otherwise much like Bahama, Bermuda and Cayman.

Location. Turks and Caicos is a British colony located in the Atlantic Ocean, approximately 575 miles southeast of Miami and less than 100 miles north of the Dominican Republic and Haiti. It comprises two groups of islands with a total land area of approximately 166 square miles. Between the two groups is a 22-mile-wide deep-water channel.

At this point, it is not as well-traveled as are other, more established, havens. Three flights a week are made between Miami and Grand Turk, a flight of two hours. You may also reach Grand Turk by means of the Bahamas, Haiti or the Dominican Republic.

Direct-dial telephone service is in place; you may call Grand Turk using 809 plus local prefix 946. It is equipped for both telex and cable. The time is the same as New York throughout the year.

It provides good mail service, considering the limited number of flights in and out of the country. Using local courier services, you may deliver documents to any part of the world within two or three days.

Culture. The population is about 12,000 and predominantly black. About half of the population lives on Grand Turk Island. Although a large number of islanders have emigrated in recent years seeking better opportunity elsewhere, an expected boom in the local economy has attracted quite a few of them back to the islands. English is the official language.

Political System. Turks and Caicos came under control of the United Kingdom in 1963, following dependencies at one time or another under both Bahama and Jamaica. Until 1973, it shared a governor with Bahama but now has its own governor.

As a separate British colony, Turks and Caicos operates under a constitution adopted in 1976 and amended in 1986 which provides for a ministerial form of government with substantial internal self-government.[1] England appoints the governor, acting through the Queen. The Legislative Council has 11 members elected by districts, three appointed members, a Speaker and three official members: the Chief Secretary, the Attorney General and the Financial Secretary. The Governor, the Chief Secretary, the Attorney General, the Financial Secretary and the Foreign Ministers of Turks and Caicos are separately called the Executive Council and function as a cabinet for the governor. The governor and the British government are responsible for defense, external affairs and internal security.

In 1974, the legislature sought to replace Britain with Canada but was turned down. If it had succeeded, Turks and Caicos would have lost its tax haven status. It remained a British colony, and there is no noticeable interest in seeking independence from Britain today. As a consequence, Turks and Caicos may be considered politically stable.

The government employs more people than any other organization in the colony. The unemployment rate is low. It is burdened by a large trade deficit, but it is so far covered by British government grants. Import duties, fees paid by companies, stamp duty on land transfers and income from the sale of stamps and coins generate the bulk of the government's revenues.

Legal System. Turks and Caicos is an English common law jurisdiction. As is the case with other British-related tax havens, the Privy Council in England serves as the court of last resort for appeals.

Except for a small crayfish export industry, there is virtually no local economy outside the tax haven service group. The Turks and Caicos business development law[2] is heavily promoted in order to encourage all forms of new business by granting relief from import duties (as high as 26%) and income taxes (up to 35 years).

It is a signatory of the 1961 Hague Convention. Accordingly, documents executed in Turks and Caicos are authenticated by an Apostille, the standard certificate provided by the convention. The Apostille should be signed by the Governor of the Turks and Caicos Islands.

Local Support Services. I find little published on support services. So all there is to relate is the opinion of a Cayman bank officer with long experience in the havens. His view is that the government and professional infrastructure is thin and relatively unsophisticated, compared to Cayman, Bermuda and Bahama. You may wish to take this opinion with a grain of salt, but this sort of thing is his business. I would investigate the Turks and Caicos personally before committing your resources to it.

Currency. The currency in use is the US dollar. No exchange controls exist, so there is no disclosure to any exchange control authority and no restriction on the repatriation of funds. Bank accounts may be maintained in any of several currencies.

Secrecy. Turks and Caicos law[3] authorizes exempted companies and imposes financial and criminal sanctions for breach of commercial secrecy. The secrecy provisions are based on Cayman law and are so strictly enforced that a bank may not even provide a credit reference without first obtaining customer authorization.

General Corporate Law. As noted, Turks and Caicos is one of the few countries that authorize corporate redomiciliation. That law permits the transfer of a corporate domicile without resulting in constructive dissolution of the corporation for tax purposes. Because of this modern tool, Turks and Caicos successfully attracted a large number of corporations from other tax havens, principally the Bahamas.

The 1981 Companies Ordinance authorizes exempted companies (those domiciled in Turks and Caicos but operating offshore). Its provisions are copied from Cayman law and improvements added, such as: the redomiciliation privilege; no requirement for local board meetings; the right to redeem shares; a modern "any legal purpose" purposes and powers clause for exempted companies; a 20-year tax exemption (at an optional extra cost) along with a guarantee against increases in governmental fees during that 20-year period; a generally lower level of incorporation and annual fees than those imposed in other tax havens; the ability to operate with one shareholder and one director; the right to issue shares to bearer, instead of registered in the names of the shareholders; the right to issue shares for no par value; a well-developed set of statutory bylaws that may be incorporated by reference, thereby shortening the incorporation documents for an exempted company; and near-complete anonymity due to minimal public records, records which include no indication of the shareholders, directors or officers of the exempt company.

In order to use the redomiciliation provisions, the Registrar General of Turks and Caicos must conclude that no law of the originating country prevents the corporation from transferring its domicile to Turks and Caicos. The country of origin need not expressly authorize redomiciliation; it must simply have no law preventing it. The process for transferring a corporate domicile into Turks and Caicos is much simpler than the process for transferring it out to another jurisdiction; the latter could prove to be a problem if the attitude of the government changes materially. Once a permit is issued permitting redomiciliation from another jurisdiction into Turks and Caicos, the permit is valid for three years following date of issuance. There is nothing to prevent seriatim procurement of permits, so as to maintain a running option to transfer from another jurisdiction. A company that cannot be incorporated in Turks and Caicos cannot be redomiciled there without making the changes required to conform to local law.

A corporation may be formed in Turks and Caicos within a few days. Three different types are provided under local law. They include a "company limited by shares" (the only kind that qualifies as an exempted corporation), "companies limited by guarantee" and "companies with unlimited liability," neither of the last two are of interest to Target Defendants.

Corporations conducting local business are designated as "ordinary companies." Otherwise, they are registered as "exempted companies."

Although no minimum capital is required to form a corporation in Turks and Caicos, the schedule setting the fee paid to the Registrar General on incorporation sets the usual minimum paid-in capital as a matter of local custom and practice at US$5,000. Turks and Caicos imposes no restrictions on the residence or nationality of shareholders.

Either common or preferred shares of exempted companies, or both, may be redeemed if authorized under the Articles of Incorporation.

Currently, Turks and Caicos imposes no income tax, no capital gains tax, no corporate income tax, no gift tax, no property tax and no sales tax. For so long as it pursues its status as a tax haven, it is unlikely that this will change. The only taxes include a small probate fee (maximum US$500), import duties, stamp duties on documents and on local real estate transactions, a bed tax for local hotel accommodations and a departure tax.

Turks and Caicos has no income tax treaties and is disinterested in qualifying as a beneficiary country under the US *Caribbean Basin Initiative*. As a consequence, there is no legal basis or procedure on or by which US authorities may obtain information from Turks and Caicos.

Special Corporations. The banking ordinance[4] treats banks separately from other financial institutions. Although any can conduct a banking business, only a bank can offer checking accounts. Class

A licenses are for local operations and Class B licenses are limited to offshore operations.

Class A licensees must capitalize for at least US$500,000, whereas Class B licensees need only capitalize for US$125,000. If the bank head office is maintained elsewhere, however, a higher capitalization rate is required. Annual license fees range from US$7,500 to $17,000. Because of stringent requirements generally, and specifically the requirement that audited annual financial statements be not only filed but published, local banking law is not as attractive to captive or offshore banks as is that of Cayman and elsewhere.

Trusts. Turks and Caicos, as a common law jurisdiction, may serve as a useful domicile for trusts. Especially so, since enacting its first trust law in 1985.[5] That law provides for approved trustees, for the right to be governed by the *United Kingdom 1925 Trustee Act*, for no restrictions on income accumulations and for disclaimer of the Rule Against Perpetuities. The last feature means you can keep the trust in place for as many generations as you please, letting family wealth compound over long periods of time without the need for descendants yet unknown to periodically terminate and replace the trust.

Cost Comparisons. The cost of organizing a Turks and Caicos company is lower than for most offshore jurisdictions. The incorporation fee paid to the Registrar General is based on the amount of authorized capital, typically US$325.00 on capitalization of US$5,000.00.[6] The fee is set on a sliding scale for a higher capitalization, with no maximum.

In order to obtain from the Governor an undertaking that no taxes or increased fees will be imposed for 20 years, the exempt corporation must pay an extra US$500 initially and $150 per year thereafter. The annual fee for an exempted company, regardless of capitalization, is presently $300 (plus the $150 for the tax and fee guarantee, if desired).

Prospects. Since the current system appears to meet the needs of

Turks and Caicos as a country, and in light of no prospects for a major change in the British affiliation, it seems likely that the present attractive tax climate will continue for the foreseeable future.

Endnotes

1. Turks and Caicos Constitution Order 1976, as amended
2. Encouragement of Development Ordinance 1972 (No. 2 of 1972), as amended
3. Companies Ordinance 1981 (No. 11 of 1981)
4. Banking Ordinance 1979 (No. 1 of 1979)
5. Trusts (Special Provisions) Ordinance 1985 (No. 10 of 1985)
6. Companies (Fees) Regulations 1983, Sec. 2(d)

The British Virgin Islands

Summary. *Prior to termination of the United States Income Tax Treaty, January 1, 1983, the British Virgin Islands ("BVI") marketed its low tax rates and favorable tax treaty provisions to serve as an attractive base from which to carry on offshore business. Since termination, BVI enacted an International Business Companies Ordinance in an attempt to cope with its loss. The action may prove effective in retaining some substantial portion of its prior business and in attracting business from other nontreaty tax havens.*

Location. The BVI is located on the northern edge of the Caribbean Sea, near Puerto Rico and the American Virgin Islands. No direct passenger flights from the US mainland are available, but it may be reached through Puerto Rico or the American Virgin Islands. Telephone and telex service is good. To dial direct from the mainland, use 809 and the prefix 49. The BVI is on Atlantic Standard Time all year, the same as New York time in the summer and Chicago in the winter. The capital is Road Town, Tortola, about nine miles from the Beef Island Airport.

Culture. The BVI has a population of about 11,000, about three-quarters of whom live on Tortola. The population is mostly black. The language is English.

Political System. The BVI is a politically stable and substantially self-governing British territory, a state of affairs now continuing for more than 300 years. The British government appoints the governor, and is responsible for defense, internal security, external affairs, public service and court administration. Under the 1976 constitution, all other matters, including finance, are the domain of the Chief Minister of the BVI, three other ministers and an elected legislative council. There is no demonstrated interest in pursuing full independence from Britain.

Legal System. The BVI is an English common law jurisdiction, as amended by local statute. As is the case with other British colonies and territories, the Privy Council in England serves as the court of final appeal from BVI courts.

Permits are required for an alien to take up residence in the BVI, to work or to acquire land.

Being a signatory to the 1961 Hague Convention, documents executed in the BVI are authenticated by an Apostille, the standard certificate provided by the convention. The Apostille should be signed by the Governor of the BVI.

Local Support Services. The reports are in conflict, here. Published descriptions suggest that with four major and four local banks licensed to operate under its banking ordinances,[1] along with several lawyers and two accounting firms, the professional infrastructure is able to service the present volume of business in this country. Other reports I have received from nearby havens, though, are that the infrastructure is wholly inadequate to the task. Specifically, that the government hands out corporate names by the dozen with no records to back them up, that a disproportionately large number of the CFCs are formed for one transaction then dissolved or stricken for non-renewal. Before using it, I suggest a personal investigation trip there, to see which reports are the more accurate.

Currency. The US dollar serves as the currency of the BVI. There are no exchange controls.

Secrecy. There is no secrecy legislation in effect. Consequently, the common law rules requiring confidentiality by the bank as a fiduciary of the customer constitute the sole source of the secrecy law. Local corporations are required to register the names of shareholders and directors for public inspection. Those operating strictly offshore, however, are not required to disclose such information.

General Corporate Law. New corporations may be established under either of two sets of law.[2] The international business corporation features compare favorably with those forms of corporation found in nontreaty tax havens such as Cayman; it is the one you are most likely to use. An international business corporation may not conduct a local business, own BVI real estate, conduct a banking or insurance business, or claim benefits under any of the BVI's tax treaties.

The characteristics of the BVI international business corporation include: the right to issue either registered or bearer shares; a modern "any legal activity" purposes and powers clause; freedom to amend the Memorandum of Association (Articles of Incorporation) and Articles of Association (Bylaws); the right to redeem its own shares; the ability to form the corporation with only one shareholder; the ability to operate with only one director; the ability to transfer domicile to the BVI from another jurisdiction and vice versa; exemption from BVI income tax, as well as from withholding on dividends, interest and other amounts paid to nonresidents of the BVI; exemption from estate or gift taxes; exemption from BVI stamp duty; and limited filing requirements that protect the identity of its shareholders and directors.

Incorporation fees to the BVI government are in two bands: US$300 if capitalized for $50,000 or less, and $1,000 if capitalized for more than $50,000.

A local registered agent is required, for service of process. Only lawyers, chartered accountants or specially qualified companies are permitted to serve in that capacity.

The international business corporation may be moved to continue its operations elsewhere, although it is not clear from the reference material examined that formal redomiciliation is contemplated. It is clear, however, that a foreign corporation may be redomiciled in the BVI as an international business corporation, even if doing so is against the law in the other country. In fact, in an apparent move to attract business from Panama, the BVI law was amended in 1988 to permit an international business corporation to include in its name the initials "N.A."[3]

An international business corporation is exempt from the BVI income tax otherwise applicable to local corporations and resident individuals. The BVI income tax rates follow classic United Kingdom patterns, including taxing only income that arises in or remitted to the BVI. They are low by world standards: local corporations are taxed at a flat rate of 15% and individuals at 20%.

In order to determine the tax treatment of a corporation, you must first determine its domicile and residence status. If a corporation is incorporated in the BVI, it is domiciled there. If its affairs are managed and controlled there, or if a majority of its directors reside in the BVI, it is resident there. A corporation both domiciled and resident in the BVI is taxed on its worldwide income, whether or not remitted to the BVI; a corporation that is domiciled there but resident outside the BVI is taxed only on income arising from the BVI and on foreign-source income remitted to the BVI.

Accordingly, the foreign-source income of your international business corporation incorporated or resident in the BVI (not both) is taxed only on funds remitted into that jurisdiction.

The BVI maintains five tax treaties through its affiliation with the United Kingdom: Denmark, Japan, Norway, Sweden and Switzerland. In certain cases, the BVI operates under an earlier form of treaty, that earlier form having been superseded by new treaties between the United Kingdom and its treaty partners.

The income tax treaty with the US was terminated effective January 1, 1983 and replaced by a proposed new treaty signed in 1981. The US Senate, however, refused to ratify it and it now appears unlikely that it will be put into effect.

Special Corporations. As was the case with the Bahamas, the BVI early found itself grossly abused by shell-bank promoters and racketeers in the formation of offshore private banks. Enactment of its banking ordinance in 1972 imposed modern banking regulations on such activity and eliminated those unable to meet the strict licensing requirements.

Trusts. As a common law jurisdiction, the BVI is a reliable domicile for your offshore trust. The common law is buttressed by local trust law.[4]

Cost Comparisons. Overall, the BVI constitutes a low-cost tax haven for both formation and annual maintenance of corporations, compared to most other tax havens and offshore financial centers.

Prospects. The attitude of the BVI government in response to the loss of its US tax treaty demonstrates a continuing and serious interest in maintaining its status as a tax haven. Its 1984 *International Business Companies Ordinance* demonstrates an aggressive attitude in building on existing gains. Hence, the future bodes well for continued support from the BVI government for offshore investing and business operations.

Endnotes

1. Banking Ordinance 1972 (No. 17 of 1972), as amended
2. The Companies Act 1984, or the International Business Companies Ordinance 1984 (No. 8 of 1984)
3. *ibid*
4. Trustee Ordinance 1961, Ch. 260, Revised Laws of the Virgin Islands 1961

Antigua

Summary. *Antigua is a small island nation in the Atlantic Ocean, just east of the American Virgin Islands. Although newly independent, it remains part of the British Commonwealth. It is a poor nation, under intense economic pressure to establish a sufficient revenue base. For that reason, it is likely that, before it can fully establish itself as a tax haven, it will succumb to US Treasury Department blandishments and enter into the exchange of information and mutual assistance agreements offered under the* Caribbean Basin Initiative. *Consequently, this section is more a brief status report than a structured review.*

As a small island nation without noticeable resources and deeply in debt, Antigua relies heavily on tourism to meet its economic needs. Revenues of any kind are important, thus, bank licensing fees are viewed as holding the promise of a service industry built around Eurobanking. To that end, new banking and corporation legislation reflecting Barbados' law and Cayman's secrecy provisions is under consideration. Whether the adoption of a new law will offset a history of bank insolvencies and associated offshore criminality is open to some debate. Antigua lacks certain of the fundamental requirements for a successful offshore financial center: it has a desperate need for income; trained personnel to govern and administer the law is almost totally lacking; informal practices detrimental to enforcement of the law require change; there is no enforced ethical code among attorneys; and there is no system of records or tradition upon which to base business operations.

Antigua recognizes its shortcomings and is eager to improve US relations, presumably as an alternative to the risk of failure in establishing itself as a tax haven.

Banks are simply corporations domiciled there which are authorized to include the term "bank" in the name, and are endorsed for either commercial bank or offshore operations. There are no registration requirements other than payment of fees, no capitalization requirement and no screening of applicants.

The Register of Corporations exists, but is incomplete. As a consequence, governmental authorities have no adequate records of the number of registered companies domiciled in Antigua, notwithstanding a regulation requiring annual reporting. Reportedly, the number of Antigua corporations is in the hundreds or thousands. Most are approved as banks but have no visible activities on the island. Offshore activities are wholly unknown. The records are so poorly maintained that authorities learn of a registered company acting as a bank only when a police inquiry or criminal complaint from abroad is received.

Antigua is patently cooperative with regular visitors from the Federal Bureau of Investigation and others investigating crimes and tax evasion from the US. The problem is that the government itself has no idea who owns the Antigua-domiciled corporations.

In short, Antigua is without funds to the point of desperation and lacks the local skills with which to create a central banking authority and establish a dependable offshore banking industry. Accordingly, the *Caribbean Basin Initiative* is welcomed as an expression of interest in Antigua. The issue will turn upon the revenues to be derived from the tax concessions made under the *Caribbean Basin Initiative* as compared to those revenues that may be derived from continuing tax haven activities, together with the timing involved.

In virtually the same posture, except that they are economically self-sufficient and their citizens demonstrate a stronger work ethic, are Montserrat, Anguilla and St. Vincent. Consequently, the uncontrolled offshore banking industries of those three jurisdictions are likely to be soon brought to gaff by the US Treasury Department, through its *Caribbean Basin Initiative.*

Panama

Summary. *Moving from the Atlantic and Caribbean areas into Central America, Panama constitutes the most important Euro-banking center for Latin America. Because of the Panama Canal, the US maintains close military and political ties with it and has embarked on a policy of national development, with its financial industry as the keystone. It imposes a system of high tax rates generally, but bases its status as a haven on the exemption of foreign-source income. Among its advantages are long standing as a recognized tax haven, a history of never taxing income from outside sources, a liberal corporation law with low formation costs and quick service, location at the crossroads of the Americas with excellent air and sea transportation and a large free-trade zone, the use of the US dollar as its de facto domestic currency, and a major international banking infrastructure.*

Location. The Republic of Panama lies between Costa Rica and Colombia at the point where South America joins Central America. It may be reached in 3 1/2 hours by air from Miami. Flight connections are excellent with all parts of the world, as is its telephone and telex service. To dial direct from the US to Panama, use country code 507. Panama operates under the same time as Eastern Standard Time all year, so it is the same as New York in the winter and Chicago in the summer.

Culture. The population is approximately 2.1 million, of whom 700,000 live in the capital, Panama City. A large proportion of the population is of mixed racial background, primarily European. The official language of Panama is Spanish, although most corporate documents may be written in any language and translation facilities are readily available.

Panama's agricultural industry is declining, and its labor force is expensive. It has few natural resources. As a consequence, it has difficulty attracting light or heavy industrial investment. The financial industry directly employs more than 8,000 people and provides a payroll exceeding $60 million per year. Until the US invasion in 1989, it was growing at the rate of 22% per year, compared to an overall national rate of 3.6%, so it provided considerable support to building, technology and other service industries. At more than $40 billion, the assets of the banking system equal Cayman's and are second only to the Bahamas among offshore and Western Hemisphere financial centers.

Unemployment, officially reported at 10%, may be nearer 20% and is complicated by serious underemployment. A substantial portion of the population is under age 18, and many of those young people are frustrated by a high aspirational level but poor career opportunities. In the absence of successful development programs, Panama is at risk due to poverty and dissatisfaction — issues which quickly translate into political action.

Political System. Until 1903, Panama was part of Colombia. Upon obtaining its independence, it suffered continuing political instability for many years. Panama moved from a military government in 1968 to a democratic system with an elected president and legislative council under which matters were relatively quiet until shortly before the US invasion. Historically, changes in government have no noticeable effect on the tax haven industry, but the invasion produced substantial disruptions.

Legal System. Panama operates under a civil law system. It is not a signatory to the 1961 Hague Convention. Accordingly, documents executed in Panama for use in the US must be authenticated by our consulate.

Few restrictions are imposed on aliens in Panama. It does, however, restrict certain professions to nationals and prohibits foreigners from engaging in retail trade.

As is the case with certain Caribbean nations and other Central America jurisdictions, Panama encourages pensioners from other countries to retire in Panama. In less troubled times, its Colon Free Zone tax incentives make that an attractive proposition.

Local Support Services. Panama boasts more than 3,000 lawyers whose skills are well-regarded. In addition, it has a large number of accounting firms and major international banks, the latter operating through branches, subsidiaries and representative offices.

Currency. The authorized currency, the Balboa, was never issued in paper form. Coin-denominated Balboas are in circulation. The US dollar is legal tender in Panama, circulates freely and serves as its *de facto* currency. Panama has no exchange controls.

Secrecy. Being a major repository for flight capital from Latin America, Panama has a comprehensive secrecy law, including numbered bank accounts. While financial authorities claim that only 20% of the Panamanian accounts are private, the figure is much larger when the practice of local accounts held by corporations in other jurisdictions is taken into account; that technique successfully precludes disclosure of the beneficial account owner. Secrecy is viewed as a necessity for the continued success of Panama in attracting three classes of assets: private local registered company accounts, interbank accounts (nonbank assets on deposit in Panama), and personal accounts containing flight capital. The central bank authority (which is not a monetary authority because of the predominance of the US dollar) is denied by secrecy laws any right to audit deposits. That presents a profound flaw in attaining stable, respectable banking practices. Stability may be assessed only by examining the creditworthiness of loans, not by any accounting tests of bank reports regarding funds on hand or deposit transactions. A bank management may therefore engage in extensive laundering, looting or asset kiting, the only measure of which would be an internal audit by a foreign headquarters bank or publication of the defalcation upon discovery. While aware of the risk to reputation, Panamanian bankers regard any threat to secrecy of greater importance.

Panama does not police, or allow anyone else to police, offshore activities by exempt companies. Present procedures provide that any foreign individual, company or authority complaining or inquiring about the activities of a Panamanian offshore company is directed to the Ministry of Commerce. The Ministry examines its files to identify the local agent, usually a Panamanian attorney, and communicates only that information to the foreign correspondent. The foreign correspondent has only one avenue to pursue: deal with the agent provided for notice purposes. Ministry officials agree that they receive many complaints of various frauds perpetrated abroad, but no action is taken unless the case is brought in Panama itself.

Panamanian law does not recognize crimes committed abroad as the basis for any action in Panama. Until June 1987, the foregoing served as the response to all requests for information by foreign governments and their enforcement authorities. Panama's position was that there can be no release of information with respect to any crime when the crime was not committed in Panama. Both the bank secrecy law and this fundamental territorial posture of the criminal law were intended to protect account holders from disclosure or prosecution. In June 1987, however, the Panamanian government suddenly allowed the US Drug Enforcement Administration full access to formerly secret bank records, resulting in the rapid withdrawal of $1.6 billion within two weeks. The banking hemorrhage continued at a rate estimated to remove US$15 to $28 billion by year-end 1987.

General Corporate Law. Panama is a major corporate tax haven. It may have more offshore corporations domiciled there than all the other tax havens in the Americas combined, an estimated 50,000 corporations. Two Panamanian law firms alone are believed to represent more than 5,000 corporations each.

The corporation law[1] is liberal, providing easy formation of corporations. It derives from Delaware law as it existed in 1927. In order to provide stability, few changes have been made, none of which include changes made by Delaware since 1927.

Two incorporators (usually nominees) execute the Articles of Incorporation before a Notary Public. The articles are then recorded at the Public Registry Office. A local registered agent is required, usually a lawyer or law firm.[2] The prevailing minimum fee for a registered agent ranges from US$150 to $200 per year.

Under a rule of evidence peculiar to Panama, corporate minutes are not admissible unless maintained in a special bound book, rather than a loose-leaf minute book. Assuming your corporation will not conduct local business and you do not expect to be involved in local litigation, you may safely ignore that requirement.

Using a local director may be convenient, but probably unnecessary, since shareholders and directors meetings may be held anywhere in the world. Minutes reflecting the election of new directors or the appointment of new officers must be authenticated before the Panamanian Counsel and registered in Panama, but if the secretary who signs the minutes is registered as the secretary of the corporation in the Mercantile Registry of Panama, you may dispense with that formality. Accordingly, you may wish to use a local attorney as the corporate secretary.

Aside from the foregoing, each Panamanian corporation must have at least three directors and three officers: as to the latter, a President, Secretary and Treasurer. There are no nationality or residence requirements for either directors or officers. Should you choose to use one or more local persons as director or officer, the prevailing fee is approximately $200 per year.

The annual flat tax on corporations imposed by Panama is currently $150.[3] It is payable within three months following registration, and each year thereafter within three months after the anniversary of the date on which it was registered. Payments are made by the corporation's registered agent in Panama, who also files a sworn statement as to the date of registration. Late payment penalties are imposed, and a corporation in default may not register any documents or obtain a "good-standing" certificate.

Under Panamanian law, a foreign corporation may transfer its domicile to Panama and out again,[4] but there is no provision authorizing a Panamanian corporation to move its domicile to another jurisdiction. It is, however, possible for a Panamanian corporation to accomplish the same result by merger with a foreign corporation where the foreign corporation is the surviving entity.

Panama is not a no-tax jurisdiction; it imposes an income tax with relatively high rates. It is characterized as a tax haven because all income of a Panamanian corporation from foreign sources is exempt from Panamanian income tax.

Because Panama derives major benefits from its status as a tax haven, it is unlikely that the exemption of foreign-source income will be changed in the foreseeable future. There is a 10% withholding tax on dividends paid by Panamanian corporations, but no withholding on the redistribution of foreign-source income. There is no estate or inheritance tax on shares of a Panamanian corporation owned by a nonresident decedent. Panama is not a party to any tax treaties.

The Colon Free Zone is a segregated area located in Colon on the Caribbean side of Panama, in which foreign merchandise may be landed without payment of customs duties. Approximately $3 billion of business is conducted each year from the Colon Free Zone, and some 15,000 people are employed there.

Corporations operating from the Colon Free Zone pay a maximum tax of 8 1/2% on net profits over US$100,000 derived from re-exporting goods abroad.[5] The rate is reduced if the company generates substantial local employment. Full Panamanian corporate tax is imposed on sales made within Panama, although sales from one free zone company to another are treated as foreign sales.

Local law firms routinely market "shelf" corporations already formed, which can be placed in effect within a few hours. An old company can be bought, if needed, in order to back-date transactions documented abroad. Attorneys form and hold these "vintage" corporate shelfs charging, as with good wine, for the age. A registered shelf company in Panama costs less than US$1,000 to form and about $250 annually to maintain. Panamanian law firms maintain European offices for the convenience of their European clients. Shelf corporations purchased there are generally less costly, because the competition is more intense.

Special Corporations. As recently as 1982, Panama was the domicile for 126 banks, eight of which are important retail commercial institutions. There are 20 banks located in the free zone. Fourteen new banks were formed in 1981, five were formed in 1982 and five more were in registration at the end of that year. Bank licensing procedures are strict due to the unhappy experiences of the early 1970s. Panama prefers to license only major international banks already headquartered in responsible foreign countries. It will not only reject applications from banks headquartered elsewhere in the Caribbean, but will reject applications from subsidiaries of major international banks if those subsidiaries are in the Caribbean. The paid-in capital requirement is US$250,000. Fifty-five of the banks operating in 1982 were international banks headquartered abroad, many of which operated in the wholesale Euro-currency market. A number of the newly chartered banks are Japanese. Panama imposes no income tax on bank deposit interest.

Panama is a major shipping haven, with hundreds of American-owned ships registered under the Panamanian flag. Most of the ships are owned by Panamanian corporations.

Trusts. Panama is a civil law jurisdiction. Thus, notwithstanding its 1984 trust law,[6] it is not an attractive jurisdiction in which to establish your tax haven trust.

The 1984 trust law does permit revocable trusts. It also provides for trust secrecy, with major penalties for disclosure. A Panamanian trust may be redomiciled if the trust declaration authorizes it. The trust must have a resident agent and a US$100 annual tax is imposed in much the same manner as a corporation.

Cost Comparisons. Especially with the competition-driven price differential of shell corporations sold to European clients, Panama is a low-cost country in which to form and maintain a foreign corporation. You may incorporate a simple offshore corporation with minimum capital of US$700 to $800. Annual maintenance, including the registered agent, three local directors and the annual corporation tax will cost approximately $900.

Prospects. The short-term effect of the US invasion is still being evaluated. But in due course, Panama will again become popular with Latin Americans and Europeans for the incorporation of holding companies where tax treaty benefits are of no significance. The only serious question about Panama's future is related to the Panama Canal treaties. Questions also remain about the new government; you may prefer not to use Panamanian corporations to hold real estate or other assets that might be difficult to transfer quickly in the event of political turmoil. More comfort is provided by using them to hold bank deposits and securities.

Endnotes

1. Panama Law No. 32 of 1927, as amended
2. Panama Decree No. 147 of 1966
3. Panama Law No. 9 of 1980, as amended by Law No. 1 of February 28, 1985
4. Panama Decree No. 16 of 1958
5. Panama Law No. 24 of 1975
6. Panama Law No. 1 of 1984

Costa Rica

Summary. *Like Panama, Costa Rica taxes only income from sources within the country; it does not tax foreign-source income. Among other advantages: it is a stable, democratic government, it is host to a large number of American and European retirees, it has long-term stability as to its tax posture, and it has virtually no restrictions on resident foreigners.*

Costa Rica may be useful as a tax haven for corporations conducting their business entirely offshore. Corporations are inexpensive to form and maintain.

Location. Costa Rica lies between Nicaragua on the north and Panama on the south in Central America. It is a three-hour flight from Miami. The telephone and telex service are good. To dial direct from the United States, use country code 506. Costa Rican time is the same as Central Standard Time all year, so it is the same as Chicago in the winter and Denver in the summer. A high mountain spine runs its length. It is semi-tropical and lush, relatively cool at its higher elevations. It has long stretches of virtually unused beaches. The coastlines are hot and humid. Its pride is its large, national rain forest.

Culture. The Costa Rican population is approximately 2.7 million, of which 500,000 live in the capital city of San José. Most Costa Ricans are of European origin. The literacy rate is above 90%. The official language is Spanish.

Political System. Unlike a large part of Latin America — Nicaragua and El Salvador in particular — Costa Rica is a peaceful oasis. It has no army and relies on the Organization of American States for any defense required. It is rightly regarded as the most stable and democratic country in all of Latin America. Like the US, political power passes from one party to another with some frequency, but changes from one elected president to a successor are always orderly.

Legal System. All corporate documents must be in Spanish, the official language, but translations are easily obtainable.

Costa Rica operates under a civil law system.

It is not a signatory to the 1961 Hague Convention. Accordingly, your Costa Rican documents still require authentication by the US consul.

Except for the power to vote or hold political office, foreigners enjoy the same rights as Costa Ricans. Costa Rica is unique in the freedom provided to resident foreigners. An individual or family may not only enter the country as permanent residents, but may also obtain provisional passports.[1] The passports are identical to those given Costa Rican citizens and are perfectly satisfactory for international travel. A political controversy in 1983 brought about the suspension of new issuances, though. How long it will last is unknown.

The law[2] is used (successfully) to attract retirees to Costa Rica. The immigrant must either demonstrate a permanent, regular income from outside Costa Rica of at least US$1,000 per month or maintain a bank balance there of US$100,000. The qualifying income is specifically exempt from Costa Rican income tax, as is all income from outside the country. In the absence of some special dispensation, a retiree resident in Costa Rica may not engage in any occupation other than with respect to personal investments.

Local Support Services. All commercial banks in Costa Rica are owned by the government. A large number of high-quality law and accounting firms are available.

Currency. The currency of Costa Rica is the Colon. The exchange rate for the Colon has dropped in value from US$.12 to less than two cents in recent years. Good time to buy real estate.

Exchange controls require that all foreign currency transactions be affected through the Central Bank or an approved commercial bank. The free market rate is used for the purchase of US dollars, payment for imports, and for the payment of dividends, interest and royalties.

Secrecy. Bank accounts are confidential; information concerning them may be provided only upon written authorization by the account owner or by order of a competent court.[3] Notwithstanding nontaxation of foreign-source income, Costa Rica requires an income tax return each year from every Costa Rica corporation. The names of the officers and directors of a Costa Rican corporation are part of the public record.

Bearer shares were in wide use until 1980, at which time the legislature prohibited their use.[4] You may use shares registered in the names of nominees and endorsed in blank as *de facto* bearer shares, if that sort of privacy is important to your needs.

General Corporate Law. Under the law governing Costa Rican corporations,[5] par value is required for corporate shares; those values may be expressed in any currency if the equivalent is expressed in Costa Rican Colones. No minimum capitalization is required.

The code permits broad corporate powers, authorizing the corporation to engage generally in agriculture, industry and commerce; categorics broad enough to cover any lawful business activity.

A Costa Rican corporation may not exist in perpetuity. Most are established for terms of 99 years.

Local procedure for corporate formation is elaborate. Two incorporators (usually nominees) appear before a Costa Rican Notary, the proposed articles are published, following which they are registered. The procedure usually takes at least three weeks. Unlike other civil law countries, most Costa Rican attorneys are also Notaries Public. The registration fee, as well as legal fees, are low in comparison to other tax havens.

Meetings of shareholders and directors may be held anywhere in the world. The corporation must have at least three directors and the fiscal, or guardian. The officers, directors and shareholders may all be foreigners, but each corporation must appoint a local representative for service of process. The president of a Costa Rican corporation is given power to bind the company in all transactions, unless the power is deleted in the articles.

There is no provision in the law authorizing a Costa Rican corporation to transfer its domicile to another jurisdiction, nor is there any provision expressly prohibiting it. Thus, there is a risk that doing so may be treated as a constructive dissolution for tax purposes. There is, however, a provision authorizing the transfer of a foreign corporation to Costa Rica if its country of origin permits it to do so.[6] Such a company may also move its domicile from Costa Rica to another jurisdiction.

Each Costa Rican corporation must close its fiscal year on September 30. As noted, each must file an annual income tax return, even if all of its income is foreign-source. No other annual reports are required and the government imposes no annual fees.

In light of the fact that four of the five countries comprising the Central American Common Market tax corporations only on domestic-source income, it is unlikely that any change will come about from eventual tax harmonization. Costa Rica imposes no capital gains tax on the sale of shares of a Costa Rican corporation.

There is a withholding tax on dividends; it apparently applies even to corporate earnings entirely from foreign sources, although a 1988 change raises the hope that this was not intended.[7] The rate is 15% on dividends paid to nonresidents, but that withheld from dividends paid to a person domiciled in Costa Rica, including a Costa Rican trust, is only 5%. Since a trust can apparently remit the dividends to a nonresident beneficiary without further withholding tax, it may be useful to use a Costa Rican trust to receive the corporate dividends and reduce the effective rate of withholding from 15% to 5%.

Costa Rica has no income tax treaties. It is an "eligible beneficiary country" under the US *Caribbean Basin Initiative*. In November 1984, the US Treasury announced that Costa Rica and the US had agreed in principle on the text of a *Caribbean Basin Initiative* agreement to exchange tax information.[8] The agreement is now signed and enables IRS to obtain any form of tax information needed for its investigations. Costa Rica benefits under it from tax-deductible American business conventions and from becoming a qualified jurisdiction for Foreign Sales Corporations.

The former succession tax on Costa Rican corporation shares

owned by nonresident aliens was repealed in 1976 and replaced with a culture stamp tax.[9]

Special Corporations. All Costa Rican banks are owned and operated by the government. It is possible, reportedly, to establish a privately-owned bank there, but such a bank may not offer checking accounts.

Trusts. Being a civil law jurisdiction, it is not suitable for trusts as a general rule. An exception may be for a trust to hold shares in a Costa Rican corporation in order to reduce the withholding tax as already noted.

Cost Comparisons. Compared to other tax havens, the formation and operation of corporations and trusts in Costa Rica is noticeably less expensive.

Prospects. Unlike classic tax havens, Costa Rica has never promoted itself as such, nor as an offshore financial center. Few people within or without the country even recognize its potential as a base for offshore investing in business operations. While there is no indication of a serious effort to change the present circumstances, if such an effort were to develop, there would be no entrenched lobby to oppose it. As a consequence, Costa Rica is excellent for the moment, but there can be no assurance that it will last. Mounting pressures from conflicts in nearby countries are eroding Costa Rica's 40 years of political and economic stability. That problem notwithstanding, approximately 15,000 US expatriates enjoy a happy, low-cost retirement there. At 1987 prices, one may purchase a two-bedroom furnished home on five acres with maid's quarters, gardens, a lawn, pool and automobile for about US$125,000. Escaza is a suburb of the capital city, San José, favored by the more affluent Americans. They pay up to $250,000 for a luxury home there. At the other end of the spectrum, comfortable two and three-bedroom houses in the El Bosque development in San Francisco de Dos Rios sell for about $20,000. Except for gasoline, living costs are about one-half those in the US.

Endnotes

1. Costa Rican Law No. 4812 of 1971
2. *ibid*
3. Costa Rican Commercial Code, Art. 615
4. Costa Rican Law No. 6450 of 1980
5. Costa Rican Commercial Code, Arts. 17-32, 102-225
6. Costa Rican Commercial Code, Art. 227
7. Costa Rican Income Tax Reform Act (Law No. 7092 of 1988)
8. US Treasury Department Release R-2918, November 8, 1984
9. Costa Rican Law No. 5923 of 1976

Switzerland

Summary. *Despite its location in central Europe — surrounded by Germany, Austria, Italy, and France — Switzerland remained aloof from most European wars to date, including both world wars. Because of its carefully-preserved neutrality and the often high direct taxes imposed by its 26 cantons, Switzerland is regarded more as a capital haven than a tax haven.*

Location. Located in central Europe, Switzerland extends over approximately 16,000 square miles. Regular flights to and from Zurich and Geneva are readily available. Telephone, telex and mail services are excellent. To dial direct from the US, use country code 41, plus local code 1 for Zurich or 22 for Geneva. During most of the year, Switzerland is six hours ahead of New York time.

Culture. The population of Switzerland is approximately 6.4 million persons. About two-thirds are German-speaking; most of the rest speak French or Italian. About 700,000 people live in Zurich, the largest city. The other important cities, Bern, Geneva, Basel and Lusanne each have fewer than 400,000 people. Unemployment and underemployment are nominal.

Every major nation is identified with certain ideals. For Americans they are freedom, equality and justice; for Germans they are military strength and unity. Swiss traditions focus on hard work, privacy, self-reliance and a serious business attitude. Like most national ideals, they are unlikely to change soon. Unlike most national ideals, they are favorable to the foreign investor.

Political System. Switzerland has one of the best reputations in the world for political and economic stability. It boasts adequate secrecy laws, well-capitalized banks and enclaves among several Swiss cantons that serve as attractive holding company jurisdictions.

Power is decentralized, resulting in limited federal powers and a major portion of government concentrated at the cantonal and local levels. Taxation is imposed primarily at the canton level.

Notwithstanding a trend toward harmonization of taxes, there remain important differences from canton to canton. Changes in tax rate increases generally require approval by referendum.

Legal System. Switzerland operates under a civil law system.

It is a signatory to the 1961 Hague Convention. Accordingly, documents executed in Switzerland are authenticated by an Apostille, the standard certificate provided by the convention. The Apostille should be signed by the appropriate federal or cantonal authorities.

Non-Swiss citizens are restricted in several major respects. Work permits are required and difficult to obtain. Foreigners need special permission in order to acquire Swiss real property.

Local Support Services. Switzerland is almost without peer in providing high-quality banks, attorneys, tax consultants and accountants.

Currency. Historically, the Swiss Franc has proven to be one of the world's most stable currencies. Its current value is about US$.76. There are no restrictions preventing foreigners from holding Swiss bank deposits or bonds denominated in Swiss Francs. There are no currency controls.

Secrecy. Switzerland provides limited commercial secrecy in a complex arrangement of local practice, tax treaties and special agreements. Banking secrecy applies to both Swiss and foreign authorities. It is buttressed by substantial penalties that include both fines and imprisonment. Secrecy may be penetrated by court order but only in nontax, criminal investigations. Tax evasion is not a crime under Swiss law unless the taxpayer falsified records other than tax returns.

The tradition of bank secrecy is well-established in Switzerland, and is unlikely to substantially change. There is, however, some risk that tax evasion may soon be characterized as a criminal matter, permitting both Swiss and foreign governments to obtain banking information that is today protected.

Swiss agreements with the US include the US-Swiss Tax Treaty, the *Treaty of Mutual Assistance in Criminal Matters* and the *International Mutual Assistance in Criminal Matters.* Under the last, foreign prosecutors have the same powers in Switzerland as do Swiss prosecutors. It also contains a broadened application to tax affairs, notwithstanding the noncriminality of tax evasion under Swiss law, but tax cases not involving fraud still do not fall under provision-of-information procedures.

As to commercial secrecy, names of persons authorized to act on behalf of corporations are published in the official gazette, as are the capitalization of the corporation and its stated business purposes. Share ownership records and financial accounts, however, are not available. Bearer shares are customary and widely used.

General Corporate Law. A corporation formed under Swiss law includes in its name "AG" in the German-speaking parts of the country and "SA" in the French-speaking parts. There is no fundamental difference between those used to conduct local business and those utilized for strictly offshore activities.

Forming a corporation in Switzerland requires approximately two weeks. Three subscribers are required, usually nominees. After formation, a corporation may be owned by a single shareholder, other than qualifying directors' shares. A broad, statutory purposes and powers clause is in wide use, and the doctrine of *ultravires*[1] does not apply to Swiss corporations.

Minimum capitalization is SFr50,000 (about US$38,000). Par value required is at least SFr100 (about US$76). Switzerland does not recognize the concept of "authorized but unissued shares." If shares are issued in registered form, the issuee must pay at least 20% of the amount authorized, minimum SFr20,000 (about US$15,200), and is personally liable for the balance. For bearer-share corporations, all capital must be fully paid at the time of incorporation. Capital paid in cash must be deposited in escrow with a bank, and payments in kind are strictly limited.

Care is taken by Swiss authorities to avoid misleading corporation names. Accordingly, geographic designations are generally prohibited.

A Swiss corporation must have at least one director. A majority of the board must be Swiss citizens residing in Switzerland. To meet that requirement, bankers and lawyers often serve as directors of Swiss corporations owned by their foreign clients. Each director must hold and deposit at least one qualifying share with the corporation; the share is usually held for the beneficial owner under a nominee agreement.

As is the case with US corporations, the board determines who may sign on its behalf and how many signatures are required. Signature rights are then published in the official gazette, making them a matter of public record for all corporations.

Shareholders' and directors' meetings may be held anywhere in the world, and proxies are permitted. Annual audited accountings are required and presented at the annual shareholders' meeting.

Swiss federal law[2] provides certain circumstances under which a Swiss corporation may transfer its domicile from Switzerland to another country. There is no law permitting or prohibiting the redomiciliation of a foreign corporation to Switzerland.

Switzerland may be a low-tax or high-tax country, depending upon the form of corporation, the type of business conducted and the canton in which it is located. The tax system is complex and varies considerably from one canton to another. In fact, municipal taxes within the same canton vary widely.

A large number of the cantons and municipalities apply low tax rates to pure holding companies, to participation or mixed companies, to domiciliary companies and to service companies. Those are, accordingly, the types of businesses that might consider Switzerland as a domicile.

While the definition of a holding company differs from canton to canton, it is generally one that administers its own holdings in the shares of other corporations, either Swiss or foreign, as its exclusive or major business activity. The pure holding company generally pays no cantonal or municipal income taxes, although it may pay a small cantonal tax based on its capitalization. The rate varies from .05% to .25%, with an average of perhaps .15%. There is a generally-imposed minimum of approximately SFr300 (about

US$198) per year.

A maximum 9.8% federal tax is imposed on most pure holding companies, along with an annual federal capital tax of .0825% on net assets. A substantial interest, defined as 20% or more of the other corporations' shares or shares worth at least SFr2 million (about US$1.5 million) provides an exemption from federal income tax with respect to dividends from those interests. The exemption does not extend, however, to gains realized on their sale.

Dividends paid by a pure holding company, including liquidating dividends, are subject to a 35% federal withholding tax unless reduced by treaty.

A participation company is a mixed holding and operating company. Unlike a pure holding company, it does not limit its activity to the administration of investment interests in other businesses. A participation company with a substantial investment interest in another company is granted pro rata tax benefits with respect to the federal income tax and corresponding benefits in about 17 of the 26 cantons. As is the case with holding companies, dividends paid by a participation company are subject to the 35% federal withholding tax unless reduced by treaty.

A domiciliary company, the one you would use if you established an offshore corporation in Switzerland, only maintains a statutory domicile in Switzerland and does not engage in any local business activity there, nor does it own any real estate in Switzerland. In approximately 20 of the cantons, a domiciliary company is taxed in a manner similar to holding companies. If located in one of those cantons, it pays no cantonal income tax and only a small cantonal capital tax. It must, however, pay the federal income and capital taxes, and its dividends are subject to withholding.

The service company is a Swiss corporation that performs auxiliary functions for foreign enterprises as its major activity. It must pay regular federal income and capital taxes and, in at least five cantons, is granted a reduced rate of cantonal income tax and cantonal capital tax. As is the case with other corporations, dividends are subject to withholding.

Switzerland maintains several tax treaties and is continuously negotiating new ones. Unlike the case in the Netherlands Antilles, however, foreigners are generally prevented from using Swiss corporations as conduits to obtain benefits from their treaty network. As noted in the section on secrecy, Switzerland and the US have an income tax treaty and three supplemental agreements providing for reciprocal exchange of information. The reciprocity extends only to criminal matters, which, under Swiss law, does not include tax evasion.

Trusts. As a civil law jurisdiction, Switzerland is usable but rarely useful as a domicile for your tax haven trust.

Cost Comparisons. It is relatively expensive to organize and maintain a corporation in Switzerland due, in part, to the 3% of par value capital tax on formation. On minimum capitalization of SFr50,000 the capital tax would be SFr1,500 (about US$1,140). The total cost of forming a Swiss corporation with minimum capital of SFr50,000 would approximate SFr6,000 (approximately US$4,560). It would require approximately SFr2,000 (about US$1,520) per year to maintain.

Prospects. Along with possible recharacterization of tax evasion as a criminal matter subject to disclosure agreements and the steady increase of taxes imposed by the Swiss government at its various levels, the future holds notable change from traditional banking operations. The Swiss Franc, historically among the most stable currencies, began recovering in 1990 from the effects of a 5% inflation rate; the rate went higher than both France and Germany, and was barely lower than inflation-ridden Italy. The Swiss central bank tightened the money supply to start the recovery.

Bank secrecy is a matter of growing concern. Some embarrassing financial scandals in the late 1980s brought down Switzerland's Justice Minister and tarnished its image. New legislation intended to repair the damage necessarily led to relaxation of bank secrecy with respect to disclosures of insider trading and money laundering, and has tightened the diligence convention (the gentleman's agreement between Swiss banks to identify the true owners of accounts).

Everyone applauds the prosecution of swindlers and drug traffickers; the nervous investors just wonder where the changes will lead. Much of the capital in Swiss banks is unreported at home. Those customers prefer not to take the risk that tax evasion may in time become a crime in Switzerland, thus leaving those records unprotected by bank secrecy laws. The money is moving out in large amounts.

The response of the banks and legislators of Switzerland is to look for ways to become more competitive. They must, because the stakes are so high. Offshore asset management in that country is 40% of the world's total. The financial services industry of Switzerland accounts for more than 10% of its gross domestic product, employs 120,000 people and pays more than US$6.5 billion in taxes.

The steps under way to become more competitive include: opening up to smaller banks the bond underwriting monopoly enjoyed for years by the big three (Union Bank of Switzerland, Swiss Bank Corporation and Credit Suisse); same with the securities trading on the seven Swiss stock exchanges; using the exchanges fully, instead of matching purchases and sales among bank customers before going to the exchange with the remaining transactions; opening up the sale of voting shares in Swiss corporations (only Nestle now permits foreign investors to trade in its voting shares); considering abolition of its stamp duty of up to 3% on financial transactions; and rationalizing the 20-odd conventions which fix prices and practices in the banking and securities markets, padding bank fees and charges since before World War II.

Switzerland installed in 1988 an automated futures and options exchange ("SOFFEX") for investment-grade securities. The Swiss Electronic Exchange is expected to be operational in mid-1991, unifying the three largest bourses (Zurich, Geneva and Basel).

These steps, if actually taken in a responsible way, will both highlight the shabby way foreign investors have been treated and materially change it for the better. Switzerland has a long and distinguished tradition and an efficient infrastructure. While it is estimated that heavy competition will cause more than half of its

630 banks to merge or close by 1995, it will recover and prosper. Consequently, serious investors will continue to give it every consideration.

Endnotes

1. Law Protecting Legal Entities, Companies and Firms, of April 12, 1957
2. The 1962 Decree of the Swiss Federal Council on Measures Against the Improper Use of Swiss Tax Conventions

The Netherlands

Summary. *Notwithstanding its high tax rates, the Netherlands is a tax haven by virtue of exempting certain categories of income from its corporate income tax. You would establish your CFC in the Netherlands if its business could be conducted entirely within exempt categories.*

Prime among the exempt categories is its "participation exemption," the Netherlands' designation for a holding company. Under its "substantial-holding privilege," a Netherlands holding company pays no corporate income tax or capital gains tax on dividends and trading gains arising from direct investments in domestic or foreign business interests. The theory behind the privilege is that double taxation of the same profit at the corporate level should be avoided.

Location. The Netherlands is in Western Europe, is more than 15,000 square miles in size (much smaller than the state of Oregon) and is bounded by Belgium, Germany and the North Sea. It has excellent service by air; it may be reached in approximately seven hours nonstop from New York. Telephone and telex services are excellent. To dial direct from the US, use country code 31 plus local code 20 for Amsterdam or 10 for Rotterdam. The Netherlands is six hours ahead of New York, Eastern Standard Time.

Culture. The Netherlands has a population of approximately 14 million people. About 2.5 million reside in the largest cities: 1 million in Amsterdam, 800,000 in Rotterdam and 700,000 in The Hague. The language of the Netherlands is Dutch.

Political System. The government of the Netherlands is a combination of monarchy and constitutional democracy. The king serves more of a ceremonial than governmental function, the latter being exercised by its elected parliament.

Legal System. The Netherlands operates under a civil law system. It is a signatory to the 1961 Hague Convention. Accordingly, documents executed in the Netherlands are authenticated by an Apostille, the standard certificate provided by the convention. The Apostille should be signed by the Registrar of the Courts of First Instance.

Local Support Services. Banking, legal, tax and auditing services available in the Netherlands are of excellent quality.

Currency. The official name for the Netherlands currency is the florin, although commonly referred to as the guilder. The Dutch guilder is exchanged at about US$.56. While the Netherlands imposes exchange controls, the regulations are lax by comparison to other jurisdictions.

Secrecy. As a civil law system, there are no inherent fiduciary concepts on which to expect secrecy as a common practice, nor is there any bank or commercial secrecy law. The Netherlands does not authorize numbered bank accounts. The tax inspector's office freely demands and receives information from banks and businesses operating in the Netherlands.

General Corporate Law. Although the Netherlands continues to provide the *naamloze vennootschap* or "NV," since 1971 it has also provided the *besloten vennootschap* or "BV." The emergence of the BV came about because of European Economic Community directives requiring publication of detailed financial data concerning corporations. The auditing and publication requirements do not apply to the BV form, so it is suitable for a closely-held corporation such as a holding company; some privacy is assured.

Existing NVs were given an opportunity to convert into BVs, and most of them did so. The conversion was tax-free, both in the Netherlands and in the US, and no advance ruling from IRS was required.[1]

As is the case with Netherlands Antilles corporations, there is a blurring of the distinctions commonly accepted in the US between the responsibilities and the functions of the board of directors as opposed to the operating officers, in that its affairs are managed by managing directors. Those managing directors may bind the corporation as to third parties and may also be corporations as well as individuals. Although NVs may issue bearer shares, BVs may not. At least 20% of the authorized capital of the BV must be issued and paid upon incorporation.

So long as at least 20% of the authorized capital remains in the corporation and required amendments are made to the Articles of Incorporation, either the NV or the BV may freely redeem its outstanding shares. The minimum capital requirements of the civil code are presently NFl35,000 (approximately US$19,600).

Netherlands law permits the transfer of the corporate domicile from the Netherlands to the Netherlands Antilles in the event of an emergency (defined as revolution or immediate threat of war).[2]

Except as so noted, the Netherlands has no law permitting a corporation to move its domicile into or out of that jurisdiction, nor any prohibiting it. Thus, there is a risk that doing so may be treated as a constructive dissolution for tax purposes.

The Netherlands is considered a high tax jurisdiction, with its corporate tax rate of 43%. If your corporation qualifies as a holding company under the "substantial-holding privilege," however, it avoids the corporate income tax.

The exemption is determined holding-by-holding (it must hold 5% or more of the company in which the investment is made); so if the holding company earns other income from nonqualifying investments, that income would be taxable at the corporate rates.

The Netherlands imposes no withholding tax on interest. In addition, income tax withholding on dividends paid from the Netherlands to a foreign parent corporation is often reduced by income tax treaties.

The Netherlands is a party to approximately 35 income tax treaties and, unlike Luxembourg and Switzerland, has no law denying the benefit of those treaties to US investors who establish a CFC within the Netherlands. If dividends from the Netherlands holding company are not brought within the ambit of an existing treaty, the withholding rate is 25%. Under various treaties it will range from zero to 15%, typically 5%.

Because of the 1973 decision of a Netherlands Antilles court imposing a business relationship requirement between the holding company and its subsidiary, the Netherlands Finance Ministry attempted in 1974 to assuage the concerns of offshore investors. It stated that the foreign affiliate paying a dividend must be engaged in some business in which there is a relationship between that business and the business of either the Netherlands holding company or its parent. That permits the Netherlands holding company to either be the parent or a link in the chain of corporate holdings. In the absence of that business relationship, the exemption for holding company status is not granted; it is also not granted as to portfolio holdings (holdings of less than 5% of the outstanding shares of another company). The business relationship test suggests that you cause your Netherlands holding company to provide certain minimal management, data processing or professional services to the companies in which it has a "substantial holding" relationship.

There is no Netherlands withholding tax on interest or royalties paid by a Netherlands corporation. Although interest or royalty income received by a Netherlands corporation is not covered by the substantial-holding privilege, thus subject to full tax, it may be reduced or fully offset by the payment out of disbursements bearing the same character (i.e., interest or royalties). Only the differential, if any, is taxed by the Netherlands. Consequently, if its offshore holdings includes such income, it should plan to receive and remit it during the same tax period to a CFC in a no-tax haven, if by doing so it may accumulate tax free.

Upon the formation of a Netherlands corporation, and upon each subsequent capital contribution, a capital tax of 1% is imposed. There is no annual capital tax.

Two of the Netherlands tax treaties are of particular interest: the US Treaty and the Netherlands-Antilles Agreement. The Netherlands-US Treaty was signed in 1948, supplemented in 1965 and is in wide use by both Netherlands residents and by "treaty shoppers" from third countries. The position of IRS is that use of the treaty by non-Netherlands citizens comes within the "letter" of the law but violates its "spirit." Consequently, the US has sought a new income tax treaty with the Netherlands for years. The

Netherlands, however, is unwilling to modify the treaty unless the US eliminates its unitary taxation system, an issue that has brought about a total impasse, with the old treaty remaining in force.

Through 1985, dividends from a Netherlands company to its Netherlands Antilles parent were tax-exempt. Consequently, non-US citizens desiring to invest in the US routinely formed a Netherlands Antilles corporation, which in turn formed a Netherlands subsidiary, which in turn made US investments. If the US investments were bought within the substantial-holding rule, payments to the Netherlands holding company were untaxed by the Netherlands, and dividends from the Netherlands holding company to the Netherlands Antilles parent were not subject to withholding tax. In 1986, however, a new tax agreement between the Netherlands and the Netherlands Antilles forces an election between a 7.5% Netherlands tax on dividends paid to a Netherlands Antilles parent corporation, or payment of a 5% tax in the Netherlands plus 5.5% on the remaining dividend in the Netherlands Antilles. Since the Netherlands Antilles tax at the 5.5% rate is imposed on net dividend income, chargeable expenses should be examined in order to determine the lowest effective tax rate. With no deductions, the rate will not exceed 10.225% (5% in the Netherlands plus 5.5% of the remaining 95% in the Antilles).

Here is the relational pattern:

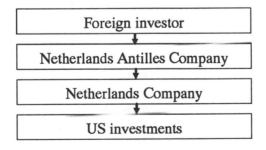

Remember, this is for non-US taxpayers, not you as a Target Defendant.

Trusts. Civil law jurisdictions do not generally contemplate the kinds of fiduciary relationships on which trust concepts depend. The Netherlands has not enacted any specific law grafting trust concepts onto its civil law system. Trust status being thus rendered uncertain, it is not an attractive jurisdiction for your tax haven trust.

Cost Comparisons. Fees and costs for establishing and operating a Netherlands corporation are higher than average. The additional cost is related directly to the importance of suitable tax rulings and more intensive use of attorneys, accountants and Notaries Public.

Prospects. One objective of the European Economic Community ("EEC") is to eventually harmonize the tax laws of its constituent countries, including the Netherlands. If that ever happens, the current favorable treatment of Netherlands holding companies may be impaired. Until that time, it remains an attractive enclave for offshore holding companies owned by non-US taxpayers.

Endnotes

1. Rev Rul 72-420, 1972-2 CG 473
2. Supra-National Act Governing the Voluntary Transfer of Seats of Legal Entities, as amended

Luxembourg

Summary. *Although some tax harmonization steps have been taken by Luxembourg with respect to its fellow members of the EEC, Luxembourg holding companies remain exempt from corporate income tax. Only a small annual capital tax is imposed on such holding companies, determined by the value of issued shares and debentures. There is no withholding tax on either dividends or interest paid by a holding company, nor is there any estate or inheritance tax on the shares of a holding company held by nonresident decedents. Luxembourg is highly regarded as an offshore financial center.*

Location. Luxembourg is smaller than Rhode Island and is bounded by Belgium, France and Germany. The country is easily and conveniently accessible by air from all major capitals of the world. In addition, it provides excellent train service to most of Europe, along with modern telephone, telex and mail communications. To dial direct from the US to Luxembourg use country code 352. Luxembourg is six hours later than New York time, except during daylight savings time.

Culture. Of the 370,000 persons living in the Grand Duchy of Luxembourg, approximately 80,000 reside in the capital city, also called Luxembourg. Several languages are commonly spoken in Luxembourg, but the principal ones are German, French and Letzeburgesch.

Political System. Luxembourg is politically stable and boasts an extraordinarily high level of wealth. The European Court of Justice is located there, as well as the Common Markets Monetary Fund. Unlike Switzerland, it was occupied by German forces during both world wars.

Legal System. Luxembourg operates under a civil law system.
    It is a signatory of the 1961 Hague Convention. Accordingly, documents executed in Luxembourg are authenticated by an Apos-

tille, the standard certificate provided by the convention. The Apostille should be signed by the Ministry of Foreign Affairs.

Residence and work permits are required for foreigners, but may be obtained without difficulty. No permits are required of citizens from EEC countries.

Local Support Services. With more than 90 banks, Luxembourg is a major international banking center. Those banks and its stock exchange play an important role in the Eurobond market, as well. It boasts a large number of high-quality law and accounting firms, as well as management companies specializing in holding company service requirements.

Currency. The local currency is the Luxembourg Franc, which is worth about US$.03. Although no exchange control restrictions are presently in place, its close ties to Belgium would probably cause it to apply any imposed by that country.

Secrecy. Luxembourg has taken a clear position in favor of bank and commercial secrecy, the position extending well beyond either the Netherlands or Switzerland. Numbered bank accounts are common and bank secrecy is respected as a matter of practice. Luxembourg corporations may be established with either registered or bearer shares.

General Corporate Law. Its basic corporate law was last amended in 1983.[1] Corporations must have two shareholders — either individuals or corporations. The creating instrument is called a "Deed of Incorporation"; it is executed before a Luxembourg Notary Public and published in the official gazette. The authorized capital may be denominated in any currency, must be fully subscribed and at least 20% paid-in. Minimum capitalization for a holding company is LFr1.25 million (about US$37,500).

At least three directors are required, as well as an auditor. There are no citizenship requirements for officers, directors, auditors or shareholders.

The tax structure for holding companies is found in a 1929 law on the tax status of holding companies enacted July 31, 1929, rather than *The 1915 Company Act.* That law exempts corporate tax as to corporations that conduct no business other than simply holding, managing and disposing of interests in other corporations. Unlike the Netherlands, holding companies may not engage in any commercial or industrial operations or the exemption is lost. Luxembourg hosts an estimated 6,500 holding companies.

Each holding company files an annual financial statement with the Luxembourg authorities; most must also publish the statements in the official gazette. The holding company portfolio need not be included in those disclosures.

A Luxembourg holding company is permitted to acquire and hold shares of both domestic and foreign corporations without a minimum percentage requirement (compared to the substantial-holding requirement of the Netherlands), bonds and debentures, government securities, cash, foreign currencies and gold, deposits with banks and other financial institutions, shares and other interests in real estate companies, notes evidencing loans made to corporations in which it holds an equity interest and patents, but not usually trademarks.

A Luxembourg holding company is prohibited from holding interests in partnerships, an interest in an *anstalt* (a combination corporation and trust peculiar to European countries), real estate (other than for its own office requirements), patent licenses (other than those related to patents already owned) and commodities.

A Luxembourg holding company is also prohibited from acting as a bank. Commercial borrowings are limited to three times its capitalization, and bond issues are limited to 10 times that figure.

A 1973 report of the EEC Commission implies that no pressure will be placed on EEC members to harmonize taxes in a manner detrimental to holding companies in Luxembourg, the Netherlands and Switzerland until the other countries affiliated with its members and offering privileged treatment to holding companies (the Netherlands Antilles, the Bahamas, Bermuda, the Channel Islands and the Isle of Man) can be brought along in the same process. That prospect is remote.

Upon formation, a registration tax of 1% of capitalization is imposed on Luxembourg corporations. For a holding company with a minimum share capital of LFr1.25 million (about US$37,500), the registration tax would be approximately LFr12,500 (approximately US$375). Additional costs include registration, publication, translation, notary fees, legal fees and value-added tax. Overall, the cost of forming a holding company in Luxembourg will range from US$3,000 to $4,000.

The annual cost of maintaining a Luxembourg holding company includes a capital tax of .2% of capitalization, minimum LFr2,500 (about US$75). Capitalization includes any debentures issued, as well as paid-in capital for shares. Any bonds or debentures issued are valued at market, rather than initial principal value. Other annual costs include publication of financial statements, publishing announcements of shareholders' and directors' meetings, domiciliation or registered office fees, legal and auditing fees and (if local directors are appointed) local directors' fees. The total annual expense may approximate US$5,000 for a holding company with minimum capital.

During a period of political upheaval or war, a Luxembourg corporation may temporarily transfer its registered office to another country. Except as so provided, Luxembourg has no law permitting a corporation to move its domicile into or out of that jurisdiction, nor any prohibiting it. Thus, there is a risk that doing so may be treated as a constructive dissolution for tax purposes.

Unless the Luxembourg corporation is brought under the holding company exemptions, the corporate income tax rates imposed on it may be as high as 34%; that makes it a high-tax country. As noted, a mixed holding company and operating company is not permitted to enjoy the holding company exemption.

A Luxembourg holding company is precluded from taking advantage of Luxembourg's income tax treaties. Those treaties include Austria, Belgium, Brazil, Denmark, Finland, France, Germany, Iceland, Ireland, Italy, Morocco, the Netherlands, the United Kingdom and the US. Nonetheless, Luxembourg holding companies continue to be popular in Europe.

Special Corporations. In addition to its worldwide reputation as a base for holding companies, Luxembourg is an attractive jurisdiction for finance companies. Unlike holding companies, Luxembourg's finance companies may fully employ tax treaty benefits. An example is the Luxembourg-US Income Tax Treaty which provides for a complete exemption of US tax on nonmortgage interest received by a Luxembourg corporation that does not maintain an office for the conduct of business within the US. (Mortgage interest is usually taxed by the US on a net-income basis.) The Luxembourg finance company receiving US interest is technically taxed up to 34% of its net income, but may first deduct any interest it has paid on borrowed funds. Therefore, a non-US investor may establish a corporation in a no-tax jurisdiction, use it to establish a Luxembourg finance company, cause the no-tax jurisdiction corporation to lend funds to the Luxembourg finance company which, in turn, reloans them into the US; repayments from the US are passed through Luxembourg to the no-tax haven without tax in Luxembourg and the no-tax haven corporation accumulates them in the no-tax haven. All of that, of course, is of only academic interest to you as a US Target Defendant. You would need to examine the other tax treaties of Luxembourg, since you may not lawfully establish that pair of companies and reinvest your funds in the US without personal liability for taxes.

All bond interest paid by a Luxembourg corporation to a nonresident is free of withholding tax.[2]

Bank licenses may only be obtained by major international banking organizations, upon approval by the Luxembourg Banking Commissioner. Minimum capitalization is LFr350 million (about US$10.5 million).

Notwithstanding the absence of enabling laws, Luxembourg hosts several international mutual funds. A mutual fund structure usually takes the form of three holding companies: the fund itself, a repurchase company and an investment advisory company. Minimum capitalization for the management company is LFr3 million (about US$90,000), of which two-thirds must be invested in the fund. The repurchase company repurchases shares of the fund using share premiums from the sale of fund shares at a price in excess of par value. The Luxembourg Banking Commissioner requires registration of the management company and approves any transfer of its shares.

Trusts. As a civil law country, Luxembourg is generally unsuitable for trusts. There is no special statutory law authorizing them.

Cost Comparisons. The cost of forming and operating a Luxembourg holding company, stated in US dollars, is $3,000 to $4,000 and $5,000 per year, respectively. This is comparable to most other major havens on formation costs, noticeably higher for annual maintenance.

Prospects. Luxembourg has a firmly established constituency dependent on its continuing status as a major base for holding companies. That fact, taken together with the unlikelihood that the EEC will cause other tax havens affiliated with its member-countries to change their posture on tax harmonization, bodes well for the future of Luxembourg as a base for holding companies.

Endnotes

1. Luxembourg Company Act, August 10, 1915
2. Luxembourg Law, November 30, 1978

The Channel Islands

Summary. *Jersey and Guernsey are tax havens and offshore financial centers, primarily for the British, located in the English Channel. Since 1979, non-U.K. residents have made increasing use of them. At the present time, there are no exchange controls.*

Location. Jersey and Guernsey are the two largest of the Channel Islands. They are located in the English Channel off the coast of France. The size of Jersey is approximately 45 square miles, and Guernsey 24 square miles.

The flight from London to either Jersey or Guernsey is about one hour. They are both part of the U.K. telephone system. To dial direct from the US, use country code 44, plus local code 534 for Jersey or local code 581 for Guernsey. The time in both is the same as London throughout the year, five hours later than New York time except for daylight savings time. Telephone, telex and mail facilities are excellent.

Culture. The population of Jersey is approximately 80,000 and Guernsey 55,000. The indigenous peoples are Norman French. English is the primary language, although many natives speak a French patois.

Political System. Except for matters of defense and foreign affairs, responsibilities undertaken by Britain, both Jersey and Guernsey are self-governing. Queen Elizabeth II rules as the Duke of Normandy, rather than as Queen. Politically, these jurisdictions are stable. Jersey and Guernsey have a peculiar position within the EEC: they have the benefit of the free-trade aspects, but tax harmonization policies do not apply.

Legal System. The statutory laws of Jersey and Guernsey are written partly in French and (more modernly) partly in English; local contracts are often prepared in French.

The roots of Jersey and Guernsey law are partly Norman French and partly common law. Most importantly, they have adopted common law trust concepts.[1]

They are both signatories to the 1961 Hague Convention. Accordingly, documents executed in Jersey and Guernsey are authenticated by an Apostille, the standard certificate provided by the convention. The Apostille should be signed by Her Majesty's Principal Secretary of State for Foreign and Commonwealth Affairs.

As to residency opportunities, Jersey accepts only five new residents per year. Each must have an income of more than £500,000 per year (about US$942,500) and liquid assets of at least £8 million (about US$15 million). Guernsey is less restrictive.

Local Support Services. There are ample numbers of local lawyers and accounting firms, all of whom operate at a high ethical and skill level. Experienced bankers and trust companies are also in ample supply. If a distinction must be drawn between the two, Jersey has a reputation of being slightly superior to Guernsey in terms of its financial and professional facilities. Both, however, are more than adequate.

Currency. Although both Jersey and Guernsey have their own currency notes and coins, the English pound is in free and widespread use. England floated the pound and dismantled the sterling area in 1972, leaving the Channel Islands among the few jurisdictions to remain within the scheduled territories of the sterling area. Exchange controls were extinguished in 1979 and none were since reimplemented. The pound is today exchanged at about US$1.95.

Secrecy. Bearer shares are not permitted, but corporations are not required to disclose beneficial ownership to any Jersey or Guernsey taxing agency. Consequently, the common law aspects of those jurisdictions (holding bankers liable as a fiduciary for breach of confidentiality) is the primary mode of privacy protection.

General Corporate Law. In the British mode, "companies limited by shares," and tax privileged "exempt companies" are the two forms of corporation available from Jersey and Guernsey.

Forming a corporation in either country requires three or four days. The corporate laws are written in Norman French and are similar to nineteenth century British company laws. The Memorandum of Association (Articles of Incorporation), for example, may not be amended except to increase the authorized capital. It may not even be amended to enlarge the purposes and powers clause to avoid nullification of a particular corporate action that exceeds those purposes and powers. The corporate capital may be denominated in any currency. Jersey is the domicile for more than 24,000 corporations, Guernsey about 12,000. New corporations are formed in Jersey at a rate of approximately 250 per month, about 90 in Guernsey.

Neither Jersey nor Guernsey has a law permitting a corporation to move its domicile into or out of its jurisdiction, nor any prohibiting it. Thus, there is a risk that doing so may be treated as a constructive dissolution for tax purposes.

Corporations that conduct local business or which are managed locally are subject to a flat 20% income tax on worldwide income. Those managed and controlled from outside the jurisdiction are corporation tax companies and subject to a flat fee of £300 per year in lieu of income tax. Jersey and Guernsey impose an annual service charge on corporation tax companies. Although the tax rates of Jersey and Guernsey are the same, their methods of imposing the tax vary.

Jersey replaced its former "corporation tax companies" law in 1989 with one for "exempt companies."[2] Now, every corporation domiciled in Jersey is deemed "resident" for tax purposes unless it obtains exempt company status.[3] If the requirements are met, the corporation becomes nonresident for tax purposes, exempting from tax its foreign-source income.

To qualify, you establish that the corporation is nonresident-owned by disclosing to Jersey's Commercial Relations Department your identity as beneficial owner. You pay an annual tax of £500 for the exemption, along with a registration fee each year of £100. The annual tax is due by March 31.

Prior to creation of exempt companies, local bank account interest was subject to taxation. Under present law, it is exempted, thus avoiding the task of maintaining accounts in some other country in order to classify the interest as "foreign source" income.

An exempt company may, but is not required to, have local directors. Directors may meet there or abroad.

Guernsey expects to have a similar law in place soon. At such time as it is adopted, it will probably be applied retroactively to 1989, to coordinate with the effective date of Jersey's law.

Both Jersey and Guernsey have tax treaties with England and with each other. They have no other tax treaties and are not covered by any others of the United Kingdom. No estate or inheritance taxes are imposed by either Jersey or Guernsey on corporation shares held by nonresident decedents. There are no guarantees against future taxes and fees available.

Special Corporations. The law and bureaucracy regulating banking operations in both Jersey and Guernsey are well established, providing close internal supervision over banks and related financial institutions conducting business in the Islands. Jersey now hosts approximately 40 merchant banks and financial institutions, as well as branches of the main United Kingdom banks. Jersey attempted to slow the growth rate in recent years, because it was producing staff shortages, and housing shortages created difficulties with respect to importing trained personnel from outside. The growth continues, however, with major banks regularly acquiring smaller local banks.

Jersey does not welcome and lacks the legal and management support for the administration of offshore captive insurance companies. That is not the case, however, for Guernsey. It is a popular base for such carriers, hosting more than 100, and continues to be interested in this type of business.

Trusts. Guernsey has no express law authorizing and controlling the establishment and operation of trusts. Jersey, however, enacted the *Trusts (Jersey) Law,* effective March 1984. Generally accepted common law concepts, however, permit the formation and operation of trusts in both jurisdictions. The Channel Islands are the domicile for thousands of trusts, but if you choose to make one the domicile for yours, take extra care in its preparation to be certain it comports with local law. Local trust services in both Jersey and Guernsey are excellent.

Once satisfying the Jersey or Guernsey tax authorities that both the grantors and the beneficiaries are nonresidents, no local tax will be payable except on local income. The local income tax is avoided by the convenient expedience of establishing the trust in one jurisdiction and banking in the other. Any tax paid, of course, is taken as a credit against any US tax due.

Cost Comparisons. When professional fees are added to the annual governmental fees of £600 (US$1,130) per year in both Jersey and Guernsey, the annual cost of operating an exempt company in the Channel Islands will often exceed £1,300 (US$2,450) per year. That is neither high nor low by comparison to the European and Caribbean tax havens.

Prospects. Following termination of a threatened capital transfer tax by the United Kingdom on British citizens moving to the Channel Islands (and the Isle of Man), the growth rate has appreciated noticeably, from both British and non-British investors. The long period in which these two jurisdictions have governed themselves and conducted their affairs without substantial change suggests that the prospects for the future contain more of the same.

Endnotes

1. At this writing, Jersey is nearing passage of another amendment to its 1984 Trusts Law. The changes involved are of no concern to US taxpayers.
2. Repealing the Corporation Tax (Jersey) Law 1956, as amended
3. Income Tax (Jersey) Law 1961, as amended, Art. 123A

The Isle of Man

Summary. *Geographically, the Isle of Man is part of the British Isles. It boasts over 1,000 years of stable, democratic political independence. It provides personal income tax at a flat 20% and low or no corporation tax, as well as no capital gains or estate taxes. Its legislature is committed to creation of an environment attractive to offshore development. Its operating costs are reasonable, and an investor interested in living there will find it an attractive retirement location. Major promotional interests include: its freeport zone, its Isle of Man ship register, finance, insurance, manufacturing, trusts, and company formation.*

Location. The Isle of Man is located 50 miles from England in the temperate climate of the Gulf Stream, south of Scotland, west of England, north of Wales and east of Ireland. Flying time to London is one hour. The area of the Isle of Man is 221 square miles. Telephone, telex and mail service is excellent. Part of the U.K. telephone system, you may dial the Isle of Man direct using country code 44 plus local code 624. Time in the Isle of Man is the same as London, generally five hours later than New York except for daylight savings time.

Culture. The population of the Isle of Man is approximately 65,000; it is of Celtic and Norse heritage. Unemployment is low by any standard. English is the primary language, although Manx — a separate and distinct Celtic language derived from Scots Gaelic — is in use to a minor extent.

Political System. The Isle of Man is a self-governing state. It is not a part of the United Kingdom, but is a member of the British Commonwealth. The Lord of Man serves as its head of state; he is a British sovereign and is represented by a Lieutenant Governor appointed for a five-year term.

The Isle of Man is ruled by its 1,000-year-old parliament, the Court of Tynwald. Tynwald comprises the democratically-elected House of Keys and an upper house, the Legislative

Council; the latter legislates on any issue affecting the Isle of Man, although the United Kingdom government traditionally deals with those issues which transcend its frontiers. The Court of Tynwald is the oldest functioning parliament in the British Commonwealth.

Legal System. Except for its commercial law, which is similar to that of England, the Isle of Man employs its own common law. The similarities are such, however, that it may reasonably be considered a common law jurisdiction.

It is a signatory to the 1961 Hague Convention. Accordingly, documents executed in the Isle of Man are authenticated by an Apostille, the standard certificate provided by the convention. The Apostille should be signed by Her Majesty's Principal Secretary of State for Foreign and Commonwealth Affairs.

Noncitizens of the Isle of Man are required to obtain a work permit before engaging in any business or employment within that country.[1] Nonresidents are permitted to own Manx real estate.

Local Support Services. The Isle of Man has an adequate supply of lawyers, accountants, banks and trust companies. The quality of the services provided is excellent. Among the accounting firms are several of the "Big Six."

Currency. Like the Channel Islands, the Isle of Man was part of the scheduled territories of the sterling area from World War II until 1979. Thereafter, exchange controls imposed by the Bank of England were terminated; there are presently no exchange controls. The local currency is the English Pound, although it issues its own currency in notes and coins.

Secrecy. Bearer shares are now permitted in the Isle of Man. There are no financial disclosure requirements for nonresident companies but also no specific secrecy laws. Therefore, the fiduciary concepts peculiar to common law jurisdictions serve as the primary source of privacy protection.

General Corporate Law. The corporate law is much like that of Great Britain. Formation of a new corporation requires approximately one week. Tax-privileged nonresident companies are subject to a flat annual registration tax of £450 (US$848). Corporate laws by which they are regulated are the same for both nonresident companies and resident companies. There is a distinction between public and private companies: a private company must have at least two and not more than 50 shareholders, whereas a public company has more.

Court approval is required in order to amend the Memorandum of Association (Articles of Incorporation). As a consequence, the purposes and powers clause is broad.

At least two directors are required, although they need not be residents. All or a majority of the tax-privileged nonresident company directors must reside outside the Isle of Man.

The Isle of Man has no law permitting a corporation to move its domicile into or out of that jurisdiction, nor any prohibiting it. Thus, there is a risk that doing so may be treated as a constructive dissolution for tax purposes.

A flat 20% income tax is applied to the worldwide income of resident corporations and individuals.[2] Banks are permitted to pay interest to nonresidents without withholding. There is no property tax, death tax or gift tax of any kind. Although no capital gains tax is imposed as such, a land speculation tax enacted in 1974 imposes a short-term profit tax on the sale of local real property.

The only double-tax agreement of the Isle of Man is with the United Kingdom. That agreement provides for little or no exchange of information.

A tax-privileged resident corporation established in the Isle of Man requires care to avoid a double taxation problem that still awaits a legislative solution. All resident and nonresident shareholders of a resident Manx corporation are liable for income tax on its dividends. A 100% tax credit passed through from the corporation to its shareholders ordinarily cancels the tax, since the shareholders are taxable at the same rate as the corporation. With a dividend that is paid from foreign earnings, however, earnings that have been taxed in the country of origin, the Manx corporation is not permitted to pass the foreign tax credit through to its shareholders along with the dividend. As a consequence, a dividend of foreign-source income produces double taxation. Pending a legislative solution, the local practice is for Manx corporations to lend their foreign-source profits to the shareholders instead of paying dividends.

A tax-privileged nonresident corporation, one domiciled in the Isle of Man but managed and controlled from abroad, is exempt from Manx income tax on its foreign-source income. It is similar to a Jersey or Guernsey corporation in that the only tax or fee is a registration tax of £450 (US$848) per year.[3] It is deemed nonresident for tax purposes if a majority of its directors reside outside the country and all of its board meetings are held outside the island.

A 1984 law permits a private company incorporated in the Isle of Man or elsewhere to be exempt from Manx income tax even if it is resident for tax purposes.[4] Company operations are limited to investing in securities, commodities, property or managing ships. One local director is required, and a qualified local individual must serve as its corporate secretary. It must apply for the exemption within the time constraints provided, and pay a £450 (US$848) annual fee. A penalty of £650 (US$1,225) is imposed for late payment, and the exemption may be lost if payment is more than three months late. Such an exempt company may be required (but not presently) to produce financial statements and to disclose in private the identity of the beneficial owner.

A customs union agreement was terminated in 1980, following growing concern on the Island that U.K. customs officers operating under it to administer to its value-added tax might disclose information to the U.K. Inland Revenue, notwithstanding that they were forbidden to do so by law.

Special Corporations. The Isle of Man has enjoyed a dramatic and sustained increase in its financial services sector in recent years. That sector now employs 6% of the Manx work force and contributes 21% of its gross nationa income. The Isle of Man Bank, which has the largest branch network on the island, is an independent subsidiary of the National Westminster Group. In 1982, the Isle of Man had £1.2 billion in total bank deposits and was regarded as a quiet backwater among the second-tier offshore financial centers. It was startled into regulatory action at that time by the failure of its Savings and Investment Bank, a failure widely attributed to loose governmental regulation. The Financial Supervision Commission, galvanized by the damage to its reputation, set out to improve its modern regulatory framework by amendment and to aggressively employ it, with the result that the Isle of Man is now the envy of the offshore banking world. Deposits grew in the next eight years to £6 billion (US$11.3 billion) in mid-1990. That is a far cry from the £40 billion-plus on deposit in the Channel Islands, but certainly makes the Isle of Man a force with which the major havens must reckon. 58 full-service banks and 52 "Section 7" banks (held by investment companies) now operate there. They include all the major British banks, although none from the US.

The government takes a personal, unbureaucratic approach to regulation that banks, merchant banks, licensed deposit takers and trust companies find attractive.[5] A bank inspector closely supervises bank operations. Licenses are granted, as a rule, only to established banks. Minimum capitalization is £500,000 (US$944,000). The banking business is defined as one which is engaged in the receipt of money in any form of running account, the advancing of loans and the payment of collection of checks. Banking licenses are issued on the recommendation of the Financial Supervision Commission.

The Isle of Man is an established base for captive offshore insurance companies.[6] An insurance company producing only offshore business is subject to an annual license fee of £2,000 (US$3,770) and is exempt from tax on its profits from that offshore business, as well as its investment income. The government provides a full-time insurance inspector to monitor insurance company operations.

Trusts. With its comprehensive trust laws,[7] the Isle of Man is an excellent jurisdiction in which to establish a common law trust. No restriction on accumulations is imposed, nor are there any registration requirements or stamp duties for living trusts. Under local practice, no income tax is imposed on foreign-source income of a Manx trust which has only nonresident beneficiaries.

Cost Comparisons. The Isle of Man is an effective tax haven and offshore financial center for international investors from all over the world, not just for residents of the United Kingdom. Overall, the costs are noticeably lower than most other tax haven or financial center jurisdictions, particularly if local staffing for CFC business operations is required.

Prospects. Given the ten centuries of self-government, the high literacy rate, the well-trained work force, the diversified local economy and the serious attitude of the government toward becoming a major player as a tax haven and offshore financial center, it may reasonably be assumed that the present desirable features of the Isle of Man will remain available well into the future.

Endnotes

1. Isle of Man Control of Employment Act 1975, as amended
2. Isle of Man Income Tax Act 1970, as amended
3. Isle of Man Company Registration Act 1974, as amended
4. Isle of Man Income Tax (Exempt Companies) Act 1984
5. Isle of Man Banking Act 1975, as amended, and Banking License Regulations
6. Isle of Man Exempt Insurance Companies Act 1981; Exempt Insurance Companies Rules 1981; and Insurance Act 1986
7. Isle of Man Trustee Act 1961

Gibraltar

Summary. *Gibraltar remains firmly aligned with the United Kingdom, notwithstanding pressure by Spain for annexation. Although tax advantages may be obtained under its exempt companies laws, its political difficulties with Spain bear watching.*

Location. Gibraltar is a small peninsula comprising 2 1/4 square miles on the southern shore of Spain. Located at the mouth of the Mediterranean Sea and separated from Africa by the Strait of Gibraltar, its historical value as a military vantage point cannot be overstated.

It is accessible by air from London with a flight time of less than three hours. Regular flights are also available between Gibraltar and Morocco.

Telephone, telex and mail communications facilities are good. You may dial direct to Gibraltar from the United Kingdom, but not from the United States, using country code 350. The time in Gibraltar is six hours later than New York, except during daylight savings time.

Culture. Gibraltar has a population of approximately 30,000. The official language is English, although most Gibraltarians are bilingual, speaking Spanish as well.

Political System. Gibraltar became a British colony in 1704 and retains that status to this day. The preamble to the 1969 Constitution includes the assurance of the United Kingdom that sovereignty over Gibraltar will not be given to another state against their wishes.[1] In 1967 a referendum was conducted, posing the question whether Gibraltar should become part of Spain; the proposal was soundly rejected.

Gibraltar is governed in a bicameral structure by a House of Assembly with 15 elected members, two official members (the Attorney General and the Financial Secretary) and the Council of Ministers. The Governor is appointed by the Queen. England is responsible for foreign affairs, defense and internal security.

The border between Gibraltar and Spain was closed by Spain in 1969 in an attempt to put pressure on Gibraltar for annexation. It was reopened in 1985.

Legal System. Gibraltar is a common law jurisdiction. The Privy Council in London serves as the Court of Last Appeal from the Gibraltar trial and appellate courts.

It is a signatory to the Hague Convention. Accordingly, documents executed in Gibraltar are authenticated by an Apostille, the standard certificate provided by the convention. The Apostille should be signed by the Governor and the Commander-in-Chief of the City and Garrison of Gibraltar.

Local Support Services. Gibraltar has a large number of qualified lawyers and several firms of chartered accountants, as well as seven local banks that provide an excellent level of service.

Currency. The currency in use is the English Pound. Exchange controls were terminated in 1979 and have not been reinstated.

Secrecy. Provision is made in local law for the nonpublic disclosure of confidential information to the officials directly involved in the various matters. Beyond that, privacy is a function of established common law concepts of fiduciary duty. Specifically, an applicant for an exemption certificate must furnish information to the Financial and Development Secretary, including the names of the beneficial owners of the shares. Similar information is provided on transfer of those shares, since the approval of the Financial and Development Secretary is required for the transfer. Confidentiality is observed as to those disclosures.

General Corporate Law. A Gibraltar corporation requires no local directors. The capital structure of an exempt company may be denominated in any currency.

Gibraltar has no law permitting a corporation to move its domicile into or out of that jurisdiction, nor any prohibiting it. Thus, there is a risk that doing so may be treated as a constructive dissolution for tax purposes.

As is the case with most tax havens, Gibraltar separates corporations into two categories: those that conduct local business (taxed at a flat 35%), and those conducting only offshore business. Gibraltar imposes no capital gains tax.

An "exempt company" may conduct business anywhere except Gibraltar, and is not subject to the Gibraltar income tax unless it elects to pay it. It may maintain a local office for purposes of conducting its offshore business without jeopardizing its exempt company status. An exempt company may usually be formed within a few days.

Formation of an exempt company is similar to a Gibraltar corporation engaged in local business. Following formation, it applies for registration as an exempt company.[2] Upon approval it receives an exemption certificate with a term of 25 years, conditioned upon payment of certain annual fees and compliance with all other requirements. If the Application for Exemption is declined, the corporation is subject to regular income tax. Exempt company status is not affected by local management and control. Accordingly, it may function with local directors and hold its meetings in Gibraltar.

If management is located in Gibraltar, the annual government fee is £225 (US$425); if not, it is £200 (US$377). Presently, approximately 1,000 exempt companies are domiciled in Gibraltar. The exemption certificate extends beyond income taxes to include all death taxes otherwise imposed on shares owned by a nonresident decedent.

The election to pay the local tax of 35% is relevant only to controlled foreign corporations owned by United Kingdom citizens. The U.K. taxes their CFCs unless they opt to pay the tax applicable in the jurisdiction in which the CFC is domiciled; that tax rate, however, must be at least 27% — more than half the normal U.K. corporate tax rate. Consequently, U.K.-controlled CFCs will elect to pay the local tax at 35%, rather than the U.K. tax of 54%.

All that is of only academic interest to you, since there is no compelling reason to pay any tax for a US-controlled CFC.

If, for any reason, your application for an exemption certificate is denied, there is an alternative. A Gibraltar corporation will pay no income tax if it is managed from outside Gibraltar and has only foreign-source income, none of which is remitted to Gibraltar.

Special Corporations. Different, but similar, exemption certificates are available to ships and shipping companies. The Europeans have flocked to Gibraltar to avail themselves of registration and tax exempt certification for pleasure yachts.

Trusts. As a common law jurisdiction, Gibraltar is imminently suitable as a trust domicile. In addition, its *Gibraltar Trustee Ordinance*[3] improves on the common law, particularly with respect to broadened investment powers. Income of a Gibraltar trust payable to a nonresident beneficiary, or if accumulated for his or her benefit, is tax-free in Gibraltar. Remember, of course, that it is not tax-free in the US.

Cost Comparisons. The cost of incorporating a Gibraltar company as an exempt corporation with minimum capital is about £350 (about US$560). Annual costs are about £250 (US$470). Costs are thus noticeably lower than those of competing jurisdictions.

Prospects. While Spain continues to consider ways of annexing Gibraltar, it is unlikely to reimpose the blockade or to invade the country. In light of the near-unanimous attitude of its citizenry to continue its alliance with the United Kingdom, the environment in which your offshore trust or corporation would operate will probably remain unchanged for years to come.

Endnotes

1. Gibraltar Constitution Order 1969
2. Gibraltar Companies (Taxation and Concessions) Ordinance 1983
3. Gibraltar Trustee Ordinance, based largely on the English Trustee Act; Gibraltar Trustee Investment Ordinance. The 1958 U.K. Variation of

Trusts Act applies to Gibraltar under the Gibraltar English Law (Amendment) Ordinance 1970

The United Kingdom

Summary. *Like Costa Rica, the United Kingdom is not widely regarded as a tax haven. However, a nonresident U.K. corporation pays no tax on its foreign profits unless they are remitted to the United Kingdom.*

There is no annual flat tax, although there is no assurance that this will continue to be the case. The U.K. is less dependent upon revenues from nonresident corporations, thus has less incentive to retain them than do the Channel Islands, the Isle of Man and Gibraltar.

Location. The component parts of the United Kingdom are England, Wales, Scotland and Northern Ireland. Consequently, a nonresident corporation may be formed anywhere among those jurisdictions. In London, where excellent transportation and communication facilities with all parts of the world are found, you may dial direct from the United States using country code 44 plus local code 1. Time in the United Kingdom is five hours later than New York, except during daylight savings time.

Culture. The population is, of course, almost entirely Anglo-Saxon and English-speaking.

Political System. It is a combination monarchy (primarily ceremonial) and a democratic republic. The parliament functions as its legislature.

Legal System. The United Kingdom is the seat of common law.

It is a signatory to the 1961 Hague Convention. Accordingly, documents executed in the United Kingdom are authenticated by an Apostille, the standard certificate provided by the convention. The Apostille should be signed by Her Majesty's Principal Secretary of State for Foreign and Commonwealth Affairs.

Local Support Services. United Kingdom attorneys, accounting firms, banks and trust companies are in ample supply and of excellent quality. Our "Big Six" is fully represented.

Currency. The currency of the United Kingdom is the English Pound, currently trading at about US$1.95. Exchange controls were abandoned in 1979.

Secrecy. The United Kingdom, under virtually all of its many income tax treaties, has agreed to exchange information with its treaty partners. The information maintained by the Inland Revenue, however, includes little more than correspondence verifying that the company is, in fact, nonresident. The question then becomes, Will it act on behalf of the inquiring treaty partner to investigate and seek out information not required for its own needs? Milton Grundy[1] believes that it will not take any such action and that it lacks the power to do so. If true, a reliable level of privacy should be afforded by the application of general common law fiduciary concepts.

General Corporate Law. There is little apparent difference in a U.K. corporation conducting local business and a nonresident U.K. company. Either may be formed with or without limited liability on the part of its shareholders. Typically, the nonresident U.K. corporation will be a company "limited by shares" and, as such, will be required to file annual balance sheets that are open to public inspection. It may be preferable to avoid that by forming the corporation with unlimited liability but held by a tax haven corporation so that liability is *de facto* limited.

   U.K. nonresident corporations are not required to utilize local directors; indeed, it is preferable not to do so. Records must be maintained to prove that all meetings of directors have taken place outside the United Kingdom. It is prudent to conduct each board meeting in the same place so as to avoid classification as an itinerant corporation.

   The March 1988 Budget Speech included a call for termination of nonresident U.K. corporations: no new ones to be allowed, and existing ones to become resident in 1993. Actual implementation of this change is unclear at this writing.

The United Kingdom has no law permitting the corporation to move its domicile into or out of that jurisdiction nor any prohibiting it. Thus, there is a risk that doing so may be treated as a constructive dissolution for tax purposes.

Trusts. As a common law jurisdiction, the United Kingdom is an excellent choice as the domicile for your trust.

Cost Comparisons. Cost of formation and operation of the U.K.-domiciled CFC are typically modest. They are comparable to those of the Channel Islands and the Isle of Man.

Prospects. Inland Revenue may succeed in its efforts to do away with the nonresident U.K. corporation. It will become clear by 1993.

Endnotes

1. *The World of International Tax Planning*, Cambridge University Press, 1984, p.127, note 6

Liechtenstein

Summary. *Liechtenstein is a tiny country in Western Europe, located between Switzerland and Austria. It maintains close economic ties with Switzerland, particularly in the banking business, and uses the Swiss Franc as its currency. Your Liechtenstein-domiciled CFC conducting all of its business abroad will pay only a small capital tax and is exempt from all other taxes. Liechtenstein is favored as a tax haven by wealthy Europeans, particularly for use as a holding company or investment company domicile. Its corporation law is flexible and several types of entities are peculiar to that jurisdiction.*

Location. As noted, Liechtenstein is bounded by Switzerland and Austria. It may be reached in one hour by train from Zurich, Switzerland. The trains run almost every hour from Zurich to Sargans, Switzerland, where you continue by taxi or bus to Vaduz, the capital of Liechtenstein. The total land area of this small country is only 62 square miles, approximately the size of Washington, D.C. Telephone, telex and mail communications facilities are excellent. To dial direct from the US to Liechtenstein use the Swiss country code 41 plus the prefix 75. Liechtenstein is six hours ahead of New York, except during daylight savings time.

Culture. Liechtenstein has a population of 27,000, about 5,000 of whom live in its capital city, Vaduz. German is the primary language.

Political System. Liechtenstein has long enjoyed a stable government. The homogeneous quality of its population presents no prospects for political unrest. It has maintained a customs union with Switzerland since the 1920s.

Legal System. Liechtenstein operates under a civil law system. It is a signatory to the 1961 Hague Convention. Accordingly, documents executed in Liechtenstein are authenticated by an Apostille, the standard certificate provided by the convention. The Apostille should be signed by the Office of the Government of the Prince, at Vaduz.

Non-Liechtenstein citizens are not permitted to conduct local business in Liechtenstein. There is no restriction, however, on the conduct of foreign operations by noncitizens from facilities in Liechtenstein.

Local Support Services. Liechtenstein has an ample supply of trained and qualified attorneys, accountants, bank and trust officers accustomed to dealing with the needs of international investors.

Currency. Liechtenstein uses the Swiss Franc as its currency. Although exchange controls have existed from time to time in the past, there are none in existence at this time.

Secrecy. Liechtenstein operates its banking and commercial affairs under strict bank secrecy laws patterned after those of Switzerland. It has no tax treaty with the US, thus no obligation to exchange information.

General Corporate Law. Liechtenstein law[1] authorizes some 20 different forms of business entity. Generally, the shares issued by a Liechtenstein corporation must be fully paid for prior to formation by depositing the funds with either a Swiss or a Liechtenstein bank. Under a 1982 regulation, all business entities engaged in commercial activities within Liechtenstein must appoint an auditor.[2]

Of those 20 forms of business entity, the "domiciliary company" is the one you would select as your CFC. It is expressly authorized to function as a Liechtenstein-domiciled corporation but conduct only foreign business operations from an office within Liechtenstein. It is treated as a holding company if it holds only shares of other corporations or intangible property rights (*e.g.*, patents, trademarks and copyrights). At least one director is required, and at least one must be domiciled in Liechtenstein; that local director must also meet certain professional requirements. All business operations are conducted by the directors, who represent it and are authorized to bind it as to all third parties. The domiciliary company is also required to appoint a legal representative in that jurisdiction and to authorize that legal representative to represent it before Liechtenstein governmental authorities.

It must establish and maintain adequate books and records, but need not file financial statements with authorities unless it engages in local business activities. If limited to offshore operations, the only tax is an annual capital tax of one-tenth of 1% on both its capital and reserves, minimum SFr1,000 (about US$760).

Liechtenstein permits a corporation to move its domicile into or out of that jurisdiction.[3] That provides some assurance that doing so will not be treated as a constructive dissolution for tax purposes. Advance consent in writing is required, and the consent is based on political, legal or other reasons. Similarly, a transfer of domicile into Liechtenstein requires the prior approval of a Liechtenstein court.

Liechtenstein is a low-tax haven in which residents are taxed on worldwide income at rates ranging from 7 1/2 to 20%. Your CFC, however, whether or not operating as a holding company, is exempted from Liechtenstein income taxes.

Liechtenstein also imposes on domestic corporations doing local business a withholding tax on certain dividends and interest of 4% and a stamp duty on the creation of a new corporation or an increase in its capital. The application of those taxes varies, depending upon the business activity being conducted.

There is an estate, inheritance and gift tax, but only on assets located in the country owned by persons domiciled there.

Future tax limitation guarantees are no longer provided, although it is still possible to purchase shell companies that acquired those benefits in earlier years. They sell at a premium, of course, and the remaining life of the guarantee is limited.

Special Corporations. Among the forms of business entity peculiar to Liechtenstein are the *anstalt* and the *stiftung*. The former is a hybrid corporation and trust that would probably be disregarded as a separate tax-paying entity by IRS, and the latter is essentially a family charitable foundation. Consequently, neither serves your purpose as an international investor.

Related in form and effect to the *anstalt* is the "trust enterprise." It is a business enterprise independent of its trustee, with segregated assets and liabilities. Taxed in the same manner as an *anstalt*, it, too, offers little utility to the international investor.

Trusts. Even though it is a civil law country, Liechtenstein has statutory law expressly authorizing and regulating trusts. Trusts are generally created by a written instrument between the grantor and the trustee, as is the case in common law jurisdictions. There is no Rule Against Perpetuities, and income accumulations are permitted.

You may, if you choose to use Liechtenstein as a trust domicile, elect to have it governed by the law of a common law jurisdiction. If so, a dispute is arbitrated by a Liechtenstein court under selected law.

Cost Comparisons. Costs are generally comparable to the Netherlands and less than Switzerland for both the formation and the maintenance of a CFC.

Prospects. The long, stable history and the consistent attitude toward supporting and protecting its tax haven and offshore financial center status suggest that present conditions may be safely projected well into the future.

Endnotes

1. Law on Persons and Companies of 1926, as amended in 1928
2. Liechtenstein Law Gazette 1982
3. Law on Persons and Companies of 1926, Art. 234

Liberia

Summary. *Africa's only active tax haven, Liberia serves as the domicile for the world's largest merchant shipping fleet: more than 75 million gross tons of shipping are registered in Liberia.*

Among its advantages as a tax haven are the following: worldwide recognition as such since the early 1950s, no tax on foreign-source income of foreign-owned nonresident Liberian corporations, a modern maritime code, a liberal, US-style corporation law permitting quick formation and low cost, correspondent offices in the US and Switzerland to facilitate corporate formations and ship registrations; use of the US dollar as its national currency; no exchange controls; and English as the official language.

Location. Located on the west coast of Africa, Liberia enjoys modern air transportation facilities. It may be reached by air in approximately nine hours from New York. Its time zone is the same as London, about five hours later than New York, except during daylight savings time. Telephone, telex and mail service are good. To dial direct, use country code 231.

Culture. Liberia has a population of 1.8 million, about 10% of whom reside in the capital city of Monrovia. The population is almost entirely of African descent; many are descended from slaves who returned to Africa from the US several generations ago. The principal language is English. As a people, Liberia identifies in almost every respect with the US.

Political System. The Republic of Liberia was established in 1847 and it constitutes the oldest independent nation in Africa. A military coup in 1980 brought about major changes in the government, but little impact is noticed as to its tax haven functions.

Legal System. Although Liberia was established and operates under laws peculiar to that jurisdiction, those laws firmly recognize the concept of *stare decisis* (a requirement that judgments conform to prior judgments on the same issue unless clearly distinguishable on the facts and in the absence of contrary legislation or grounds for reversal or modification). A review of the appellate opinions of Liberia discloses the consistent and widespread use of US law as persuasive in construing Liberian law. Taken together, there are notable parallels between US and Liberian law that provide a large measure of comfort to the US investor conducting business in that jurisdiction.

Liberia is not a signatory to the 1961 Hague Convention. Accordingly, documents executed in that country are authenticated by the US consul.

Legal Support Services. Although limited, the number and quality of attorneys, accountants, bank and trust facilities of Liberia are sufficient to meet the needs of the US international investor.

Currency. As noted, the US Dollar serves as the currency of Liberia. It has no exchange control laws.

Secrecy. Liberia has no special bank secrecy legislation and, in the absence of clear applicability of common law concepts, traditional fiduciary law provides little assurance of privacy protection as a matter of business practice. In addition, corporate records are available for public inspection, presumably including shareholder identification. Accordingly, few offshore corporations conduct banking activities in that jurisdiction.

General Corporate Law. The law governing Liberian corporations established in 1948 was fully replaced in 1977.[1] The new law is more comprehensive and carefully preserves the features found so attractive by shipping companies and offshore investors.

Liberian corporations may be quickly formed, using procedures with which the US investor is familiar. Typically, the corporation is formed without actually traveling to Liberia, by using US service companies. The information is transmitted to Liberia by telex and the corporation usually formed within 48 hours. A return telex advises as to the date of incorporation.

The form of corporation identified in the Liberian Corporate Law as a "Non-Resident Domestic Corporation" is the form preferred by most offshore investors. It conducts no business in Liberia. A single incorporator may be used; that incorporator may be a natural person, partnership or corporation. The articles of incorporation may authorize the conduct of any lawful business, so as to avoid the risk of engaging in a business activity not falling within the ambit of the purposes and powers clause required under less modern law. There is no minimum capitalization requirement for the corporation.

A local registered agent must be appointed in the Articles of Incorporation so as to permit local service of process. That function is usually performed by a local trust company. There are no annual reporting requirements. The annual government fee is $150; that of the registered agent is $200.

Corporations formed under prior law may elect to be governed by either the prior law or the new law; the latter is evidenced by an amendment to the Articles of Incorporation in the same way as is the case in most states of the US.

While the corporation must have three or more directors, they need not be named in the Articles of Incorporation and none need be Liberian nationals or residents. If the corporation has fewer than three shareholders, the number of directors may correspond to the number of shareholders. Each corporation must have a president, a secretary and a treasurer. For a one-shareholder corporation, that person may hold all offices.

The corporation may issue either registered or bearer shares. If the latter, they must be authorized and described, along with required notice to bearer shareholders, in the Articles of Incorporation. Shareholders' and directors' meetings may be conducted and records kept anywhere in the world.

Liberia has no law permitting a corporation to move its domicile into or out of that jurisdiction, nor any prohibiting it. Thus, there is a risk that doing so may be treated as a constructive dissolution for tax purposes.

There is a Liberian income tax on domestic-source income of Liberian corporations. It bases its tax haven status on the fact that all foreign-source income, as well as shipping income, of a Liberian corporation is exempt from income tax if 75% or more of the shares are held by non-Liberian citizens.[2] The consensus of those doing business with and in Liberia is that, notwithstanding the absence of long-term tax guarantees, the exemption for foreign-controlled Liberian corporations is likely to continue indefinitely.

Although Liberia imposes a 15% withholding tax on dividends, those paid from tax-exempt foreign-source income or shipping income of foreign-controlled Liberian corporations are exempt.[3] The exemption extends to dividends paid by one nonresident Liberian corporation to another.[4] The Federal Republic of Germany and Sweden both have income tax treaties with Liberia. They do not, however, affect nonresident Liberian corporations.

Since 1982, Liberia and the United States have provided reciprocal tax exemptions for shipping and aircraft earnings without benefit of a formal agreement.[5]

Special Corporations. The Liberian merchant and tanker fleet is 2 1/2 times larger than that of Japan, its nearest competitor. A majority of the Liberian tonnage is less than 10 years old. Under local law, a Liberian ship must be owned by a Liberian corporation.[6] The annual fee for ship registration was substantially increased in 1974 in order to finance Liberia's maritime safety program. It is $725 per year plus 4 cents per net registered ton. The annual tonnage taxes have also been gradually increased since 1981 in order to compensate for the effects of inflation.

Trusts. The statutory law of Liberia is not a hospitable domicile for the trust of the US international investor, except as a means of avoiding probate by holding the stock of a Liberian corporation. The available body of law for establishing and operating trusts is generally inadequate.

Cost Comparisons. Compared to other tax havens, Liberia is an inexpensive jurisdiction in which to form and maintain corporations.

Prospects. There is a widely acknowledged vested interest in maintaining Liberia's status as a tax haven; witness the negligible impact of its military coup in 1980. Revenues from corporations and ship registrations constitute a major source of income for that country, as well as a highly elastic pricing area that permits periodic adjustments to compensate for the effects of inflation. Given its relative importance, the operating environment is likely to continue into the indefinite future.

Endnotes

1. Liberian Business Corporation Act, 1977
2. Liberian Internal Revenue Code, Secs. 11.81, 11.83
3. Liberian Internal Revenue Code, Secs. 11.23, 11.83
4. Liberian Internal Revenue Code, Sec. 11.82
5. US Treasury Department Release R-960, September 24, 1982
6. Liberian Maritime Code, Sec. 51, as amended

Hong Kong

Summary. *The role of Hong Kong as one of the most important financial centers of the Far East was considerably enhanced by the opening of trade and establishment of diplomatic relations between the United States and the People's Republic of China; it serves as the gateway to the Chinese mainland. Hong Kong is a politically stable British colony that for many years has served as the leading manufacturing and trading center of Southeast Asia. A high level of concern was demonstrated by businesses operating from Hong Kong at the prospect of it becoming part of the People's Republic of China in 1997 on expiration of the current lease. That concern was assuaged by a subsequent agreement between Great Britain and China permitting Hong Kong to remain as an enclave of capitalism for an additional 50 years beyond that date, but Tiananmen Square upset them all over again.*

As is often found in low-tax financial center jurisdictions, Hong Kong taxes under the territorial principle: it has no corporate income tax other than that imposed upon domestic-source profits, salaries, interest and the rental value of Hong Kong real estate. The tax rate on individuals is 15% and that on corporations is 16.5%. There is no tax of any consequence on foreign-source income, nor is there any death tax on the non-Hong Kong property of a resident decedent. Dividends, capital and capital gains are not taxed, nor is bank deposit interest for those doing no local business. Hong Kong has no tax treaties and no exchange control restrictions.

While regulatory friction causes corporations to move their headquarters to Hong Kong, the high price of real estate and office rentals causes them to move out almost as fast. There are always more corporations ready to take their place, however. Hong Kong is second only to Tokyo as the most expensive city in the Far East. Apartment rent levels are among the highest in the world.

Location. Hong Kong is located on the southern coast of the People's Republic of China, facing the South China Sea. A few hundred miles to the east lies Taiwan, and to the southeast, the

Philippine Republic. It is accessible by air from all parts of the world. Flying time from San Francisco to Hong Kong is approximately 14 hours. Excellent telephone, telex and mail services are available. To dial direct, use country code 852, plus city code 5 for Hong Kong Island or city code 3 for Kowloon.

Logistical problems arise from the vast time difference between the US and Hong Kong. The time difference is 13 hours between Hong Kong and New York, except during daylight savings time when it is reduced to 12 hours.

Culture. Hong Kong has a population of more than 5 million people, 98% Chinese. British territory includes 35 square miles of Hong Kong; the remaining 370 square miles are leased from the People's Republic of China.

The primary language is Cantonese, although English is used for virtually all business transactions.

Only recently have Hong Kong and the People's Republic of China stemmed the flow of Chinese refugees. Refugees continue to pour in, however, from Chinese enclaves in Vietnam, Cambodia and other parts of Asia.

Political System. Hong Kong is a British Crown Colony, so government is vested in the governor and the executive and legislative councils over which he presides. Neither council includes any elected members; their members are either civil servants whose position requires service in that capacity, or they are appointed by the governor. The British government appoints the governor, of course.

The lease between Britain and China for the Hong Kong territory expires in 1997, leading to major concerns about the future by businesses operating from that base. After some delay, and after a large number of businesses began shifting key operations to Singapore, Britain and the People's Republic of China entered into an agreement under which Hong Kong will become a self-governing capitalistic enclave of the People's Republic of China for 50 years, commencing in 1997. Redomiciliation of Hong Kong CFCs, however, continues apace.

Legal System. Hong Kong presently operates under English common law, modified by certain United Kingdom statutes, local ordinance and Chinese law that applies where Chinese customary rights are involved. Until 1997, the Privy Council in London will continue to serve as the Court of Last Appeal for the Hong Kong courts. The only changes in the law after the lease expires will be the replacement of those incorporating English law by reference. For sovereignty reasons, the People's Republic of China will pass substantially the same laws but without reference to England.

It is a signatory to the 1961 Hague Convention. Accordingly, documents executed in Hong Kong are authenticated by an Apostille, the standard certificate provided by the convention. The Apostille should be signed by the Governor and Commander-in-Chief of the Colony of Hong Kong.

Noncitizen residents of Hong Kong (including British subjects) require work permits in order to engage in any lawful occupation there. Permits are normally granted for an initial period of six months and thereafter extended for three-year periods. After seven years of residence, a person may become a "belonger," following which a work permit is no longer required.

Local Support Services. An abundant supply of high-quality attorneys, accountants, banking and trust firms are found in Hong Kong. There are more than 130 licensed banks and more than 300 other deposit-taking financial institutions of one sort or another, together with a large number of trust companies.

Currency. Hong Kong has no central bank. The currency of the colony is provided by three large commercial banks which issue bank notes for that purpose. They are the Hong Kong and Shanghai Banking Corporation, the Chartered Bank and the Mercantile Bank. The value of the Hong Kong dollar is tied to the US dollar, currently equal to US$.13. There are no exchange controls.

Secrecy. There are no statutes providing commercial or bank secrecy in Hong Kong. Consequently, the international investor is left to rely on fiduciary duty concepts found in the common law, obligating those with whom he does business to maintain his secrets or face civil liability.

General Corporate Law. As might be expected, the corporation law of Hong Kong is similar to that of the United Kingdom.[1] Hong Kong serves as the domicile for approximately 130,000 corporations. Under the law, a distinction is made between public and private corporations in which the latter is limited to no more than 50 shareholders and the transfer of shares is restricted, usually requiring approval by the directors. The formation of a new Hong Kong corporation requires approximately four weeks. That is due in no small part to the requirement that the Memorandum of Association (Articles of Incorporation) and the Articles of Association (Bylaws) must be printed.

Turning from the applicable corporate law to the applicable tax law, every Hong Kong corporation must file an annual income tax return. It may be able to obtain an exemption, however, if it conducts no local business and earns no profits from Hong Kong sources.

Private companies must prepare audited balance sheets annually, and must submit them to the shareholders and file them with the Inland Revenue Department. The balance sheets of a public company are open to public inspection, but those for private companies are not.

Each corporation must have at least two directors and a secretary. There are no nationality requirements for directors or shareholders and meetings may be held anywhere in the world. Shares must have a par value and the law does not provide for the issuance of bearer shares, at least for private companies.

A non-Hong Kong corporation that qualifies to do business in Hong Kong must register and pay a filing fee. Tax treatment is, at least in theory, the same as for a Hong Kong-domiciled corporation. In the course of registration, the foreign corporation must appoint a resident agent in Hong Kong for service of process.

If the non-Hong Kong corporation operating through a Hong Kong office is required in its jurisdiction of domicile to file annual reports, Hong Kong requires that those same reports be filed there. Such reports are available for public inspection.

Hong Kong has no law permitting a corporation to move its domicile into or out of that jurisdiction nor any prohibiting it. Thus, there is a risk that doing so may be treated as a constructive dissolution for tax purposes.

Since World War II, Hong Kong has imposed taxes on four categories of income and profits: those arising from property, salaries, profits and interest. The standard tax rate is 15%, except for the 16.5% imposed on business profits. Whether income is local or foreign-source is a question of fact to be determined by the taxing agency or the courts, as the case may be. Dividends paid from taxed profits are exempt from further tax. In a deviation from the territorial principle of taxation otherwise employed, bank account interest income received by a business conducted in Hong Kong is not taxed regardless of its source. That is in response to competition from Singapore; prior to 1982, Hong Kong taxed such interest and Singapore did not, resulting in a pattern in which Hong Kong banks established branches in Singapore and booked their Hong Kong transactions there in order to avoid the tax.

Hong Kong is a party to no tax treaties, they being deemed unnecessary under its territorial basis for taxation. Hong Kong imposes no gift tax, although stamp duties may apply to transfers of marketable securities and interests in local real estate. It does, however, impose an estate tax of as much as 18% on assets situated in the colony and owned by a decedent, whether or not that decedent was a resident of the colony.

Special Corporations. Special licenses are required for banking, deposit taking, money lending and insurance businesses. Before the *Deposit-Taking Companies Ordinance of 1976* was passed, virtually anyone could incorporate a finance company, accept deposits from the public and issue letters of credit, bills of exchange and other bank instruments. The only material difference between a deposit-taking company and a commercial bank were found in the rules governing checking account deposits. After enactment of the *Deposit-Taking Companies Ordinance of 1976,*

the banking functions of deposit-taking companies continued unchanged except: that they were not permitted to accept a deposit
for less than HK$50,000 (US$6500); the deposit term could be no
less than 90 days; a minimum capitalization of HK$2.5 million
(US$325,000) was imposed; and no more than 25% of capital
could be committed to any one borrower. Those restrictions were
not viewed as particularly onerous, as a consequence of which two
years later roughly 25% of total Hong Kong deposits were held by
deposit-taking companies. In an effort to stem the competition,
local commercial banks caused Great Britain to impose stricter
regulations on deposit-taking companies and to grant no more
charters for that purpose. Today, as a practical matter, the apparent
advantages given deposit-taking companies no longer exist.

In 1978, the Hong Kong and Shanghai Bank tendered for
control of Marine Midland Bank of New York. As an inducement,
they persuaded Great Britain to enact legislation authorizing banking charters for large banks wishing to establish branches or
affiliates in Hong Kong. The issuance of Hong Kong charters,
however, was dependent upon reciprocity and limited to banks
with a deposit base of $1 billion or more. So the oligarchy
continues.

Trusts. As a common law jurisdiction, Hong Kong is ordinarily
viewed as a satisfactory domicile for trusts. Local trust services are
of good quality and the trust law is substantial and favorable. You
should not lose sight, however, of the death tax imposed on Hong
Kong property of nonresident decedents.

While it is often suggested that the Hong Kong death tax may
be avoided by causing the trust to limit its investments to areas
outside that jurisdiction, it is a common practice for Hong Kong
trusts to hold their assets in holding companies incorporated elsewhere. The stock of such holding companies constitutes personal
property within Hong Kong, so it seems logical that Hong Kong
may insist upon imposing its death duty on those shares.

Under Hong Kong trust law,[2] accumulations are restricted and
the Rule Against Perpetuities applies. While no legislation authorizes or permits transfer of the trust domicile into or out of Hong

Kong, the consensus of local practitioners is that it may be authorized in the trust declaration itself.

Cost Comparisons. With formation costs of a Hong Kong corporation ranging from US$800 to $1,000 and annual operating costs
of $800 to $1,500, including maintenance, two local directors, a
secretary and auditing fees, Hong Kong costs compare favorably
with other tax haven jurisdictions.

Prospects. Under the 50-year lease extension with the People's
Republic of China, Hong Kong will remain a self-governing
capitalistic enclave until 2,047. The present environment will
probably continue, relatively unchanged, not as much because of
the lease as because of the increasing use of Hong Kong made by
the People's Republic of China as its "window on the outside
world."

It is not assured, though. The afternoon of June 4, 1989 in
Tiananmen Square shook the confidence of Hong Kong residents
that China would let this enclave of capitalism continue undis-
turbed after 1997. Business can tolerate almost any adversity but
uncertainty.

The real gross domestic product of Hong Kong grew at an
average annual rate of 7.8% between 1979 and 1986, reaching its
economic crescendo in 1987 at an astonishing 13.8%. But it then
tailed off to 7% in 1988, a mere 2.5% in 1989 and 3% in 1990.
Hong Kong's economy is strong and resilient, so it would bounce
back under normal circumstances. But these are not normal circumstances.

Hong Kong is losing much of its best and brightest talent. More
than 42,000 left in 1989 and 45,000 in 1990. A loss of managerial
skills and skilled labor in such numbers is a serious matter.

The outcome will turn on the fundamental strength of the Hong
Kong economy. It is robust, with 135 foreign banks and 167
representative offices of other financial institutions. Witness the
major civil projects undertaken in 1990: the new airport with
associated port, road and tunnel networks are impressive. The
willingness of England to issue passports to those who chose to

leave should give many the confidence to stay. And in no small measure, the continuance of Most Favored Nation status for China will serve to avoid serious disruptions to the Hong Kong economy.

All things considered, Hong Kong will probably continue to be one of the most powerful economic engines in the Far East for many years to come. I would watch and wait until the outcome becomes more clear, however.

Endnotes

1. The Companies Ordinance, Laws of Hong Kong, Ch. 32, as amended
2. The Trustee Ordinance, Laws of Hong Kong, Ch. 19, as amended

Singapore

Summary. *Singapore is a high-tax country which became a major banking center in the years shortly before 1982 by trading on the fact that Hong Kong taxed bank interest; it did so by not taxing bank interest, thus attracting branches and a large banking volume from Hong Kong.*

Location. Singapore is an island nation just off the southern tip of the Malay Peninsula, between the South China Sea and the Indian Ocean. It is readily accessible by air, using major international airlines. Flying time from San Francisco is approximately 18 hours. Telephone, telex and mail services are excellent. To call Singapore, use country code 65.

Singapore time is 13 hours ahead of New York, except during daylight savings time.

Culture. While population statistics are not as reliable as is the case in more industrialized countries, the Singapore population is estimated at about 2.5 million people. About 75% are Chinese, the rest either Malay or of Indian origin.

The principal languages are Mandarin Chinese, Malay, Tamil and English. Most people speak English, the language most widely used in business.

Political System. While independent since 1965, Singapore remains a member of the British Commonwealth. The only political party in the country has been in power since about 1960, for most of that time under the able leadership of Lee Kuan Yew. Singapore is regarded as one of the most stable countries in the developing world.

Legal System. Singapore operates under English common law. The Privy Council in England serves as its Court of Last Appeal.

It is not a signatory to the 1961 Hague Convention. Accordingly, documents executed in Singapore are authenticated by the US Consul.

Local Support Services. As a major offshore financial center, the banks, legal and accounting firms of Singapore are in abundant supply and provide high-quality services.

Currency. Singapore imposes no exchange controls; prior controls were abolished in 1978. The Singapore Dollar is currently equal to approximately US$.57.

Secrecy. Singapore has no bank or commercial secrecy laws, as such. Consequently, you are left to rely on common law concepts of fiduciary obligations imposing civil liability upon bankers and others for consequential damages arising from disclosure of confidential information.

General Corporate Law. As might be expected, the laws regulating corporations in Singapore follow British patterns. A distinction is made between public and private corporations, the latter defined as having no more than 50 shareholders. Public companies are required to file financial statements annually with the Registrar of Companies; private companies do not.

A Singapore corporation must have at least two directors. Although there are no nationality requirements, at least one director must be a Singapore resident. The secretary must be both a citizen and a resident of Singapore. Aside from those restrictions, no shareholder need be either a citizen or a resident of that jurisdiction. The law does not contemplate the issuance of bearer shares.

Singapore has no law permitting a corporation to move its domicile into or out of that jurisdiction, nor any prohibiting it. Thus, there is a risk that doing so may be treated as a constructive dissolution for tax purposes.

As noted, Singapore is a high-tax country. An examination of its tax incentives, reveals opportunities through which to conduct business exempt or almost exempt from local taxation. For example: notwithstanding the corporate tax rate of 32%, banks pay only 10% income tax on profits earned from offshore loans; the same is true for Asiadollar operations (financial houses dealing in

Asiadollars); an offshore reinsurance business is subject to a tax of only 10%. Nonresidents depositing Asia currency units in Singapore are not taxed at all on the interest, and there is no death tax on those deposits.

It appears possible to use a nonresident corporation incorporated in Singapore as a tax haven if the corporation is managed and controlled from offshore and if all its directors' meetings are held outside Singapore. Such a corporation is not taxed on its foreign-source income unless actually remitted to Singapore. Dividends attributable to foreign-source income not remitted into Singapore are also free of income tax.

Singapore has enacted an incentive for pioneer industries and for the expansion of new ones.[1] The special focus is on production for export. Singapore has not enacted any laws expressly authorizing the establishment of exempt corporations, nor does it provide guarantees against future taxes.

Singapore has income tax treaties with Australia, Bangladesh, Belgium, Canada, the Republic of China, Denmark, Finland, France, Germany, India, Israel, Italy, Japan, Korea, Malaysia, the Netherlands, New Zealand, Norway, Philippines, Sri Lanka, Sweden, Switzerland, Thailand and the United Kingdom. It has no tax treaty with the US.

Trusts. Notwithstanding its common law tradition, Singapore does not lend itself as a useful domicile for your offshore trusts due to its high-tax environment.

Cost Comparisons. The cost of forming and maintaining a Singapore corporation is neither high nor low, in comparison to other tax haven jurisdictions.

Prospects. Singapore celebrated 25 years of independence in 1990, all under a remarkable leader, Prime Minister Lee Kuan Yew. Upon his retirement in 1991, he was able to look back on the development of Singapore into a bustling, modern country in the midst of a massive building boom, with huge hotels, office buildings, convention centers and art museums under construction. He put in place the infrastructure to clean polluted rivers and harbors and maintain them, and allocated $53 million to restore the famed Raffles Hotel. The Changi airport will soon be enlarged to accommodate 20 million passengers per year, and a $21 million passenger ship terminal was completed in 1991.

The highest priority of Prime Minister Lee was to ensure the continuation of US and European investment in Singapore. His success is attested by a gross national product growth rate of 6.5% for 1979-86, 8.8% in 1987, 11% in 1988, 9.2% in 1989 and again in 1990. Under the leadership of his chosen successor, Goh Chuk Tong, he is certain that this remarkable growth rate will continue to about 2005 before stabilizing. It is a good place for the investment of foreign capital.

For so long as Singapore continues to enjoy substantial revenues from its offshore banking operations and to acquire new industry to support domestic employment needs, the present environment should continue.

Endnotes

1. Economic Expansion Incentives (Relief from Income Tax) Act, Singapore Laws, Ch.135

Nauru

Summary. *Like Turks and Caicos, Nauru recently established itself as a modern tax haven using business strategic planning techniques and heavy promotion. It imposes no stamp duties and no taxes. It attempts to offset its distant location with modern laws and special inducements.*

Location. Nauru is a tiny island country comprising slightly more than eight square miles, located in the Central Pacific. It is approximately 40 miles south of the equator and 2,500 northeast of Sydney, Australia. It has no capital and no cities.

Notwithstanding its remote location in the Central Pacific, it is conveniently served by air with its own airline, Air Nauru. Its planes are acquired from major airlines, as are its flight crews. Several flights are available each week between Guam and Nauru and one to two flights each week between Nauru and Auckland, Hong Kong, Honolulu, Manila, Melbourne, Nandi, Noumea, Port Vila, Sydney and Taipei. Visas are required for visitors and are available through its overseas offices. There is one hotel, the Meneng, providing 60 rooms.

Satellite service now permits good telephone and telex service between Nauru and Hong Kong and Australia. Mail service is reasonably good. The time difference with other financial centers can be so great as to seriously impair the ordinary conduct of business. For example, two o'clock Pacific Standard Time in California is 10 the next day in Nauru, permitting only three hours in which to conduct business each day, and only two hours in the summer because Nauru does not observe daylight savings time.

Culture. Of its 7,000 people, more than 4,000 are native Nauruans, ethnically similar to Polynesians. The remaining population comprises a variety of other Pacific Islanders (and to a lesser extent, Asians) imported to mine phosphate. The phosphate deposits that cover most of the island have produced a high per capita income and virtually no unemployment. The island is circled by a single,

12-mile-long road. The population is largely bilingual: Nauruan and English. English is the official language.

Political System. Prior to World War II, Nauru was a German protectorate. It then became a mandated territory under the League of Nations. During World War II, it was occupied by the Japanese. Then it became a trusteeship of the United Nations, administered by Australia. It became an independent republic in 1968.

Because all of the native Nauruans benefit from the enormous income earned by exporting phosphate, Nauru is economically stable. Each property owner receives a royalty payment from phosphate sales and, notwithstanding the wealthy circumstances in which the natives find themselves, many of the men are regularly employed. Employment is primarily with the government, the phosphate industry or related service organizations.

The emergence of Nauru as a modern tax haven is based on a clearly expressed concern about the circumstances in which the country will find itself in 1995, when the phosphate deposits are expected to be fully mined. The country has established a trust for the benefit of its people, which in turn built Nauru House, a 50-story building in the central business district of Melbourne, Australia. That investment, together with other investments from retained government earnings deposited in trust, is intended to provide long-term security for native Nauruans.

Legal System. Local law is unique to Nauru, although patterned to some extent after those of England and Australia.[1] An unwritten law based on custom and practice applies to land and inheritance matters affecting only Nauruans. All legal documents are prepared in English.

Nauru is not a signatory to the 1961 Hague Convention. Accordingly, those of your documents executed in Nauru are authenticated by the US Consul.

Land and local businesses must be owned solely by native Nauruans. The country is not interested in attracting immigrants and does not encourage visitors. There is no incentive legislation intended to attract industry.

Local Support Services. There is only one commercial bank, the Bank of Nauru. The local needs of nonresident Nauru corporations (registered agent, etc.) are provided by two local corporations. Originally tax haven business was derived principally from Australia. That country took strong legislative measures to cut off the flow of funds, however, leaving Nauru turning to other markets for replacement business. It is guided by consulting advice from a major international bank.

In addition to the two registered corporation agents acting on behalf of nonresident Nauru corporations, local management services are also provided by a nominee corporation, a secretary's corporation, and a trustee corporation. To all appearances, all are owned by the same principal. There are no local accountants in private practice in Nauru, and the only two lawyers do not practice privately.

Currency. The Australian Dollar serves as the currency of Nauru. It is currently exchanged at approximately US$.83. There are no exchange controls in effect, although controls imposed by Australia in the future could be placed in effect in Nauru. That is considered unlikely.

Secrecy. The privacy of nonresident Nauru corporations is protected to some extent by statutory restrictions on the inspection or copying of documents relating to holding companies, and by the requirement that all civil proceedings relating to them permit the inspection of corporate records only in chambers. While each Nauru corporation must file an annual return containing certain corporate information, public disclosure of financial information — other than licensed banks and insurance companies — is not required. The latter two must file annual audited financial statements with the regulatory authorities.

Aside from the foregoing, the common law mainsprings of Nauru law suggest that widely-held concepts of fiduciary duty will serve to protect privacy by imposing on bankers' civil liability for consequential damages flowing from disclosure of confidential information.

General Corporate Law. The law regulating corporations in Nauru[2] is the novel product of an Australian attorney engaged by Nauru to draft it. Generally following British concepts, it is contained in a single, 200-page volume and may be obtained from the overseas offices of Nauru.

Nauru now serves as the domicile for several hundred corporations. Although none are public companies, some may be subsidiaries of publicly-held companies.

A "holding corporation" is not permitted to issue securities to the public. It is limited to holding portfolio interests in other corporations and may not have more than 20 shareholders. It must indicate in its name that it is a holding company.

A "trading corporation," unlike a holding corporation, may issue securities to the public upon approval of a prospectus by the Registrar of Corporations. Also unlike a holding corporation, a trading corporation may conduct active business.

Each nonresident Nauru corporation must appoint one local registered director from an approved list provided by the government, in the absence of special Articles of Association (Bylaws) providing otherwise. Meetings of shareholders and directors may be held anywhere. Trading corporations are specifically required to convene annual shareholders' meetings, but that requirement is not imposed on holding corporations.

The Corporation Act expressly authorizes the issuance of bearer shares. Capitalization must be denominated in Australian dollars or in a limited number of other currencies. A Nauru corporation is expressly authorized to redeem its own shares.

Formation of a new corporation takes one or two days after the papers reach Nauru, due to standard corporation forms and procedures. No preclearance of beneficial owners is required, except for offshore banks and insurance companies. (But see §3.2 on the mail-order banks from this haven.) Each corporation must appoint a Registered Secretary in Nauru.

A corporation domiciled elsewhere may transfer its domicile to Nauru upon satisfying the Nauru Registrar of Corporations that the original jurisdiction permits it. Following the transfer, the corporation continues as if originally incorporated in Nauru.

In similar manner, a Nauru corporation may transfer its domicile to any other jurisdiction if its continuance there is authorized under the laws of that jurisdiction. Before doing so, the transfer out must be approved by the Nauru Minister for Island Development and Industry. Upon securing an instrument of continuation in the transferee jurisdiction, the former Nauru corporation ceases to exist as such.

There is a deep dislike for taxes by the local populace. Nauru does not, however, offer guarantees against possible future taxes. It has no tax treaties.

Special Corporations. Presumably because of the greater price elasticity for governmental fees, Nauru is particularly interested in offshore bank and trust companies. The law[3] permits the establishment of banks and trust companies upon application and issuance of special licenses. No minimum capitalization is required. The annual government fees may range as high as $A1,000 (about US$830), depending on the nature of the business undertaken. Although the law is designed to attract undercapitalized banking business, Nauru claims it is not interested in attracting racketeers and swindlers.

Nauru now hosts a small number of offshore captive insurance companies, authorized under its insurance law.[4] As with banks, special licenses are required. The annual government fee is $A250 (about US$207).

If a nonresident Nauru corporation owns ships, they may be registered.[5] The initial registration fee for a ship is Australian $1 per net ton with a minimum of $A500 (about US$415). There is no annual registration fee.

Trusts. Under its trust law,[6] Nauru abolished both the Rule Against Perpetuities and restrictions on accumulations of income. That, at least in theory, permits a Nauru accumulation trust to run forever. The grantor must appoint a licensed Nauru trust corporation as trustee. At present, only one such corporation is qualified in that jurisdiction.

Cost Comparisons. With costs of approximately US$700 to establish a corporation and slightly less for annual maintenance thereafter, operating costs in Nauru compare favorably with other modern tax haven jurisdictions.

Prospects. Australia has already taken firm action to stem the flow of funds from its own citizens to Nauru, so it could conceivably take further action to impair tax haven business between Nauru and other jurisdictions. Having avoided damage to its own economy, however, further action is unlikely. The fears of the Nauru government that its citizens may be exploited by more sophisticated visitors constitutes a limiting factor on its potential as a tax haven, but one which may be offset by enlightened legislation and promotion. In the absence of a long tradition as a tax haven, it is difficult to project the present environment into the future. The relative affluence of its citizenry and the decisive action taken once the strategy was developed militate in favor of the conclusion that little will change.

Endnotes

1. Nauru Custom and Adopted Laws Act (No. 11 of 1971), as amended
2. Nauru Corporation Act (No. 5 of 1972), as amended
3. Nauru Banking Act (No. 4 of 1975), as amended
4. Nauru Insurance Act (No. 6 of 1974), as amended
5. Nauru Registration of Shipping Act (No. 7 of 1968), as amended
6. Nauru Foreign Trusts, Estates and Wills Act (No. 7 of 1972)

Vanuatu

Summary. *Like Nauru, Vanuatu is in a remote location in the South Pacific. It recently obtained its independence, and since has held itself out as a tax haven and offshore financial center featuring modern corporate laws designed around that standing. Unlike Nauru, it is a beautiful tropical paradise. It was featured in the book* South Pacific, *by Michener, and by the play and movie of the same name, written and scored by Rodgers and Hammerstein.*

Location. Vanuatu is the former New Hebrides, as it was known from 1906 until independence was granted in 1980. It is located between Fiji and New Caledonia. Air service into its capital, Port Vila, is available from Brisbane, Melbourne and Sydney, Australia, from Nandi, Fiji or Noumea in New Caledonia. A flight from Los Angeles to Port Vila takes approximately 14 hours plus a layover of several hours at Nandi, Fiji. Telex and international telephone services by satellite are available, but not direct-dial telephone service. Mail between Vanuatu and the United States usually takes a week. Overall, communications facilities are good.

Vanuatu observes daylight savings time from October through March, so the time difference between there and the United States varies between 15 hours during US summer and 17 hours during the US winter. For example, two o'clock Pacific Standard Time is 10 the following day in Vanuatu. That permits a three-hour business day between the two countries.

Culture. Of the 130,000 people residing in Vanuatu, 96% are Melanesian; the remainder are of European origin. More than 100 different dialects are spoken, as a consequence of which natives are often unable to communicate with one another. To some extent, the absence of a common language is mitigated by a form of Pidgin English in wide use, called Bislama. The culture is a throwback to an earlier time, but neither that fact nor the lack of a common language impairs the success of Vanuatu as a recently established tax haven. Although all visitors are required to present passports, US citizens do not require visas.

The capital city of Port Vila has a population of 17,000. It is flat, box-like, with uninspired architecture. That fact, however, is transcended by the inherent beauty of this typical South Pacific island.

Political System. Until 1980, Vanuatu operated under an unique condominium form of government jointly administered by the British and the French. Upon obtaining independence in 1980, it was reconstituted as a republic. The new government includes an elected President, a Prime Minister, a Cabinet of Ministers and an elected legislature. There are two active political parties in Vanuatu; both actively and publicly support its status as a tax haven.

Legal System. The official languages of Vanuatu are English and French, as are local commercial laws. Under the law prior to independence, French citizens were subject to French law, U.K. citizens were subject to British law, and all other citizens were required to elect one or the other. Natives were governed by native law, interpreted by native courts. Since natives were neither British nor French, they were technically stateless.

Vanuatu is a signatory to the 1961 Hague Convention. Accordingly, documents executed in Vanuatu are authenticated by an Apostille, the standard certificate provided by the convention.

Local Support Services. The number of attorneys, accountants, banks and trust companies in Port Vila is limited, but adequate for the present level of business. The quality of training and service is good.

Currency. The local currency is the Vatu, trading at approximately US$.01. Vanuatu imposes no currency controls, and bank accounts may be denominated in any major currency.

Secrecy. Each corporation domiciled in Vanuatu must keep a proper set of books and records. Unless excused, each must also have them audited annually and a copy attached to the annual return filed with the government. Exempted companies are generally excused from the audit requirement, although they must still file the annual return. These filings are confidential as a matter of law[1] and may not be disclosed by the government. Disclosure of the return contents by anyone gives rise to criminal sanctions.

General Corporate Law. Under the enabling legislation,[2] satisfactory references are required for individuals forming Vanuatu corporations. The preclearance system is similar to that of Bermuda. The process, however, is expedited by virtue of the fact that it is conducted by the trust company or law firm representing the incorporators. A corporation may ordinarily be formed within a week after receipt of the necessary documentation in Port Vila.

The principal means of attracting offshore business to Vanuatu is its authorization of exempted companies. Virtually all international investors establish their presence in Vanuatu through exempted corporations, now numbering more than 1,000.

No guarantees against future taxes are provided; rather, the attraction is secrecy. The prospect of taxes being imposed, however, is remote.

Local law requires that at least one meeting of directors be convened in Vanuatu annually, although alternate local directors may be used for that purpose.

The law does not permit the issuance of bearer shares, although an unwieldy and generally unsatisfactory substitute in the form of share warrants may be used to accomplish that purpose.

The screening requirements for persons forming Vanuatu corporations require suitable references by which to qualify the beneficial owners. Those references will ordinarily be from a well-known bank or law firm. Full names and addresses of each beneficial owner are required. References are now spot-checked, although originally everyone received scrutiny. The government now relies on the trust companies and law firms to protect against any influx of racketeers and swindlers.

Local law firms and trust companies also serve as an arm of government in policing the activities of a Vanuatu corporation after formation. Generally, that is accomplished by either furnishing a majority of the directors (thus obtaining control of corporate activities), or furnishing one local director and insisting on receiving copies of all minutes of shareholders' and directors' meetings. If any corporate action is disapproved by the local director, he resigns and informs the government, resulting in the corporation being stricken from the Register of Corporations. Any such disapproved corporate activity would be in the nature of crimes, rather than normal business activity. Any change in either registered or beneficial shareholders must be reported to the government.

Among the modern provisions used by Vanuatu in attracting offshore business is its Redomiciliation Law.[3] Current law permits a foreign corporation to transfer its domicile into Vanuatu, and a Vanuatu corporation to transfer its domicile out to another jurisdiction. A permit is required from the Vanuatu Registrar of Companies, either way. The permit has a term of three years, and may be renewed for a successive three-year period. Thus, it may serve as a stand-by permit in the event of political or economic change. A corporation transferring its domicile to Vanuatu may elect within six months after registration to become subject to the laws of the original jurisdiction, rather than local law.

Transfer of domicile is available not only to corporations, but to other legal entities distinguishable from its beneficial owners; presumably, that includes trusts.

Vanuatu has neither direct taxation nor tax treaties.

Special Corporations. Vanuatu directs its legislative focus to the attraction of banking and insurance business by means of its *Vanuatu Banking Regulation,*[4] and its *Vanuatu Insurance Regulation.*[5]

Special licenses are required to conduct banking and trust business. Banks and trust companies may be established by a reputable overseas bank, a business corporation or an individual. They may be classified as exempted corporations by conducting only offshore banking or trust business.

Similarly, insurers may be categorized as exempted corporations by conducting only offshore business. The law is designed to attract captive offshore insurance and reinsurance companies. Exempted insurers are not permitted to solicit business from the citizens of Vanuatu, although they may insure affiliated corporations domiciled in that jurisdiction. Regulation is nominal, and exempt insurance and reinsurance companies are not subject to any minimum capitalization requirements, nor to any of the controls applicable to the insurance companies conducting domestic business.

The *Vanuatu Prevention of Fraud (Investment) Regulation 1971 Act*[6] establishes a body of statutory law governing the formation and operation of offshore mutual funds. Little is known about the success enjoyed by Vanuatu in attracting that business to date.

The *Vanuatu Maritime Act*[7] was enacted shortly after obtaining independence as a means of attracting ship registrations in competition with Panama, Liberia and other major shipping havens. As is the case in those other havens, the ship registered will also be owned by an exempted company. The Deputy Commissioner of Maritime Affairs of the Republic of Vanuatu, in New York, is principally responsible for shipper registrations. Dual registration is available so that, typically, a bareboat charter company may register its vessels in Vanuatu without giving up registration in another jurisdiction.

Trusts. English common law, supported by the statutes governing trusts placed in force January 1, 1961 and modified by the *Vanuatu Perpetuities and Accumulations Regulation 1974,*[8] classifies Vanuatu as a useful domicile for your tax haven trust. A trust may be and remain in effect for as long as 80 years, the Rule Against Perpetuities having been abolished. Several qualified and well-established trust companies operate out of Port Vila.

Cost Comparisons. The costs associated with corporate formation and maintenance in Vanuatu is competitive with those of other tax havens and offshore financial centers; about US$2,000 to form and US$1,200 per year to maintain.

Prospects. Continued improvements to its transportation and communication facilities should bring about greater use and recognition of Vanuatu as a tax haven. Its principal market is offshore business from within the Pacific Basin, since there are relatively few no-tax havens in the Pacific, and since time differences are nominal.

Endnotes

1. Vanuatu Companies Act 1986 (No. 12 of 1986)
2. Vanuatu Companies Regulation 1971 (No. 4 of 1971), as amended
3. Vanuatu Companies Act 1986, Secs. 374-75
4. (No. 4 of 1970), as amended
5. (No. 18 of 1973)
6. (No. 9 of 1971)
7. (No. 8 of 1981), as amended
8. Regulation No. 3 of 1975

Glossary

Ab Initio. Latin. From the beginning; from the first act; entirely; as to all acts done; in the inception.

Charging Order. An order imposing a judgment lien on the asset and requiring all distributions made on account of that asset to be delivered to the judgment creditor. The property remains in the possession of the debtor and, unless exempted, may be subject to a further order for execution.

Comity. Courtesy, respect; a willingness to grant a privilege, not as a matter of right, but out of deference and goodwill.

Common Law. As distinguished from the Roman law, the modern civil law, the canon law and other systems, the common law is that body of law and juristic theory which was originated, developed and formulated and is administered in England, and obtains among most of the states and peoples of Anglo-Saxon stock.

De Minimis Non Curat Lex. Latin. The law does not take notice of trifling matters.

De Novo. Latin. Anew, afresh. A trial *de novo* is a complete second trial of the same matter.

Dictum, Dicta. Latin. Generally used as an abbreviated form of *obiter dictum*, meaning "a remark by the way"; *i.e.*, an observation or remark by a judge in rendering an opinion or judgment concerning some rule, principle or application of law, that is not necessarily essential to determination of the case at hand.

Et Sic Pendet. Latin. "And so it hangs." A term used in the old reports that a point was left undetermined.

Ex Parte. Latin. On one side only; by or for one party; done for, on behalf of, or on the application of, one party only.

Execution. A levy that includes an order of sale, so as to sell the property taken by levy and apply the proceeds to satisfaction of a judgment.

In Propria Persona. Latin. In one's own proper person. The common meaning is one who acts as his or her own attorney of record in pending litigation.

Inchoate. Imperfect; partial; unfinished; begun but not completed; as a contract not executed by all the parties.

Levy. To take the property, including money, to satisfy a judgment.

Mens Rea. Latin. A guilty mind; a guilty or wrongful purpose; criminal intent.

Pendente Lite. Latin. Pending the suit; during the actual progress of a suit; during litigation.

Raison d'être. French. Reason to exist.

Settlor. One who creates a trust. Other terms with the same meaning are grantor and trustor.

Trust. A right of property, real or personal, held for the benefit of another. Any arrangement whereby property is transferred with the intent that it be administered by a trustee for another's benefit.

Index

About the Author

F. Bentley Mooney, Jr., is a California attorney and managing
shareholder of Mooney & Murphy in North Hollywood. His "a.v.-
rated" firm of four attorneys practices exclusively in the areas of
business law and litigation, estate planning and probate. Mr. Mooney
entered private practice in 1972, following fourteen years in life
insurance sales and management. He is a frequent guest speaker
within areas of practice concentration and author of numerous articles and books. Among the latter are *Handcuff the Taxman, Going
Bare, The Artful Use of Offshore Tax Havens, Cluster! A Flexible
Approach to the Cluster Agency Maze* and *When Health is Lost:
Providing for Long-Term Nursing Care.* Mr. Mooney received his
Chartered Life Underwriter designation from The American College
of Life Underwriters (1963) and his Bachelor of Laws (LLB, with
honors in taxation) from the University of San Fernando Valley,
College of Law, in 1972.

About the Publisher

PROBUS PUBLISHING COMPANY

Probus Publishing Company fills the informational needs of today's business professional by publishing authoritative, quality books on timely and relevant topics, including:

- Investing
- Futures/Options Trading
- Banking
- Finance
- Marketing and Sales
- Manufacturing and Project Management
- Personal Finance, Real Estate, Insurance and Estate Planning
- Entrepreneurship
- Management

Probus books are available at quantity discounts when purchased for business, educational or sales promotional use. For more information, please call the Director, Corporate/Institutional Sales at 1-800-PROBUS-1, or write:

Director, Corporate/Institutional Sales
Probus Publishing Company
1925 N. Clybourn Avenue
Chicago, Illinois 60614
FAX (312) 868-6250